LET THE READER UNDERSTAND

A GUIDE TO INTERPRETING AND APPLYING THE BIBLE

BridgePoint,
the academic
imprint of
Victor Books, is
your connection
for the best in
serious reading
that integrates
the passion of
the heart with
the scholarship
of the mind.

LET THE READER UNDERSTAND

A GUIDE TO INTERPRETING AND APPLYING THE BIBLE

DAN McCARTNEY
CHARLES CLAYTON

A
BRIDGEPOINT
BOOK

Copyediting: Robert N. Hosack
Cover Design: Joe DeLeon

Library of Congress Cataloging-in-Publication Data

McCartney, Dan.
    Let the reader understand: a guide to interpreting and applying the Bible / Dan McCartney & Charles Clayton.
        P.   cm.
    Includes bibliographical references.
    ISBN: 1-56476-266-1
    1. Bible—Hermeneutics. I. Clayton, Charles. II. Title
BS476.M333   1994   93-45514
220.6'01—dc20   CIP

BridgePoint is the academic imprint of Victor Books.

1   2   3   4   5   6   7   8   9   10   Printing/Year   98   97   96   95   94

CONTENTS

Dedicated to
the men and women who valiantly proclaim, teach,
and defend the Gospel on university and
college campuses throughout the world,

and in memory of
Raymond B. Dillard
teacher, mentor, friend.

"In thy light shall we see light" — *Psalm 36:9*

INTRODUCTION

GOD'S WORD AND HUMAN UNDERSTANDING:
What Is the Problem?

Recently a campus minister approached a couple in the campus Christian fellowship group. The couple had been sleeping together even though they were not married. When he confronted them with some biblical texts about fornication and marital commitment they responded: "Well, that's *your* interpretation; everybody is entitled to their own interpretation."

How often are those words spoken every day? Many people want to say they believe the Bible, but not so many wish to heed its message. "Interpretation" often appears to be a way of getting the Bible to say what someone wants it to say.

Of course, if we want to understand the Bible, we must expend at least some mental effort, and this mental effort is interpretation. And it is true that each person must do his or her own understanding, even if he or she depends on someone else to explain things, and so everyone who reads the Bible must be an interpreter. But does this mean that "everybody is entitled to their *own* interpretation"? Is interpretation simply a matter of subjective feelings about the Bible?

Even for Christians, or perhaps especially for Christians, this is a problem. Does the Bible teach something in particular, or is the meaning of a text simply "what I get out of it"? Is a particular interpretation right, and are others wrong? How do we know whether an interpretation is wrong or right? On the other hand, how do we explain how different Christians can read the same text and reach contradictory conclusions about what the text teaches? How can we challenge someone's interpretation, and say, "Your interpretation is wrong"?

If we regard the Bible as the fountainhead of our faith, it is *crucial* that we resolve this problem. If we are to obey God, we must first understand what He said. If we are to believe, there must be something there for us to believe.

Perhaps the reader is at this point thinking, "Yes, there are always people who twist and contort the Bible to say what they want it to say, but there is a *plain* or literal meaning to Scripture, and the problems come from not paying attention to the plain

11

meaning." But different people see different "plain" meanings in a text. And the "plain" meaning is not always literal. What is the "plain" meaning of "If your right eye causes you to sin, tear it out"? (Matt. 5:29) How does one *know* that the "plain" meaning here is not literal? It is with these questions in mind that this book has been written. "Hermeneutics," the science of interpretation, is not a lightweight subject. But some modern books on hermeneutics make it far more difficult than it needs to be. They sometimes seem to be dedicated more to "the art of giving incomprehensible answers to insoluble questions"[1] than to helping people understand. But those who trust in the self-revealing God *can* answer these questions, and we will strive to give some comprehensible (though hardly comprehensive) answers.[2] In the midst of Jesus' discourse on the last things (Mark 13 and Matthew 24) are the words, "let the reader understand." God Himself wants His people to understand His book. It is our prayer that He will use our book to help some of His people understand His book just a bit better.

We have organized our material into three parts. The first part has to do with our "presuppositions," the things we assume when we begin trying to understand a text. How these presuppositions operate, how we may critique our *own* presuppositions, and the assumptions which the Bible itself makes, are the topics addressed in the three chapters which make up this section.

The second part deals more directly with the *theory* of interpretation. After a brief look at the way some Christians have in the past dealt with the interpretation of the Bible, we will examine both "grammatical-historical" exegesis, which is focused on determining the *original* meaning, and the questions of later meaning and application today.

The third part focuses on the *practice* of interpretation. Here is the "nitty-gritty" of exegesis and interpretation, with examples of how, and how not, to interpret. Here too are suggestions regarding the interpretation of various literary genres found in the Bible.

Finally, this last section also broadens out to the *application* of interpretation, or how to use the Bible, especially with regard to worship, witness, and guidance. Two appendices discuss the rather technical matters of where the meaning of a text resides and a description and critique of various "critical" methods of interpretation.

PART ONE

INTERPRETATION AND PRESUPPOSITIONS

C an a Christian and a Jew agree on the meaning of Isaiah 53? If they suspend their Christianity and Judaism, are they then able to agree? If so, is it because they have come to the text without presuppositions, or is it because they now share a new presupposition (e.g., rationalism)? Is the new presupposition inherently superior to the Christian or Jewish one?

The reformer John Calvin began his *Institutes of the Christian Religion* with the observation that to know God one must know one's self, and to know one's self one must know God.[1] Something like this is true as well for interpreting the Bible. We must begin by asking who we are who read the book. In other words we must look at ourselves rather critically, to see what kind of intellectual baggage, and what sort of ideological agenda we are bringing with us, consciously or unconsciously, and how these presuppositions influence, for good or ill, our understanding of the Bible.

Interpreting any text involves two different types of assumptions. First, underlying all our thinking and interpreting are our presuppositions[2] about life and ultimate realities, our worldview. These provide the basic foundation for how we understand everything. Second are the assumptions which we make about the nature of the text we are reading.

Because they are so central to our understanding, the first of these are held tenaciously; to relinquish or change our basic presuppositions means a reordering and reevaluation of our lives. It calls into question all that we think we know.

On the other hand, our assumptions about texts are usually held loosely and are easily adapted according to the character of a text. When we start reading a book, we have in mind a certain paradigm, or preconception of what the book is about. If we think the book is history, and then discover it has the marks of fiction, we simply discard the first paradigm and reorder our understanding of the book according to the new one.

But in the case of the Bible, which deals with the fundamental questions of our lives and worldviews, our assumptions about the text move into the first category of presuppositions. The Christian presupposition is that Isaiah 53 is part of God's revelation in both the Old and New Testaments; the orthodox Jew presupposes that God's revelation is in the Hebrew Bible as mediated through the Talmud. The Christian believes the Old Testament is primarily a prophetic book which leads up to a historical fulfillment in Christ; the orthodox Jew sees the Hebrew Bible as primarily a law book which provides the constitution for the Jewish people. Hence, the Jew and the Christian are going to see Isaiah 53 differently. And for either one to change views on the nature of the text would mean a complete reordering of worldview.[3]

But why do we not simply suspend all our presuppositions and just stick to the facts? Would this not remove the uncertainty in interpretation and provide an unshakeable ground upon which to understand things?

We will argue later that there is a right way to understand Isaiah 53 or any other passage and that the right way is indicated by the nature of the text itself. However, discerning this is not a matter of escaping or suspending our presuppositions, but changing and adapting them. We really cannot escape them. Since the things we assume are to us self-evident, we may be unconscious of them, but they still determine our understanding, and without them there is no understanding. Any time we find "meaning" in a text, we arrive at that "meaning" by fitting it in with our previous knowledge. And this involves assumptions or presuppositions about such things as the nature of the text we are reading, the meaning of life, and how we know things. All our interpreting activity in life involves assumptions, just as in geometry every theorem can only be proven on the basis of previous theorems and "self-evident" assumptions.[4] Presuppositions form the basis of the "interpretive framework" by which we understand things.

Jesus says in Matthew 6:22, "The eye is the lamp of the body. So, if your eye is healthy, your whole body will be full of light; but if your eye is bad, your whole body will be full of darkness. If then the light in you is darkness, how great is that darkness!" He was talking about the root commitments around which one orients his or her life, or what we are calling "basic presuppositions."[5] If the principles which enable us to "see" and understand are wrong, then our understanding is no understanding at all.

This is a devastating judgment. Which of us has all his or her presuppositions right? Fortunately we do not have to have *all* our presuppositions right in order to begin. There is a difference between blindness and the need for wearing glasses. But we do need to make sure our eyes are working. In other words, we must make sure that our most basic presupposition, whether conscious or unconscious, is sound. But what should this most basic presupposition be?

For most modern people, the conscious or unconscious starting point is their own existence and their own reason. The philosopher Descartes basically set the tone for the modern way of thinking when he decided that the only thing he could not doubt was the fact that he was doubting, and concluded that, since he was thinking, therefore he must exist. People thus start from themselves, and assume that only their own human reason can decide whether something is true.[6] But more recently philosophers have realized that reason never exists apart from a person who is reasoning, and thus "reason" is subject to other interests of the reasoner. Otherwise all reasoning human beings would be able to agree on everything.

Further, if humans claim to be the ones who ultimately decide what is true, they are claiming to be able to make an absolute judgment. But to make an absolute judgment,

> man will . . . have to seek to make a system for himself that will relate all the facts of his environment to one another in such a way as will enable him to see exhaustively all the relations that obtain between them. In other words, the system that the non-Christian has to seek on his assumption is one in which he himself virtually occupies the place that God occupies in Christian theology. Man must, in short, be virtually omniscient.[7]

But no human can ever have *all* the facts, and further, as we shall point out in 2.4.1, "facts" can only be stated in relation to other facts. So how can anyone know anything on this presuppositional basis? This is why non-Christians today frequently deny that there is any "absolute truth."

The Christian, on the other hand, affirms the validity of human reason, but maintains that it can only have a proper ground if we acknowledge first that God the Creator exists, that He has communicated with humanity, and that He constituted our "reason" as an effective tool for comprehension of language and all else in the created world.[8] This Christian starting point is not a groundless assumption. According to Romans 1:19-21, all human beings are constituted such that they *know* the essential attributes of God, because the creation screams at them that it, and they themselves, have been made by God. That is, everyone has a built-in ability to recognize the plain, self-evident God by the created universe. But rather than proceed on the basis of this self-evident presupposition, unregenerate men and women prefer other starting points for reason, and in the process destroy the real ground for reason.

When it comes to the Bible, this means that the modern non-Christian's basic presupposition will result in an approach different from that of the Christian. For the non-Christian, statements which say they come from God cannot be allowed to escape testing by a human reason which has begun by *assuming that it has no need of God*; they assume that reason would operate the same whether or not the true God exists. Thus, many modern students of the Bible evaluate whether biblical statements are true on the basis of criteria which are external to the Bible itself,[9] and this cuts them off from having their own thinking critiqued by God's Word. This is like children who cannot learn because they believe they know everything already. But Christians are persuaded by the Holy Spirit that the Bible is God's true voice.[10] Christians, under the Holy Spirit's tutelage, use reason to decide *what* God is saying in His Word, and their reason, starting from the correct presuppositions, can recognize the wisdom and truthfulness of what is said,[11] but they do not use reason to decide *whether* what He says is true on the basis of some external criteria. What criteria could be more ultimate than God's speech? Are our thoughts higher than God's thoughts?

For Jesus and the New Testament writers, the Scripture is inviolable ("Scripture cannot be broken," John 10:35, NIV); we cannot decide whether it is true on the basis of some external criteria. Yet the evangelists like Paul and Apollos *"argued . . . from the Scriptures*, explaining and proving that it was necessary for the Christ to suffer and to rise from the dead" (Acts 17:2-3 [RSV]; see also 18:28; 19:8).

If truth exists outside of ourselves, we will not know it by pretending that we have no presuppositions, nor will we attain it by embracing all our presuppositions as unchangeable parts of ourselves; we will achieve it only if we submit ourselves, presuppositions and all, to the One who understands and interprets all things rightly. The goal therefore is to become, not presuppositionless, but presuppositionally self-critical. Obviously we have been presupposing a great deal. But if the Bible communicates the truth, and if we wish to learn it from the Bible, we must at least share that most basic of its presuppositions, that submission to God who speaks in His word is the first step in understanding Him. The fear of the Lord is the beginning of both knowledge and wisdom (Prov. 1:7; Ps. 111:10).

It is not only our most basic presupposition that should be brought into line with that of the biblical writers; subordinate presuppositions need to be examined as well. Of course, this too is never easy, because our presuppositions are going to influence how we look at our presuppositions, but it is not hopeless. Although it is an exceedingly difficult process, the attempt to recognize one's presuppositions, and evaluate whether and to what degree they are in harmony with those of the Bible,[12] must continually be undertaken throughout life. In fact, we could say that *the key to interpreting the Bible is to allow it to change and mold our presuppositions* into an interpretive framework compatible with the Bible.

What causes our presuppositions to change? More to the point, what causes our assumptions regarding the meaning or interpretation of the Bible or a part of it to change? If a paradigm or set of assumptions about a text is yielding little understanding, eventually we may shift them to a new set which works better. Elements of discord or "cognitive dissonance"[13] may also provoke a reevaluation of assumptions. In mystery novels, a good detective who is bothered by the "little" discords in the "obvious" solution is often thereby motivated to discover the correct solution. The hermeneutical process is similar. Even after our "rock-bottom" presupposition is right, constant reevaluation is still a necessary and healthy process and should continue throughout life. It is what enables us to understand the truth and to grow in our understanding of God's Word.

We can think of this as a "hermeneutical spiral" or a "spiral of understanding." Although one must know the forest in order to understand the trees, it is also true that a knowledge of the trees builds up the understanding of the forest. Our presuppositions about the overall meaning of the Bible, and life in general for that matter, form the interpretive framework for understanding particular texts of the Bible, which in turn act as a corrective to the overall interpretive presuppositions. This continual interaction moves us up a spiral toward a "meeting of meaning" and understanding of the truth.

Unfortunately, in our day the very relevance of this task is seen as rather questionable. Not only do many people deny the existence of absolute truth, they claim that even if there were "absolute truth" it would be incommunicable, because language is relative. So our first chapter will look at the general presuppositions regarding truth and language. The discussion may get a bit technical in this chapter, but the reader is urged to persevere, because all the discussion these days about "hermeneutics" has largely to do with presuppositions about truth and language. In chapter 2 we shall focus on presuppositions regarding the Bible, and chapter 3 will raise the question of how presuppositions relate to our methods of interpretation.

ONE

TRUTH, LANGUAGE, AND SIN

When we approach the Bible, there are three aspects of our worldview, of our general outlook on life, that profoundly affect and even determine what meaning we find there. The first of these is our view of truth: is there such a thing as absolute truth, and if there is, are we capable of knowing it? Truth is the pillar upon which proper understanding is built. Second, how does language, the vehicle of understanding, work? What are our assumptions about how language works; how can a text that is thousands of years old "say" anything to us today? Finally, we must reckon with the fact of our own sin, and the degree to which it spoils our understanding by coloring our *desire* to read the text one way as opposed to another.

1.1 The Pillar of Understanding: Truth

The presuppositions of most people today include: (1) an *ideological* presupposition that man[1] is the measure of all things and that human reason must be entirely autonomous; (2) the *methodological* assumption that the "scientific" method is the only valid means for ascertaining truth; and (3) an assumption of *attitude* that there is no knowable "absolute" truth, but that "truth" is always relative to the knower.[2]

But if we wish to understand the Bible's message on its own terms we cannot use these presuppositions. They are incompatible with the Scriptures, which presuppose that God, not man, measures all things (Job 38–41), that human reason is dependent and cannot penetrate to the very bottom of things, but that ultimate and absolute truth is knowable, by way of personal relationship (1 Cor. 8:2-3). With regard to method, the Scriptures claim that things do not always work the same way, and that some events have non-earthly or supernatural causes (e.g., Heb. 2:4). Now if these claims are true, then it is inappropriate to apply to Scripture a modern naturalistic "scientific" approach which assumes in advance that there is not supernatural intervention. One cannot evaluate the Bible's claims to truth by using methods which assume in advance that these claims are impossible.

19

1.1.1 Can we know the truth?

Anyone who has tried to testify to the truth of the Gospel on a secular university campus knows that many students believe it is impossible to know "the truth." They can give three reasons for this belief: first, knowledge is limited to this world; second, all knowledge is relative to the knower; and third, language is relative and thus incapable of expressing "absolute truth."

1.1.1.1 Is knowledge limited to this world?

Ever since Plato philosophers generally made a distinction between ultimate or transcendent truth (the "ideal world"), and worldly or proximate realities (the "real" or phenomenal world, which our senses experience), but until the Enlightenment they believed both could be known, and both were capable of being understood by reason. The philosopher Immanuel Kant, as a child of the Enlightenment, was committed to the sovereignty of human reason, but he showed, at least to the satisfaction of most philosophers since, that pure human reason, proceeding by *a posteriori* argument, could not of itself penetrate to any ultimate truth, certainly not to the "transcendent" realm of morals and theology. "Knowledge" to Kant was never more than a synthesis between sense experience and the structures of understanding coming out of a person's mind.[3] So Kant drew the line between "ideal" and "real" much more sharply, dividing knowledge between the *noumenal* world (the world of mental structure) and the *phenomenal* world (the world of sense experience). The only knowledge achievable by critical scientific investigation is of the phenomenal; it is limited to our synthetic understanding of this world, and all knowledge of this world must be acquired through (inductive) reasoning, not by way of any external authority. On the other hand, God, the soul, and freedom were noumenal constructs, "ideas," pure *a priori* concepts which exceed the possibility of experience, and which were innate in the human mind.[4] In this view, ultimate realities are not discoverable, but only believable, and thus whatever "knowledge" we do have is subjectively determined. Nietzsche drew this to its logical conclusion, that any speaking about truth is illusory.

What, then, is truth? A mobile army of metaphors, metonyms, and anthropomorphisms—in short, a sum of human relations, which have been enhanced, transposed, and embellished poetically and rhetorically, and which after long use seem firm, canonical, and obligatory to a people: truths are illusions about which one has forgotten that this is what they are: metaphors which are worn out and without sensuous power.[5]

The secularist Enlightenment began in hopes of finding absolute truth without a God who acts in this world.[6] It ended up denying the possibility of truth.

But was not the Enlightenment validated by the history of human thought subsequently? The physical sciences have been rather successful in their inductive analysis of and resultant control over the physical world; the world seems to be reasonable and knowable as long as we stick within the bounds of reason and science.[7] On the other hand, philosophy and theology have become increasingly confused and confusing, often degenerating into exercises in "sesquipedalian obfuscation."[8] So increasing numbers of people have come to view science as the only source of truth and think that truth is limited to descriptions of this world.[9] Questions of God, or ultimate meaning, are regarded as simply unknowable, or "knowable" only by intuition or subjective "feeling," and should be left alone.

But in spite of this, people cannot stop thinking about reality beyond the physical world, and many strange cults and a plethora of religious ideas have cropped up, demanding and often obtaining the allegiance of large numbers of people disaffected with the purely materialistic scientific approach. Certain elements of experience (not just thought), particularly those having to do with human relationships, cannot be fit into the purely material universe, and yet are undeniably real. Personality is more basic in the universe than physics.[10] Further, science itself is starting to recognize that even in the physical universe there are limits to what rationality can accomplish.[11] The existence of truth which transcends this universe can no longer be denied simply because "science" cannot analyze it.

1.1.1.2 Is all knowledge relative?

But even if this be true, is not all human knowledge, even that of the physical world, relative to the knower? Knowledge necessarily entails a paradigm or theory of order (an *a priori*; a person always

21

knows "facts" in relation to other facts which he or she knows), and since everyone's total knowledge and experience is different, each person's total worldview is unique, and hence his or her knowledge of something is never identical to any other person's knowledge of that same thing.

It must be acknowledged that human knowledge is always relative to the knower, and is always based on that human being's experience and presuppositions, but *there is an important distinction between knowing an absolute truth and knowing a truth absolutely*. Humans can know an absolute, transcendent truth if that truth is known by an absolute Person whose knowledge does *not* depend on experience and if that absolute Person shares His knowledge with humans. It is a conviction, indeed a basic assumption, of the biblical writers that such a Person indeed is there and that He has communicated truth in Scripture.[12] Scripture writers assume God is there and that He has spoken. Thus we may know absolute truth, albeit not absolutely; we may know it truly, even though only partially and imperfectly. The atheist or agnostic may cry "presupposition" at us, but we may point out that they are presupposing that God has *not* spoken.

In fact, the proponent of the idea that "all truth is relative" really can say nothing, for if all truth is relative, then the statement that all truth is relative must be relative, which means no such absolute statement can be made. The difference between the Bible and the modern approach is that the modern person regards knowledge as the provenance only of beings who are finite and relative, and thus for them "truth" can only be a relative term. But the Bible recognizes One who transcends relative knowledge, so there is absolute truth, and He speaks to His people, so they may know it.[13]

1.1.1.3 Can truth be expressed in language?

Perhaps the most forceful argument against the knowability of absolute truth is the argument that, since human language is always relative, therefore language is incapable of expressing or formulating an "absolute truth." One extreme form of this view was held by the great linguistic philosopher Ludwig Wittgenstein. In his *Tractatus Logico-Philosophicus*[14] he asserts, "ethics cannot be put into words" (6.421), and declares a little later, "God does not reveal himself in the world" (6.432). Wittgenstein does acknowledge that there are "things" which cannot be put into words, which he calls "the mystical" (6.522), but since they cannot be put into words no certain knowledge can be had of them, nor can they be shared via language. Thus, the final section of his *Tractatus,* on this mystical, consists of a single sentence which simply claims that nothing can be said.

From a different perspective the German philosopher Martin Heidegger also challenges the possibility of knowing absolute truth because knowledge is linguistic and always "on the way," being disclosed in language. In his most influential work, *Being and Time,*[15] Heidegger insisted that language reveals Being, but every disclosure of "Being" is also a concealment. Any language which spoke of positive and absolute truth as something that could be had rather than striven for was "fallen" and inauthentic, because it was not anchored in the existential moment.[16]

Both Wittgenstein and Heidegger are operating on a presuppositional base which excludes direct communication by the transcendent God.[17] On such a base they are being consistent in rejecting the knowability of absolute truth.[18]

But although modern presuppositions lead to a denial of any absolute truth, biblical assumptions affirm and support that there is indeed truth that is absolute and transcends the relativity of human knowing. What God has said is absolutely true. If we wish to know that truth truly, our only avenue is to know the One who knows absolutely, and this means adopting an attitude of submission to God and a recognition of what reason cannot do. It also means cultivating our relationship to God if we wish to increase our understanding of the truth, and it means maintaining humility, in recognition that, while by God's grace we may know some absolutes, we shall never know them perfectly.[19]

1.1.2 How do we know transcendent truth?

All the above might give the impression that reason or the mind has nothing to do with knowing the truth and that truth is simply apprehended mystically. But although our *basis* for knowledge is a relationship to God, the actual *content* of knowledge and its acquisition is not a mystical experience, but involves communication, thinking, and a conscious positive response to the knowledge we thereby acquire. In other words, it involves language, reason, and faith, considered here in reverse order.

1.1.2.1 Faith

Anselm rightly said, *"credo ut intelligam,"* "I believe in order that I might understand,"[20] referring to Isaiah 7:9b. Anselm recognized that unless we approach knowledge, especially knowledge of the Scriptures, from a standpoint of submission to its teaching, we will not be able properly to understand it.[21] But in some sense the reverse is also true: we must understand in order to believe. Faith is a response to *something*, not *nothing*. True faith is not simply an irrational leap in the dark, a submission to nothing in particular, or to the *"mysterium tremendum et fascinans."*[22] It is a knowledgeable response to God's communication with us.

We are thus confronted with another circle or spiral.[23] If true knowing requires faith and faith requires knowing, how does one get started on the spiral? The answer is twofold. First, every human being, by virtue of being in the image of God, has an awareness of deity as soon as he or she has self-awareness. This *sensus deitatis*, which is built into people, provides a ground for knowledge, whether it is acknowledged or not. All creation, including humanity itself, shouts of its Creator, and thus everyone knows enough about God to be condemned for not obeying Him. The problem is that people suppress this awareness and by doing so they distort the truth they know (see Rom. 1:19-23).

Secondly, God initiates a special relationship with His people by special revelation (see sec. 2.4). "No one knows the Father except the Son and anyone to whom the Son chooses to reveal Him" (Matt. 11:27). It was quite appropriate for the father of the demon-possessed boy to cry out, "I believe; help my unbelief!" (Mark 9:24) Faith ceases suppressing the truth and instead seeks it and is nourished by it.

1.1.2.2 Language

In order to understand what anyone is saying, one must first of all have some idea of what the other person is talking about.

> Words produce understanding by appealing to experience and leading to experience. Only where word has already taken place can word take place. Only where there is already previous understanding can understanding take place.[24]

How then is communication possible?

When children learn language they must already know something about the language in order to know what to make of the diverse sounds. But to know the language they must first learn it.[25] How do children get started on this "linguistic competence spiral"? They must have some innate linguistic capacity, an inherent recognition which places them already in the spiral of understanding. Even non-Christians recognize this inherent linguisticality in children, though they cannot explain it.[26]

The Bible indicates that humans are created in God's image. This implies many things, but it certainly includes our ability to communicate with God and each other,[27] and this involves competence in language, as well as the ability to understand concepts.

1.1.2.3 Reason

Like linguisticality and faith, and implied by them, our reasoning and understanding capacities also come from God and act as responses to God. The Book of Proverbs lays down the principle that "the fear of the Lord is the beginning [i.e., the starting point] of knowledge" (Prov. 1:7). God calls to Israel, "Come now, let us reason together" (Isa. 1:18). The context in Isaiah indicates that God is not inviting Israel to argue with God, but to consider and understand the redemptive purposes of God.

Language and reason are inextricably linked. One might even argue that they are simply two aspects of the same innate human ability.[28] Reason must work with *predications* or statements about reality. Even the law of noncontradiction,[29] the most basic predicate of rationality, is a linguistic entity. And evaluating, relating, and ordering predications, that is, using reason, all happen linguistically. There is indeed pre-linguistic perception, but the "making sense" of such perception is the process of putting it into language. Raw sense experience must be linguistically interpreted.

Likewise faith and reason are linked and when properly understood and used are not in opposition, but are co-functional. Even for those who disclaim Christianity, some belief system or presuppositional framework of understanding provides a basis for reason, and reason applied to data within that framework provides the content for their belief. If faith and reason are perceived to be in opposition, it is because of a dichotomy between the faith upon which one's reasoning is based and the faith which is professed. The mind must be used (1 Peter 1:13), but it must also recognize its dependency and its limitations (Isa. 55:8-9; 1 Cor. 1:18-25).

In summary, our knowledge is possible because: (1) God first creates us as thinking and speaking beings with self-awareness and awareness of Him, (2) He speaks to us, and (3) He enables us to believe. As Paul says in 1 Corinthians 8:2-3, it is not the one who thinks he knows who knows as he ought to know, but the one who *loves* God who is known by Him. We know because God first knew us, just as we love because God first loved us (1 John 4:19). Those who do not know God only "know" on borrowed capital; they really do know things, but only because they are made in God's image. They have no justification for their knowledge.

1.2 The Vehicle of Understanding: Language

Although we noted above that language is one of the elements involved in knowing the absolute Knower, the problem of language is of special importance, first, because it has all but taken over philosophical thinking in the West in the last century, and second, because questions about how to interpret a book are going to be directly affected by the theory of language adopted. Although we cannot now expound much on the intricacies of this subject,[30] we do need to address at least in cursory fashion the question, "What is a text?" and the related question, "Wherein does the meaning of a text lie?"

1.2.1 What is a text?

Sometimes a text is defined simply as "a piece of language." This may appear obvious to some degree but it is also misleading, because it obscures the more personal nature of a text.[31] Like speech,[32] serious writing is communication,[33] a means of conveying thought and feeling, and of facilitating the sharing of experience, and hence the broadening of experience and knowledge.[34] When an author writes, she produces a linguistic representation or reflection of her thought.[35] When a reader reads, this analogue is "re-presented" in his mind.[36] Thus the reader communes with the author's ideas. Even if the reader criticizes or rejects those ideas, he first attempts to understand or set up in his own mind thoughts analogous to those of the producer of the text.[37] He aims for a "meeting of meaning" with the author.

We might illustrate by means of the now almost obsolete vinyl record. The little waves and ripples in the groove are not music, nor are they a perfect analogue to the performance, but they do truly convey the music. Just as a reader converts the little black marks on a page into words, and the words into a sequence of ideas and arguments, a record player can "read" the waves and ripples and reconvert them into musical sounds, so that the hearer experiences an analogue to the original performance. The listener may reject the music as being too raucous or incomprehensible, or may reject the performance as too lush or too austere, but for the hearer to do so, the music must first be reestablished from its analogue form on the record.

Now this illustration has certain weaknesses, because it too is an analogy. A vinyl record cannot even theoretically be as good as the original performance, no matter how high the quality of the reproduction equipment. Further, the author's thought may in fact not even exist apart from its linguistic form. If thought needs language in order to be formed in the first place (see p. 25), then a language event cannot be simply an externalization of a non-linguistic or pre-linguistic thought. Language, along with the rest of the world experience of the thinker, provides the interpretive framework for thought, not just its encoding form.[38] Nevertheless, the vinyl record is like language in its being an analogous but imprecise medium of conveying human expression.

Imprecision in a vinyl record means that something is lost. But imprecision in language is in some ways its strength. Ambiguity and open-endedness mean that language is flexible enough to express thought accurately.[39] Of course, the difficulty at the other end remains; the interpreter can never understand perfectly the exact original thought of the writer, even though the theoretical possibility of it forever remains in the text. But, just as any record player can reproduce with some fidelity the original performance, any reader can with some degree of fidelity reproduce the original thought. And finally, a text, like a record, is permanent, and the thought, like the performance, can be reproduced over and over again, each time deepening the total apprehension of the original on the part of the hearer, coming ever closer to a "meeting of meaning."

This is quite a different question than how reality is transmitted through an author's language. When an author transmits his perception of reality the transmission is not identical to the reality itself, because he is using a medium, language. A text is, to use Paul Ricoeur's words, not a reproduction of reality but a "representation" of it.[40] Thus Ricoeur likens a text to a painting rather than a photograph.[41] If we remained with our record-player illustration, it would be more like the relationship of the performance which is recorded to the notes written on the composer's manuscript. A conductor "re-presents" the "reality" of the composer's product. Solti, Szell, Toscanini, and Furtwängler all gave valid but different readings of Beethoven's symphonies. But some readings could conceivably ignore the notes or present them in such an insensitive and unmusical way that most listeners would call them "poor."

The application to the Bible should be clear. Language is adequate to convey God's thought accurately and truly, though not comprehensively,[42] because our abilities to receive it are always imperfect. But the advantages flowing from the facts that any reader can get some more or less faithful understanding (just as any record player can play any record, albeit with greater or less fidelity) and that the message can be heard over and over, mean that the textuality of the Bible is not its weakness but its strength. Further, like the several conductors, different biblical human authors may "re-present" the same reality differently, and yet each presentation be a valid rendition (such as with the four Gospels).

So a text is first of all an encoding of thought in such a fashion as it may be replayed, "re-presented," reexperienced. But texts are also intentional acts.[43] Just as a conductor makes a recording for some purpose (such as to register his ideas on how a piece should be performed or to make money), texts are "uttered" by people who wish to accomplish something by their utterance. They can project a world (as in fiction), they can assert things, and by such projections or assertions they can attempt to generate changes in behavior or perception in the hearers. This is certainly true of the Bible: "So shall my word be that goes out from my mouth; it shall not return to me empty, but it shall accomplish that which I purpose" (Isa. 55:11).

Now if a text is an act, does it follow that meaning is the intent of the initial actor (i.e., the author)? Where does the meaning of a text lie? Again, at first glance this appears to be obvious, but the issue is not as simple as it seems.

1.2.2 What and where is meaning?
The word *meaning* is somewhat slippery. If we ask, "What do you mean?" we are usually requesting an expanded paraphrase or re-

phrasing of something. It is the idea of sense or thought which is most commonly identified with meaning. But the question "What do you mean?" could also be used to ask someone to specify the *referent* or the specific application to the sense which the speaker has in mind. More of this is discussed in 5.1.2.

Meaning can also indicate what something entails. "This means war!" expresses the idea that some act *entails* war. Meaning can refer to the *value* of something. ("My job means a lot to me.") And sometimes the purpose or *intention* of the speaker or author is indicated by the word *meaning*. If I tell my daughter "the milk is sour," my meaning is that she should not drink it.[44]

But most often meaning is taken to refer to the linguistic sense of what is said. In oral speech, this is often identical with the *referent*, the specific person, thing, or circumstance which is being talked about. With written texts, however, although they frequently are generated by a specific referential circumstance, their meaning is more generally applicable. Fiction, of course, has no referent at all, unless it is allegorical. The meaning is how a discourse, sentence, or word functions in language as a whole. With this idea of "meaning" in mind, we can ask the question, "Where is meaning?" or "Where does meaning come from?"

One of the aims of the Enlightenment was to get back to the sources, to recover the original primitive ideas of early writers. Theologians of the late Middle Ages had tended to read even the ancient pagan philosophers through a Christian grid, placing the most Christian interpretation possible upon their works. This was rejected in the Enlightenment. The "meaning" of a text was to be understood only by reference to the original author and his immediate audience. The assumption was that the author's intent was what one should attempt to uncover in the process of interpretation.[45]

But this focus on the author as the source of meaning was not only a feature of the Enlightenment. As we shall see in chapter 4, the Reformers also rejected the church tradition approach and strove to recover the meaning intended by the original authors of Scripture. Unlike the Enlightenment secularists, the Reformers recognized that God was the ultimate author of Scripture and that He as author was the source of its meaning. But they looked to the original human author's situation and intent as the basis for discovering God's meaning. To understand the divine sense of a text, it was necessary to recover as much of its original human referent as possible, as a contextual guide to that sense. Any alleged sense of Scripture which is unrelated to the original referent must be suspect. Focusing on the author's intent provides both a key and a control to meaning.

But does "author's intent" cover all there is in the meaning of a text? An objection sometimes raised is that if the author is deceased or unavailable for direct comment, the only meaning possible is a reconstruction on the part of the reader. Thus the "author's intent" cannot be some kind of criterion for evaluating a reading, because that intent is only knowable by way of a reading.[46] Although the authority of meaning may rest in the author's thought, we have no way of accessing that thought except through the actual words and what we know of the situation of the original hearers. In the case of the Bible, if the text had any authority for its original hearers, it must have been expressed in a way understandable to them, so that they would be responsible to act on the teaching.

Further, an author's intent or purpose is not quite the same as the sense, as was noted above. When a young child says, "why?" the intent may be simply, "Please keep talking"; although the meaning or sense of, "Why?" is, "What are the causes behind the previous assertion." Finally, not everything that an utterance or text might legitimately mean in every situation has to be in the author's consciousness.[47] As an historical phenomenon, a text, like any other thing in history, can mean something on its own. The Battle of Hastings means something, not because an author "wrote" the battle but because it had and has a determining effect on the present. Similarly, a classic text changes things and has a determining effect on the present. The way a text has influenced history might have little to do with an author's conscious intent.

These problems led to a development of three more modern theories: (1) the autonomous text theory of interpretation, (2) the so-called reader-response theory, and (3) the socio-linguistic community theory. The autonomous-text theory finds meaning in the text itself, apart from author or reader. The reader-response view argues that meaning is only found in the mind of the reader. Even the author becomes only another reader on this view. The community theory argues that meaning is an unreflected awareness of meaning generated by the conventions and expectations of the socio-linguistic community to which the reader belongs.

A more detailed discussion of these may be found in Appendix A, but at this point we simply suggest that, although all of these theories have certain aspects of truth, all of them also suppress other aspects. Particularly, what many of them frequently understress is that all types of speech, texts included, are forms of *personal* communication, and therefore bear the character of inter-personal acts,[48] acts which necessarily involve both speaker and hearer as well as the medium of communication. But more importantly in our view, the question of the locus of meaning as well as even the very possibility of meaning cannot be answered without reference to a truly transcendent interpreter. Meaning and understanding presuppose order, coherency, and purpose. For there to be order, coherency, and purpose there must be One who orders, holds things together, and intends. It is the understanding which this One has which makes possible the communication of meaning in language. By itself, this does not help us to know what the true meaning of a text is, but it does give a basis for expecting that there is a knowable true meaning outside of ourselves (see p. 21), a universally valid standard of meaning toward which we must strive. There is a determinate meaning; it is intended by the author, inherent in the text within its context, *and* apprehended with more or less fidelity by the more or less informed reader, all of these being under the linguistic standard of God's interpretation of all acts, linguistic and otherwise.[49]

However, each of these loci functions in a somewhat different way. The author is the one who made certain choices regarding what to say. The language or social environment may determine what *way* he or she says something, but it does not determine *what* is said.[50] Thus the meaning that inheres in the reader's mind strives for congruity with the thought of the author, and the text itself has meaning only as a tool to establish communication between an author and his or her audience.

When it comes to the Bible, this matter becomes even more crucial because the Bible professes, and the church confesses it, to be God's own utterance. For most of the church's history Christians assumed that the Bible had been authored by God, with human writers to a greater or lesser degree simply acting as mouthpieces for His speech.[51] So interpretation was a question of understanding what God meant. The assumption was that God expressed absolute truth in language. The interpreter sought to hear God speaking in the Scripture. But after the Enlightenment, the divine authorship, although not always explicitly denied, was deemed more or less irrelevant for the task of ascertaining the "meaning." Interpretation focused on the human author exclusively.

If the Bible is God's Word, is not He, rather than the human author, the One who gives the Bible its determinate meaning? But if this is the case, how can we know what that determinate meaning is? All speech with which we are familiar here on earth occurs in *human* contexts, and the meaning of a set of words is different from that same set of words uttered in a different context. For this reason, even the Protestant Reformers, Luther, Calvin, and Zwingli, emphasized that the meaning of a text had to be rooted in the human author's situation and linguistic environment.[52] Unlike the later Enlightenment figures, however, they did not regard the human author's situational meaning as the limit but as the *foundation* for our knowledge of the text's meaning. Certainly the biblical authors themselves, when they used earlier biblical materials, almost unreflectively assumed that the words addressed to previous generations in earlier circumstances were nevertheless also addressed to them (e.g., see 1 Cor. 9:10 and 1 Peter 1:12).

In conclusion, God as ultimate author of Scripture is the One who determines its meaning. Not only is He its author (and thus the "author-ity" behind it), but also He is the sovereign God who interprets all things rightly. He invented language, and He created humans with their linguistic capacity. With respect to our knowledge of the divine meaning, since the Scriptures function in human contexts, *our access to that divine meaning can only be by way of the human authors and their contexts*. The human author's meaning and his concrete socio-linguistic situation provide the starting point for understanding God's meaning for all His people. We "get to know" the human author's point in order to grasp God's point.

1.3 The Spoiler of Understanding: Sin

What has sin to do with interpretation? In most people's minds, sin has to do with behavior, whereas interpretation has to do with understanding. Most modern literary criticism avoids deriving from any text an ethical teaching about life in general. Such didacticism is derogated as "moralism" and is shunned as inappropriate for the task of interpretation. But texts themselves, biblical and non-biblical, are only valuable to humans as they provide help in dealing with life. Even artistic or entertainment texts are appreciated and entertaining to us because they in some way help us cope with life, and so the implied moral questions, questions of what is right (not just those within the narrative structure but in life generally), are as important to a real-life understanding of the purpose of a text as is the analysis of its own internal meaning. Hence, interpretation of any serious writing sooner or later becomes ethical in its outcome.

Also, we have argued that texts are communicative acts, and communicative acts are acts of the will. Thus there is a motive behind the production of a text, and motivation can never be morally neutral. Further, a communicative venture involves not just the utterer or author but also the hearer or interpreter. Just as the author's act cannot be morally neutral, neither can interpretation be ethically neutral. This should be obvious at certain levels. Deliberately misconstruing some text to misrepresent its author is a morally reprehensible act; it is a kind of lying, a "bearing false testimony."

The ethicality of interpretation is supremely important when it comes to interpreting the Bible. The Scriptures repeatedly warn that wrong thinking is ethically and morally evil, and ineluctably leads to more evil and less understanding.[53] Thus, misinterpreting the Scripture is sin. Since the Bible frequently addresses questions of behavioral morality, misunderstanding can lead to incorrect behavior[54] and thus more sin. Third, since the Bible's subject matter directly addresses our life orientation, our interpretation is bound to be heavily influenced by our attempts to justify our own behavior. Finally, we note that biblical interpretation touches directly on questions of truth. Truth and ethics are inseparable.[55] A false interpretation of a true statement is a lie, and lies are evil. A false interpretation of a true statement which is a matter of life and death is therefore a great evil. The Bible even declares that a lie on the part of the serpent was the sin which perpetrated the Fall of man (Gen. 3), and Jesus castigates the devil as the "father of lies" (John 8:44). Satan lied by *misconstruing* the Word of God before he blatantly contradicted it. Bad interpretation is bad.

It therefore seems strange that so much of biblical studies and even books on biblical interpretation seem to operate on the assumption that interpretation can be an ethically neutral and value-free scientific enterprise. There is no escaping the fact that the Bible addresses moral truth, and this automatically means that no reader who understands its message can remain neutral in his or her understanding.

Actually we have probably understated it so far. The problem of sin is the central problem which the Bible addresses. If the chief subject matter of the Bible is the relationship between God and man, the chief obstacle to that relationship is not human finitude or God's invisibility, but human sin.[56] Jesus Christ came into the world to save sinners (1 Tim. 1:15).

Now if sin is such a problem in the biblical frame of reference, one should expect that sin, if the Bible is correct, is going to be a hindrance in any communication, especially in interpretation. Recognition of this may not help directly in the practical matter of finding out the correct interpretation of a passage, but it does help indirectly. It first means that our abilities to communicate linguistically as well as in other ways are weakened. The story of the Tower of Babel illustrates this graphically. It also means that it is extremely unlikely that any interpretation we make will be entirely free from error. Our interpretation is too inescapably beset by unconscious motivations of self-interest. Thus we learn to hold our interpretations, particularly on matters on which the church has very little consensus (such as infant baptism or the millennium), as more or less tentative, and we are slow to brand those who hold differing interpretations as willful suppressors of the truth.

We are also able to understand why certain problems may not hold tidy solutions. For example, in church history the issue of divine sovereignty and human responsibility has often generated more heat than light. The Bible affirms both and does not try to accommodate one by weakening the other. Sometimes well-meaning Christians misstate this as though it were a contradiction, that God is both sovereign and not sovereign. But this is not what Scripture does. Only if God is sovereign, and *exercises* that sovereignty, does *any* human act have purpose. Human responsibility is established, not undermined, by God's sovereignty.

The juxtaposition of divine sovereignty and human responsibility was not a problem with Jesus Christ (and would not have been for humankind had Adam not sinned); Jesus was fully responsible for His actions as a human, His temptations were real (Heb. 4:15), and yet He was unalterably God's chosen Messiah. Interpretation would not be a problem for us were it not for our sin. False interpretations are sinful and are generated by sin. But as we say this, we also reemphasize that an interpretation different from our own may not be sinful; it might be *our* interpretation which is sinful.

But are not at least some texts of the Bible plain and clear? Certainly it often appears to Christians as they read the Bible that they are simply reading the "plain" meaning of a text; and we will even argue later that Scripture is indeed perspicuous. But what is plain to one person may not be plain to another, and in fact might be totally false. The "plain" meaning of Matthew 5:29 appears to command self-mutilation in order to isolate oneself from temptation, but few would suggest that the "plain" meaning here is the correct one. In fact, most people would not even call this a plain meaning, since plainly it is not meant to be taken literally. But there are no explicit indications in the text itself that its meaning is nonliteral. Again the point is to warn against concluding that, because others do not see what is "obvious" to us, *they* are the ones who are willfully suppressing or sidestepping the truth. What is "obvious" to us might be wrong.

In other words, recognition of the problem of sin in interpretation should result in a deep humility about our own interpretations, and a recognition of our need continually to repent of the sinfulness which we may not even recognize in our interpretive endeavors. Perhaps this is why James warns teachers so harshly (James 3:1). When one teaches, one passes on one's interpretations, and the falsity within those interpretations is perpetuated. However, *humility should not lead to inaction*. To withhold the truth also brings judgment, because, "Where there is no revelation the people cast off restraint" (Prov. 29:18), and "my people go into exile for want of knowledge" (Isa. 5:13, RSV). God's people yearn for revealed truth, and if this yearning is not satisfied, they may accept its counterfeit. Fortunately God is gracious and has provided a sacrifice for all our sins, even our sinful misinterpretations.

1.4 Summary
We have been examining how our presuppositions, worldviews, and expectations of the Bible affect and determine our understanding of it. Our understanding of what truth is, whether it is absolute

or relative, and whether it is knowable, sets the stage for our approach to Scripture. We argued that Scripture's own understanding is that truth is indeed transcendent and nonrelative, and that it can be known because God makes it known and because He has created us with minds capable of receiving it. But we also observed that our knowledge of absolute truth is not itself absolute. Our knowledge is derivative and dependent. Although everyone by virtue of the indelible awareness of God and the ineluctable force of general revelation has *some* knowledge of the truth, to know truth *truly* is impossible apart from an attitude of faith and a recognition of the limits of human reason. Therefore, we must affirm both the objectivity of truth in itself and the subjectivity of truth in our apprehension of it.

We also looked at the problem of language as a medium of communication. We concluded that language events such as texts are interpersonal communicative acts. Meaning is a function of the entire matrix of the author, the author's linguistic community, the text, the reader, and the reader's linguistic community. But the direction of interpretation is the reader seeking to understand the author, for which reference must be made to the author's context. If the reader seeks simply to understand herself, there is no communication but only solipsistic omphaloskepsis (navel contemplation).

In the case of the Bible, the ultimate author is God, and so He determines the meaning of the whole. However, since we can only determine the meaning of any utterance by reference to a human situation, the starting point for understanding the divine meaning is always the attempt to recover the meaning determined by the context of the human author.

Finally, we noted that interpretation is an inherently and inescapably ethical activity, particularly when the subject of interpretation is the Bible, which purports to instruct on ethics and truth. Interpretation is never value-free, just as it is never presupposition-free, and decisions on what is right and wrong are necessarily as ethical as the acting upon those decisions. Because of this, if the Bible is correct in its evaluation of sin as the chief problem of humans, sin becomes the chief problem of interpretation. We also warned that this should result not in the condemnation of those who disagree with us but a recognition of the sinfulness inherent in our own interpretation and a constant need to subject our interpretations to reevaluation in the spirit of repentance.

In considering our general presuppositions regarding truth, language, and sin, which provide a context for meaning, we also made reference to God's revelation, both by way of His word and in His world. Since our assumptions about God's revelation have an even greater and more immediate affect on our interpretation, in chapter 2 we will look more closely at our presuppositions about the Bible and creation.

TWO

KNOWING GOD:
PRESUPPOSITIONS ABOUT THE
BIBLE AND CREATION

Most Christians would agree that the Bible plays a unique role in connection with the relationship of God and man. But what kind of role, and what is the precise nature of the Bible's consequent authority? This is an important question for interpretation, because the nature of the Bible's authority will directly affect how we understand and apply it.

In this chapter we shall focus on four questions: (1) What is the relationship between the text of Scripture and the self-revelation of God? (i.e., is the Bible the Word of God, and if so in what sense?) (2) Is the Bible true? (what is the nature and extent of biblical truth?); (3) Is the Bible coherent? (particularly, what is the Bible chiefly about, and how does the Bible interpret itself?); and (4) What is the relationship between the Bible and the world? (in particular the relationship of the truth of the Bible to truth discovered by other means, especially historical material)

2.1 Is the Bible the Word of God?
At the risk of being overly simplistic, those who profess Christianity usually answer in one of three ways.[1]

View 1: The Bible *is* the Word of God. The older orthodox view which prevailed in a more or less unreflected fashion for most of the church's life was that the Bible was directly inspired by God and thus was God's speech to humanity. Sometimes this was stated baldly, the human authors being regarded as little more than scribes taking down the Holy Spirit's words as though by dictation. But often it was more nuanced, reckoning that it was God's sovereign oversight which produced the genuinely human situations and created the human authors in such a way that in truly addressing their real human situations they mediated the truth of God.[2]

View 2: The Bible *becomes* the Word of God. The position sometimes referred to as neo-orthodoxy argues that the text by itself is no more than any other human writing, but that when it encoun-

ters faith, the words of the Bible become for the believing person
God's Word to him or her. God, who is infinite and holy, can only
*in*directly communicate with humans who are finite and sinful. In
this view there is only *indirect* revelation of God in the Scripture.[3]

View 3: The Bible *testifies to* or *contains* the Word of God. This
can actually take different forms. Some see the saving and revealing activity of God in history, especially in the acts of Jesus Christ,
as the Word of God (i.e., the Gospel), and the Bible is simply the
testimony of God's people in response to this self-revealing activity of God. The Bible is the primary source which relates that
activity.[4] Another form views Jesus Christ the person as the Word
of God, and again the Bible is our primary source material for
perceiving and encountering the person of Jesus Christ.[5] Others
think that certain passages of the Bible convey religiously powerful moral force, and in that sense the Bible contains the Word of
God.

Now these views would not necessarily be in conflict if they
were not stated in an exclusive way. This book on hermeneutics
does not become our words *only* when it is read by someone who
knows us personally. Earlier theologians believed the Bible *is* the
Word of God, and yet also regarded Christ as the living Word, and
knew that only the believer can hear the Word of God in the Bible
(see 2 Cor. 3:14-18). Some modern Bible scholars and theologians,
however, contrast the first view with views two and three. They
want to hold to the Bible as the source of our relationship to God
and at the same time to escape the problems generated when the
Bible appears to be in conflict with modern critical views, particularly modern scientific theories and ethical opinions. Those who
hold to the first of these views are then often castigated as "bibli-
cists" who refuse to recognize the historical determinedness of
the several writings of the Bible, and turn the Bible into an idol.[6]
But to recognize that the Bible testifies to the living and true
person who is the Word of God, and that it recites the acts of God
in history, and that it becomes dynamic in believers' lives as they
read it in faith, does not necessarily entail a denial that God has
directly and sovereignly determined the text of the Bible, addressing therein His people during all ages. And to deny that the Bible
is the Word of God inevitably vitiates its authority. If the Bible *only*
becomes or *only* testifies to the Word of God (views two and
three), then the individual reader is free, indeed obligated, to de-

cide which parts truly "become" or truly "testify" to God's Word. He or she must extrapolate the true Word of God from the chaff of the errant text. So the authority ultimately rests with the reader and not with the Bible itself. How then can believers hear what they do not wish to hear? How can the wrong presuppositions and outlooks of the current age and culture be corrected?

Even more important is the uniform assertion of the Bible itself, whenever it quotes itself, that it has unmitigated and direct authority since it comes from God Himself (2 Tim. 3:16).[7] Note how the author of Hebrews, when he quotes the OT, introduces quotations with words like "as the Holy Spirit says" (Heb. 3:7); or note how both Hebrews and Paul indicate that God was speaking directly (Heb. 5:5; 2 Cor. 6:16); or note how Jesus indicates that David spoke words under the inspiration of the Holy Spirit (Mark 12:36). These examples could be multiplied.

But if we adopt the Bible's own viewpoint that it is authored by God, we must raise the question of language again.[8] When humans use language they must formulate what they say in terms of the language they are using. The language enables them to "objectify" their subjective experience so that others can share it. But does it not then follow that the language in which the speaker formulates his thought will to some extent determine the particular objective form of his thought?[9] And will not this influence of language become even more determinative for the reader who attempts to understand the meaning?

If we acknowledge this, then the question arises whether God, if He has spoken in Scripture, has by objectifying His thought in language so limited or "adjusted" His statements according to the linguistic and cultural situation that they are no longer perfectly true? Is direct revelation even possible?

To answer this we refer to three indications from the Bible itself:

First, Jesus Christ was here, and interacted with people face to face. If God can reveal Himself truly in the person of Jesus Christ, with all the limitations of being human, then He can certainly reveal Himself truly in language. Jesus Christ was "determined" as an individual in a particular historical context (He even expressed Himself in one or more human languages) and yet even when He was on earth He was truly and unequivocally God. The incarnation serves as the ultimate foundation for God's linguistic communication with us (see Heb. 1:1-3).

Second, people can speak because God speaks. Language was not a human invention according to the Bible. God spoke first and by speaking created (Gen. 1). Further, God named the most basic distinctions of the created world, light and dark (day and night; Gen. 1:5), and heaven, earth, and sea (Gen. 1:8, 10).[10] After God created man He spoke to man (Gen. 2). He did assign to man the task of naming the animals and perhaps most things, but linguisticality itself was given to man.[11] Thus language need not be totally relative to a social context or to the particular form of the language. Anything that can be said in one language and culture can be said in any other (although it may take longer in some languages than others). Translation, although it may be difficult, is always possible. Thus, although a particular language may influence the thought's form, it does not limit or determine thought.[12]

Third, according to the Bible, humans were made "in God's image." Therefore they have an innate ability to think thoughts patterned after God's thoughts. Linguistic communication from God to humans is possible, though never exhaustive, just as communication between people is possible though never exhaustive.

The astute reader will observe that in this chapter we have presupposed that the author of a text is its source of meaning, even though we acknowledged in the previous chapter that to some extent a text's meaning also has a subjective aspect in the reader. If God is the author of the Bible He is trebly the source of its meaning, for God has determined not only the specific verbal content, but also the linguistic situation and the human understanding. Furthermore, in the case of living authors it is usually recognized that they have at least some moral authority over their works—even deconstructionists[13] are prone to copyright their books and insist that people not deliberately misunderstand them. If God is the ultimate author of Scripture then He as living author retains the moral right to define its meaning. But how does God exercise this right?

There are three means whereby living human authors expect to be able to control the meanings of their texts. One means is further speech; another means is the expectation that the reader will at least begin by assuming an internal consistency in the work; finally the author expects one's readers to understand the particular situation he or she originally addressed as the context for his or her words. Similarly, God, the author of Scripture, exercises authority over the meaning of His words. In fact, He did engage repeatedly in further speech; later revelation (the NT) interpreted and completed the earlier (the OT). He undoubtedly also expects His readers to assume that His speech has an internal coherency and consistency, and He also expects readers to be aware of the historical contexts in which the particular speech first occurred.

Naturally, therefore, where we stand on the issue of God's relationship to the Bible will have at least some effect on the way we interpret it. Particularly, the remaining three questions of this chapter will be answered differently by people who hold varying views on the authorship question. The truth of the Bible, if God's direct authorship is denied, will be perceived as only relative or partial; the truth will have to be critically gleaned from the Bible. If there is only indirect revelation, that is, if there are only human words *about* God's (nonverbal) revelation, then the coherency of the Bible will be only general; one will expect inconsistencies or even contradictions, and the reader will have to make priority judgments when they are perceived. The problems of the Bible's truth in relationship to science and history will be less consequential if we adopt this viewpoint.

But we prefer to retain the viewpoint which the biblical writers themselves evidenced. This may lead to more work, but on the other hand it allows for the text, when we do not understand it, to compel us to reexamine our interpretations and presuppositions. We have something outside of ourselves which controls us, and serves as a sure ground for our interpretations, namely the Bible itself.[14]

2.2 Is the Bible True?

We begin this section with a reminder about what truth is. At least truth involves a linguistic correspondence to extra-linguistic realities as they are constituted by and known by their Creator. This does not mean truth is relative; it is to be sure dependent on God's knowledge, but truth is not dependent on human knowledge. Truth, or rather our experience of it, may indeed be linguistic in form, but not in content. Nevertheless, this linguistic correspondence idea is important because *truth is expressed in propositions.* We shall argue later that truth is more than just propositions, but certainly the Bible makes many assertions about ultimate realities, God, human behavior, and humankind's situation before God which claim to be *true*. By "the Bible's propositions" we do not mean statements in the Bible isolated from their contexts. In fact, divorcing a proposition from its context can distort its meaning and make it an untruth. But the Bible's propositions, considered within the context of the entire Bible, are the completely reliable food supply for doctrine, the crucial elements for teaching the truth about God and humanity. The theology of the Bible is found in its propositions.

Particularly in America, many Christians have attempted to maintain the propositional truth of the Bible and the concept of direct revelation by reference to the Bible's "inerrancy."[15] This happened because the older term "infallibility" was in some quarters being deprived of its semantic value by restricting it to matters of "faith or religious practice" ("faith" and "religion" also being narrowly understood).[16] Now the term inerrancy is particularly oriented toward propositional truth.[17] The authors of this book wish to affirm strongly that everything the Bible *actually says* is true, and that therefore the Bible is without error, but the use of the term inerrancy can be misleading. Some proponents as well as opponents of biblical inerrancy often take the term to mean that every assertion of the Bible must maintain a modern scientific or mathematical *precision*, that historical statements in the Bible must be identical in kind to those of modern historiography, or that all the Bible's assertions are intended in a strictly *literalistic* sense. So clever scholars can set up an "either-or" situation whereby one must opt either for a kind of inerrancy which is totally insensitive to the genre or nature of the particular biblical text or for an acceptance of errors in the Bible.[18] But this is a false dichotomy. Being sensitive to the biblical writer's historiographic purpose, being aware of the use of approximate or symbolic numbers, and being sensitive to the intentional use of different kinds of metaphor are keys to understanding what the Bible's actual assertions are. An erroneous misunderstanding of a text is an error on the part of the *reader*, not of the text or its author.[19] Galileo's opponents thought that the Bible taught that the sun revolved around the earth, but the error was not in the Bible; it was in their understanding of it.

Nevertheless, the term inerrancy does not really go far enough.

The Bible, like human communication in general, is certainly more than true assertions. Communication not only involves the intellectual apprehension of propositions, but also involves the emotions, the aesthetic abilities, and the will. Is praise a proposition? While a psalm may include declarations of God's faithfulness, it is not principally a proposition, and yet it is true.[20] Is a command "without error"? Certainly, if what is meant is that it is indeed a genuine command of the one reported to have commanded it, but it is not a proposition; it is a demand for action. So certainly the Bible is not strictly a set of propositions. Further, Jesus calls Himself "the truth" (John 14:6), and surely He means more than that He is a true proposition or set of propositions, or even the sum of all true propositions. Jesus says to His disciples that "the truth will make you free" (John 8:32). If we acknowledge that saving faith is more than intellectual apprehension of propositions (see James 2:19) then the truth in which we believe must be more than propositions. Especially it must entail imperatives and personal relationship. So although one could define truth as strictly "propositional truth" and then tautologously say that all truth is propositional, it would appear that when Jesus prays, "Your word is truth" (John 17:17), it means more than that it makes true assertions. So although we acknowledge the inerrancy of the Bible with respect to those propositions which it actually makes, the term is really inadequate to indicate the total trustworthiness or urgency or uniqueness of the Bible. A telephone directory might conceivably be inerrant, but its truth is not likely to set anyone free.

Nevertheless, although truth is more than propositional, it is certainly not less than propositional. The meaning of biblical texts is expressible in propositions; biblical truth is not just some mystical experience or a vague feeling of dependency. The fact that truth is more than doctrine should never be used to suggest that doctrine does not matter. Without its propositions, not only would the truth be unknowable and incommunicable, whatever else truth is would collapse in meaninglessness.

2.3 Is the Bible Coherent?

This actually entails many questions; we are here going to focus on two of them: (1) the *perspicuity* or natural clarity of the Bible, and (2) the *unity* of the Bible, or what the Bible is all about. For the latter question we shall look especially at the way in which the NT writers used the OT, since this points up what they regarded as the main message of the (earlier) Scriptures.

2.3.1 Perspicuity

During the Reformation, Protestants were anxious to get the Bible back in the hands of the people and waged war against the doctrine that it could only be properly interpreted by sanctioned experts. They therefore taught that the Bible was clear enough in its important teachings to be properly understood by anyone. For example, in response to the assertion of Erasmus that nothing can be clearly known, even in Scripture, Luther says boldly, "The Holy Spirit is no sceptic, and the things he has written in our hearts are not doubts or opinion, but assertions — surer and more certain than sense and life itself."[21] The Reformers were not saying that all parts of the Bible were equally clear, nor were they denying that some passages in the Bible are so closely tied to their own culture and historical situation that the text is difficult to understand. But they did believe that the primary matter of the Bible was clear enough, and the experience of men and women everywhere was common enough for the Bible's main teachings to be understood without need of expertise or ecclesiastically sanctioned teaching.[22] They also argued that, once the main teachings were understood, the more obscure portions could be properly understood in relation to the clear ones.

We concur heartily with this basic thesis. With all the technical discussion in this book, the reader might conclude that interpreting Scripture is too complicated a matter and that it should be left to experts, but we want to encourage all Christians that they can understand the Bible. Scripture as a whole, as the voice of God, truly communicates without need of intermediaries. God does not play cat and mouse with people; He desires that we understand (1 Tim. 2:4), and if God does indeed oversee all interpretation and give humans their linguisticality, then God's speech is accessible to any who can understand language, and it has an intrinsic vitality that can break through clouds of even self-imposed darkness. Further, God's people are given the Holy Spirit to aid them in their attempts to understand (1 John 2:20).

One of the most important hermeneutical principles is that of repeated reading. One of the authors of this book became enamored at a young age with J.R.R. Tolkien's *Lord of the Rings*. He read that trilogy, along with *The Hobbit*, a total of five times. The reason he did so was because each time through, more of the overarching and underlying history of "Middle Earth" became evident, and the story's subtleties became clearer.

Now the Bible has far more underlying history and far more complexity than Tolkien's trilogy and has the further quality of being a true story. It stands to reason that repeated reading will clarify its message more and more.

Is repeated reading under the tutelage of the Holy Spirit all we need? Well, it is all we absolutely need but it may not be all that is helpful. Good teachers can help us understand better, if for no other reason than that repeated readings by others can compound understanding and give us a head start. This is why, in spite of the dangers of "traditionalism," we should be very slow to reject the tradition of the church. The church's tradition reflects a great deal of repeated readings by godly men and women.

It is also true that in many counselors there is much wisdom (Prov. 24:6), and there are experts in the biblical languages, in the historical and geographical background of the Bible, in the history of the church's understanding of the Bible, in Palestinian archaeology, and other disciplines that can assist us in our understanding (see sec. 7.2.3). Knowing that Laodicea was famous for its wealth, fine textiles, and medical salves may help one to appreciate the irony of Revelation 3:17-18. Greater knowledge of the context enhances and clarifies understanding. Some of these experts may be more accessible to our teachers than to ourselves, but even without this expert's knowledge, any reader can recognize that Laodicea was being upbraided for its delusions of self-sufficiency, and *each individual reader bears responsibility for his or her interpretation*. Teachers are doubly responsible (thus the warning in James 3:1), but no one can escape this responsibility; dependence on another interpreter is itself a decision.

Recognition of this personal responsibility should prevent the all too common overdependency that many Christians develop, even toward good teachers. Good teachers can be a bad influence if dependence on them inhibits one's own initiative in learning. The best teacher inspires students to learn independently and to make their own progress on the hermeneutical spiral.

It is our hope that this book will, among other things, assist in the task of choosing and evaluating "counselors," especially books, to build confidence that the meaning of the Bible is not only accessible but *must* be accessed, and to begin to construct an interpretive framework around the primary message of the Bible.

2.3.2 What is the Bible all about?

Tolkien's trilogy was the product of a single human mind; the Bible was written by many different humans spread out over more than a millennium. One might ask, if this were purely a human book, how it could have any coherency at all. But if, as we claimed earlier, God is the ultimate and original author, then it does have a unity and coherency.

This is not the same as *uniformity*. The human authors of Scripture addressed real situations in history; they had their own particular concerns and backgrounds, and most of all they occupied different places in redemptive history.[23] But God's sovereignty also produces and guides the human authors and their situations, and even directly influences and teaches them (2 Peter 1:21), so the resultant whole has a single mind behind it, and Scripture performs His purpose.

The nature of the coherency of Scripture in the midst of its diversity has led to many debates. The coherency of a discourse involves both a sequential ordering and a relation to a topic.[24] But what is that ordering, and what is the topic? Is it simply a unity of its thematic concerns? Is the unity a matter of how the OT moves progressively toward the person of Jesus Christ? Is it the continual movement from promise to fulfillment? Is it a progressive revelation of true religion? Or is its unity simply a function of tradition which has established a "canon" for the community's life?

Jesus Himself answered this question in Luke 24:44-47. Right before His ascension Jesus told His disciples:

> This is what I told you while I was still with you: everything written about me in the Law of Moses, in the Prophets, and in the Psalms, must be fulfilled." And then he opened their minds so they could understand the Scriptures. And he told them, "This is what is written: The Christ will suffer, and be raised from the dead on the third day, and repentance for the forgiveness of sins will be preached in his name to all the nations, starting from Jerusalem (authors' trans.).

Note first of all that Jesus seems to be providing a reminder of His earthly teaching (v. 44a; see Luke 9:22). He indicates that the content of this teaching is derived from the Scriptures (which of course at that time was the OT), and not just from a few verses but the entirety of Scripture. "Law, Prophets, and Psalms" was a way of referring to the entirety of Scripture. Jews still refer to the (OT) Bible as "Tenakh," an acronym from the first letters of Torah (law), Nevi'im (prophets), and Khethuvim (writings). Further, there is no single OT text which says that the Messiah will be raised on the third day. Just as the later church derived the doctrine of the Trinity not from a particular verse but from the whole of Scripture,[25] so Jesus, and the NT writers after Him (see 1 Cor. 15:4), perceived the resurrection of the Christ in the OT as a whole.

Secondly, the disciples had to have their minds opened by Jesus' instruction (v. 45). Now the attitudinal opening of our minds is something done by the Holy Spirit (2 Cor. 3:16-17; 1 John 2:20), but what is our access to the verbal *content* of Jesus' instruction? Indeed, it is the NT. *To understand the OT properly, it must be read in the light of the NT.*

Thirdly, in the Greek (as in the NIV), the words "the Christ will suffer and rise from the dead" and "repentance and forgiveness of sins will be preached in his name to all nations" are syntactically dependent on "it is written." In other words, "what is written" in the OT consists of two main elements: the death and resurrection of Jesus, and the preaching of this good news to the nations, including Gentiles.[26]

If Jesus knew what the Bible was about, we must conclude that (1) the purpose of the Bible is redemptive, that is, its subject matter is God's redemption of His people which He accomplished in history; (2) the focus of this whole redemptive activity, and consequently of the Scripture which recounts it, is the person of Jesus Christ, especially His death, resurrection, and ascension; and (3) the divinely intended application of this redemptive activity, and hence of Scripture, is the redeemed people of God, which in this age we call the church.

2.3.2.1 The Bible is redemptive-historical in character

Christian theologians sometimes speak of the Bible as "special revelation." It is God's unique revealing of Himself and the truth about His relationship to His creation, especially humans. General revelation is the manifestation of God in creation (see sec. 2.4.1). The primary difference between them is that special revelation communicates God's special dealing with a selected people. (Sometimes this special dealing is in Scripture called His covenant — see e.g., Ex. 19:5.) Special revelation focuses on God's rescuing and redeeming His people from their sin and its consequences. The self-revelation of God in Scripture is uniquely redemptive.

This redemptive self-revelation is also historical. The biblical authors understand God as revealing Himself in history, and He is made known to later generations by that history. The record of the process by which God successively does the things that make possible human relationship to Him is called "redemptive history." God's self revelation is redemptive historical, and the redemptive history of the Bible is what reveals God. The history of God's redeeming His people shows us who God is, and this redeems us.

Even apart from the word of Jesus in Luke 24 noted above, this fact should be clear from the nature of the Bible itself. Why else should it exist? The acts of God which are recorded in the Bible have to do with God's calling a people who will know Him and be known by His name (Ex. 19:5-6; 1 Peter 2:9). God rescues them from their enemies, reveals His own character, teaches them His precepts, punishes them for disobedience — in short, treats them as His children. But because of sin and rebellion against God, they repeatedly fall back into various forms of slavery, and God must again and again rescue them.

The Bible itself is an act of God, given for this purpose. The books of Moses both teach and warn. And the covenant given through Moses explicitly indicates that the relationship must be maintained by continual rereading of the words of the covenant (Deut. 6:7-9). The historical books (in English Bibles, the books from Joshua to Esther) recount Israel's vacillation and God's constancy, so that new generations can learn and be faithful. And it is the rereading of the earlier redemptive history that brings about repentance (see 2 Kings 22). The prophets denounce sin and rebellion and announce future punishment as well as redemption and deliverance, but they also continually hearken back to the earlier record of God's dealings with His people. The Psalms praise God for His redemption, both individual and corporate. And of course the NT announces God's ultimate provision of deliverance from sin.

But it is easy to forget this purpose of the Bible. In Jesus' day many of the Pharisees had lost the historical and redemptive nature of the Bible, treating it primarily as a source for "laws."[27] They missed the fact that its primary intent was to point to God's past and future redemption. Consequently their interpretation of the history of the Bible tended to bypass its historical character and instead became a strange kind of "case book," used to solve the sticky problems of applying the Law to the contemporary situation.[28]

The result was that, by isolating the Law of God from the covenantal relationship to God, the Law became an enslaver that worked against the redemptive purpose. This is why Paul can say he upholds the Law (Rom. 3:31) even though he calls it a slavemaster, and says that circumcision no longer matters (Gal. 6:15). Paul is not simply "vacillating in his theological attitude toward the law,"[29] he is reading the OT according to its redemptive purpose and historical character. The Law's true function can only be carried through as subsidiary to God's redemption of His people and establishment of relationship with them. This happens, Paul says, by faith, that is, by acceptance of the relationship as accomplished by God and by submission to His terms for that relationship, not by "works of the law."

In an entirely different way, the great Alexandrian Jewish philosopher Philo also neglected this historical redemptive nature of the Bible, attempting to find in it not law but the philosophical concepts and ideology of a variety of Platonism. Since the historical reading of the Bible did not provide much in the way of Platonic philosophy, Philo found primarily allegorical or symbolic meaning in the history, and even in the legal material, often denying the historicity of the biblical events.[30]

People today also tend to forget this historical redemptive character of the Bible. For some the Bible is primarily a book that somehow magically gives guidance to personal problems, or is simply a source book for ethics or politics, or is a mysterious or poetic guide to meaningful personal existence. While the Bible does indeed provide guidance, speak on ethics, and provide the key to the meaning of one's existence, it can do all those things precisely because it is not simply a guidebook or ethics manual or philosophical treatise; it is rather a book which recounts and applies God's redemptive activity in history. If we lose sight of the historicity of the Bible, we lose the framework of understanding which the biblical writers themselves maintained, and we are cast adrift in a sea where meaning is purely subjective, and is thus no meaning at all.[31]

Now by stressing the redemptive-historical character of the Bible we are focusing on its purpose and hence the most comprehensive category for understanding the whole. We do not mean to deny that the Bible contains both legal precepts and theological (and metaphysical) concepts, nor do we deny that the Bible gives us guidance. But the precepts and concepts are all part of the redemptive-historical activity of God, and this redemptive-historical activity is *covenantal*. By this we mean that God has *verbally declared* and *formally ratified* an indication of the nature and responsibilities of the relationship between Himself and His people.[32] It is by virtue of our being part of this formally declared relationship that we learn ethics and theology and obtain guidance from the Bible. This redemptive-historical covenant is established and ratified by a mediator, Jesus Christ (Heb. 9:15), and it is therefore on Him that this redemptive history focuses.

2.3.2.2 The Bible's focus is on Jesus Christ

We noted above that the Pharisees forgot the redemptive-historical purpose of the OT, and so missed its chief point. On the other hand, the people of Qumran who wrote the Dead Sea Scrolls kept that redemptive-historical dimension of the OT. They remembered that the OT constantly and as a whole looked forward to God's ultimate deliverance of His people. But the Qumran sectarians as well as the Pharisees forgot that God's deliverance activity was ultimately focused on a representative individual. They overlooked the *christocentric* character of the future redemption.[33]

Paul had to learn this in a dramatic fashion. Prior to his conversion he as a Pharisee had strongly opposed the "news" that Jesus fulfilled the OT (see Acts 8:1; 9:1-2). On the other hand, after his experience on the road to Damascus, he began to understand the OT christologically (see Acts 13:16-41). So, in Romans 10:4 Paul tells us that Christ is the "end" of the Law. This might be understood to mean that when Christ comes the Law ceases to be valid, but Paul seems to want to "uphold the Law" (Rom. 3:31). Although in the new era of Christ's fulfillment the Law is no longer our slavemaster, it has always pointed to Christ and leads to Christ (Gal. 3:19, 21; 4:21; Rom. 3:19). It also indicates what righteous behavior is (Eph. 6:2) and thus is fulfilled by those who walk according to the Spirit (Rom. 8:4). It is more likely, therefore, that Romans 10:4 means that Christ is the goal or purpose of the Law.

This enables us to see what Paul is doing with Deuteronomy 30:12-14 which he cites later in Romans 10. Note how Paul interjects explanatory notes to explain the christological point of Deuteronomy:

> The righteousness that is by faith says: "Do not say in your heart, 'Who will ascend into heaven?' " (that is, to bring Christ down) "or 'Who will descend into the abyss?' " (that is, to bring Christ up from the dead). But what does it say? "The word is near you, on your lips and in your heart" (that is, the word of faith which we preach) (Rom. 10:6-7).

The christological reading of the OT begins with Jesus Himself, as we saw in Luke 24. Throughout His ministry on earth, Jesus cited the OT and applied it to Himself (e.g., Matt. 22:41-45). Furthermore He specified that He had come to fulfill the "Law and the Prophets" (Matt. 5:17-18), suggesting that in His view the OT has its ultimate purpose in Him. Jesus' application of texts to Himself becomes clearer and clearer as His ministry progresses. His citation during His trial (Matt. 26:64, citing Dan. 7:13) and the cry of dereliction (Matt. 27:46 = Ps. 22:1) are directly and unambiguously self-referential.[34]

Jesus applies the OT to Himself because He finds His own death and resurrection as something which the Scriptures mandate and move toward.[35] The Synoptic Gospels all recount His reiterated passion predictions, and these are all characterized by statements of the *necessity* of His death and resurrection: "The Son of man must suffer many things" (Mark 8:31). This necessity appears rooted in Scripture. This is explicit in Luke 18:31 which mentions "the prophets" as indicating this necessity. Further, when Jesus is arrested and Peter wants to engage in battle, Jesus says that He could call upon twelve legions of angels, "but then how should the Scriptures be fulfilled?" (Matt. 26:54; cf. Mark 14:49)

Thus too, in Luke 9:31 when Christ is transfigured and is discussing His forthcoming death, resurrection, and ascension with Moses and Elijah, He discussed His forthcoming departure (the Greek word is *exodon*, or "exodus") which He was about to bring to fulfillment in Jerusalem. The Exodus theme, which in the OT was repeatedly taken up and applied to God's future deliverance of His people, comes to full fruition in Jesus' departure. Again, Jesus is the focal point and culmination of Israel's history. As we already noted, He understood Himself as the fulfillment of the OT (Matt. 5:17-18). This is why He could freely associate His own redemptive activity with such things as the bronze serpent in the wilderness (John 3:14, alluding to Num. 21). Paul, along with the other NT writers, has simply echoed the approach of Jesus.

This program of exegesis is carried on right from the beginning of the church in Acts. In his very first sermon, Peter cites Psalm 16 (Acts 2:25-28), demonstrates that it cannot apply strictly to David, and then says that David "was a prophet, and knew that God had promised him on oath that He would place one of his descendants on his throne. Seeing what was ahead, he spoke of the resurrection of the Christ, that he was not abandoned to the grave, nor did his body see decay" (Acts 2:30-31).

Matthew's Gospel was written some time after Peter's speech was given, and develops this approach in an especially interesting way. Matthew seems very concerned with showing that Jesus fulfills not just the words of the OT, but the history of Israel. Especially in chapters 1 and 2, but also scattered elsewhere (12:18-21; 13:35; 21:4-5), Matthew interjects OT references to show how Jesus is fulfilling the OT expectation. These fulfillments are not always altogether clear to us when we go back and read them in the OT context. Is Matthew doing what we earlier said and subsequently will say again should not be done? Is Matthew ignoring the original historical context?

To answer this question, let us look at one of the most problematic of these citations. In Matthew 2:15 he refers to Jesus' family fleeing to Egypt in order to escape Herod, and indicates that this fulfills the prophecy of Hosea 11:1: "Out of Egypt I called my son." The context in Hosea, however, does not easily yield any sense of prophecy of what will happen to the Messiah. It rather has to do, first, with the historical event of God's calling Israel (His son) out of Egypt, and second, with the parallel to the implied future deliverance of Israel from the forthcoming exile in Egypt and Assyria (see Hosea 11:5, 11; 12:9). Hosea 11:1 by itself does not look like a messianic prophecy.

The solution lies in understanding Matthew's concept of fulfillment. Fulfill here does not mean simply to bring to historical reality some event that had been prophesied; it rather means to *bring to fruition*. This meaning of "bring to fruition" is clearly illustrated in James 2:23-24: when Abraham's justification is said to be "fulfilled," James does not mean that the prophetic word, "it was reckoned to him as righteousness" (RSV) was a prediction of Abraham's sacrifice of Isaac, but that the righteousness conveyed in God's declaration in Genesis 15:6 bore fruit in his obedience in Genesis 22. Matthew 2:15 is saying that God's deliverance of His people from Egypt in the Exodus, and His promise of future deliverance from exile, has borne fruit or come to full fruition in the deliverance of Jesus Christ from Egypt.[36] The coming of Jesus does not just fulfill verses here and there; *Christ fulfills the whole history of Israel*. All the history as well as the prophecy of the OT, all the Law as well as the wisdom, point beyond themselves to God's forthcoming redemption of His people by the Christ. It is this christocentric character of the Bible which the NT claims is its principal thematic unity.[37]

Now this is not to say that the Bible never talks about anything other than Jesus Christ.[38] When in Genesis 14 Abraham and his 318 trained men rescue Lot from Kedorlaomer, the text is not speaking *directly* about Jesus Christ.[39] But this story, as part of the whole message of the Book of Genesis and the promises to Abraham, does point indirectly to Him. This is a difficult but important principle. Individual verses must be understood in their immediate historical and literary context, and may *as* individual verses have little to do with the messianic expectation. But as part of the whole, they do relate in some way to the christological goal of this redemptive history.

Perhaps another way to say this is that, according to the NT, the OT as a whole points to Christ and that its parts teach about various things including Christ. But of course a part of a book only takes on its full meaning in relation to the whole. Even with the NT, not every single verse is directly referential to Christ, but as a whole it only has meaning in relation to Him. The person of Christ lies at the heart of both testaments, even when they are discussing something else.[40]

2.3.2.3 The Bible's application is to the church

If the Bible is focused on Christ, we have a coherent picture of God's redemptive activity; but how can such a book apply to us in our daily lives? The NT writers in fact do not stop with the focus on Christ. The NT operates with a principle that believers are identified with Christ, or, to use Paul's phrase, they are "in Christ." (Paul uses the phrase a host of times, but especially see Rom. 8:1-17; Eph. 2:5-6, 13; Phil. 3:9-10.) As a consequence the NT frequently extends the OT to apply to Christians. This is so pronounced a tendency in Paul that Richard B. Hays claims that Paul's use of the OT is principally ecclesiocentric rather than christocentric.[41]

Paul rather explicitly tells his readers that the OT was written "for us" (1 Cor. 10:11; cf. Rom. 15:4), that is, "for our instruction." Paul therefore frequently addresses the problems of his churches by applying Scripture in a fairly direct way to them.

Some of these seem reasonably obvious. Ephesians 6:2 is a straightforward application of the fifth commandment. But some are not so obvious. Just a few verses earlier in Ephesians, Paul cites Genesis 2:24 ("a man will leave his mother and father and be united to his wife") and then declares that "this is a profound mystery — but I am talking about Christ and the church" (Eph. 5:32, RSV). To all appearances Genesis 2:24 refers simply to the pattern of continual generation of nuclear families which is based on the fact that husband and wife are "one flesh." Paul, by referring it to Christ and the church, goes beyond this on the basis of the similarity of marriage to the relationship between Christ and His people. This concept too did not originate with him; the Prophets Hosea and Isaiah already had likened the relationship of God and Israel to marriage, and the Jews usually understood the Song of Songs to be an allegory of God's relationship to Israel.[42] But Paul's application is both christocentric and ecclesiological. God's love for His people is Christ's love for His people.

Now how did Paul make the shift from the christological focus which Jesus Himself evidenced to the ecclesiological application? Some indication may be given by his odd reference in Galatians 3:16 to the promise to Abraham "and to his seed" in Genesis 12:7 and 13:15. Paul informs us that since "seed" is singular, it therefore refers to Christ. Now Paul knows as well as anyone that "seed" in the singular in Genesis meant "the descendants" in the plural, because in Galatians 3:29 he says that "you [plural] are Abraham's seed [singular]." His point is that Jesus Christ is the ultimate fulfillment of the promise to Abraham and that Abraham's seed (plural) are so by virtue of their relationship to the one seed. The whole passage is predicated on the union of believers with Jesus Christ. Hence, if the OT is christocentric, it will also apply to those who are united to Christ by faith, who are baptized into Christ, who have put on Christ, and are thus heirs according to the promise (Gal. 3:26-29).

Another verse where Paul's use of the OT seems "strange" to us is 1 Corinthians 9:9. Paul indicates that Moses' commandment "do not muzzle an ox while it is treading out grain" applies not primarily to oxen but "on our account" (see 1 Tim. 5:18). This is sometimes taken as an example of a rabbinic technique of legal exegesis known as *qal wahomer*,[43] roughly equivalent to an *a minore ad maius* argument. What is true for oxen must be all the more true for people. But this is not quite what Paul says he is doing. He rather indicates that the ultimate purpose of this OT text has nothing to do with oxen. Its purpose is to instruct the church with regard to how it should take care of those who labor for the church.

Paul can do this because he understands the ultimate purpose of the whole of Scripture as informing and exhorting the church. It thus should not surprise us when he in Galatians 4 understands the story of Sarah and Hagar of Genesis 16 and 21 as applying to the church's situation. He understands this allegorically (Gal. 4:24) as applying to the present situation of his readers. Those who appeared to be the heirs as a result of human endeavor (Ishmael = the Judaizers) were actually cast out; the true heirs were those whom God blessed apart from human effort (Isaac = Christians by faith). Although Paul even refers to this as an allegorical interpretation of Genesis, it is not a haphazard allegory.[44] Ishmael was the result of Abraham's effort at fulfilling the promise in his own power; Isaac was miraculous and came by virtue of God's promise. Doubtless the Judaizers were thinking in reverse; for them it was the children of the circumcision who were the true descendants of Abraham. Paul showed that these Judaizers had the spiritual intent of the story topsy-turvy.[45] Our point here, however, is that Paul shows no reluctance to apply the OT to the church, because that is its purpose.[46]

First Peter also operates on this principle as in 2:4-9.

[Christ] to whom you have come is the living stone, rejected by men but chosen by God as precious. And you too are as living stones being built up into a spiritual house, to be a holy priesthood, that you may through Jesus Christ offer spiritual sacrifices which are acceptable to God. For this is what it says in Scripture: *Behold I lay in Zion a stone, a cornerstone, elect, precious, and the one who believes on him will never be put to shame. Thus,* there is honor to you who believe, but for those who do not believe, *the stone which the builders rejected has become the cornerstone, and a stone of stumbling and a rock which brings offense.* They stumble at the word, because they do not believe. For this they were appointed. But you are *a chosen race, a royal priesthood, a holy nation, a people for God's own possession, so that you may proclaim the wondrous deeds* of him who called you out of darkness into his marvelous light (authors' trans.).

Clearly the "stone" here is Jesus Christ. But verse 5 informs us that believers are also like "living stones." Just as the cornerstone is "precious" or "honored" in verse 6, so believers also receive "honor" (from God) in verse 7.[47]

In fact 1 Peter spelled out this hermeneutical move in his echo of the passage we looked at earlier, Luke 24:44-47. According to 1 Peter 1:10-12:

This salvation [i.e., the "salvation of your souls," v. 9] is what the prophets who prophesied of the grace which was intended for you searched and inquired about. They inquired what person or what time the Spirit of Christ within them was indicating when the Spirit testified in advance to the sufferings intended for the Christ[48] and the subsequent glorious things. It was revealed to them that they were serving not themselves but you, in the things which have now been announced to you by those who preached the good news to you through the Holy Spirit sent from heaven, things into which angels long to look (authors' trans.).

Note that: (1) the subject matter of the prophets is salvation (redemption), (2) the subject of their testimony was the sufferings intended for the Messiah and the glorious things following them, and (3) they were intended for you (v. 10), and the prophets even knew they were ultimately serving "you," that is, the church.

Since Peter's audience was most likely Gentile in origin[49] the hermeneutical principle of 1 Peter, although entirely dissimilar in wording, appears to be virtually identical in content with that of Jesus in Luke 24.

Since the prophets were serving "not themselves but you," the other uses of the OT in 1 Peter follow the same kind of ecclesiological application model that was evidenced in Paul. According to 1 Peter in 3:10-12, Psalm 34 applies to Christian behavior; the Flood is a type of baptism in 3:21; and the Proverbs point to God's judgment of the wicked and grace toward His people in 4:18 (Prov. 11:31, LXX [Septuagint]) and 5:5 (Prov. 3:34).

2.3.3 Conclusion

Taking the lead from Jesus' own teaching, the NT authors understand the OT as redemptive in character, focused on Christ, and written for the benefit of the church. Certainly the same can be said of the NT itself; it too is redemptive in purpose, focused on Christ, and is written for the church.[50] If we wish to be faithful to the NT teaching, we cannot do otherwise. This will be a key factor in any Christian interpretation of the Bible. Ultimately, any interpretation of a biblical passage is incomplete until it asks:

(1) How does this passage function in God's plan of redemption for His people, and where does it fit in the unfolding history of that plan?

(2) How does the passage point to Jesus Christ; that is, how does this (OT) passage participate in the entire OT's movement toward, and focus on, Jesus Christ; or how does this (NT) passage build on the completed fulfillment of God's plan in Jesus Christ?

(3) How does this passage, having been focused on Christ, instruct those who are in Christ, the church? How does it help us to follow Him, know Him, or grow in Him?

All the methods and procedures that we shall discuss later in this book are worthless unless they help to answer these questions.

2.4 The Bible and the World

The Bible is God's communication to humans in the world. As such it is part of the world. It is written in earthly languages, and it speaks not just of extraworldly things, but also of things which we can and do experience in the world. Naturally, therefore, our interpretation of it is going to be influenced and determined by the world in which we now live.

This section will address two special problems: (1) the interrelationship of the Bible's teaching (special revelation) and what we learn from looking at the world (general revelation), and (2) the relationship of the Bible's history to human history as a whole.

2.4.1 The interrelationship of general and special revelation

In section 1 we mentioned the fact that all interpretation works within a "hermeneutical spiral." We interpret any experience, including the reading of a text, by what we already "know" about its meaning, and this in turn informs and perhaps alters what we know, which gives us a better standpoint to interpret the next time around. It is like learning a language. Here we wish further to specify the nature of that spiral, in terms of the relationship between what we know by exposure to the world around us and what we know by reading Scripture.

We must start by pointing out that all our knowledge is related not only to "facts" but also to other knowledge. When we encounter a "fact" it only has meaning in relation to other facts and to our framework of understanding. So far as our knowledge is concerned, there are no "brute facts."[51]

When we first come to Scripture, we start interpreting[52] in terms of our initial framework of understanding, which comprises what we "know" by general revelation, especially our presuppositions. General revelation usually is taken to refer to the revelation of God's attributes (such as His invisibility, power, and transcendence; see Rom. 1:19-20) which is mediated by creation itself apart from linguistic communication (Ps. 19:1-4). But such general revelation presupposes an ability of the recipient to perceive, interpret, and understand the significance of creation. Since knowledge of ourselves, language, and the ability to reason (see sec. 1.1.1) are indispensable to understanding anything, and thus are a prerequisite to reception of the more precisely defined content of general revelation, we are including such things as part of the process of God's self-revelation which occurs apart from Scripture.[53] Fortunately for us humans, this initial revelation of God is, to use Milton's phrase, "never unperceived, ever understood." Unfortunately, we then go on to suppress this knowledge. Although we cannot destroy such knowledge, we can be fiendishly inconsistent in our knowledge by denying it.

Nevertheless, a person's prescriptural worldview, based on an interpretation of general revelation, is a primitive "systematic theology." Everyone, even a non-Christian who has never thought about God much, has an operative systematic theology. People live their lives on the basis of belief systems which they think do justice to themselves, the world in which they live, and ultimate realities (including God) so far as they may be known.

When we then encounter Scripture, we understand what we read by way of the language we use in general life. If a believer has a submissive attitude to Scripture, the interaction of the data of Scripture further informs his or her systematic theology. This newly informed theological system now can look back at general revelation and understand it better. The "objective" material of general and special revelation are continually interpreted by, interact with, and influence the "subjective" lens of one's systematic theology.[54]

Perhaps this interaction of general and special revelation can be thought of as a double spiral. It is a spiral rather than a circle because the understanding can keep improving. Scripture or aspects of general revelation that we do not understand are not understood because our systematic theology is defective or deficient at some point. So to deal with the new piece of revelation, some modification is made in the system in order to incorporate and understand it. Occasionally enough material from either general or special revelation will build up to cause a large scale reordering of part of the system. An analogous event in the development of scientific theory is called a "paradigm shift."[55] By continual refinement and occasional paradigm shifts our understanding gets closer and closer to a "meeting of meaning," a perfectly centered knowledge or understanding of both Scripture and the world. Of course, we can never get all the way; perhaps not even very close. Even had Adam and Eve not fallen, they would have had to grow bit by bit and perhaps never reach total understanding of God's speech with them, although their understanding would always have been true so far as it went. And we have not only the problem of finitude but the problem of sin. However, we can approach hermeneutical congruence, and the important thing is that we keep getting closer.

Now this "inter-relatability" of general and special revelation presupposes that they both have to do with the same world, which is both spiritual (ultimate) and physical (phenomenal). If general and special revelation are both revelation from God, they are both inherently infallible and indispensable.[56] If this is the case, there is a corollary to this idea, namely, that our understanding of general revelation (knowledge of the world in general) must be open to correction by the Word of God. Since our knowledge of the world can never be complete, it is always susceptible to error, and Scripture may inform us at a point where our limited knowledge of the world breaks down. More controversial to many is the opposite: *our understanding* of Scripture (*not* Scripture in itself), subject as it is to a misinterpretation and sinful perversion of what Scripture actually says, must be open to correction by general revelation. In other words, if there is a tension between our understanding of special and general revelation, one cannot decide ahead of time which understanding is at fault. General and special revelation when properly understood are perfectly harmonious! Our understanding of one or the other may be wrong, but not the revelation itself.

We stress this because people often give pride of place to one or the other. This is quite proper with regard to certain areas. One would not go to the Bible to learn details about the human anatomy in preparation for a medical degree. Neither would one go to a scientific study of anatomy to find out the ultimate purpose or significance of the body.

Further, the Bible speaks in language, and is thus already conceptual, whereas the created world must be conceptualized and described by its observers. And when people conceptualize, all kinds of presuppositions, biases, and sociological and cultural factors influence and sometimes distort those conceptualizations. Of course the Bible must also be interpreted, and its concepts may be distorted by the interpreter, but learning by listening to a Teacher who knows what He is talking about, even if we misunderstand His words sometimes, is far more reliable than trying to learn by building up an understanding from the limited perspective of personal experience.

But there likely always will be points at which our understanding of general and special revelation may be in conflict. And this tension can be very useful in refining and correcting our understanding — our systematic theology.[57]

This systematic theology is the working presupposition which provides the interpretive framework within which our understanding of the Bible is accomplished. This is why there are so many areas of biblical interpretation where intelligent and godly interpreters may differ. Hopefully, the spiral will keep improving the theology and thus the interpretive framework. But there is some danger of solidification. If the interpreter stops moving in the spiral, if one assumes that his or her systematic theology has "arrived," or that one's interpretation of the whole world or the whole Bible is "plain" with no room for discussion, that is, if one loses his or her interpretive humility, then the spiral is frozen and no further improvement in understanding can take place. We hope that the readers of this book will be willing throughout their lives to continue spiraling, that their understanding of God's Word, as well as His world, may never cease to deepen.[58] Since both the knowledge of the world and the available knowledge of the historical background and context of Scripture never cease to increase, neither should our need to spiral. This would be true even if we were perfect interpreters untainted by sin. We further hope that our readers will learn how to recognize that some differences of interpretation stem not from willful rejection of what the text clearly says, but from being in a different spot on the spiral.[59] We must insist that Scripture be interpreted correctly, but we do this not by impugning the motives of those who disagree with us, but by showing how their interpretation is incorrect and how their interpretive framework does not conform to Scripture.

2.4.2 The importance of world history

The Bible is related to the world in another way. Not only is it written in history, and not only does it record historical incidents, but, as we indicated in section 2.3.2.1, its principal content is the relating of a history. As such, its material can be related to history which is known from extrabiblical sources, which for the sake of convenience we shall here call "world history." In a way this is a special application of the problem just discussed. And therefore again, when a tension arises between our interpretations of biblical history and world history, we cannot prejudge which of our interpretations is incorrect. But here we have a slightly different situation, because world history is not known by direct measurement but by way of human interpreters. And its source material is derived from the interpretations of earlier "historians" who interpreted and recorded events. History is not simply an aimless listing of events; it is the connection of events into a cause-effect chain; it is a rational interpretation of events. If there are no brute facts in the world at large, there are certainly no brute facts in history. Thus, any account of world history or a part thereof is, like the Bible, already conceptualized, but unlike the Bible it is not infallible. No historian can ever have all the facts, and even when two historians have access to exactly the same set of facts, they may give completely different, sometimes contradictory, accounts.[60] And the same biases and misconstruals to which our interpretation is subject operate on the historians on whom we depend for world history.[61]

But even with this caveat in mind, we want to affirm that biblical history does "fit" into world history. Actually, it would be better to say, world history "fits" into biblical history. *Redemptive* history is also redemptive *history*. The Bible's own testimony is that all of the things that have ever happened in the world at large are under the sovereign control of God, who is using it all to accomplish His redemptive purposes.[62] Note Acts 4:27-28, where the early church prayed:

Indeed, Herod and Pontius Pilate met together with the Gentiles and the people of Israel in this city to conspire against your holy servant Jesus, whom you anointed. They did what your power and will had decided beforehand should happen.

God's hand and plan generated the political events of Rome for His own purposes. This was an application of Psalm 2:1-2, which had just been cited in the previous verses in Acts.[63]

God is not only working in history; He is working out history. This means that world history can be very useful for increasing our understanding of biblical history, and that the biblical history must provide the platform for evaluating and understanding world history.

A recurring problem for Bible students is the nature of correspondence between biblical accounts of historical events and the events themselves as they actually happened.[64] Biblical history is not concerned with recounting "brute facts" even if such a thing were possible; it reveals the divine meaning to events. But we expect such interpretation of events to resonate with the perceptions of people who were there.[65] There are no "brute facts" but there are true facts. And if humans can know anything at all, their perceptions must have at least some resonance with these true facts.[66] The limits to our knowing a fact "in itself," or rather "according to its perception by God," are not due to the nonexistence of the fact but because of the dependency of our knowledge.

Hence, on the one hand, we cannot critique the truth value of the Bible simply because its statements are different than or even contrary to some judgment of a historian. On the other hand, neither can we isolate biblical history from the events of the world, within which context the biblical historical events occurred.

For these reasons, any approach to the Bible which, faced with tensions between the Bible and world history, either shifts the ground of biblical revelation from history to subjective experience, or ignores world history as the irrelevant musings of unbelievers, forfeits the unique character of biblical religion and vitiates its integrity. Redemption is historical in character. It does no good to call this some other kind of history, a "history for me," for example, for this also reverts to subjective experience. The Bible is timeless, because its ultimate truths transcend history, but the form of communication God uses in the Bible is clearly historical.

THREE

THE FOUNDATION AND THE FRAME: PRESUPPOSITIONS AND INTERPRETATION

In 1980 a book appeared with the title *You Take Jesus, I'll Take God: How to Refute Christian Missionaries*, by Samuel Levine. In the opening pages, the author argues that the best way to refute Christians who argue that Jesus is prophesied in the OT is to use grammatical-historical exegesis to determine what the text "really" means. Levine suggests that this procedure will conclusively demonstrate that the original meaning of the OT prophecies have nothing to do with Jesus. He is advocating the same method espoused in most Christian books on biblical interpretation, but is coming to entirely different conclusions. How can this be?

The reason is that method of interpretation does not really determine the end result of interpretation. Hermeneutical methods are the tools we use to find out what a Scripture text means. That is, they help us to extricate meaning not only from texts that appear dark, confusing, or remote from us, but even from texts that at first appear "plain." They help to control what meaning may legitimately be derived from a text. But as tools they do not themselves determine what meaning will be found in a text, any more than a woodcarver's tools determine what the artisan will do with a piece of wood.[1] The analogy is imperfect, because of course hermeneutics is supposed to be helping us understand what someone else has created, but tools remain only tools, which are wielded by a person with certain motivations (see sec. 1.3). As Bruce Chilton noted,[2] of the great families of OT interpreters (the Rabbis, Philo, the Qumran community, and the NT church), it is not the method that governs the different results so much as the intent. Hermeneutical goal is more important than and antecedent to method.

We saw in chapter 2 that the NT writers understood the OT to speak of Jesus, and they indeed found Him in its pages. In contrast, the Qumran sectaries, even though their exegetical methods resembled those of the NT writers,[3] regarded their community as the primary target of Scripture, and so found themselves in its pages. Philo thought that the OT spoke Platonic philosophy, and of course he found it.

So, can a Christian and a non-Christian Jew agree on the true and ultimate meaning of Isaiah 53? Their disagreement is not because they disagree on method. It is because their interpretive goals are different. Paul puts the matter in an interesting way in 2 Corinthians 3. By drawing an analogy between the Israelites' inability to look on Moses' face after his encounter with God (Ex. 34:33-35), Paul points out that "to this day when Moses is read a veil covers their hearts. But whenever anyone turns to the Lord, the veil is taken away" (2 Cor. 3:15-16). Only repentance and trust in Christ, as Paul knew from personal experience, can enable a person to understand the OT truly, because humans are dependent on the Holy Spirit to "unveil" the meaning of Scripture. Just as Jesus showed the true import of the OT to His disciples in Luke 24, so the Holy Spirit now must show that import to His people today, by pointing to the correct hermeneutical goal, which is more important to the result than hermeneutical methods.

But this should not be taken to mean that method is unimportant. A person's systematic theology forms the grid for his or her interpretation of biblical texts, and a crucial part of this interpretive grid is the particular methodology by which a reader expects to obtain an understanding of what is read. Methodology, like the rest of one's systematic theology, whether conscious or unconscious, is a product of the interface between experience and what one already knows of special revelation. Method is important, because it assists in keeping the spiral spiraling.

Further, method gives a discipline to inquiry. And when both goal and method are agreed upon, it provides a means of resolving certain differences in interpretation.

But too much weight can be given to method. Method is a function of theological necessity; it is chosen according to two criteria: first, the degree to which it corresponds to one's overall view of texts, language, and the world; second, its fruitfulness and the degree to which it produces results in harmony with previous results. As we shall see in chapter 4, methods have varied from age to age and situation to situation, in accordance with the dominant theological concerns and commitments.

If the hermeneutical *goals* of the NT writers are the ones we should adopt in our own exegesis, we must further ask, what *methods* are most compatible with the presuppositions, goals, and methods of the NT. We should as well address the role of the pre-exegetical matters that are especially important to the Christian's interpretive framework: tradition and the church. Finally, if the Holy Spirit "unveils" Scripture, we must ask, what is His role in interpretation?

3.1 Presuppositions and Method

What methods or approaches are appropriate in view of our Christian presuppositions? This is not an easy question. But if the Bible is indeed coherent and divinely authored, we should be able to draw from it this principle: the Bible is its own best interpreter, not only in a general sense, and not only with respect to the passages specifically quoted and interpreted later. In other words, *the Bible's interpretation of itself should indicate to us the nature of our own interpretation.* That is, our hermeneutic should have as its standard the hermeneutic of the biblical writers, particularly the NT writers as they interpreted the OT. This is above all true with regard to the goal of our interpretation. Biblical interpretation should be redemptive-historical in character, christological in focus, and ecclesiological in application. But in addition, the NT writers' use of the OT should also provide some indications for what our methods should be.

This is not to say that every specific thing which the NT writers happened to do in the course of their use of the OT is a model for us. For example, the fact that the NT writers most frequently used the Septuagint does not mean that we should. The use of the Septuagint was an incidental matter stemming from what translation was available and useful. Nor is it to say that the NT's definable methods are the only ones we may use, if for no other reason than that the NT writers did not deal with every OT text. But at least the NT's use of the OT provides us with a preliminary framework for constructing a methodology of exegesis which is compatible with and suitable for Scripture. Most particularly, recognition of and submission to the Bible's ultimate divine authorship means that we, like the NT writers, may be bold in seeing clues of the end in the beginning.

Even with these caveats, to say that we should take our methodological cue from the NT writers is rather a controversial statement, because the NT writers do not always conform to the methods which our age deems legitimate. Some wag once commented
that Paul would certainly have failed a standard hermeneutics
course at seminary. In fact, the biblical writers used methods quite
similar to those of their contemporaries. Richard Longenecker's
important study of *Biblical Exegesis in the Apostolic Period*[4] demonstrates many similarities between the NT's exegesis and that of
the Qumran community and rabbinic tradition. He also points out
that although the NT writers have a much greater sense of the
historical meaning than either of these groups, "fulfillment" exegesis, the NT's dominant exegetical motif, is also found in the
Qumran texts. Thus one could argue that even if we accept that
their exegetical *goal* was right, the apostles' *methods* were time-
bound, determined by their social context, and thus they might be
inappropriate for our different context. Longenecker himself con-
cludes:

> What then can be said to our question, "Can we reproduce the
> exegesis of the New Testament?" I suggest that we must answer
> both "No" and "Yes." Where that exegesis is based upon a revela-
> tory stance, where it evidences itself to be merely cultural, or
> where it shows itself to be circumstantial or *ad hominem* in nature,
> "No." Where, however, it treats the Old Testament in a more
> literal fashion, following the course of what we speak of today as
> historico-grammatical exegesis, "Yes." Our commitment as Chris-
> tians is to the reproduction of the apostolic faith and doctrine, and
> not necessarily to the specific apostolic exegetical practices.[5]

That is, as long as the NT writers conform to what we have
already decided is correct (grammatical-historical exegesis) we
may "follow" them. But this is equivalent to saying, "I will follow
you wherever you go, so long as you go in my direction." What
kind of "following" is that? What transcendent authority rests exclusively upon the grammatical-historical method of exegesis?

If the NT writers may determine the goal of our interpretation,
they may also be expected to have something to say about our
methods, because methods are not wholly unrelated to goals. We
observed that other groups were interpreting the OT at the same
time as the NT writers and reached differing results primarily

because of differing goals. But the methods employed also differed, because different methods work better when different goals are being pursued.

The "scribes and Pharisees" of the time of Jesus did not write down their interpretations, but their interpretive heirs[6] eventually did, and we see that their legal casuistic concerns resulted in a rather atomistic and (to us) very strange methodology, used primarily to justify the legal tradition.[7] In "gematria," for example, the numerical value of the letters in certain words was thought to be full of meaning.

On a different front, the Alexandrian Jewish philosopher Philo believed that Neoplatonic philosophy was the absolute truth, and he wished to find it, therefore, in the pages of the Bible. The assumption of a hidden "ideal" world which explains the physical world, coupled with the assumption that the Bible is divine and absolute truth, gives the expectation that the "physical" stories and events of the Bible "really" point to some ideal truth in a "hidden" manner. Philo therefore resorted to a speculative, allegorical method, but there is not a hint from reading Philo that he ever envisioned himself doing anything other than explaining what was "really there" on the pages of the Bible.[8]

From the documents found less than fifty years ago in the Dead Sea area, it appears that the community at Qumran saw themselves as the eschatological people of Israel, awaiting the final denouement of God's history, and they interpret by reading their own community and its history as the focus of the OT texts.[9] The Qumran people primarily used a typological approach not dissimilar to that of the church (which also regarded itself as the fulfillment of OT prophecy).[10] But their method was to treat each item of a text as in some way prophetic of the Qumran community's present circumstance, recent history, or near future.[11] In all these cases — Philo, the Rabbis, and Qumran — the goal has to some extent determined the method.

That goals influence what methods are used can also be documented from more recent history. Luther insisted on a literal method of interpretation of Jesus' words in the Lord's Supper, "this is my body," but berated the Anabaptists for taking too literally the millennial prophecies. Luther's methods in these particular cases were determined by what he was looking for. Certain Christians have insisted that everything in the Bible be taken literally unless it is absurd to do so, but they disagree among themselves as what constitutes absurdity. Methods are chosen according to what produces results in line with what is already known, or what makes sense of a text.[12]

We must be honest about this. The NT writers also used methods which obtained the results which they knew already to be true. They *knew* Jesus Christ; they saw what He had done and they heard Him explain the OT Scriptures as being about Him (Luke 24:44-47; see sec. 3.3.2). They did indeed adopt the method which produced the results Jesus had told them were correct. Their hermeneutical goal certainly determined their method.

Does all this mean there is no way to evaluate what goals and methods are most suitable to a text? Are we trapped in some vicious hermeneutical circle?

By no means. If God uses human language in the way language ordinarily works, so that humans can understand it, then the circle is not vicious but a spiral, because the text has a built-in corrective power, so long as we reckon on its internal consistency. Now if that "normal" use of language in the OT carries with it a genuine purpose of looking toward the person of the Redeemer, then the NT's interpretive goal is the proper framework for reading the OT, and the NT's exegesis, in line with that goal, is true. And if the NT is indeed the Word of God, we should follow it, not only with respect to its goal, but also the method sanctioned by the inspired biblical writers.

Of course all this assumes that the NT is indeed the proper understanding of the OT. This is a presupposition. Knowing the author enables us to recognize his voice, and the voice we hear in the OT is the same voice we hear in the NT. But it is also a conclusion. The OT does indeed look forward; this is scarcely deniable. And the outline of God's redemptive activity and His character which we find in the OT does indeed reflect the greater redemption and fuller manifestation of His character we find in the NT.[13] The NT writers continue the spiral on which they themselves were traveling. It is good that we travel the same spiral.

Further, if we do not operate on the inspired biblical writers' methods, then whose interpretive methods shall we use? Strictly grammatical-historical exegesis, some say.[14] But on what ground? The Enlightenment insisted on "pure" grammatical-historical exegesis because of the assumption that such exegesis was based on reason and is rationally controllable and that a scientifically restricted approach to a text could result in a consensus. The past 200 years have shown both of these to be false. Just as a hammer by itself cannot build anything, "reason" by itself is a basis for nothing (see sec. 1.1.2.3.), and no consensus has been reached even amongst professional descriptive exegetes on the problems of the Bible.[15] Thus we agree with Markus Barth:

> I am not yet convinced that the hermeneutical methods developed since the Enlightenment have yielded results so superior to those employed by the authors of the NT that we are entitled to put their hermeneutics on a Schandpfahl or into a museum for good.[16]

We do not wish to deny the value of grammatical-historical exegesis; indeed we believe it is crucial, but we deny that it should ultimately be grounded on human reason, or that it is totally adequate. It is rather best grounded on the NT writers' use of the OT, which is itself based on the principle of the consistency of redemptive history. God's revelation in the historical events of the OT really does look forward to the Christ.

But we cannot talk about a "pure" grammatical-historical exegesis. All results are determined by the goal, even if only one "method" is used. Nor can we limit the meaning of a text to what could demonstrably have been understood from it by its original readers, for the NT writers are not so restricted in their approach to the OT. Such limitation precludes that God meant to teach something by the history itself (which would not be perceptible to the people who were in it), and it flies in the face of the explicit statements of Paul (1 Cor. 9:9; Rom. 4:23; 15:4), Hebrews (11:39-40), and Peter (1 Peter 1:12) that the OT events and writings are for the benefit of Christians. The most important thing is to have the correct goal in interpretation, but that goal will also indicate method. For the NT writers, the goal was Jesus the Christ and His representative redemptive work by the cross and resurrection; the most basic methodological consideration, therefore, was to look to see how the OT spoke of Jesus' person and work, and the life of His people that would grow out of it. If we share that goal, shall we not also share that basic consideration?

What are the methods characteristic of the NT's use of the OT?[17]

1. Generally, the NT cites from the LXX, but not exclusively. Thus we have warrant for using translations.

2. Often introductory formulas are used, such as "it is written" or "the Holy Spirit says" — indicating that (OT) Scripture confirms NT revelation, and that the OT is therefore prophetic in character. Thus the NT indicates a high regard for Scripture as God's speech.

3. The NT treats the OT events as genuine history, constitutive for the present state of affairs. Thus the NT warrants a grammatical-historical method.

4. History is understood as being under divine control; it is going somewhere: God accomplishes salvation in history. Thus we look for a redemptive-historical meaning.

5. The OT history is understood as indicating *where* it was going. Thus the OT should be typologically and eschatologically understood.

6. As in the OT, humans are regarded both individually and corporately (the body of Christ). Thus we apply a covenantal understanding.

7. Christ fulfills the role and character of the corporate entities mankind (Adam) and Israel (see Heb. 2:8; Rom. 5; 1 Cor. 15:27), and thus those who are united to Him become true Israel (Gal. 6:16; Phil. 3:3), the perfect man (Eph. 4:13; Col. 1:28). Thus Scripture is interpreted christocentrically and ecclesiologically.

8. Scripture is regarded as a mystery now revealed (Mark 4:11; Eph. 3:3), an "uncovered secret." Thus we use an expositional method.

Although these provide the methodological guidelines for our own exegesis, as we indicated before, the much more important matter is the interpretive framework or presuppositional goals for which we are aiming. Also, as indicated earlier, this interpretive goal for the NT writers was Jesus Christ's person and work. But even with this goal in mind, we still have a wide open field of interpretive framework, including method, to develop rightly if we wish to understand Scripture rightly. The fact that there are within the church so many different interpretations of various passages indicates that other subordinate interpretive goals are at work. These unspoken subordinate goals may come from a variety of sources and ought now to be addressed.

3.2 Tradition and the Church

3.2.1 Tradition

Tradition is often in our day identified as something "bad." And of course one can find plenty of instances where tradition has stifled thought, creativity, and progress, or even wrought heresy or discord (Col. 2:8). Who can forget Tevye in the musical *Fiddler on the Roof,* so dominated by tradition that new situations tear his world apart. Tradition is often binding and turns the hermeneutical spiral into a vicious circle. Tradition was quite binding, even blinding, in the Judaism of Jesus' day, as He pointed out in Mark 7:8-12: "You have a fine way of setting aside the commands of God in order to observe your own traditions" (v. 9).

That it was tradition and not exegesis that really formed the basis for Jewish religion is illustrated in a story about the famous Rabbi Hillel. Hillel was arguing that it was legal to sacrifice the Passover lamb on the weekly Sabbath if the Passover fell on the first day of the week. At great length he argued by exegeting various Scripture passages in creative ways, and each exegesis was rejected by his colleagues. Finally Hillel ceased all exegesis and simply said that he had received the oral tradition from his teachers, whereupon his argument was immediately accepted and Hillel was elected president of the assembly.[18]

The church too has been subject to tradition which can blind as well as bind. Note the avowal of Pope Pius I at the first Vatican Council:

> I accept sacred scripture according to that sense which holy mother church held and holds, since it is her right to judge of the true sense and interpretation of the holy scriptures; nor will I ever receive and interpret them except according to the unanimous consent of the fathers.[19]

In other words, to some people, the Bible can only be allowed to mean what tradition says it means, and that is the end of the matter. Tradition can, if not continually challenged, lull people into a comfortable dogmatic slumber from which they may never wake.

In our age, the primary objection raised against tradition is that it is an externally imposed authority. The Enlightenment could tolerate no authority except human reason, and so reason overthrows tradition. But to the biblical writers, tradition is not all bad. Paul refers positively to the "tradition" (1 Cor. 11:2; 2 Thes. 2:15; 3:6). Tradition preserves what has been learned in the church about the biblical text and its theological framework over centuries, and it is folly to insist on standing on our own two feet rather than on giants' shoulders. It is important to note that although the Reformers rejected tradition as the final authority (a place reserved for Scripture alone), they did not reject tradition itself except where such tradition was demonstrably out of harmony with Scripture. On the other hand, the Enlightenment did reject tradition as being prejudice, never recognizing that it had its own prejudice against tradition.[20]

Actually tradition is inescapable even for the Enlightenment person; every human being acquires something of his or her way of looking at life from other human beings; and every reader of the Bible is inescapably going to be influenced by his or her surrounding community's preconceived notions of what the Bible is about.[21] In God's providence this means that each human being does not have to start from scratch. Interpreting must be done within an interpretive framework; tradition gives one a head start on the hermeneutical spiral, and inhibits spinning off of it. Yet we must also be always ready to stand back and evaluate tradition, without necessarily rejecting it.

3.2.2 The church

The church, or God's people, is the primary carrier of tradition about the Bible. It certainly is not infallible[22] and must be continually critiqued, but this tradition is maintained and critiqued not by individuals working separately but by the church as a whole. Even in our age of fragmented churches, where interpretive traditions vary widely, one's own church is still an instrument of maintaining the tradition.

This function of the church led to a certain tension in early Protestantism, because whereas the Reformers wished to make the individual conscience free and unbound in its interpretation of the Bible, they also wished to maintain a doctrinal standard for the particular church. The result was an acknowledgment that each person has not only a right but a responsibility to interpret the Bible for himself according to his own conscience, but that if the individual wished to teach in a church, he must adhere to its doctrinal tradition. The tradition could be improved or changed, but only by the careful consideration of that church in assembly. No church's tradition can define the meaning of every verse in Scripture, but it does set boundaries on the theological interpretive framework within which interpretation is done. A church's standards thus act as a check on "new" interpretations the consequences of which have not been adequately thought through.

In our age, of course, the church is fragmented, and a variety of interpretive traditions (frameworks) provide a variety of subordinate interpretive goals, which result in a variety of interpretations. Although the fragmentation of God's church is a tragedy, it is also a blessing, because while tradition can remain strong and functional within a church, the constant encounter with different traditions never permits the church to slip into a dogmatic slumber. Interpretive frameworks of tradition are constantly being tested.[23]

3.3 The Holy Spirit: The Ultimate Interpreter

The church's tradition is not wholly in the hands of human beings. The Holy Spirit who authored Scripture (2 Peter 1:21) enables the church to perceive, first, that Scripture is indeed the Word of God.[24] He also promised to guide the church with regard to His meaning (John 16:13-15).

Two difficulties proceed from an acknowledgment of this activity of the Holy Spirit. First is the great diversity of opinion in the church regarding doctrines and interpretations. This diversity suggests to some that the Holy Spirit has done nothing of the sort, or if He has, we have no way to distinguish the Holy Spirit's interpretation from its competitors. Just how is the Holy Spirit leading the church into truth? Second, the revealing activity of the Holy Spirit in Scripture raises the question of whether revelation continues today.

The first of these should be answered by reference to those passages which deal with the interpretive activity of the Spirit. The principle passages are: John 14:25-26, John 16:13-15, 1 John 2:20 and 27, and 1 Corinthians 2:6-16.[25]

Both John 14 and 16 occur in the context of Jesus' last discourse with His disciples before His crucifixion, preparing them for the future, when they must carry on without His physical presence, but with the power of His Spirit. He is thus speaking to His inner circle, the apostles. Certain of the things He tells His apostles obviously apply also to those who would believe later through their testimony (John 17:20), but equally obviously not all so apply (e.g., John 16:16). Do these passages relate directly to us?

John 14:25-26 has a degree of specificity to it. "These things I have spoken to you, while I am still with you" (RSV). This is certainly specific to those who knew the physical presence of Jesus. So there is a contextual disposition to regard the next verse as also specific: "The Counselor, the Holy Spirit, whom the Father will send in my name, he will teach you all things, and bring to your remembrance all that I have said to you." In other words, the Holy Spirit will *remind* the apostles of the things they heard from the mouth of the earthly Jesus; and the Spirit will also enable them to *understand* all things. This passage says nothing about the Holy Spirit enabling "us" to remember or understand everything the earthly Jesus said.

On the other hand, the verse is not meaningless to us. It rather gives assurance that the remembrances and teachings of the apostles are authoritative and sanctioned by the Spirit of the living God. Thus the NT is a trustworthy text, both in regards to its historical account (remembrance) and its theological interpretation.

John 16:13-15 appears to be a less specific context. The preceding verses (8-11) speak of the activity of the Spirit in convincing the world regarding sin, righteousness, and judgment. This is certainly an activity of the Spirit which extends beyond the bounds of the apostolic band. But Jesus does not there refer to "you" (the apostles) as the object of such convincing, but "the world." On the other hand, verse 12 focuses again on the people present in the Upper Room—"I have yet many things to say to you, but you cannot bear them now" (RSV). This only applies to disciples prior to Jesus' resurrection and ascension. And verse 16, immediately following, is also specific to those who historically lived through the death and resurrection of Jesus. So the Spirit of truth guiding "you" into all truth is limited to His guidance of the *apostles* into all truth; thus the passage is parallel to 14:26. In both of these passages, Jesus teaches that the Spirit authenticates the testimony of the apostles. This testimony is now our NT. Neither of these passages indicates the role of the Holy Spirit in *our* present-day interpretive processes.

On the other hand, John himself suggests in 1 John that the interpretive activity by which the Holy Spirit guided and sanctioned the teaching and words of the apostles also extends in some ways to all Christians. In 1 John 2:20 he tells his readers (who were not apostles), "But you have an anointing from the Holy One, and all of you know the truth."[26] And in verses 26-27 following he expands it a bit: "As for you, the anointing you received from him remains in you, and you do not need anyone to teach you. But as his anointing teaches you about all things, and as that anointing is real, not counterfeit—just as it has taught you, remain in him." Since divine anointing is the activity of the Holy Spirit (Acts 10:38), we can expect that "the holy one" of verse 20 is the Holy Spirit. The point here is that John is reassuring his readers that their personal knowledge of the truth has come about by the activity of God in them (compare the words to what Jesus says of Peter's words in Matt. 16:17). The promise of John 14:26 that the Spirit would teach the apostles is extended to all believers, but the context of that extension (particularly 1 John 2:18–3:10) is specifically the *maintenance of personal relationship with Jesus* (remaining in Him and trusting Him). The Spirit teaches us that we really do know Him and His truth (see Gal. 4:6), in spite of the fact that some have departed from the faith (1 John 2:19). So the point here is not that the Spirit informs us directly of the precise content of God's truth, but that the Spirit convicts and assures us of the truthfulness and trustworthiness of that content found in Scripture.

First Corinthians 2 is dealing with a different matter. Paul is facing a congregation where at least some people have been denigrating Paul's teaching because it was not rhetorically powerful. Paul writes to remind the Corinthians that rhetorical splendor is not the criterion of truth, but the Spirit of God. His first point is that the Spirit of God has authenticated his preaching by accompanying miracles (v. 4). Miracles verified the apostolic testimony (see Heb. 2:4). Second, Paul claims that his teaching was "revealed by the Spirit" (v. 10). Like the other apostles included in the John 14 and 16 promises, Paul is recipient of "God's secret wisdom, a wisdom that has been hidden and that God destined for our glory before time began" (v. 7). But Paul ends by implying that the Corinthian believers too have "not received the spirit of the world but the Spirit who is from God, that we may understand what God has freely given us" (v. 12). But for the Corinthians the Spirit does not *generate* the content of the truths of the faith; He *enables* their reception of it. Verse 13: "And we [i.e., the apostles] impart this in words not taught by human wisdom but taught by the Spirit, interpreting spiritual truths to those who possess the Spirit" (RSV).[27] Again, whereas the Holy Spirit enables every believer to recognize and submit to the truth of Scripture, the direct revelation of the content of that truth is only through the apostles.[28]

Our conclusion must be that the Holy Spirit continues to guide His people in their ability to recognize, understand, and apply "all truth," but that the direct revelation of "all truth" comes not to every believer apart from Scripture but by way of the apostle's words, which we find in Scripture. Just as the believer must work at *obedience* to God, even though it is the Holy Spirit who produces that obedience, so he or she must work at *understanding* God's words.

Does this mean the Holy Spirit has stopped revealing truth to His people? Has He simply "closed shop" so far as guidance into truth is concerned? Or does revelation somehow continue today?

This can be answered by comparing revelation with redemption. Redemption has an accomplished aspect and an applied aspect. There is an objective, completed redemptive activity of Christ in cross and resurrection that can never and need never be repeated. It is "once for all" and finished forever (e.g., Heb. 9:28; 10:10, 12). But redemption also has a continuing, subjective, experiential aspect; believers experience their own justification and sanctification in their own time. Likewise with special revelation, the Word of God. Revelation has an accomplished, objective, definitive, and unrepeatable dimension. We thus have a "canon" of Scripture. But the Word is also continuously applied to individuals, who subjectively experience the Word of God coming alive to them, meeting their needs in their special situations. Thus we have "hermeneutics," which is concerned with ascertaining not just the once-for-all meaning of Scripture, but also the way to apply that once-for-all meaning in one's own life. But just as the objective redemption must always be the ground of applied redemption (no one can be saved apart from the work of Christ on the cross), so objective revelation must always be the ground of "applied revelation."

This similarity of redemption (accomplished and applied) with revelation (accomplished and applied) is not accidental. Verbal revelation in Scripture accompanies God's redemptive deeds in history. The foundation of God's people in the OT Exodus is the redemptive-historical occasion for the Pentateuch. The conquest sets the stage for Joshua, Judges, and Ruth. The typological theocracy under David and his line is the occasion for the historical books, the Psalms, and many of the prophetical books. And the Exile provides a context for Daniel, Ezekiel, and some scattered other works. In contrast, during the hiatus of redemptive-historical deeds in the intertestamental period, revelation did not occur. But when redemptive history reached its climax in the NT, verbal revelation reached its culmination. God's Word and God's deeds go together; His Word explains His deeds.

Further, note that when verbal revelation is given in the Bible, its purpose is never private—it is always given for the benefit of God's people as a whole. Even the few "personal" letters of Paul are really intended for the church, as is indicated by, among other things, the use of the plural "you" in 1 Timothy 6:21, 2 Timothy 4:22, and Titus 3:15. And the few instances of direct personal guidance by prophecy recorded in the OT are commands for action for some redemptive historical purpose, not the revealing of truth or the ethical will of God.

It is for this reason that we need to be exceedingly careful about accepting alleged personal revelations by the Holy Spirit. The human mind, even the believer's mind, can deceive itself very easily, and a person can genuinely believe that he or she has received a vision from the Holy Spirit which is no such thing. Jeremiah, who knew the genuine revelation from the Holy Spirit, says in 23:28 of his book: "Let the dreamer tell his dream, but let him who has my word speak my word faithfully: Chaff and grain are quite distinct, says the Lord" (authors' trans.). Even if a vision, dream, prophecy, or picturing is genuinely from God, the only way to test such "revelation" is by the revelation that already is known, the Bible. One should never interpret Scripture by way of an alleged prophecy, whether such prophecy be genuine or not. No reputed vision can possibly compete with the Bible. The Bible alone is sufficient for whatever knowledge of the truth we need, and this Word of God alone is reliable and guaranteed.

This is not to deny that the Holy Spirit does work, sometimes in unexpected ways, in enabling the believer to understand, and to believe, Scripture. In fact, if the Holy Spirit did not work to change our minds, we would never be capable of understanding it. But again we may compare with the process of redemption. The Holy Spirit *sanctifies* the believer, but the individual is responsible to be holy (1 Peter 1:16). The believer must apply oneself to obedience, and may often be wrong in his or her moral decisions. In similar manner, the Holy Spirit continually *illumines* and convicts the mind of the believer, but he or she is also responsible to interpret and to believe and may often be wrong regarding the meaning of a text (see sec. 2.4). One can never appeal to subjective illumination by the Holy Spirit as a means of bypassing the labor of exegesis, for this would be to interpret Scripture by subjective feeling rather than to interpret the subjective experience by God's Word.

Finally, we may mention that, although Scripture gives no indication that the Holy Spirit *directly* reveals the meaning of Scripture now, the Spirit does give gifts to the church by enabling some people to be teachers (Eph. 4). That is, He does impart to some special abilities in discerning historical and textual backgrounds, awareness of the entirety of Scripture, and insights into how Scripture applies to the contemporary culture. But again this is never a guarantee to an individual that his or her interpretation is correct, but a guarantee that the Holy Spirit will ensure the continuation of sound doctrine in the church, God's people. So there is great cause for confidence that the Holy Spirit leads His church into truth, but no ground for arrogance that one's own unique interpretation at any specific point is absolutely correct. As individuals, we will always be on the hermeneutical spiral.

PART TWO
INTERPRETATION IN THEORY

Many books on Bible interpretation assert that it should be read "like any other book." In one sense, it should certainly be read like any other book, because, as we argued in the previous chapter, the Bible is written in ordinary human language. We should therefore go about understanding its discourse content in the same way we would with other books. But in another sense, by arguing for divine authorship we also implied that the Bible is no more like "any other book" than the death of Christ is like any other death. The only way to understand the Bible as it is meant to be understood is to submit to it as God's Word.

If the Bible is divine speech, is it in some respects a genre by itself and subject to different rules of interpretation? Although God is its ultimate author, the Bible is still genuinely human speech, not just divine speech in a human guise. Thus we must first look at the discourse of the Bible in the same way we would attempt to understand other human speech. Just as a preliminary knowledge of general revelation is necessary to understand special revelation, so a knowledge of the human meaning of Scripture must serve as a base for knowing the divine meaning. What the human author said in his original context must be intrinsically linked to what God intends to say for all time — they must be organically related — otherwise we would have no means of understanding the speech, no socio-linguistic framework in which to arrive at a "meeting of meaning."

When examining biblical discourse, however, we must bear in mind that God's past actions and words are of a piece with His later actions and words. Thus the NT writers are free to refer to the historical meaning as something which of itself, in its original historical context, looked forward to the Christ. Notice how the author of Hebrews argues that the OT itself foresaw that the sacrificial system was temporary, because it pointed beyond itself to a more perfect sacrifice (Heb. 10:1-18). This does not imply that the christological meaning was necessarily directly in the mind of either the OT writer or his first hearers. (Neither is there reason to deny that they often were aware of the promise of Christ.)

Certainly it is impossible to demonstrate that the OT writers and first readers *always* understood the christological meaning which the NT writers unfold. But the christological meaning is inherent in the history and revelation itself. Biblical revelation in the OT was always going somewhere (see Heb. 11:39-40). Abraham, for example, knew that God was doing things with a view to the future. He bought the field at Machpelah (which was in Canaan) because he expected the fulfillment of God's promises (Gen. 23). He himself may have understood very little of all that those promises would entail, but Hebrews indicates that in a sense Abraham believed in the resurrection, because of his obedience in offering his son Isaac (Heb. 11:19). Moses also knew that biblical revelation was going somewhere. Deuteronomy indicates that Moses looked forward to a prophet like him but even greater than he (Deut. 18:15, 18).

So if we wish to obtain a sound understanding of what God *is* saying in a text, we must first understand what the human author *was* saying. In other words, we cannot cite a text as a proof text for some teaching until first we find out what that text was saying in its original setting, both textual and historical. Neither can we simply assume that our subjective impression of a text is the meaning God intends for us. The task of "grammatical-historical exegesis," which will be explained in chapter 5, is the first step to understanding God's Word.[1]

Nevertheless, as divine speech the Bible is qualitatively different from ordinary human utterances in its effectual power, its absolute trustworthiness and consistency, its fullness of meaning, and its applicability to all God's people everywhere at all times. So although grammatical-historical exegesis may exhaust the accessible meaning of an ancient inscription on a potsherd, the limits imposed by this method cannot do full justice to Scripture. Thus chapter 6 will look at how we may learn from the Bible more than pure grammatical-historical exegesis would reveal.

No one comes to a text without a background; this book is written for Christians, and Christians operate within the context of God's people, the church. This is significant because it means our interpretation will be influenced first by the traditions and methods of interpretation of our predecessors and by the fact that the Holy Spirit is active in leading the church in its understanding of Scripture. In chapter 4 we shall notice how the apparent tension between the necessity of reading the Bible like other books and the commitment to reading it as the transcendent Word of God has occupied the church's thinking about biblical interpretation throughout its history.

FOUR

THE CHURCH AND BIBLICAL INTERPRETATION

This chapter does not so much survey the history of biblical interpretation as highlight the principal ways in which the church has attempted to resolve the problem of interpreting a book that is both earthly and transcendent. We shall therefore focus on the key figures in the church's history who not only interpreted the Bible but set the interpretive agenda for subsequent discussions on how the Bible should be interpreted.

4.1 The Early Church: Justin Martyr and Irenaeus

The early church took its cue from a variety of sources. Most important was the NT itself. Since the NT saw the OT as pointing to Christ, early church exegesis did likewise. They believed that God had genuinely foretold of the Christ in prophecy and interpreted particularly the Prophets and Psalms as referring directly to Christ. Unfortunately, sometimes the efforts to find Christ in the OT proved fanciful, and allegorical interpretation, which was an accepted technique in Hellenism for interpreting sacred texts, also became common among Christians. *Justin Martyr* (d. ca. 165), for example, in his *Dialogue with Trypho* (77–78) argued with a Jewish non-Christian about the meaning of Isaiah 7:14.

"I admit," said Trypho, "that your arguments are so numerous and forceful that they suffice to make me confused, but I again call to your attention that I want the proof of that Scriptural passage which you have so often promised. Please go on now and show us how that passage refers to your Christ, and not to Hezekiah, as we Jews believe."

"I will do as you wish," I replied, "but, first, prove to me that Hezekiah was the one spoken of in the following words: 'Before he had known how to call father or mother, he received the power of Damascus and the spoils of Samaria in the presence of the king of Assyria.'. . . Now, you cannot prove that this ever happened to any of you Jews, but we Christians can show that it did happen to our Christ. For at the time of His birth, the Magi came from Arabia and

85

worshipped Him, after they had met Herod, then king of your country, whom Scripture calls king of Assyria because of His wicked ungodliness. For you well know that the Holy Spirit often speaks in parables and similitudes, just as He did to all the people of Jerusalem when He frequently said to them: 'Thy father was an Amorite and thy mother a Hittite.' . . . The words of Isaias, 'He shall take the power of Damascus and the spoils of Samaria,' meant that the power of the wicked demon that dwelt in Damascus should be crushed by Christ at his birth. This is shown to have taken place. For the Magi, held in servitude (as spoils) for the commission of every wicked deed through the power of that demon, by coming and worshipping Christ, openly revolted against the power that had held them as spoils, which power the Scripture indicated by parable to be located in Damascus. And in the parables that sinful and wicked power is fittingly called Samaria. . . ."[1]

This kind of argument would convince few modern Westerners, but in Justin's day allegorical meaning of sacred texts was taken for granted. But in spite of the allegorism, note that Justin also preserves a historical dimension; certain events actually happened in fulfillment of certain OT prophecies.

Irenaeus (d. ca. 200) is another well-known Christian of the second century, and Irenaeus developed the historical approach in a *typological* direction. The coming of Christ clarifies what was previously only hinted at.

For every prophecy, before it comes about, is an enigma and a contradiction to men; but when the time comes, and what was prophesied takes place, it receives a most certain exegesis. And therefore when the Law is read by Jews at the present time, it is like a myth; for they do not have the explanation of everything, which is the coming of the Son of God as man. But when it is read by Christians, it is a treasure, hidden in the field but revealed by the cross of Christ. . . . The true exegesis was taught by the Lord himself after his resurrection.[2]

Irenaeus also formulated the principle that obscure passages should be interpreted in the light of clear ones. In taking some early Gnostic Christian heretics to task for focusing on the obscure, he says: "If anything is clear in Scripture, it is that there is only one God who created the world through his Word."[3] This is an article of scriptural faith which the Gnostics denied most vehemently. Irenaeus, in his battles against groups on the fringes of Christianity who had perverted its main teachings, also introduced the idea of authoritative exegesis. The true meaning of Scripture is invested in the church, where apostolic authority was preserved. Although part of what he said was true (the church is invested with the knowledge of Scripture's meaning), this began a long tradition of finding authoritative meanings in the early church leaders rather than in careful exegesis of the biblical text itself, which culminated after the Reformation in the Council of Trent's affirmations of ecclesiastical infallibility.

4.2 The Developing Church: Origen and Theodore

Origen (d. 254) stands at the apex of a tradition of interpretation developed at Alexandria.[4] Philo of Alexandria (d. ca. A.D. 50) had championed a highly developed allegorical approach to the OT by which he was able to find the philosophical ideas of Greek idealism in the Books of Moses. Origen's immediate Christian predecessor at Alexandria, Clement (d. 215), brought this idealist allegorism to Christian interpretation, especially at Alexandria.

According to Clement, the "true" meaning of the Bible was hidden in allegories so that the "higher" Christian, the one who had genuine understanding, would be able to discern things, whereas the commoner would be kept from knowledge which might be harmful to him. Unlike the Gnostics, however, Clement viewed "true knowledge" as equivalent to Christian doctrine, not secret knowledge of the hierarchies of spiritual beings. Knowledge was for Clement equivalent to salvation. He did therefore engage in explanations of the true knowledge, and he laid down some principles of interpretation, namely that: (1) nothing is literally true which is unworthy of God; (2) no interpretation can be accepted which contradicts the Bible as a whole, and (3) literal meaning is meant to excite interest in understanding the deeper meaning.[5]

Origen did not share Clement's secretive ideas and devoted himself to making the Bible known to anyone who would listen. Unlike Philo, Origen was not concerned to show how the Bible spoke Platonic philosophy, but he did use Platonic philosophy as a grid for understanding the Bible and for talking about and presenting Christ. Of course, a problem is that the grid does not work too well. Since Origen's presuppositions about the Bible as God's

Word were more central to him than his Neoplatonic philosophy, it could be hoped that Origen would have moved closer to a biblical worldview had he lived longer. In fact, by the time of his later works (such as the *Commentary on Matthew* and *Against Celsus*), he is not nearly as fanciful in his allegorizing as in his earlier.

Origen is important because he is the first to have formulated his principles of biblical interpretation. These are recorded in book 4 of Origen's *On First Principles*. In chapters 1 and 2 of this fourth book, Origen's principles are:

Assumption 1: Scripture is divinely inspired.
Therefore:
   (a) Its legal precepts are superior
   (b) It is powerful in changing lives
   (c) Biblical prophecy comes true
   (d) Like Jesus, the Bible is divine but in human form
   (e) The Bible contains hidden secrets.
Assumption 2: Scripture should be interpreted according to its nature.
Therefore:
   (a) Not every text has a literal meaning, but every text does have a spiritual meaning
   (b) The spiritual meaning is not always plain or easily understood
   (c) Scripture has a threefold meaning, a body (literal meaning), a soul (a psychical meaning relating to the will), and a spirit (spiritual meaning which speaks of Christ).
   (d) The problems in Scripture are there to hinder us from being too enamored of the literal meaning.

Chapter three of book four is then a demonstration of the "impossibilities" that result from taking all Scripture literally. For example, if the sun was created on the fourth day, how could there have been evening and morning on the first three? Anthropomorphisms such as the "face" of God could not be literal. According to Origen, the prohibition to eat vultures if taken literally is ridiculous, because no one would think of doing it. Certain animals in the OT are mentioned which Origen thought were mythological and therefore must be allegorical. Similarly, casting only the right eye out when it caused one to sin, becoming "uncircumcised," and other things in Scripture can only be interpreted as metaphors for something else.

Origen also has an apologetic motivation for allegorical interpretation. For Origen, the prayer of Psalm 137:8-9 was so contrary to the Gospel that it had to be explained.

> The infants of Babylon, which means "confusion," are the confused thoughts caused by evil which have just been implanted and are growing up in the soul. The man who takes hold of them, so that he breaks their heads by the firmness and solidity of the Word, is dashing the infants of Babylon against the rock.[6]

But Origen does wish to retain a literal value for many things, especially the moral injunctions, and he admits there are times when it is difficult to decide whether something bears a literal meaning, an allegorical, or both. It is sometimes forgotten that Origen admits that "the passages which are historically true far outnumber those which are composed with purely spiritual meanings" (*First Principles* 4.3.4), and he found the fact that the Bible is literally true to be a support for its allegorical meanings (*Against Celsus* 8.67). Christianity is superior to paganism because Christ *literally* exists and *literally* rose from the dead.[7] And when it came to defending the faith, Origen relied almost exclusively on the literal meaning.[8]

Origen's argument for a divine meaning which is different from the literal and is allegorically discerned set the tone for most biblical interpretation up through the Middle Ages. Augustine of Hippo (d. 430), for example, could understand the door of Noah's ark as symbolizing the wound in Christ's side (*City of God* 15.26). By the time of Cyril (d. 444) the *Quadrigam*, the fourfold meaning scheme employed by the scholastics, had developed. Scripture could have a literal meaning (what God did in the past), an allegorical meaning (the meaning having to do with faith), a tropological meaning (for moral guidance), and/or an anagogical meaning (pertaining to the Christian hope).

But in the third century Origen's was not the only exegetical option. At Syrian Antioch a different kind of Christian scholarship developed, whose best representative is probably *Theodore of Mopsuestia* (d. 428).[9] Not much is known of Theodore, and few of his works remain. But he and others of the "Antiochene" school opposed the allegorism of Alexandria in favor of literal interpretation. He wrote a treatise against allegorism called *Concerning Allegory and History Against Origen* in which he argued that Origen's approach deprived biblical history of its reality. If Adam was not a real person, argued Theodore, then how did death enter the world? The "allegorical interpretation" of Paul in Galatians 4 did not deny the historical events but used them as an example or illustration.

Theodore apparently attempted to achieve consistency in his commitment against allegorism. From his commentary on the minor prophets,[10] his principle appears to be: unless the NT actually cites the text it is not messianic. Allusion is not sufficient to establish a text as messianic. Even when the NT does cite an OT text, it may be only illustrative rather than an indication of a messianic meaning; Hosea 11:1 itself, says Theodore, makes no reference to Christ in spite of Matthew 2:15. On the other hand, Joel 2 does contain information that is only unveiled in the coming of Jesus.[11]

Theodore does not deny, however, that the NT gives indication of actual literal fulfillments of OT prophecy. The prophets actually foresaw Christ and thus their prophecies had a double sense, a historical and a messianic. Psalms 2, 8, 95, and 110 literally refer to Christ. Theodore developed Irenaeus' idea of typology, but kept it limited to a historical correspondence. The meaning of a text was its historical meaning. Later in redemptive history, one might notice historical correspondences (types), which stem from patterns in God's plan. Thus Psalm 22 is in itself historical only and only tangentially applies to Christ as it would apply to any sufferer. It only applies to Christ par excellence because He is the ultimate sufferer.

Unfortunately for the church, Theodore was declared heretical, partly because of the alleged christological errors of his pupil Nestorius, and partly because he rejected certain canonical books as not inspired, but his influence was widely felt for a while in Eastern Christianity. Especially the famous preacher John Chrysostom (d. 407) focused on the historical meaning. He does find Christ in the OT, but usually restricts himself to historical typology. Chrysostom found warrant for typological understanding of the OT in the refrain of Psalm 117, "his truth endures forever" (Gk. trans.). Thus the OT history has some meaning for today as well.[12] For

Chrysostom, the historical meaning is the outline of God's truth; the final form (the full portrait) is found in the typological meaning.[13]

4.3 The Middle Ages: Aquinas[14]

Although the Middle Ages represents a mixture of several different opinions on all issues (including the interpretation of Scripture), standing at the apex of late medieval thought, and representative of medieval exegetical theory, is *Thomas Aquinas* (d. 1274). For Aquinas, the principal hermeneutical consideration was that the Catholic Church was the authoritative interpreter. Like most of his contemporaries and predecessors, Thomas held to the fourfold exegetical method.

Thomas, however, insisted that the literal should be the basis of the other three. He explains his position in *Summa Theologica* 1.1.10.

> The author of Holy Writ is God, in whose power it is to signify his meaning, not by words only (as man also can do) but by things themselves. So, whereas in every other science things are signified by words, this science has the property that the things signified by the words have themselves also a signification. Therefore that first signification whereby words signify things belongs to the first sense, the historical or literal. That signification whereby things signified by words have themselves also a signification is called the spiritual sense, which is based on the literal, and pre-supposes it. For as the apostle says (Heb.x. 1) the Old Law is a figure of the New Law and [Pseudo-]Dionysius says: "The New Law itself is a figure of future glory." Again, in the New Law, whatever our Head has done is a type of what we ought to do. Therefore, so far as the things of the Old Law signify the things of the New Law, there is the allegorical sense; so far as the things done in Christ, or so far as the things which signify Christ, are types of what we ought to do, there is the moral sense. But so far as they signify what relates to eternal glory, there is the anagogical sense. Since the literal sense is that which the author intends, and since the author of Holy Writ is God, Who by one act comprehends all things by His intellect, it is not unfitting, as Augustine says (Confess. xii), if, even according to the literal sense, one word in Holy Writ should have several senses.[15]

Thus Aquinas argued that the history itself, not just words about history, was prophetic.

Aquinas recognizes the problem with Scripture having "several senses."

> Many different senses in one text produce confusion and deception and destroy all force of argument. Hence no argument, but only fallacies, can be deduced from a multiplicity of propositions. But Holy Writ ought to be able to state the truth without any fallacy.[16]

To this he responds:

> The multiplicity of these senses does not produce equivocation or any other kind of multiplicity, seeing that these senses are not multiplied because one word signifies several things; but because the things signified by the words can themselves be types of other things. Thus in Holy Writ no confusion results, for *all the senses are founded on one—the literal—from which alone can any argument be drawn,* and not from those intended in allegory, as Augustine says (Epist. xlviii). Nevertheless, nothing of Holy Scripture perishes on account of this, since nothing necessary to faith is contained under the spiritual sense which is not elsewhere put forward by the Scripture in its literal sense (emphasis ours).[17]

Aquinas was remarkably close to the Reformation on the question of Scripture's meaning. Even though he and other late medieval theologians generally stressed deductive reason (reasoning from the generals to the particulars) rather than inductive examination as the means to obtaining an objective exegesis, since most of the church's theology had been built up by Christians paying attention to Scripture, his framework was a Christian framework. But on the other hand, his concerns were systematic and philosophical, and his questions were often drawn from an Aristotelian framework. Also, for Aquinas, interpretation of Scripture requires no special grace, because theology and the knowledge of God (which did require grace) were not the direct result of interpretation of Scripture. The knowledge of God was more wedded to philosophy and tradition than to exegesis (unlike the Reformation, which thought of theology as dependent strictly on exegesis).

4.4 The Reformation: Luther and Calvin

The two watchwords of the Reformation were *sola fide* and *sola scriptura*, faith alone and Scripture alone. As Melancthon pointed out, these were the material and formal principles of the Reformation.

4.4.1 Martin Luther

Martin Luther[18] (1483–1546) derived several hermeneutical principles from these commitments. From the principle of *sola scriptura*, Luther felt he must stress first of all that the historical sense is the true sense: "Only the historical sense gives the true and sound doctrine."[19]

In this Luther followed the lead not only of the exegetical *theory* of Aquinas, but more particularly the *practice* of Nicholas of Lyra (d. 1340) and Jacques Lefevre d'Etaples (known in Latin as Jacobus Faber Stapulensis; d. 1536).

Holding to *sola scriptura* and the historic sense also meant a rejection of traditionalism: "The teachings of the Fathers are useful only to lead us to the Scriptures as they were led, and then we must hold to the Scriptures alone."[20]

Hence he also rejected the fourfold method, particularly allegorism as a source of doctrine.[21]

When I was a monk I allegorized everything. But after lecturing on the epistle to the Romans I came to have some knowledge of Christ. For therein I saw that Christ is not an allegory, and I learned to know what Christ actually was.

Because the esoterism of allegorical interpretation was no longer primary, the Bible became accessible to ordinary thought and so Luther saw the meaning of the Bible as simple and clear.[22] This was not to say that there were not some difficult passages, but that the main matters of the Bible as a whole were understandable to the mind of the ordinary man or woman.

Luther's second principle derived from *sola scriptura* was that Scripture is its own interpreter: *Scriptura sui ipsius interpres* says Luther,[23] citing Augustine's dictum. As A.S. Wood says:

Luther . . . insists that the Bible itself must teach us how to interpret the Bible. The first hermeneutical circle is to be drawn from the design of the Word. The sphere from which the methodology of hermeneutics is to be derived is that of Scripture itself. The true principles of biblical interpretation are themselves quarried from biblical sources. To break this circuit is to deprive interpretation of its essential dynamic and authority."[24]

The other Reformation principle was *sola fide,* from which Luther concluded, first, that true understanding of Scripture can only occur by experiencing the Word and second that the whole Bible is about Christ.

Scripture can only be apprehended spiritually and experientially:

> If God does not open and explain Holy Writ, no one can understand it; it will remain a closed book, enveloped in darkness.[25]

On the other hand, when God does open the human heart to the meaning of Scripture, it is a sure and certain word.

> The Holy Spirit is no sceptic, and the things he has written in our hearts are not doubts or opinion, but assertions — surer and more certain than sense and life itself.[26]

Thus, in accord with passages such as Luke 24:44-46, there is a christological meaning to the whole. Of course, a christological reading of the OT was not new, but Luther focused on the fact that Christ, the true spiritual sense of Scripture, is communicated by the *historical* sense. Commenting on the fact that Paul uses Deuteronomy 30:12 in a different sense than the historical (Rom. 10:6-8), Luther claims that:

> [Paul is] teaching us that the entire Scripture deals only with Christ everywhere, if it is looked at inwardly, even though on the face of it it may sound differently, by the use of shadows and figures.[27]

Again following Lefevre, who had insisted on a twofold literal sense, a literal historic and a literal prophetic, Luther held to the historical sense in two ways, first as an account of the history of what God has done, and second as having a history which pointed to what God was going to do.

For Luther, the importance of Christ was God's imputation to us of His righteousness, and so the christocentric focus to the word also meant that the hermeneutical key was the imputed righteousness of God which was given to the believer through faith alone.[28]

Occasionally Luther's understanding of the *sola fide* and the *sola scriptura* principles came in conflict. The conflict could be resolved in two ways: by submission of one's faith to the Scripture, or by critiquing the Scripture so that it conformed to one's faith.

Now Luther's *theory* presupposes that Scripture is the Word; therefore Scripture is above all human thinking.

> Scripture is the Word of God.[29]
>
> The Holy Scriptures have been spoken by the Holy Ghost.[30]
>
> No living Christian can be forced to recognize any authority beyond the sacred Scripture, which is exclusively invested with divine right, unless indeed there should come a new and attested revelation.[31]
>
> The God of Truth speaks to us in the Scriptures, and therefore we must simply accept what stands there.[32]
>
> The Scripture is God's word, not man's, and not one jot or tittle of it is in vain.[33]
>
> The more you distrust yourself and your thoughts, the better a theologian and a Christian you will become.[34]
>
> In it [the Bible] not one word is of so small an account as to allow of our understanding it by reason.[35]

In theory, Luther differentiated between the magisterial and ministerial use of reason. "Our intellect must adjust itself to the Word of God and to Holy Scripture." Thus reason cannot adjudge the truth value of the Scriptures. But reason must be employed in order to understand the truth.[36]

However, his practice treats some Scriptures as being more important or clearer than others, and some Scriptures do not fit his theological assumptions (e.g., James) so he practices criticism, placing reason above the Bible.

> We should throw the Epistle of James out of this school [Wittenberg], for it doesn't amount to much. It contains not a syllable about Christ. . . . I maintain that some Jew wrote it who probably heard about Christian people but never encountered any.[37]

It is well known that Luther thought that Esther, James, and Jude were unimportant because he could not see how they spoke of Christ, and he was dubious about Revelation, because of its "Jewish" imagery. Further, some Scripture was dismissed as no longer relevant. Luther's Law and Gospel distinction in his theology was so sharp that he argued, for example, that the Ten Commandments did not apply to Christians, being addressed only to the Jews who had come out of Egypt.[38]

Post-Reformation theologians of both Lutheran and Calvinist affiliation stressed Luther's theoretical commitments and worked out the implications by rejecting Luther's unsubmissive criticism. The theology had to be brought in line with the Bible rather than the Bible critiqued to fit the theology. But the Enlightenment in Germany stressed rather Luther's practice and rejected his own theoretical ideas about the Bible as retaining the trappings of medieval thought. It was not until some time later, however, that such people realized they were thus bringing the Bible into line with their theology, which undercut the Reformation principle of deriving theology from exegesis.

It is the former group which is faithful to Luther. It is those who follow through on the implications of someone's theory that are the heirs to that person's thought, not those who reject the theory and develop a new theory out of the person's practice.

4.4.2 John Calvin

One of the greatest early developers of Luther's theoretical principle of *sola scriptura* was *John Calvin* (1509–1564).[39] To a large degree Calvin agreed with Luther, both on the formal principle of *sola scriptura* and on the material principle of *sola fide*. On the authority of Scripture he says:

> Before I go any farther, it is worthwhile to say something about the authority of Scripture, not only to prepare our hearts to reverence it, but to banish all doubt. When that which is set forth is acknowledged as the Word of God, there is no one so deplorably insolent — unless devoid also both of common sense and of humanity itself — as to dare impugn the credibility of Him who speaks. Now daily oracles are not sent from heaven, for it pleased the Lord to hallow his truth to everlasting remembrance in the Scriptures alone [cf. John 5:39].[40]

The authority of Scripture "derives in general from the fact that God in person speaks in it,"[41] and "Scripture exhibits fully as clear evidence of its own truth as white and black things do of their color. . . ."[42] Therefore "it is not right to subject it to proof and reasoning."[43]

Also as in Luther, Scripture was inherently clear, and the job of the preacher or teacher was simply to present the clear and simple teaching of Scripture in a clear and simple manner. Calvin's last address before his death included his assertion: "Though I might have introduced subtle senses, had I studied subtlety, I cast that temptation under my feet and always aimed at simplicity.[44] For Calvin, the ideal exposition was clear, simple, and brief. Some of the harshest language in Calvin is reserved for the convoluted verbal machinations and hermeneutical sophistry of the "school men" of his day.

Calvin was more consistent than Luther, however, in working through a theology based solely on Scripture. In that sense we can say he "out-Luthered" Luther.

First, Calvin engaged in much less allegorizing than Luther. Although Luther railed against allegorism, he continued to indulge in it from time to time. But Calvin, almost in the spirit of Theodore, is very slow to find direct references to Christ (even typologically) in the OT, unless the NT gives specific warrant, or the teaching is clearly in the context of the expectation of the future Messiah. And Calvin avoids even the "illustrative" or "adornment" use of allegorical interpretation.

Furthermore, Calvin's adherence to *sola scriptura* made him less free with his criticism of Scripture. Rather than reject James, Calvin attempted a synthesis of James and Paul. His closer examination of what James was actually saying removed much of the apparent conflict between the two. And instead of focusing on the rather narrow matter of justification by faith, Calvin took the much larger rubric of the glory of God as his interpretive viewpoint and was able to hold together the array of biblical teaching much more easily.

Calvin, like Luther, did recognize problems in Scripture, and if he had no solution he simply let a problem stand, rather than give an artificial solution or question Scripture's authority. For example, in his commentary on the Synoptic Gospels, he notes that Matthew 27:9 quotes Zechariah 13:7, but identifies it as Jeremiah. Calvin says, "How the name of Jeremiah crept in I cannot confess to know nor do I make much of it."[45] On the other hand, where he can harmonize a difficulty he does not hesitate. On the identity of "Zechariah son of Barachiah" in Matthew 23:35, he indicates that "there is no doubt about the matter at all that Christ refers to the impious stoning of that Zechariah which is described in 2 Chron.

24.22," that is, Zechariah son of Jehoiada, but Calvin suggests that perhaps this latter Zechariah held the name "son of Barachiah" (literally, "son of God's blessing") as an "honorific."[46] At no time does Calvin suggest that the original text was in error.

Distinctive to Calvin was his development of the doctrine of the conviction of the Holy Spirit.

> The testimony of the Spirit is more excellent than all reason. For as God alone is a fit witness of himself in his Word, so also the Word will not find acceptance in men's hearts before it is sealed by the inward testimony of the Spirit. The same Spirit, therefore, who has spoken through the mouths of the prophets must penetrate into our hearts to persuade us that they faithfully proclaimed what had been divinely commanded.[47]

> Even if it wins reverence for itself by its own majesty, it seriously affects us only when it is sealed upon our hearts through the Spirit. Therefore, illumined by his power, we believe neither by our own nor by anyone else's judgment that Scripture is from God; but above human judgment we affirm with utter certainty . . . that it has flowed to us from the very mouth of God by the ministry of men.[48]

Not only the conviction of the truth of Scripture, but its very understanding, is a gift to the elect.

> Whenever we are disturbed at the paucity of believers, let us . . . remember that none but those to whom it was given have any apprehension of the mysteries of God.[49]

Thus Calvin, like Luther, believed that the Word must ultimately be experienced in order to be truly and redemptively understood.

4.5 The "Modern" Church: From Schleiermacher to Bultmann

The nineteenth and twentieth centuries have seen a great deal of development in the methods of interpreting the Bible, largely due to the increasing ascendancy of the "historical-critical" method (see Appendix B). Furthermore, much has been written on hermeneutics, with a great deal in the way of modern philosophy being given over to the subject. Several works give a detailed account of biblical interpretation during the modern period and interested readers may refer to them,[50] but the two figures who set the tone for biblical hermeneutics during this time were Friedrich Schleiermacher in the early nineteenth century, and Rudolf Bultmann in the early twentieth.

4.5.1 Friedrich Schleiermacher

Although many Christian scholars had undertaken to interpret the Bible, and a few had attempted to spell out the methods for biblical interpretation, no one had thought about the relation of biblical interpretation to the processes of interpreting texts in general before German liberal Protestant theologian *Friedrich Schleiermacher* (1768–1834). In fact, few had thought about the problem of how meaning was conveyed in texts. Up until Kant, readers generally assumed that there was an objective content to a text, and this is what was directly perceived by the interpreter. But Kant's dialectic which set human freedom and understanding over against nature as object had introduced a gap between an interpreter's understanding of a text and its scientifically describable character. One of the great contributions of Schleiermacher was to think through some of these matters.

First, Schleiermacher argued that, although in some respects the Bible was unique, since it was written to humans it must partake of the character of linguistic communication in general. "No text is intended in such a way that its hearers could not possibly have understood it."[51] Therefore, the problem of understanding texts in general was not different than the problem of understanding the Bible.

Second, he recognized that presuppositions and background determine understanding: "The understanding of a given statement is always based on something prior, of two sorts—a preliminary knowledge of human beings, and a preliminary knowledge of the subject matter."[52] Preliminary knowledge of human beings involves especially some awareness of the speaker or author. Where an author is remote in time and culture, or where the reader is unfamiliar with the subject matter, some background work is necessary, and in all cases the gap between an author and the readers must be bridged. Schleiermacher thus identified two sides to the process of understanding a text: an objective side, which focused on the text itself, its words, grammar, and such, which he called "grammatical interpretation," and a subjective side, which attempts to "step out of one's own frame of mind into that of the

author."[53] This "subjective" side he called "technical interpretation."

> Strictly speaking, grammatical interpretation is the objective side;
> technical, the subjective. Consequently, grammatical interpretation
> plays a negative role in hermeneutical construction, marking the
> boundaries; technical interpretation is positive.[54]

Grammatical interpretation proceeds according to two canons.
The first is:

> one should construe the meaning from the total pre-given value of
> language and the heritage common to the author and his
> reader. . . .[55]

In other words, the characteristics of the language in which the
author and his readers operated must determine the semantic value of the author's statements.

The second canon is:

> the meaning of each word of a passage must be determined by the
> context in which it occurs.[56]

Essentially, Schleiermacher laid the methodological groundwork
for grammatical-historical exegesis as it is practiced today and
which is described in our chapter 5. Although this kind of investigation had been done intuitively before, particularly by Calvin,
Schleiermacher was the first to codify the method, and to present
it as a means of overcoming the distance between the author and
the present-day interpreter.

The other procedure in interpretation which complements the
"grammatical" was the "technical":

> Technical interpretation is chiefly concerned with the over-all co-
> herence and with its relation to the universal laws for combining
> thoughts. At the very beginning, therefore, one must immediately
> grasp over-all coherence. The only way to do this is by quickly
> reading over the whole text.[57]

Thus Schleiermacher recognized one of the hermeneutical "circles," "that each part can be understood only out of the whole to
which it belongs, and vice versa."[58]

Elsewhere he identifies this "technical" interpretation as the attempt to develop an empathic, "subjective" appreciation for the author: "The goal of technical interpretation should be formulated as the complete understanding of style."[59]

By "style," Schleiermacher means not just the way an author handles language, but also the way of thinking that is bound up with his way of saying. To discover an author's unique style, Schleiermacher commends a two-pronged approach, a "divinatory" and a "comparative" method, which support each other. The divinatory method leads the interpreter "to transform himself, so to speak, into the author . . . to gain an immediate comprehension of the author as an individual."[60] The comparative method, on the other hand, proceeds by comparing an author with similar authors and texts. It "tries to find [an author's] distinctive traits by comparing him with the others of the same general type."[61] The divinatory method tries to gain an intuitive grasp of the author's style or way of thinking and saying as a whole, and the comparative method tries analytically to identify an author's style by setting his work in contrast to the style of other authors.

It was Schleiermacher's hope that, by "combining the objective and subjective . . . the interpreter can put himself 'inside' the author," even to the point of "understanding an author better than he understands himself."[62] The problem is, of course, that "these two sides of interpretation cannot always coincide, for that would presuppose both a complete knowledge of and completely correct use of the language."[63] Therefore, the process of interpretation is an "art" of balancing the two conflicting processes. "Because of this double-character of understanding, interpretation is an art. Neither aspect can be completed by itself.[64] "The 'art' lies in knowing when one side should give way to the other."[65]

In many ways, Schleiermacher anticipated much that would happen in our own time. It is significant that his work on hermeneutics, which only existed in the form of unpublished notes until the 1950s, has now taken on great importance, and is being frequently cited in literature on hermeneutics. But Schleiermacher raised some issues more successfully than he answered them. Particularly, the emphasis on the "technical" or subjective side of exegesis led him to look for an "inner consciousness" within the NT, which Schleiermacher identified as the mind of Jesus being reflected in His disciples.[66] The actual verbal structure of the Gospels and letters of Paul was then subjugated to this overall impression and provided for Schleiermacher and other theologians of the nineteenth century an excuse for deriving one's general knowledge of theology not from the text of Scripture but from reason. Scripture then was read in the light of reason, rather than the theological truths being derived from Scripture.

Schleiermacher has often been called the "father of modern theology." He was not the first, of course, to apply a rational criticism to the Bible, but he was a key early figure in the struggle to integrate a deep personal Christian faith with the "modern" way of thinking. In hermeneutics he began the story of a twofold tension in biblical interpretation which occupies hermeneutical thought up to the present day. Biblical interpretation is now seen as, first, a historical-critical study which attempts to establish a text's boundaries of meaning in its original historical context, and second, a theological-believing study which tries to *understand* the text and integrate it with the overall worldview of the interpreter.[67] He also in particular was a father to the so-called theological liberalism of the nineteenth century, which attempted to derive from a synthesis of historical and sympathetic study an "understanding" of the inner moral life and ideals of Jesus.

Schleiermacher had conceived of the task of the interpreter as establishing a link with the author via the two paths of scientific study of the text and the exercise of human empathy. A more rigorous application of Kant's dialectic of nature and freedom could not allow for this however; the author is actually unknowable. Thus at the end of the nineteenth century Wilhelm Dilthey had shifted the ground away from the author and onto the interpreter. Dilthey spoke of the interpreter as engaged in

a mode of re-experiencing (Nacherleben) which is to be understood as a re-creation (Nach-bildung) of an expressed meaning rather than as a psychologistically conceived re-production (Abbildung). The creative understanding involved in Nacherleben is a function of the historian's imagination.[68]

This set the stage for the present view of hermeneutics as ultimately a matter of *self*-understanding. Whereas Schleiermacher and nineteenth-century theologians tried to synthesize the critical historical investigation and theological thought, twentieth-century theologians increasingly realized their essential incompatibility. And with this we come to the most influential biblical interpreter of the twentieth century, Rudolf Bultmann.

4.5.2 Rudolf Bultmann

German neo-orthodox theologian *Rudolf Bultmann* (1884–1976)[69] was not only extremely vigorous and thorough in his critical analysis of the NT documents, setting the lead for NT historical study up until the present day, he also attempted a massive theological synthesis, a description of Christianity as a whole, which continues to influence theologians.

This influence must be at least partly because of Bultmann's success in developing a way to relate his historical work to his theological enterprise through "de-mythologization," which we will discuss later. But the starting point for Bultmann's work is his acceptance of the dictum of Kant that divides reality into two mutually exclusive kinds. There is a phenomenal world which can be studied scientifically, and a noumenal world of human meaning, but, *contra* Schleiermacher and the nineteenth-century theologians, these two realms cannot be directly synthesized.

In 1896 Martin Kähler had written a book entitled (in English) *The So-Called Historical Jesus and the Historic, Biblical Christ.*[70] Kähler pointed out that the Jesus which liberalism had constructed on the basis of Schleiermacher's program of attempting to recover the "mind" of Jesus through a "modern" reading of the Gospels was really a product of the modern spirit and that the Gospel texts themselves presented Jesus rather as a unique, fully sovereign Lord. Kähler argued that historical-critical methods are simply inappropriate for discovering the actual person of Christ who lives and reigns today just as He did then. The "Jesus" reconstructed by modern historical-critical methods is not the actual historic Christ.

In presenting his argument, Kähler made a distinction between a *critical, scientifically demonstrable* history, which he called *Historie*, and true, real, transcendent history, which he called *Geschichte*. Although Bultmann could not follow the orthodox Kähler in simply rejecting the historical-critical venture, he did pick up on this distinction. On the one hand, there is a "historical Jesus," about which we can know very little, but even if we knew more it would not ultimately be helpful.

All historical phenomena which are subject to this kind of historical investigation are only relative entities, *entities which exist only within an immense inter-related complex*. Nothing which stands within this inter-relationship can claim absolute value. Even the historical Jesus is a phenomenon among other phenomena, not an absolute entity.[71]

Thus, the Jesus who is the object of historical-critical research is only a Jesus "after the flesh," and is irrelevant to faith.

On the other hand is the Jesus Christ who speaks to us in the Bible, calling us to repentance and faith, which are ways of addressing our self-understanding and our awareness of who we are as historic beings (beings in context). So a dichotomy is made between *factual* knowledge and historic *self-understanding*.

In all such factual knowledge or knowledge of principles the world is presumed to have the character of something objective, passive, accessible to simple observation. That is, the world is conceived in conformity with the Greek understanding of being. . . . In such a conception of the world as an objective entity, man himself is regarded as an object (as a fragment of the cosmos); his self-understanding is achieved along with the understanding of the world (and vice versa). . . . [But] the existence of man does not have the character of an objective entity but is *historic* existence; where it is recognized that man in his history can *become a new person and consequently* can also newly understand himself; where, therefore, it is recognized that the being of man is a potentiality to be. That potentiality to be is always at risk; its possibilities are grasped each time by man in resolve, in decision. An understanding of these possibilities of man's existence here and now would obviously be a new understanding each time, since a historical situation with its character of possibility is not understood if it is conceived as a "case" illustrating a general law. The historical situation cannot possibly be "seen" in the Greek sense as an objective fact; it can only be heard as a summons.[72]

Because such a sharp division was made between phenomenal scientific historical study and the faith, Bultmann was free to engage in as consistent and radical historical criticism as he deemed necessary. His starting point was the results of the newly successful "history of religions" school in Germany, of which three are of special importance.

(1) As other ancient religions began to be studied, scholars noticed certain parallels and similarities to Christianity in the religions of Hellenism and the East. Phenomena such as demon possession and "divine men" in the Greco-Roman world were said to be the context for the NT's teaching on demon possession and the Man who was also God. Christianity was not so unique after all, on this approach.

From this, Bultmann developed a way of discerning the genuinely historical material from its later accretions. If something in the Gospels which Jesus says or did is (a) not like what first-century Jews said and did, and (b) not like what later Christians said and did, *and* if such material is probable within the strictures of a scientific worldview, then such a saying *may* be genuinely authentic. This was called the "criterion of dissimilarity."

(2) Researches in the Gospels themselves by Johannes Weiss, William Wrede, and Albert Schweitzer suggested that the Jesus which genuine historical research uncovers was not a nineteenth-century liberal moralist but a charismatic rabbi of first-century Hellenistic Judaism who foresaw the end of the world and regarded Himself as its judge.

(3) Finally, the history of religions school had noted that in primitive societies, the mythology and legends of that society are a dynamic store of lore, which grows and adapts itself to ever changing situations. The oral "literature" is thus constantly relevant.

From this, Bultmann developed what was his most significant contribution to the historical-critical venture. He began to look at the Gospels not for historical material about Jesus (the criterion of dissimilarity effectively eliminated most of it, but for material about how the early church used the traditions about Jesus. To do this meant identifying within the Gospels the pieces of the oral tradition which were elaborated and developed and asking how such elaboration met the needs of the early Christian communities. Although certain other individuals also developed this approach independently at about the same time, Bultmann was the most successful and thorough, and he became the chief proponent and exponent of the so-called "form critical" approach to historical study of the Gospels. No longer did historical research look for the historical Jesus, about whom we have little data; it looked at the way the early church used the stories about Jesus.

Bultmann was not only concerned about historical criticism

however; he regarded himself as a Christian and wanted to be able to talk about faith in God. He achieved this by reference to the existentialism being put forward by Martin Heidegger.[73] This existentialism regarded the meaningfulness of man as focusing on the continuous acts of decision. Man's existence is not so much what man *is*, as what man can be. It is not what man has, but what man does. As Robert C. Roberts put it, "the authentically and specifically human kind of reality . . . has its true being only in 'decisions,' which he also calls 'acts.' A human being has his true reality so exhaustively in his acts that Bultmann can say 'only in act are we ourselves.' "[74]

Bultmann regarded it as the genius of Christianity to recognize that, for a human being to have a meaningful life, he or she cannot look for that life in the world or in security within what can be physically experienced, but must look for it in the will, in self-realizing decisions.

Whereas to ancient man the world had been home—in the Old Testament as God's creation, to classic Greece as the cosmos pervaded by the deity—the utter difference of human existence from all worldly existence was recognized for the first time in Gnosticism and Christianity, and thus the world became foreign soil to the human self.[75]

In the modern understanding of history, *reality* is understood in another way than in that of objectifying sight, namely as the *reality of historically existing man*. The being of man is fundamentally different from the being of nature which can be perceived in objectifying sight. Today we are accustomed to designate the specifically human kind of being as *existence*.[76]

Bultmann found the NT's emphasis on the future especially compatible with existentialism's insistence on the potential, the possibilities of the future. For him, NT eschatology becomes no longer the end of the physical world, but the end of the existential world—the end of *my* world. Therefore the "end" of the visible quantifiable world is a deliverance from sin.

The world indeed is simply the sphere which men have made into a power over themselves by whatever they have done in the past. To live on the basis of the world, that is, of the past, is what is called sin. To live on the basis of the future is called living in dependence on God.[77]

Therein is the basis for the Christian hope. By deciding to grasp firmly the future as possibility, rather than take security in the past, man finds true freedom. Life determined by the world is bondage to the flesh; true freedom comes "when he can free himself from the world and soar up to the eternal as his home."[78]

Thus the Christian cannot delight in what has happened or what he or she has accomplished in the past. Not even the knowledge of "existential truth" is a "possession." One cannot "carry its truth with him as a possession. Such a mistaken opinion would turn Christian truth precisely into a general truth . . . the truth has to be laid hold of ever anew. . . ."[79]

Bultmann therefore believed that a "worldview" is counter to existence, since it seeks to grasp everything under controllable categories. "It is the effort to find security in generalizations, whereas insecurity is what characterizes the real nature of human existence."[80]

Here is perhaps the heart of existentialism. All effort to seek the meaning of one's life in this world, whether by money, or relationships, or accomplishments, or tradition, or anything else that one can *have*, is inauthentic existence, and doomed to death. Only when one looks to one's future possibility, to what one can be, and continually decides to act on the basis of that future possibility, does one live authentically. This, says Bultmann, is love. Love seeks nothing for itself, but always denies one's self, not seeking one's own security, but in faith choosing insecurity, the insecurity of faith in what is not phenomenally experienced.

Of course, there are many items in the NT which do not conform to Bultmann's ideas of true Christian existence. In particular, the NT writers put a decisive emphasis on the past historical event of Christ's physical resurrection as the keystone in their preaching. While Bultmann acknowledges a *spiritual* resurrection as the escape from worldly thinking, such emphasis on a worldly resurrection goes counter to what Bultmann regards as the Gospel. Furthermore, the biblical writers held to a view of the physical world which, according to Bultmann, modern man can no longer hold. Even though the NT writers recognized a category of existence, they still retained a primitive cosmology and expressed much of their existential truth in mythological terms. "Sometimes we are told that human life is determined by cosmic forces, at others we are challenged to a decision."[81] Thus, according to

Bultmann, the form of the NT teaching (its christology) is bound up with the worldview of its authors, which is highly primitive and mythological. Bultmann describes the NT cosmology in this way.

> The cosmology of the New Testament is essentially mythical in character. The world is viewed as a three-storied structure, with the earth in the centre, the heaven above, and the underworld beneath. Heaven is the abode of God and of celestial beings—the angels. The underworld is hell, the place of torment. Even the earth . . . is the scene of the super-natural activity of God and his angels on the one hand, and of Satan and his daemons on the other. These supernatural forces intervene in the course of nature and in all that men think and will and do. Miracles are by no means rare. Man is not in control of his own life. Evil spirits may take possession of him. Satan may inspire him with evil thoughts.
>
> Alternatively, God may inspire his thought, and guide his purposes. He may grant him heavenly visions. He may allow him to hear his word of succour or demand. He may give him the supernatural power of his Spirit. History . . . is set in motion and controlled by these supernatural powers. This aeon is held in bondage by Satan, sin, and death . . . and hastens toward the end. That end will come very soon, and will take the form of a cosmic catastrophe. . . . The judge will come from heaven, the dead will rise, the last judgement will take place, and men will enter into eternal salvation or damnation.[82]

Bultmann insists that this "myth" is entirely incompatible with the modern man and that there can be no picking and choosing: "The mythical view of the world must be accepted or rejected in its entirety," and to accept the mythical view is a sacrifice of the intellect.[83]

Now "meaning," as Dilthey pointed out, is a function of the interpreter and so is determined by the *interpreter's* understanding of life.

> Every interpretation incorporates a particular prior understanding, namely, that which arises out of the context of living experience to which the subject belongs.[84]

So what is needed according to Bultmann is an interpretation of the Bible that expresses its (existential) truth in terms which modern people can accept. Thus, for Bultmann, "hermeneutics" is not just explaining the original meaning of a passage and showing how it applies to life generally, it is the interpretation of the event of Jesus Himself *into* the existential framework of the contemporary believer.

Bultmann's primary means of accomplishing this was his program of "demythologization." This meant primarily not so much simply removing the "mythology" of the NT as restating the existential truth contained within the myth in a modern way. The German word *Entmythologisierung* implies *replacing* the myth, not simply removing it. Even modern man operates with a certain "myth," a cosmology and philosophy that is not yet "at the bottom of things." But our understanding right now is determined by our "context of living experience," and the Gospel must be expressed in those terms.

Such effort to replace the "primitive cosmology" of the Bible is in Bultmann's thought entirely compatible with, even demanded by, the Gospel.

> Demythologizing is the radical application of the doctrine of justification by faith to the sphere of knowledge and thought. Like the doctrine of justification, de-mythologizing destroys every longing for security. There is no difference between security based on good works and security built on objectifying knowledge. The man who desires to believe in God must know that he has nothing at his disposal on which to build his faith, that he is, so to speak, in a vacuum."[85]

> The restatement of mythology is a requirement of faith itself. For faith needs to be emancipated from its association with every worldview expressed in objective terms, whether it be a mythical or a scientific one . . . it has tried to project God and his acts into the sphere of objective reality.[86]

Perhaps we can see why in Bultmann's eyes the idea of a literal physical resurrection is not only ridiculous from a scientific point of view, but undesirable from an existential point of view. A literal physical resurrection would be a datum of security in the world and would take away man's freedom. Likewise, "the incarnation should not be conceived of as a miracle that happened about 1,950 years ago, but as an eschatological happening which, beginning with Jesus, is always present in the words of men proclaiming it to be a human experience."[87]

In ethics, the idea of God's Law is anathema to Bultmann, who believes he is following Paul here. To adhere to an ethical standard is inauthentic existence: "he cannot in a moment of decision fall back upon principles, upon a general ethical theory which can relieve him of responsibility for the decision; rather, every moment of decision is essentially new. . . ."[88]

Even God Himself must not be thought of as an "object" for discussion, and hence language "about" God is not authentic faith. "If 'speaking of God' is understood as 'speaking *about* God', then such speaking has no meaning whatever, for its subject, God, is lost in the very moment it takes place."[89] In other words, when we try to speak about God, we "objectify" God, which makes Him no longer God.

Many writers from many sides have responded to Bultmann.[90] Perhaps the most important critique is that, although Bultmann decries "worldview" as something which limits possibilities and is incompatible with faith, it is precisely his post-Kantian worldview which has prohibited him from accepting what the NT actually *says*. Bultmann, along with his contemporaries, derided the early church's allegorical interpretation of Jesus' teaching, but Bultmann's program of demythologizing or "re-mythologizing" has imposed an alien framework for understanding just as much as did Origen or Augustine, in fact more so, because Origen and Augustine still believed in the literal historical truth of the Gospel stories.

It is also curious that, for all Bultmann's consistency in applying a "strict" historical method, he is still left with historical imponderables. By means of radical skepticism and form criticism (including the criterion of dissimilarity), Bultmann succeeds in denying historicity to any statement in the Gospels which would, if historical, indicate that Jesus claimed to be the Christ. But then, he is left with an enigma—how the disciples ever came to think that He was, so as to invent the stories. He even acknowledges this as "the great enigma of New Testament theology."[91]

Further, although the NT writers depicted their hope and their doctrine in the *language* of a prescientific worldview, it is not at all clear that the *substance* of their worldview or expectations or thinking was so limited that we cannot accept them today. For example, the resurrection in 1 Corinthians 15 appears to be expressed in terms of a new and different world order; no mention is made of going up or down. And even in 1 Thessalonians where resurrected believers "meet Jesus in the air," how is this made impossible by thinking of heaven as not in outer space (on the other side of the sky) or some other physical location, for he says in Ephesians 2:6 that believers now sit with Christ "in the heavenly places" (RSV).

No, the real incompatibility of the biblical cosmology and modern humanity in Bultmann's eyes is not because of an inherent incompatibility, but because of Bultmann's presupposition that the spiritual and physical "worlds" have nothing to do with each other. And this presupposition is not demanded by the successes of modern science, but by the necessity of the Kantian dialectic, which itself devolved from a commitment to human autonomy. It all comes back to man's "decision" to regard his own thought as the authority in life, rather than what God says. By firmly committing himself to a presuppositional framework of understanding apart from the Bible, and then disallowing any incompatibility with the Bible to reorient his framework, he was unable to proceed toward true understanding of the text. Bultmann more than any other demonstrates by way of counterexample the need for the Christian interpreter of the Bible to allow his or her presuppositional framework of understanding to be molded and corrected by the Bible itself.

4.6 Summary

Our historical survey has shown how the question of the relationship between a historical, human meaning of the Bible and the transhistorical divine meaning has run throughout the history of the church. It is our misfortune that so often the divine and human meanings have been seen to be in tension. It is our contention that, rather than being in tension, a genuinely submissive approach to the Bible as God's Word and a sincere inquiry into the historical meaning are mutually enhancing and that the human meaning is the key to God's meaning. Rather than allegorize like Origen or demythologize like Bultmann, if we truly understand the historical meaning it will direct us to the relevant message for today. So the next two chapters in this part will examine the means to ascertaining what the human meaning was (grammatical-historical exegesis), and how we can see the greater relevance of God's meaning in the larger context of the whole Bible and the whole of life.

FIVE

GRAMMATICAL-HISTORICAL METHOD: KNOWING WHAT IT MEANT

When we read an ordinary text we unconsciously use a variety of methods to discern meaning, and with works of our own age and culture this ordinarily presents no problems at all. These unconscious methods are a floating repertoire of facilitating devices which are applied unreflectively in the process of perceiving meaning. We simply supply the meaning that makes sense in the social and textual context. Ordinarily, only if we get stuck do we then proceed through a more methodical application of techniques. If we get badly "stuck," we are likely to cast further and further afield of our usual stock of techniques until we hit upon something that enables the text to make sense to us.

With a text as culturally remote from us as the Bible, parts of it are bound to fall into this category of demanding some techniques that are on the fringes of our interpretive repertoire, and even when our ordinary methods seem to work, they may appear to work imperfectly. The problem is that when we start going to the fringes of our usual stock of methods, and when a text is uniquely tied to its original culture, our interpretations become less secure. So it is appropriate to specify what methods are likely to yield results in line with the biblical writers' intent.

We are, of course, assuming that before we can ask, "What is God teaching me now through this passage?" we must first ask, "What did God teach the original hearers through this text?" If God speaks to us in Scripture, He certainly spoke as well to the original readers in a way that they could understand. Grammatical-historical exegesis attempts to uncover the meaning a text would have had to its original human author and readers. This involves asking: what was the cultural, social, geographical, linguistic, and historical background to the original situation; what is the usual significance of the words, phrases, and idioms used; what special circumstances or problems were the author or his original hearers facing; how does the passage fit in with what that particular human author says elsewhere; what type or genre of speech/writing is this; what was the purpose of the book as a whole; how does the passage function literarily in the larger text; and where do the original hearers stand in redemptive history. We have reduced all these to four basic classes of problems to be faced in exegesis:

(1) the problems of *semantics*;
(2) the problems of *cultural distance*;
(3) the problems of *context*;
(4) the problems of *genre*.[1]

5.1 Meaning and Understanding: Semantics

The problem of semantics, or the meaning of words and sentences, is of particular concern to translators and other professionals who use the biblical languages. Even for those without knowledge of these languages however, matters of how language works and the meaning of words and sentences are important.

In chapters 1 and 2 we argued vigorously that God is the ultimate author of Scripture and pointed out some of the implications of that fact. But here we are focusing on the fact that human beings wrote the Scriptures and did so in ordinary human language, using language in ordinary ways. Their subject matter was indeed extraordinary, but their tool of telling, if it was going to tell truly, had to function in the ordinary ways so that ordinary people would be able to understand it.

Of course, the study of how language works (linguistics) is a science in itself, with many philosophical and technical problems and controversies. This is not the place to delve into this subject very far, but in this section we are going to focus on six issues which pertain to language use, and are especially important in biblical interpretation. They are: (1) the priority of synchrony over diachrony; (2) the meaning of words as opposed to the meaning of sentences; (3) the distinction between sense and reference; (4) the fixity and flexibility of language (its precision and its ambiguity); (5) the differentiation of literal and non-literal (above all, metaphor); and (6) the problem of transcendent thought and concrete language.

5.1.1 Synchrony versus diachrony

The "father of modern linguistics" Ferdinand deSaussure made a distinction between the diachronic *development* of a language, and the synchronic *use* of a language.[2] Modern linguistics has fairly universally accepted the dictum that any speaker or author's *meaning* is governed strictly by the state of the language at the time of speaking or writing (synchrony). The process by which the language came into that state (diachrony) may be interesting, and may inform the synchronic analysis, but users of a language are usually not conscious of where or how words or phrases took on the meaning they presently have. Hence, with respect to lexical analysis (the meaning of the words used) and grammatical analysis (the syntax used), the only thing that matters is the contemporary usage, or the synchronic.

Saussure illustrates this by reference to a chess game.[3] After several moves a particular position is reached. Now in considering a best or even appropriate move, it does not matter how the board acquired its present state; the only thing that matters is the position and interrelationship of the pieces as they now stand. Language works the same way. When evaluating the meaning of an utterance, only the state of the language at the time of utterance is the linguistic framework for the meaning of that utterance.

But the emphasis on synchrony can be pressed too far. People do not often use language to talk about language itself, but they do speak about words spoken in the past. Biblical authors in particular are extremely concerned with God's utterances of the past as well as His past deeds, sometimes citing directly, more often alluding directly or indirectly to previous Scripture. And even when not clearly alluding to previous Scripture, virtually the entire NT appears self-conscious of being the fulfillment of God's previous words in the OT. So in terms of *content*, diachrony is inescapable, because it informs the synchrony.

Such diachrony occasionally affects the use of words as well as the content or meaning of sentences. For example, the word translated in the NT as "covenant" or "testament," which in ordinary synchronic Hellenistic Greek meant "will" (as in "last will and testament"), was used in the Greek OT to translate the word *berith*, which in English we translate with "covenant." Consequently, in the NT the word "covenant" can only be understood by reference to the history of its use in the Greek OT. (Note how the author of Hebrews plays on the two meanings of the word "will" and "covenant" in Heb. 9:15-22.) Where the biblical authors are clearly conscious of the term in history, diachronic analysis must be used in addition to synchronic study. In other words, when a biblical writer picks up on a certain word which previously written Scripture has given a specialized meaning, we must go back to the earlier uses of the word to see what content that word had for the later writer.[4]

A special application of diachrony is etymology, the study of the origins and derivations of words. Etymology is sometimes useful in helping to establish the meaning of rare words.[5] But etymological analysis is extremely dangerous when used to read more meaning into those words which are already known. Users of a language are hardly ever conscious of the etymological origins of the words when they are using them, and hence etymology has very little role in establishing meaning.[6] Few English speakers, when they use the word "nice," are thinking about the derivation of the word from the Latin *nescius*, which means "ignorant."

5.1.2 Word and sentence

When we speak of the meaning of a word, this is a different question from the meaning of a sentence. A sentence actually says something. It is, to be sure, understood according to its context, but it nevertheless does say something. A word, unless it constitutes a sentence by itself, does not say something; it is only a block used to build a sentence which says something. A word only marks off a potential field of concepts which are made specific by the sentences in which they occur.

This may seem obvious, but is worth stating because a great deal of biblical interpretation has tried to find *meaning* in the use of particular words, and these words are supposed to suggest theological truth *by themselves*. Much of the scholarly world was led astray in this direction during the first part of the twentieth century, finding theological "truth" in the fact that, for example, the Hebrew word *dabar* could mean either "thing," "event," or "word," which was taken as an indication that the OT writers viewed words and deeds as the same thing. This has now been given an undignified burial,[7] but it still crops up in popular works, where excessive information is sometimes found in a particular word. Some more attention will be given this matter in section 7.2.2, but it must be stressed that *the basic unit of meaning is not the word but the sentence*. Thus, though God has indeed sovereignly ordered the very words of Scripture, He has ordered the words in their particular combinations in sentences, not in isolation.

Unfortunately, sometimes our favorite passages are favorites because of some particular word, rather than what the sentence says. Of course, words as well as any details are important, but they only mean something in relation to other words in a sentence. For example, much interesting but dubious material has been extracted from the fact that Paul tells Timothy he should be "rightly dividing the word of truth" (KJV). It has been suggested that teachers should teach by dividing up everything in Scripture into certain slots or categories. Or, since the word was used in agriculture for "straight plowing," one should plow through the Bible from beginning to end rather than study themes. But in fact 2 Timothy 2:15 does not say anything like this. We would urge readers to examine some of their own favorite passages, and make sure they are gaining benefit from what the sentences say, rather than what particular word or words may be used.

5.1.3 Sense and reference

Another distinction commonly made in language study is that between the *sense* or general functional meaning of a word, phrase, sentence, etc., within the language as a whole, and its *reference*, the extra-linguistic reality to which it refers in a particular context.[8] "The 'what' of discourse is its 'sense,' the 'about what' is its 'reference.' "[9] For example, the Pharisees in Matthew 21:45 perceived that the Parable of the Tenants was "about them"; they recognized that they themselves were the *reference* of the parable, although the term Pharisees is not the *sense* of any of the words in the parable. But this is tricky because the sense of the parable as a whole is also not really vineyards and tenants; the sense of the parable is that irresponsible behavior on the part of the caretakers of God's people results in their dismissal and punishment.

The distinction is not always easy, because the sense and reference are often bound up with each other, and very often the sense cannot be known apart from the reference. Sometimes the sense and reference are so closely linked that we can speak almost of a direct relation between the word symbol and the thing referred to.

The famous triangle of Ogden and Richards may be helpful here.[10] The *word* is a symbol, which in a particular context generates a mental linguistic response, the *sense*, which in turn is connected by context to a *referent*, the extra-linguistic thing referred to.[11]

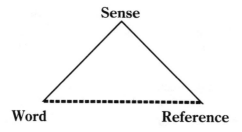

Sense

Word   **Reference**

The certain connection of the word to the referent is always by way of the sense, but the degree of connection between word and referent may vary greatly. Proper names (Julius Caesar, Republic of Ireland, World War II), and under certain circumstances scientific or technical terms (sodium, hemoglobin, justification by faith),[12] have a fairly high degree of correspondence between word and referent, and we call these words or phrases *denotative*.

Not all words, in fact probably a minority of words, are so denotative. (What does the word "beautiful" denote?) Words can refer to a variety of referents, and referents can be referred to by a variety of words. Hence the "meaning" of a word is not its reference but a range of possibilities of mental responses.

But if most words do not derive their possibilities of meaning from connection to a referent, where do they get their meaning from?

There are two approaches to this question. One approach is *concept*-oriented. Each word has a bundle of associated essential characteristics and stereotypical features. The second approach is *field*-oriented. Words get their meaning from the complex of semantic relations within the language.[13] As Cotterell and Turner point out, the main problem with the first is the difficulty "of deciding which components of the variety of discourse concepts are properly part of the lexical concept or sense of an expression."[14] The main problem with the second is that it suggests we cannot know the meaning of a word without knowing the other words in the field and their inter-field relations. Like Cotterell and Turner, we think *both* operate together.

As already noted, Saussure likened words to the pieces in a chess game.[15] Each word has a set of dynamic relations with other words "on the board," and if any word shifts places, many other words are affected in their relationships. In the words of Jost Trier:

> The value of a word is first known when we mark it off against the value of neighboring and opposing words. Only as part of the whole does the word have sense; for only in the field is there meaning.[16]

On the other hand, each chess piece also has certain inherent characteristics different from other pieces. Both the knight in itself and its position on the board in relation to the other pieces determine the meaning of the knight in the game. The "inherencies" of a word make it a candidate for usage; the relations of the word to other words in the user's vocabulary lead to its selection.

These relations can be described in terms of their variation, contrast, and specificity.

Variation involves the choice of words where meanings overlap. Words that are considered synonyms have a shared range where either word will do. "She is a strong athlete" and "She is a powerful athlete" mean the same thing. These words are not totally interchangeable in every context, however. "A powerful man is in the office" probably means someone who is politically or fiscally influential, but "A strong man is in the office" implies someone who is physically strong, or perhaps a decisive leader. Further, there are certain other words where either one or the other is inappropriate. We do not usually speak about "powerful tea" or "strong cars," but "strong tea" and "powerful cars."[17]

Contrast involves the choice of words in order to distinguish from other words. Contrast is of two types. Some words contrast by opposition (dark and light, up and down); many more words contrast by contiguity. Walk is not the opposite of run, but they are marked off from one another in sharp distinction. The sign which tells us what to do in case of fire says: Walk, Do Not Run, To The Nearest Exit."

Specificity involves the choice of words according to the degree of particularity desired. Most nouns and many verbs can be placed in hierarchical relationship. "Mystery writer" is subordinate to "novelist" which is subordinate to "author" which is subordinate to "human being." Any of these can fill in the blank in "What _____ wrote *Shroud for a Nightingale?*" The *reference* in all these sentences would be the same (the answer to the question would be "P.D. James" in all cases), but the *sense* has varying degrees of specificity.

Failure to recognize the distinction between sense and reference can lead to problems in interpretation. A word can have different references in different contexts and yet still be instances of a particular sense. G.B. Caird gives the example that in Colossians, "mystery" refers to the secret of God's incorporating people into Christ; in Ephesians it refers to God's breaking down the barrier between Jew and Gentile. But these are not different senses to the word "mystery." In both cases the sense is "God's secret which is now revealed." Only the referent is different.[18]

Similarly, the word "head" is used in Colossians 2:19 in a way that suggests that Christ as head is "source" of life from God. The *reference* or usage of "head" in this context is "source." But although "head" can occasionally *refer* to something as source, it does not bear the *sense* of "source."[19] The idea of "source" could only come from a context. Thus if one wishes to argue that in 1 Corinthians 11:3 when Paul says a husband is the "head" of the woman he means he is the "source" of the woman, rather than a divinely appointed authority over her, it is better to point to things in the context such as verses 8 and 12 rather than the meaning of the word "head." Of course, "head" does not bear the *sense* of "an authority" either. Whether "head" in 1 Corinthians 11 means "source" or "authority over" must be decided on the basis of the context in 1 Corinthians, not any supposed sense of "head" as "source."

The distinction of sense and reference comes into play with regard to sentences as well as words. For example, "Give me liberty or give me death!" originally had *reference* to Patrick Henry's preference of war, with its prospect of death, to continued subjection to the rule of George III. Its *sense*, however, is that political liberty is worth risking death to achieve. This sense can be and has been applied in innumerable other contexts where political liberty was threatened. It can have application to more than its original referent. But we would not know the sense of this sentence unless we also knew the reference. The phrase might have been uttered by a prisoner trying to commit suicide, in which case it would have nothing to do with political liberty and taking risks to achieve it. The meaning would be different.

As a biblical example, the *reference* of Jesus' statement, "I stand at the door and knock," in Revelation 3:20 is His appeal to the believers of Laodicea to repent of their pride and return to their true source of life. Its *sense* is thus a reminder to Christians of

Christ's readiness to commune with His people, and their need to receive strength from Him. It was not said in a context of inviting people to become believers, and thus it is not a general invitation to non-Christians to open their hearts to the Lord.

5.1.4 Literal and non-literal

One of us heard an address a few years ago entitled "Why I Believe the Bible Is Literally True." What the speaker meant was that he believed the Bible is *really* true. He certainly demonstrated a mastery of metaphor himself and recognized that the Bible uses metaphors and other non-literal language. Similarly, someone once wrote in an examination paper, "Our rector is literally the father of every boy and girl in the village."[20] Let us hope this person meant that the rector had a fatherlike relationship to all the village's children.

Language is considered literal when the referent in view is an instance of the ordinary meaning of the words and sentences used. That is, the usual or common meaning or *sense* directly points to the intended *referent*. A non-literal reference occurs when the connection of the referent to the *sense* of a word or sentence is *solely by context* rather than inherent within the word or sentence by itself. "Literalness" does not indicate the truth or falsity, nor the precision, of the statement. A literal statement can be false, or even fantastic ("there is a ghost in my closet"); and a non-literal statement can be true ("there is a skeleton in my closet"). Further, "literal" does not mean "expressed with scientific or mathematical precision." If the almanac reports that "The sun rises tomorrow at 6:08 A.M.," the statement is not scientifically precise (the sun does not "rise" from the astronomical point of view), but is nevertheless literal *within the understood context*.

In Scripture, the distinction between literal and non-literal is perhaps the most important, though sometimes the most difficult to make. It is here that much controversy in the church has been centered. Arguments arise over whether something is literal or non-literal (e.g., the "thousand years" of Revelation 20). Or, if a word or sentence is regarded as non-literal, what kind of non-literal symbol it is, and what the symbol stands for. Symbols are highly adaptable things. And the more symbolic a text is, the more it can yield to various interpretations.

Often literal is contrasted with metaphorical, but there are some other types of non-literal language we should mention before we discuss metaphor. These include hyperbole, sarcasm, synecdoche, metonymy, and merism.

5.1.4.1 Various non-literal types

Hyperbole, or exaggeration for effect, is common enough in the Bible, especially in poetry. For example, when David says of Saul and Jonathan in 2 Samuel 1:23 that they were swifter than eagles and stronger than lions, he is certainly not speaking literally. When Ezekiel prophesies concerning Pharaoh of Egypt that God will "strew your flesh upon the mountains and fill the valleys with your carcass" (Ezek. 32:5), he is speaking hyperbolically. When Jesus told His disciples that a person must "hate" his father and mother (Luke 14:26), He speaks in hyperbolic contrast (Matthew interprets for us: Matt. 10:37). But one needs to be a little careful with identifying hyperbole, lest one soften up the radical demands and promises of the Bible. Sometimes the Bible may sound hyperbolic when actually it is simply radical and comprehensive. When Jesus says that our righteousness must surpass that of the scribes and Pharisees, this is not hyperbole.

Sarcasm appears to be a feature of speech all over the world. In 2 Samuel 6:20, Michal exclaims to David, "How the king of Israel honored himself today" (RSV). The context indicates that Michal was not complimenting him. Paul appears to be sarcastically repeating accusations made against him in 2 Corinthians 10:1, "I who am humble when face to face with you, but bold to you when I am away" (RSV).

Synecdoche is where a part of some entity is named in place of the whole entity, or the other way around. Frequently "Ephraim," which is one half-tribe of the Northern Kingdom, can mean the whole Northern Kingdom (Jer. 31:18, 20); on the other hand "Israel," which properly includes all twelve tribes, can mean just the Northern Kingdom in opposition to Judah. Thus, when the Gospel of John uses "the Jews" to mean "those who opposed Jesus," this is not anti-Semitism on the part of John, but simply an application of synecdoche. Certainly the Gospel writer knew that Jesus and His disciples were also Jews.

A special kind of synecdoche characteristic of the ancient Near East is merism or merismus. Merism is a way of referring to the totality of a subject matter by mentioning the pair of opposites which describe the poles of that subject. "From Dan to Beersheba" was a way of referring to all Israel, and "heaven and earth" is a way of referring to the whole created order.[21]

One particularly interesting merism in the Bible is the tree of the knowledge of good and evil. Good and evil are opposites covering the sphere of ethics or morals. The "knowledge of good and evil" is thus a way of referring to the totality of ethical knowledge, including the experience of both right and wrong and the ability to decide for oneself what is right and wrong.[22] So the tree in the Garden was not a means whereby Adam and Eve became ethical creatures, for how should they have been expected to know that it was evil to disobey God? The tree represented the experiential knowledge of evil as well as good and the "knowledge" of making moral judgments apart from God's word. To eat of the tree of total moral knowledge was to claim the ability to determine on one's own what is right and wrong.

Metonymy is where something in close and definite association with something else is named in place of its associated thing. For example, "the crown" can represent the king or queen, who in turn represents the government as a whole. This is common in poetry, but frequently occurs elsewhere (see Gal. 2:7-9 [KJV and Gk.] where "circumcision" means Jews, or James 3:5ff, where the tongue represents speech).

A special form of metonymy is a circumlocution or euphemism, which is a word or phrase used to avoid direct mention of something. It is frequently used in the NT to avoid direct mention of God (e.g., the "majesty on high" (Heb. 1:3); or the "kingdom of Heaven" throughout Matthew). But it also can be used to avoid direct mention of other subjects deemed delicate. The curious OT phrase, "uncover the nakedness of" is an easily recognized metonymic euphemism for sexual intercourse.

5.1.4.2 Metaphor

The most important and common form of non-literal speech is the metaphor. The *Oxford English Dictionary* defines metaphor as: "the figure of speech in which a name or descriptive term is transferred to some object different from, but analogous to, that to which it is properly applicable." But metaphors often go beyond "objects," and can extend to actions, ideas, sentences, paragraphs, and even whole books. Further, a metaphor does not live in a single word; it is a function of a sentence and a context. Thus we prefer the view that "when we use a metaphor we have two thoughts of different things active together and supported by a single word, or phrase, whose meaning is a resultant of their interaction."[23]

This takes place to a lesser extent with metaphor's cousin "simile," even if the difference between them is simply the presence of the word "like." Some would say that "Jesus is like a good shepherd" is simile, and is basically literal, whereas "Jesus is a good shepherd" is metaphor. But the simple presence of the word "like" is not terribly important, and we prefer to think of metaphor as the juxtaposition of unrelated things in a surprising manner, whether or not the word "like" is used. It is this element of surprise that marks out a metaphor. Simile compares similar things ("mules are like donkeys," or "prawns are like tiny lobsters without claws"); metaphor compares things which at first sight are dissimilar ("men are donkeys" or "prawns are heaven on a platter"). Somehow the latter seem to "mean" more than the former, because they surprise more and highlight the less obvious characteristics. Of course there are varying degrees of surprise, and hence the line between simile and metaphor is not a sharp one. In any case a metaphor is not merely an ornament; it has a communicative power that transcends literal language.[24]

Metaphors are the lifeblood of poetry and thus are exceedingly common in the poetic sections of the Bible. Just open to any psalm, and the reader is likely to find scores of metaphors within that one psalm. Perhaps metaphor is even more common in the OT prophets, which are often poetic. But metaphor is not by any means confined to poetry. Jesus spoke in parables, which are special types of metaphors; He made statements like "I am the good shepherd and I am the vine." Even the most ordinary literal types of passages can still use metaphors.[25] It therefore is important to recognize how metaphor functions. We here mention five principles regarding metaphor.

5.1.4.2.1 Metaphor involves principal and subsidiary subjects

The first principle of metaphor is that, when a metaphor is used, there is a principal subject, which usually is literal, and a subsidiary subject. The commonplace "associated implications" of the primary and subsidiary subjects interact to expand understanding about the primary subject.[26] A metaphor is thus a "lens" (if we may use a metaphor). Ordinarily one does not notice the lens one is using; the interest is in what is being observed through the lens and the resultant expansion of information about it. So when Jesus says, "I am the vine; you are the branches" (John 15:5), the disciples would not be thinking about how this sheds light on grape plants, but on the nature of their relationship to Jesus.

However, there is no formula for indicating what is principal and what is subsidiary. Paul says that Christ's body is the church (1 Cor. 12:27, where "body" is subsidiary and metaphoric); he also says that the believer's body is a temple of the Holy Spirit (1 Cor. 6:19, where "body" is principal and literal). If we made reference to a "winged criminal," we could be referring either to a literal criminal who is adept at escaping, or to a crow who keeps plundering a vegetable garden. Identification of the principal subject is often not available within the metaphorical sentence itself, but is primarily accomplished by knowing what subject has been under discussion in the immediate context.

In some cases the principal subject lies in neither of the two juxtaposed areas of thought, but in the metaphorical activity set up by their juxtaposition. When Paul in Romans 3:13 cites Psalm 5:9 ("their throats are an open grave"), the principal subject is neither throats nor graves. The "open graves" and the "throats" interact to give an image of death which swallows up, and this image in turn applies to the evil and deadliness of people. Similarly, although we recognize disagreement among Christians on this matter, we would argue that when Christ says, "This [bread] is my body" (1 Cor. 11:24), the subject is not bread (although that is involved), nor is it really His physical body (although that too is involved); it is the presence of Jesus with His disciples based on His death which that Last Supper, and later the church's Communion service, represents and embodies.

5.1.4.2.2. Metaphor is more than comparison

Secondly, metaphors are more than just comparisons, because the power of a metaphor goes beyond obvious similarities, and in fact sometimes plays on dissimilarities. According to Isaiah 24:7, "the wine mourns and the vine languishes" (RSV). It is the dissimilarity between wine, which is associated with rejoicing, and mourning, which impacts the reader with the severity of God's judgment.

To understand the way in which a metaphor is being used involves identifying the implied associations of the two subjects which are interacting. There is no way to predict what these associations might be, or what particular characteristics of the subjects may interact in a given metaphor, but one can list certain types of interaction. G.B. Caird[27] lists four types of metaphor: *perceptual*, where there is a similarity in the perception by one or more of the five senses; *synaesthetic*, which involve a transfer from one sense to another, as when words are as "smooth as butter and slippery as oil" (cf. Ps. 55:21); *affective*, which involves feelings, as when the hearts of Joshua's troops turned to water (Josh. 7:5); and *pragmatic*, where the activity or result is similar, as when the kingdom of heaven is like yeast or a mustard seed (Matt. 13). Sometimes a metaphor may play on more than one of these, but noting the points of the interaction is what enables one to gain information about the primary subject.

5.1.4.2.3. Metaphor can have multiple levels

In Matthew 6:22 Jesus tells His disciples that "the eye is the lamp of the body." Now at first this looks like a simple pragmatic metaphor; just as a lamp enables one to see, so does the eye. But the interaction of these subjects excites a number of thoughts; about the self as a body or the relation of vision to light. As one goes on to read the whole paragraph, one discovers that the real subject is neither eyes nor lamps nor bodies. It is about what is most basic to a person's life and understanding.

Thus, to understand the metaphor one must first identify from the context the chief subject under discussion and then determine how the interaction of the two domains of thought sheds light on that subject. For the biblical student, it means first of all determining the field of associations and implications which each of the subjects in the metaphor would have had at the time of its writing and then identifying how their interrelationship fits in with the context.

5.1.4.2.4. Metaphor is fluid

It is important to realize that metaphors are fluid. That most "fluid" of metaphors, water, can mean life (Isa. 55:1), cleansing (Matt. 27:24), trouble (Ps. 46:3), judgment (1 Peter 3:20), fear (Josh. 7:5), and so on. This is important: the fact that a metaphor has a certain value in one place is no indication of the value which the same juxtaposition of words or ideas will have in another. For example, 1 Peter 2:2 tells us we should be like babies desiring milk; Hebrews 5:12-14 tells us we should stop being like babies desiring milk. These are not contradictory; the former focuses on the baby's intensity of desire; the latter on the baby's immaturity. Another example: the term "leaven" can be a metaphor for evil, as in "beware the leaven of the Pharisees" (Mark 8:15, RSV), where the point is that even a little evil will spread throughout something. But Jesus also says "the kingdom of heaven is like leaven" (Matt. 13:33, RSV), not because it has evil in it, but because it starts out small and spreads throughout something. Birds in the Parable of the Sower are a negative metaphor associated with Satan's activity; in the Parable of the Mustard Bush they are positive, associated with the growth of the kingdom of God.[28]

This flexibility of the symbolic value of metaphors implies that their interpretation must be made very carefully and rooted in things in the context but outside the metaphor. This is especially true of prophecy. During World War II, many Christians found Hitler, and various details about him, in the pages of the Book of Revelation. The symbols themselves could be made to fit, but neither the context of Revelation itself, nor the socio-historical context of the book, give any indication of the connection between the symbols of Revelation and Hitler.

5.1.4.2.5 Metaphor is descriptive

Metaphors carry descriptive and elucidating power, but not predictive power. In other words, a metaphor cannot be used to prove characteristics. Doors can keep people out, but when Jesus says "I am the door" (John 10:9), it does not mean He keeps people out. And when Paul says that the church is Christ's body (1 Cor. 12:27), that Christ is the head of the body (Col. 1:18), and also that no part of the body can say "I don't need you" (1 Cor. 12:21), we cannot infer from this that Paul taught that Christ cannot get on without the church. Certainly it would be wrong to suggest that since the church is a body it must sleep.

5.1.4.3 Special non-literal language in the Bible

There are certain kinds of metaphor or non-literal language in the Bible which deserve special mention, either because they are so frequent, or because the nature of the metaphors is not easily apprehended by modern people.

(a) The first we shall call *covenantal realism.* When Jesus held the Last Supper, He indicated to His disciples, "This cup is the new covenant in my blood" (Luke 22:20). The Supper, then as now, involved a participation by faith in the death and resurrection of Christ. Jesus was referring to the prophecy of Jeremiah 31:31-33 which spoke of God's "new covenant." A covenant, as we indicated earlier, is a formalized statement of relationship, and biblical covenants are instituted by God through individuals who represent larger groups. Our representative in the new covenant is Jesus. But this relationship between us and our covenant representative is much deeper than simply representation. Paul says we are "in Christ," and thus have "died with Christ" and are "raised with Christ." These are not mere metaphors to describe our repentance or the experience of forgiveness; they reflect a reality in God Himself. God has reckoned us as covenantally linked to Christ, so that what happened to Him happened to us. In our individualistic Western society this is sometimes hard to grasp.

(b) *Anthropomorphisms* are metaphors whereby something that God is or does is represented in language appropriate to describing what a human is or does. For example, God "repents" of having made humanity, or of the evil He was going to do Nineveh, even though God is not a man, that He should repent" (1 Sam. 15:29, KJV). The "arm" of the Lord, the "nostrils" of the Lord, are anthropomorphic metaphors. They no more indicate that the biblical writers thought that God had a body than we think a ship is female when we say "she" is on her "maiden" voyage.

(c) Similarly, *conventions* of cosmological reference may be used without indicating any necessary endorsement of particular cosmological theories. When we say "the sun rises tomorrow at 6 A.M.," we are not endorsing a cosmological theory, and when biblical writers say that Christ came "down," it does not necessarily endorse a triple-decker universe. Since Paul says in Ephesians 2:6 that we already have been raised and seated with Christ in the heavenlies, it seems evident that Paul did not think of heaven as literally "up."

(d) We mentioned *hyperbole* in our list above; this is very frequent in Semitic literature. We already noted how Jesus in Luke 14:26 commends hating father and mother (see Matt. 10:37). The word "all" or "every" is frequently hyperbolic—"all" those in Judea and in the surrounding country went out to see John and were baptized according to Matthew 3:5-6; this clearly does not mean every single person in Judea (see 3:7—the Pharisees at least were not baptized). But "all" is not necessarily hyperbole; it is defined in its context. So "all" in Romans 5:18 means in context "all who are in Christ." This is not a hyperbolic "all" but a defined "all." If we say to a class, "All are is required to write a ten-page paper and hand it in to me by December 4," we certainly do not mean everyone in the world; the context of our statement defines the "all."

A special type of hyperbole or metaphor is the prophetic hyperbole. However, some of this hyperbole is not just hyperbole, but indicates that there is some more ultimate reality lying beyond what is present and visible. The promise concerning Solomon in 2 Samuel 7 was hyperbole with respect to its immediate object, but its hyperbole pointed beyond Solomon to a real fulfillment in Christ (see Heb. 1). Isaiah 13:9-11 and Joel 2 speak of the downfall of rulers in cosmic language (earthquakes, solar and lunar eclipses, etc.). But the judgment on Babylon (Isa. 13) or on the leaders of Israel (Joel 2) was also a pointer to the greater cosmic upheavals which Christ would accomplish. Peter quotes Joel 2 in Acts 2; according to this inspired sermon, the coming of the Holy Spirit at Pentecost was a cosmic upheaval of enormous proportions. It indicated that the power of Satan and his subordinates had been broken and God's reign was now disclosed. Likewise, the threat of judgment against Babylon in Isaiah 13 was hyperbolic ("I will make the heavens tremble, and the earth will shake from its place," v. 13), but this hyperbole points beyond Babylon to God's judgment of the world, as Revelation 18 points out.

Another example of hyperbolic prophecy is the absolutely stated, but intentionally conditional prophecy. Hezekiah, when he was told he would die shortly, did not passively say, "Oh well, that's the Lord's prophecy, and the Lord's prophecies always come true," and give up; he began to pray vigorously, with the result that the prophecy did not "literally" come to pass. It did accomplish its purpose, however; the prophecy had an implied conditionality in it. Similarly, when Jonah refused to go to Nineveh, it was because he knew there was an implied conditionality to the prophecy, and that uttering the prophecy was God's way of not fulfilling it. This intended conditionality was recognized by the hearers in Nineveh as well, who did indeed repent.

(e) Sometimes language can be both metaphorical and literal. The Exodus is presented throughout the OT as a real, literal, historical event, but it also served as a metaphor for Israel's deliverance from bondage to Egyptian idolatry. The bondage in Egypt was both literal and figurative.

(f) "Dead" metaphors are metaphors which have passed into common parlance, and are now essentially literal. For example, for most people the phrase a "rule of thumb" never calls to mind the literal thumb. It now has a standardized literal meaning. Now sometimes a biblical phrase that was a dead metaphor for the original writer and readers is no longer part of our common parlance and must be explained. Caution must be exercised that not too much metaphorical baggage be carried in, simply because for us the metaphor would not be dead. For example, the injunction in Hebrews 12:15 against allowing a "root of bitterness" (RSV) to spring up might conjure up in our minds an idea of someone having a bitter attitude; but the metaphor was a biblical one (Deut. 29:18) which was probably essentially dead; it referred to hypocrites who wanted to be part of God's people but keep their own religious ideas.

Before leaving the subject of metaphor, we should point out that although the word "spiritual" is often taken in the sense of "metaphorical," this is not the usual meaning of "spiritual" in the Bible.[29] Spiritual sacrifices are not metaphorical sacrifices but nonphysical sacrifices—the physical sacrifices were themselves metaphors pointing to the true sacrifice which is sanctified by the Spirit. A spiritual body is a not-of-this-world body given by the Spirit, not a metaphorical body. Spiritual gifts are not metaphorical ones, but gifts given by the Spirit. Thus "discerning spiritual things spiritually" in 1 Corinthians 2:13 (authors' trans.) does not mean discerning metaphorical meanings by allegorical methods, but discerning things having to do with the Spirit of God by the power of that Spirit.

5.1.5 Concrete language and transcendent truth

Although the biblical writers used concrete (phenomenal) metaphors to describe God's relation to man, we must warn against a comprehensive view of metaphor that suggests that biblical writers were unable to conceive of God and religious realities except in concrete metaphorical terms. There is a difference between using concrete language and being limited to concrete thought. Sometimes an argument has been based on Hebrew language peculiarities which have little relevance: for example, the idea that the Hebrews made no distinction between "word," "event," and "thing" because the same Hebrew word was used for all three.[30] More commonly now it is sometimes argued that metaphor is our only access to ultimate reality.[31] But although we can only see "in a mirror dimly" (1 Cor. 13:12, RSV), we are also "image bearers," and thus our linguistic thinking is a genuine imprint from the divine linguistic pattern, and our relationships are patterned after God's. When 1 Peter 5:7 tells us that God cares for us, the words are being used in their normal sense, where sense and reference are directly, not just contextually, related.

Nevertheless, it is true that much of the Bible's statements about transcendent reality are expressed in terms of the concrete. Two specifics:

(a) Ordinarily only the "visible" church is addressed. This explains some difficulties, such as why NT writers envision and warn against apostasy (Heb. 6:6; 1 Cor. 8:11), even though they claim that true believers cannot be let go by God who saved them (John 10:28-29; Rom. 8:38-39). Humans cannot know who is elect and who is not; we cannot see the invisible church. Hence the NT writers speak to the visible church, in which there are hypocrites who sometimes depart from the church.[32]

(b) Promises, especially in the OT, are often given in concrete terms comprehensible to God's people at the time. Thus the promise to Abraham and his seed focused on a patch of real estate in the Middle East, although the promises went beyond that to the whole earth (Dan. 7:27; see Matt. 5:5), and had a spiritual dimension that was more important than the physical (Gal. 3:14; Rom. 4:13).

5.1.6 Fixity and flexibility

One characteristic of language that never gives us problems in everyday use, but leads to many griefs in interpreting the Bible, is that words and phrases are flexible. This allows them to fit into a variety of circumstances and be used for a variety of tasks.

What this means for interpretation, of course, is that simply because a word means something in one place does not necessarily mean that it will mean exactly that same thing in another. This is why the same Greek or Hebrew word in the original may be translated a variety of ways in the English. It is also why a literal translation is not more accurate than an idiomatic one. Quite the reverse; an idiomatic translation, if it is a good one, is much more likely to convey the exact meaning than a literal one.[33]

It should be apparent that a word does not always mean the same thing. This is especially so when more than one human author is involved. For example, the word "works" in Paul is usually shown by the context to mean "works done according to the written law with the intent of thereby winning or maintaining God's acceptance,"[34] whereas in James "works" are the evidence that one's faith is genuine. Similarly, "faith" in Paul means a living relationship to God; for James "faith" can mean "intellectual assent to a proposition as true" (James 2:19). And possibly (it is debated) Paul and James mean something different by the word "justification." The differences in the way the words are being used means that the alleged conflict between Paul's "justification through faith alone apart from works" and James' "justification by works, not by faith alone" is only an apparent conflict.[35]

Even within a particular author's work this is true.[36] Just within the confines of Galatians, Paul uses the word "flesh" to mean "physical material of which our bodies are made" (4:13), "humanity" (1:16; 2:16), "the aspect of our existence having to do with this world" (6:12), and "the aspect of our existence which reflects our evil character and rebellion against God" (5:13-24).[37] It is a mistake to try to read the same meaning into all occurrences of the word.[38]

But words are not *totally* flexible; words have finite ranges of meaning, which are fixed within the synchronic state of the language.[39] That is to say, words are flexible but not fluid. Fluids can take any shape; flexible objects retain the characteristics of their own shapes. We cannot, like the Cheshire Cat in *Alice through the Looking Glass*, make a word or phrase mean whatever we wish (unless we desire to be misunderstood). Further, although words or phrases, and even sentences, by themselves are sometimes ambiguous, almost all the time the ambiguity is resolved by the context, either the textual context or the social situation in which the utterance occurred. The *Oxford English Dictionary* lists fifty-eight meanings for the verb "run" (plus another twenty-eight for the noun "run") but ordinarily no one has any trouble immediately identifying which meaning is in view. There are very few instances in which there is ambiguity over which meaning of "flesh" Paul has in mind at a particular moment. In actual use, words and phrases usually become much more specific.[40]

Take, for example, the highly ambiguous sentence, "The officers were ordered to stop drinking at midnight." Now two words in here, "ordered" and "drinking" are in themselves ambiguous (contrast the sentence, "I *ordered* a milk shake and began *drinking* it"), but are immediately resolved simply in the context of the sentence itself, and probably the reader did not notice that they were ambiguous, because in context they were not. But with these resolved, the sentence can still mean several different things:

(a) The police officers were commanded at midnight to cease the alcoholic consumption in which they had engaged up until midnight on that particular evening.

(b) An order was given at midnight that police officers should become teetotalers.

(c) The police officers were commanded to quit the habit of getting together for drinks at midnight.

(d) The police officers were commanded to put a stop to other people's habit of consuming alcohol late at night.

(e) At midnight the police officers were commanded to put a stop to other people's alcoholic consumption.

Five more permutations can be developed by understanding "officers" as armed service officers rather than police officers and undoubtedly the reader can find other possibilities. But once the social or textual context of the statement became known, this ambiguity would evaporate.[41] And in most cases, where such ambiguous sentences are uttered, the context already exists and there is no perceived ambiguity at all.

5.1.6.1 Ambiguity in the Bible

However, interpreters of the Bible do not always know the exact social context, and thus certain texts are for us ambiguous. When Paul says that women should have an "authority" on their head (1 Cor. 11:10), although many translations understand this as being a veil (assuming a veil was a symbol of authority, which is only a guess), we are not quite sure what he meant, and endless debate has been precipitated because of it. The ambiguity would only be resolved if we had more information.

Sometimes the ambiguity may be lessened by new discoveries or careful observation. For example, Paul writes, "It is a good thing for a man not to touch a woman" (1 Cor. 7:1, RSV; the NIV is misleading here). It is well documented that "touch" in this sort of context is a euphemistic metonymy for "have sexual relations with," and this could lead to the conclusion that Paul thinks sexual intercourse is bad, or at least is something one should avoid if possible. But it could be that Paul is responding to a series of Corinthian "sayings." In 6:12 the Corinthian saying is "everything is permissable for me," but Paul responds by pointing out that not all things are helpful. And in 8:1 the saying "we all possess knowledge" is answered by "knowledge puffs up, but love builds up." If this is the case, then Paul is simply quoting the Corinthians' "it is good not to touch a woman," and responding in the next verse: "each man should have his own wife." If in fact 7:1 was a "saying" of the Corinthians being referred to by Paul, some of the difficulty is removed. But there is no way to know this for sure; the Corinthians would have known what was in their letter (see 1 Cor. 7:1); we do not.[42] The ambiguity must remain.

The problem of ambiguity is especially severe when symbolic metaphorical language is used. Symbols are highly adaptable, and symbols in one cultural situation may mean something quite different in another (see sec. 5.2).

For example, when an American has just arrived in Oxford, England, and attempts to drive north on Woodstock Road, he is confronted with the following symbols in the three lanes of traffic:

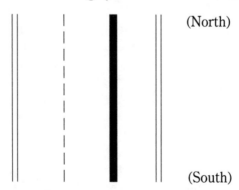

(North)

(South)

Assuming he remembers that the English drive on the left, his first thought will probably be, "Aha, I know what this means: I have two lanes of traffic going north and one traveling south." Such a meaning would appear plain to him. But this conclusion could have disastrous results, because in fact there are two lanes heading south; the dashed line divides the two opposing directions and the single solid line marks off a bus lane. The plain meaning was wrong, because the symbols involved are not universal.

5.1.6.2 Ambiguity in prophecy

Prophecy is a genre in Scripture which is particularly full of symbolic language. When prophecy is speaking of God's future for His people, much of it is cast in the terms which would have been meaningful to the original hearers, although prophecy also indicates a transcending of those terms. To interpret a prophetic symbol's subsequent historical referent unambiguously requires a thorough knowledge of how that symbol would have been perceived by the original hearers (no small feat!) and, in addition, a knowledge of how the pattern of God's redemptive activity indicated by the symbol has worked itself out in history (see sec. 8.4). There is a lot of room for "interpretive humility" here, especially with prophecy of things yet future. We may certainly draw conclusions from prophecy about the *nature* or *pattern* of God's activity and character, but to identify a precise historical referent is very difficult, and such identifications often remain ambiguous even after the historical referent has occurred.

But it is important not to overstress the problem of ambiguity,[43] particularly in non-prophetic texts. Although the particular sentence in 1 Corinthians 7:1 is ambiguous for us (not for its original readers), its function in the entire argument of Corinthians is not. It serves as part of Paul's general teaching that for some it is God's intent that they get married, and if they are married sexual intercourse is not only allowed but necessary. The ambiguity of the sentence does not render the whole discourse ambiguous.[44] And even the ambiguity of prophecy does not make the overall meaning of a prophetic utterance unavailable. The general nature of God's threats and promises can still be understood.

5.1.6.3 Ambiguity vs. inexactness

Further, there is a difference between ambiguity and inexactness. Ambiguity is where more than one meaning is linguistically possible; inexactness is where the one meaning is not precise. However, inexactness *becomes* ambiguity when one tries to remove the inexactness. For example, in the phrase "the gospel of our Lord Jesus" (2 Thes. 1:8) the "of" is inexact, not ambiguous. The word "of" simply qualifies the word "gospel" as "the one having to do with Jesus Christ." But ambiguity results if we ask what kind of "of"? Does the "of" mean Christ is the *source* of the gospel, or does it mean He is its *content*, or does it mean He *possesses* it, or something else? But this kind of question goes beyond the ordinary function of the word "of." It is not illegitimate to ask the question, and frequently the context will enable an interpreter to answer it, but the "of" itself simply does not carry precision. Had the author been concerned about such a question, he could have spelled it out, with words such as "the gospel which is about Jesus Christ."

5.1.6.4 Ambiguity is rarely intentional

Before we leave this topic of fixity and flexibility of words, a particular application should be drawn. Although words have a variety of functions, an author almost always has in mind simply one of those functions. The common exegetical practice of finding all or several of the possible meanings of a word in a particular occasional use is therefore illegitimate.[45] For example, the Greek word *katechein* can mean "to hold down, suppress" as in Romans 1:18, "men who suppress the truth by their wickedness." It can also mean "to restrain," "to hold tenaciously onto," "to occupy a position," "to possess," or "to control." If someone read Luke 14:9 "and then you will begin with shame to *katechein* the last place" (authors' trans.), it would be misleading to try to argue that Luke also meant we should suppress the last place, or control the last place, or hold tenaciously to the last place. Unless the author was deliberately making a word play we have no warrant for finding several meanings.

There are wordplays in Scripture of course. The Gospel of John is particularly rich in wordplays. For example, the word *anothen* in John 3:3 ("you must be born *anothen*) can either mean "again" or "from above." John uses the ambiguity of the word to demonstrate the confusion of Nicodemus, who thought Jesus was speaking of reentering the womb. But Jesus was speaking of being reborn into God's new age ("seeing the kingdom") which is also being born from above, by the sovereign act of God. Less clear is John 1:5, where the ambiguity is reflected in some translations which have "darkness has not understood it" (NIV) while others have "darkness has not overcome it" (RSV). But even in the cases of deliberate ambiguity or wordplay, the meaning is not in itself inherently ambiguous; the several meanings have been deliberately superimposed. And unless it can be demonstrated that the author intended a double meaning, it is dangerous to try to extract multiple meanings on the basis of alleged wordplays.

5.1.6.5 Conclusion

All this has been to show that usually words, phrases, and sentences in contexts are not in themselves ambiguous. Ambiguity results from insufficient knowledge of the context, or from asking questions of the text which it does not address, not from the flexibility of words. Our interpretive humility comes not from any inherent ambiguity of a text or the variety of meanings a word or phrase or sentence may have, but from a recognition of our of comprehensive knowledge of the contexts. Interpretive humility acknowledges the need for constant progress on the spiral of understanding, but it strives toward a goal which is real; it is not an embracing of "ambiguity forever."

Indeed, unless a reader is deliberately misconstruing, progress on the spiral is almost always possible because language is very redundant. We chose at random a word from the previous paragraph, replacing it with a blank space. Most readers supply the missing word "lack" or the equivalent with only a moment's hesitation, because the clues to meaning in the sentence are many. Redundancy usually minimizes ambiguity for the reader. *Mis*comprehension will usually result in a thought clash with other elements of the discourse and can be rectified by a shift in our understanding of the text. *Non*comprehension can be minimized by "fill" from the redundancy of the discourse. This is why most of the time readers feel reasonably confident that they understand a text. Do not let confidence become arrogance however. No earthly human's interpretive framework is so complete and perfect that his or her understanding is without error, and what seems "obvious" may not be correct. We are always in this life on the way.

5.2 Culture and Understanding

Interpreting the Bible is more difficult than interpreting something written within our own time and culture because the forms of language may function differently in different cultural contexts. This is because words are specialized symbols, and symbols are only meaningful as human convention gives them meaning.

A linguistic example of this is that in England at the time we are writing this book, the word "brilliant" is often used with the general sense of "very good." If someone produces exact change in the purchase of something, the shop assistant may say, "That's brilliant." In America, this would likely be interpreted as a sarcastic insult to the purchaser's intelligence, suggesting surprise that he or she was capable of producing the requisite combination of coins.

5.2.1 Keeping our distance
This illustration, like the earlier example of the road markings on Woodstock Road in Oxford (p. 133), demonstrates that to understand a language symbol in another culture one must first emphasize the difference between the text's cultural and linguistic environment and one's own. Just as the lane marks look familiar but in fact are not familiar at all, the American must deliberately hold lightly his judgments on what he thinks a word means, and seek more knowledge of this new environment in which he is operating by reading the "interpretive" signs at the roadside.

Similarly, although many things in the Bible are so strange that we immediately are aware of the "distance," some things may look the same as something in our own linguistic/cultural environment — but in fact are quite different — and judgment must be suspended until we see how a symbol would have functioned in its own environment.

This process is what Paul Ricoeur calls "distanciation," holding firmly to the "otherness" or strangeness of a text.[46] Like the plasterer repairing a crack in the wall, the interpreter must widen the gap before attempting to close it; otherwise his work will remain on the surface only and fail actually to close the gap. We must point out and even accentuate the socio-cultural-linguistic differences, so that we may understand the original in its own setting.

5.2.2 Bridging the cultural gap
How do we do this? Although we can never really hope to accomplish it perfectly, the two things that help us to move on the hermeneutical spiral with respect to understanding the differences

are *study* and a *sane imagination*. Study can make the interpreter aware of the cultural differences in general, and the informed and sane imagination can make good guesses about how those cultural differences would affect the meaning of a text. This is hardly warrant for a fevered imagination. To be sane an imagination must be well-informed about the cultural differences and social circumstances of the original text and will be controlled by what is actually in the text. But there is no substitute for "putting oneself in someone else's shoes" for understanding how that someone else would perceive an event or a text.[47]

Perhaps one example will suffice. When Jesus began to preach, He declared that "the kingdom of God (heaven) is near." Now the "kingdom of God" is frequently bandied about as a slogan having something to do either with a socio-political accomplishment or else with the church in some spiritual sense. More frequently perhaps, the phrase is simply passed over with incomprehension, or with some vague idea that the place where God rules is in people's hearts.[48] But study will turn up, first, that the phrase translated "kingdom of God" means actually the *sovereignty* or *power* of God. The use of the phrase in Palestine before and at the time of Jesus' ministry referred to the time when God's sovereign power would be fully manifested. So when Jesus says "the kingdom of God is near" or "has come," He is saying the manifestation of God's sovereignty is about to take place. This occurred in the redemptive historical acts of Jesus. It has nothing to do with present-day political matters, or even with the church, except insofar as God's sovereignty manifested in Christ forms the basis for the church.[49] Imagination can put the informed reader in the place of a Palestinian Jew of the first century, who groans as his parents and grandparents have groaned under harsh Roman rule, who sees the corrupt state of the priesthood interested more in worldly success than leading God's people, who wonders whether God even cares any longer. Such an imagination will perceive the excitement and awesomeness of hearing the radical proclamation, "the sovereign reign of God, His fully manifested sovereignty, is about to begin!" No wonder they called it good news!

5.2.3 The redemptive historical gap

The various parts of the Bible are not only distant from us, sometimes they are distant from each other, partly because of the great temporal distance between different parts, but especially because of the changes in redemptive historical situation which took place. With the fulfillment of the OT in the events and revelation of the NT, there is a shift in the meaning of certain symbols. The Book of Hebrews makes clear that the meaning of the sacrificial system is somewhat different from what it was before Christ came. Now that the fulfillment of that system has come, the actual practice of animal sacrifice is obsolete (Heb. 8–10). Similarly, Paul vigorously argues that circumcision, which formerly marked the people of God, is now superseded and that for a Gentile Christian to be circumcised now would be to deny the fulfillment of the law in Christ. An OT mandate cannot simply be applied directly without consideration of the difference in redemptive historical situation.

For us this means that the distance between ourselves and Paul is not the same as the distance between ourselves and Moses. Our redemptive-historical situation is essentially the same as that of Paul and the other NT writers after the resurrection, after the coming of the Spirit, but before the return of Christ in judgment.

But even though we are in the same redemptive historical age, we are still faced with cultural, social, and linguistic distance between ourselves and the NT people. For example, the command to "greet one another with a holy kiss" (1 Cor. 16:20) certainly meant a sincere literal kiss, and might still bear that meaning in some countries, but it would not mean a literal kiss in our Western culture. Similarly, women wearing head coverings in worship (1 Cor. 11) had a certain cultural meaning which no longer is evident in our Western world. The principle and concerns behind such commands is, of course, still valid, but their form might not be.

Also, although our situation after the resurrection of Jesus but before the final judgment puts us in essentially the same redemptive historical situation as the NT writers, there is still some difference. At the time the NT was being written, naturally the whole NT was not yet written, and so God's people did not have the full written revelation. God thus provided apostles and prophets who completed the NT and interpreted the OT and the events of Christ's life, death, resurrection, and present reign, providing a foundation of understanding for the church (Eph. 2:20). Now that we have the entire canon, such direct ongoing revelatory activity is no longer of critical necessity. This does not predetermine the issue of whether certain believers today are given the revelatory gifts of prophecy and apostleship, but it does indicate that our situation is not identical to that of the early church, and when Paul tells the Corinthians to desire above all the gift of prophecy we cannot apply it unreflectively to our own situation.

5.2.4 Conclusion

With all this emphasis on *distanciation,* the reader may be getting the impression that one has to be an expert in ancient Near Eastern history and Greco-Roman society to understand the Bible properly. Experts do have an advantage, but although expertise may help and may increase the ability to interpret correctly, even a nonexpert can interpret many things quite well if he or she is sensitive and tries to develop a "historical sympathy."[50] Although the cultural perspective of the original hearers may differ remarkably from our own, the human imagination can adopt another culture's different perspectives temporarily. God has made us capable of identifying with the original author's and hearers' cultural and social situation, so that we can obtain a reasonable understanding of any text. This is true because all people of any age are created after the same pattern, God's image; and our thinking and language, for all our cultural and linguistic differences, are still within this basic pattern. Translation, not only from one language to another, but also from one culture to another, is always possible, and even where a particular item may not be known, the meaning of the whole is always generally perceivable. No one really knows what a "parbar" was, but anyone can understand the basic meaning of 1 Chronicles 26:18.

Even more importantly, the Bible deals principally with the relationship of God and humans, and human beings and their relationships always remain essentially the same.[51] Culture, language, social situation, history, ideology, and worldviews may change, but people are always people, sin is sin, and God does not change. Hence we have confidence in the *perspicuity* of Scripture (see sec. 2.3.1).

In closing this section on distanciation, we should note that not only is knowledge of the original culture necessary, but a knowledge of our own culture. First, if we are unaware of our own culture, we will be unequipped to evaluate in what way our cultural conditioning is influencing our reading of a text, and second, if we wish to apply the meaning of the text to a present situation (presumably a goal in biblical interpretation for the church) we had better understand how our present culture works. John Stott entitled his excellent book on preaching *Between Two Worlds*[52] because preaching, which is properly an application of the Bible to Christians today, means not only a competence in the biblical cultures but also a competence in the culture of one's audience. It is an arduous task, but it can and must be done.

5.3 Context and Understanding

All texts have contexts; as human communicative acts they do not take place in a vacuum. One of the authors of this book was recently in a discussion group where someone said, "I agree with everything everybody has said." This might appear ridiculous apart from its context, but no one suspected he meant anything other than that "I more or less agree with the specific remarks which the people in this particular group have just addressed to the group as a whole within the preceding few moments." Meaning is not just a function of words, but of the complex of words and context. Words and sentences are set within a larger linguistic utterance or conversation, they are set within a particular historical situation, and they occur within a particular cultural, social, and linguistic setting.

5.3.1 Textual context

The importance of textual context is widely recognized. It has given rise to the aphorism, "a text without a context is a pretext." Even the seemingly isolatable pithy sayings of the Book of Proverbs are in the context of that book and can be misinterpreted if removed from that context. The fear of the Lord as the basis (not just the beginning) of understanding (Prov. 1:7) provides the foundation for all of the proverbs which follow. If this is true of Proverbs, it is certainly true of the remainder of Scripture. Often mentioned is the ridiculous example that Psalm 14:1 and 53:1 say "there is no God." The context clarifies: "The fool says in his heart, 'There is no God.' "

More difficult to spot is how larger contexts may clarify smaller units which appear to be perfectly plain in themselves. Ecclesiastes 9:1-10 by itself (like many other passages in Ecclesiastes) seems to echo an American beer advertisement's advice that, since "you only go around once, grab all the gusto you can get."

But in the context of the whole of Ecclesiastes we see this as part of the argument of the vanity of all human striving; only God's good pleasure counts. When Satan quoted Psalm 91:11 (Matt. 4:6), he seemed to be doing it right; Jesus was the Messiah, God's anointed, and God had promised to protect Him. But the psalm as a whole is about how the Lord protects the one who trusts in Him, and putting God to the test would be an evidence of distrust and not in line at all with the psalm as a whole.

All this points up the importance of understanding the overall meaning of a whole text in order to understand a part of it. When we receive a letter from a friend, we do not read it a paragraph at a time, set it down, ponder what it might mean, and wait until the next day to read the next paragraph in isolation from the first. And yet that is what we often do with the Bible. We are reserving most "how to" matters for the next chapter, but here is a basic "how to" that is so important it ought to be mentioned here: before beginning to interpret a particular text in detail, read through the entire communicative unit. This means in most cases the entire biblical book from which the text is taken.

There is, however, a hierarchy of contexts. All levels and types of context play some role in determining meaning, but the *most significant context* for the meaning of any individual unit (word, sentence, paragraph, discourse, book) is its *immediate* superior context, not its ultimate superior. If we want to know the meaning of a word, for example, the most important question is what kind of meaning is expected in the immediate sentence in which it occurs, and secondarily we look at other uses of that word elsewhere in the paragraph, chapter, and book. If we want to know the meaning of a sentence we look to see what the paragraph is about, and then secondarily to what the chapter and book are about.

5.3.2 Circumstantial context

Earlier in this chapter (sec. 5.3) we noticed how the meaning of the words "everybody" and "everything" are narrowed down by the context in which they are spoken. This is an example of the meaning being specified by the circumstances. A similar situation is recounted in 1 Kings 22:10-17. King Ahab was inviting Jehoshaphat to cooperate in a battle against Syria to recover the town of Ramoth Gilead, and Jehoshaphat insisted on obtaining prophetic advice. Four hundred prophets were brought in, who advised Ahab and Jehoshaphat to "Attack Ramoth Gilead and be victorious, for the Lord will give it into the king's hand (v. 15). When Micaiah son of Imlah is reluctantly brought in, he says virtually exactly the same words, but Ahab knows that Micaiah does not mean the same thing. Something in the circumstances indicated that Micaiah's words had a different force than those of the 400. In fact, they were a sarcastic rebuttal of the other prophets.

5.3.3 Redemptive historical context

The context within redemptive history must be understood in order to determine its meaning for today. When Moses is given the commandments on Sinai in Exodus 20, he is also given a number of case laws. Exodus 22:20 tells the Israelites, "Whoever sacrifices to any god other than the Lord must be destroyed." Similarly verse 22:18 indicates that sorcery must be punished by death. This seems incredibly harsh and out of accord with our situation now, where the idea of such religious compulsion is repugnant. Now most of this repugnance may be due to our failure to appreciate just how offensive to God idolatry and sorcery are, but there is also a difference in our redemptive historical situation. Paul does not tell his churches in the Roman Empire that they should start killing idolaters and sorcerers. On the contrary, Christians should "be subject to the governing authorities" (Rom. 13:1, RSV), even though those authorities were idolatrous.

Does this mean that Exodus 22:18 and 20 are without meaning today? No, but the meaning is indirect. Exodus laid down the covenant obligations of the theocratic nation of Israel, which was both a political entity and a spiritual entity. As its physical existence served as a pattern or "type" of its spiritual life, preexilic Israel therefore had to be not only spiritually pure (as the church must be today) but physically pure. Exodus 22:18 and 20 remind the church today of the seriousness of idolatry and sorcery and demand that any trace of them amongst Christians be expunged, but not by killing the errant Christians.

Paul dealt with an actual case of textual misinterpretation similar to this in Galatians. Some Jewish Christians had argued in their zeal that all male converts to Christianity must be circumcised. This probably seemed only logical to them. When a man became a Christian, he became a "son of Abraham" and part of the historic people of God. Therefore, they probably argued, the sign of circumcision, originally given to Abraham as a sign of his inclusion in the covenant of promise (Gen. 17), should be applied to all male believers, as it was applied to all Abraham's physical seed (Gen. 17:12).

But as Paul points out, such thinking failed to place the scriptural command of circumcision in the correct redemptive historical perspective. Circumcision was a sign of the typological covenant and indicated a situation of waiting for the coming Christ. Now that Christ has come, the religious participation in circumcision by a Gentile is essentially a denial of the completion of Christ's work (Gal. 5:2-4). It ceased to symbolize an inclusion in the covenant of Abraham and became a symbol of bondage to the Law of Moses.

A more subtle example of how the historical context affects interpretation is the heavily debated Isaiah 7:14 (cited in Matt. 1:23): "Behold a virgin (or young maiden[53]) will conceive and bear a son, and she (or you, or they[54]) shall call his name Immanuel" (authors' trans.). Many critics have argued that Matthew is misusing Isaiah 7, because the following verses speak of the coming desolation brought upon the enemies of Judah. Isaiah 8 also speaks of the desolation of Damascus and Samaria by the Assyrian king, and in this case the sign is the son of Isaiah, Maher-shalal-hash-baz, for "before the child knows how to cry 'papa' or 'mama' the wealth of Damascus and the spoil of Samaria will be carried away before the king of Assyria" (Isa. 8:4, authors' trans.). Hence, some regard the "son" of Isaiah 7:14 as either a son of Ahaz[55] (see vv. 10-12), or perhaps Isaiah's son[56] (see 8:3-4), and the "virgin" as not virgin at all, but Ahaz's or Isaiah's wife (8:3).[57]

But closer attention to both the historical and the textual situation might undermine this argument. The text speaks of the child "eating curds and honey." No evidence suggests that curds and honey were "baby food"; and 7:22 says that *everyone* left in the land after its desolation (see v. 23) eats curds and honey. This indicates a future historical situation of a remnant, returning to the land after it had lain fallow for years, living off the "fatness of the land" (as in the Exodus from Egypt and entry into Canaan — Ex. 3:8; Deut. 31:20; Josh. 5:6). It could not refer to Isaiah's own time of civilized agriculture. And as the KJV indicates, Immanuel shall eat curds and honey *in order to* know how to refuse evil and choose good, not *when* He knows.[58] The child Immanuel will know the postexilic life of direct dependence on God's provision (trust) rather than human endeavor, in order to make Him a righteous judge of His people (see Heb. 2:13-18, which quotes from Isa. 8). The text looks forward not just to the immediate future of the events of the Assyrian invasion (late eighth century B.C.), but beyond the time of Exile, that is, after the sixth century B.C.[59] Ultimately, Isaiah is looking forward to the Messianic deliverer, and Matthew did not misuse the text.[60]

In conclusion, the historical context of the Bible includes more than the immediate historical context, because biblical history points beyond its immediate situation. A redemptive-historical context is more than just the historical situation. The historical situation is itself in the context of an entire purpose or plan of God, and knowledge of both is essential to the interpretation of biblical texts. Any OT text or event will be placed at a certain point in the unfolding plan, and its meaning will depend on its place in that plan. And the interpretation of any biblical text, by virtue of its inclusion in the Bible as a whole, is informed by the whole Bible.[61]

5.3.4 Social (cultural-linguistic)

Frequently knowledge of the culture will clarify some seemingly cryptic statements in the Bible. A simple example is Jesus' statement recorded in Matthew 11:16.

> To what can I compare this generation? They are like children sitting in the marketplaces and calling to others: We played the flute and you would not dance; we sang a dirge and you did not mourn.

Now if one happened to know that the flute dance was a wedding dance for men (rather like a square dance), and the dirge was a funeral dance for women, we see the whole range of adult activity, male and female, happy and sad, reflected in the play of the children. "This generation," like truculent children, refused to participate in the activity of God, whether it be the austerity of John or the bounty of Jesus. Of course, much of this could be guessed from the context, but knowledge of the social situation clarifies.

Much more difficult examples occur in Paul's letters, some of which are responding to situations in a cultural context which Paul himself does not mention, because they were obvious to his recipients. On page 132 we mentioned Paul's culturally relative command to women that they should have an "authority" on their heads, presumably some kind of symbolic head covering (1 Cor. 11:2-16).[62] Paul is addressing a social context where it was for some reason shameful for a woman not to wear such a covering; perhaps she would thereby be declaring herself independent of all authority.[63] In any case, head coverings in our Western culture have a different social meaning, and thus discussions about whether women today should wear hats in church are rather silly.

An example from the OT is the curious behavior of Naomi's closest kinsman who had first right over redeeming the inheritance of Elimelech (Naomi's husband). At first he is willing to redeem it, but when he finds out he must marry Ruth as part of the redemption, he says, "I cannot redeem it because I might endanger my own estate" (Ruth 4:6). This seems incomprehensible until we learn that the children of the marriage would be classed as Elimelech's, and unless he could afford to have another wife as well he may have ended up with no progeny of his own line (supporting more than one wife was economically quite difficult, and there had recently been a lengthy famine in the land [Ruth 1:1]). It is interesting that another cultural custom of drawing off the sandal, recounted in 4:7, had already become culturally distant by the time Ruth was written, so an explanation is given for the original readers of Ruth for their (and our) hermeneutical enlightenment.

Occasionally, knowledge of the social situation shows how a seemingly miscellaneous event in the OT relates to God's redemptive activity. Remember when Elisha made the axhead float (2 Kings 6:4-6)? This seems to us to be a rather unnecessary miracle. But two things in the text are stressed: that the axhead was *iron*, and that it was *borrowed*. This took place right at the beginning of the iron age, when iron smelting was a military secret, and iron axes were extremely valuable. Further, since it was borrowed, the disappearance of the axhead was for the borrower a sentence of lifetime slavery. The floating of the axhead was the man's redemption.

5.4 Genre and Understanding
The fourth task in grammatical-historical exegesis is to ask what kind of literary work the text is. A parable may by itself sound like

a historical narrative, but the way in which it "means" something is quite different from history. When Jesus says "a man was on his way to Jericho" in the Parable of the Good Samaritan, it is not understood in the same way as when Matthew tells us that "Jesus was on his way into Jericho." Recognizing the particular genre is the key to understanding.[64]

This example is fairly obvious, but others, particularly in the OT, are less so. Many sincere Christians believe that the Book of Jonah is not the history genre, but the parable genre.[65] This is not a question of *whether* Jonah is true; it is a question of *how* it is true, a question about what the Book of Jonah is saying. If it is not intended as a historical narrative, interpreting it as such would be an error.

The issues in this example are, however, confused because often those who claim Jonah is not historical do so because they do not believe its miraculous elements. But this is to use a modern anti-biblical assumption to prejudge the genre issue. Miracle also characterizes the Book of Acts, which the author clearly claims is historical. If Jonah is a parable rather than history, there should be clues in the text itself to indicate that it is not history but parable.[66] We cannot relegate a text to nonhistorical genre simply because we have trouble believing something could happen.

Even with texts that seem to be at least partly historical, genre recognition is clearly necessary. In the Book of Job, the primary concern surely is not the historical record of Job's sufferings, but the theodicy question — "Why should a good God allow someone who is faithful to Him to suffer?" Unlike the recent book *Why Do Bad Things Happen to Good People?* by Rabbi Kushner, the Book of Job answers in terms of God's sovereignty. But our point is that Job is not exactly history in the modern sense of the word, but wisdom poetry. It is no more likely that Job's friends argued in lengthy complex Hebrew poetry than it is that Henry V addressed his troops in iambic pentameter (Shakespeare's meter). Further, as poetry Job uses complex imagery and metaphor, which again is different than history writing. Thus we should be very careful about deciding what Job asserts. Not only might we attribute assertions to God which He has not really made, but we may miss what God is really trying to tell us in the Book of Job.

Other questions of genre may be raised. Was Ecclesiastes written by Solomon, or is it a kind of literary genre which calls Solomon to mind but does not really claim to be by him?[67] Is the Song of Songs the historical account of something that happened in the court of Solomon, or is it a love poem which was simply set in that historical location, like a Shakespeare play? Is the Gospel of Matthew a historical narrative, or a mixture of history and theological embellishment as Robert Gundry suggests?[68] Again, these are not questions about the truth or falsehood of Scripture, but about genre. Each particular text will demand particular interpretive treatment.[69]

But now an awful specter has raised its ugly head. If we allow for variability in genre, what prevents anyone from using the genre argument to deny most of the historical value of the Bible, or to make the Bible say whatever one thinks it should say?

The answer to this lies in the dependence of the genre of a text on the author's stance, which is itself determined by the sociolinguistic conventions of his audience. Did the author of Jonah (we are not told who it was) intend to write history or to write a parable? Ordinarily the clues to the author's purpose will lie in the text itself. Otherwise how would even the original readers have recognized the genre? Occasionally the clues would have come from the cultural linguistic situation, and recovering these clues is more difficult and less certain. But usually, it is not difficult to identify genre. If we simply ask, "What was the author trying to accomplish?" we are well on our way to identifying the genre. Is the text's purpose to convey history, to illustrate, to confront, to entertain, to persuade, to develop artistically a philosophical point of view, to produce an art work, or a combination of some of these? Almost all the time the text itself will answer that question. If the author wishes to be understood, he is going to include the clues to genre within the work itself, unless the cultural context makes it obvious.[70]

Genre is both a matter of identifying the purpose and character of the work as a whole and of knowing what particular types of literary devices are being employed in smaller sections. The Gospels are historical but contain stories told by Jesus which are parables. Although the overall character of Luke is history, the story of the Prodigal Son, although not declared to be a parable, is nevertheless clearly of that genre. It is marked out by the fact that it bears contextual and literary resemblance to other parables which are so declared.

In prophecy particularly, genre identification on both the macro level (what kind of prophecy *book* is this) and the micro level (what genre is this particular *text* within the prophecy) is especially important. For example, prophecy is often stated in concrete and hyperbolic terms. The prophecy to Hezekiah in 2 Kings 20:1-6 was stated absolutely ("Put your house in order, because you are going to die; you will not recover" [v. 1]), but Hezekiah understood its genre as not pure predictive prophecy but warning; he prayed, and was spared forthwith (2 Kings 20:1-6).

It is this question of genre that enables us to address the question of allegory. There is a difference between allegory and allegorical interpretation, or allegorization. Allegory uses extended metaphor to elucidate life and is intended as such by the author.[71] In Isaiah 5:1-6 the allegory is intended, and this is clearly stated in verse 7; likewise the Parable of the Wicked Vineyard Tenants in Matthew 21 was intended as an allegory and was recognized as such by the Pharisees against whom it was directed. On the other hand, allegorization understands history as a metaphor. This appears to be what Paul does when he understands the account of Sarah and Hagar in Genesis as a metaphor for the situation of the Christians of Galatia (Gal. 4). Grammatical-historical exegesis, if it identifies the genre as being an intentional allegory, will so interpret it, but it will not interpret the genre of history as metaphorically representing something else. This does not necessarily make metaphorical interpretation illegitimate, since it may in fact be that God has constructed history in such a way that it represents something (see chap. 6). It may also be a way of illustrating something. But discovering such metaphorical meaning is a different task than ascertaining the original meaning and must therefore be reserved for the next chapter.

The meaning of words and phrases (sec. 5.1), the effort to understand the cultural distance between text and reader (sec. 5.2), the textual, historical, circumstantial, and social contexts (sec. 5.3), and the identification of genre (sec. 5.4), are the key elements of grammatical-historical exegesis which help us understand the original meaning of a text.[72] In chapter 7 we will look at the nitty-gritty of grammatical-historical exegesis; here we have simply shown the elements involved in it. But before we get to that "nitty-gritty," we need to look at how we may move from discovering what the text *meant* to ascertaining what it *means*.

SIX

REMOVING THE VEIL: FROM WHAT IT MEANT TO WHAT IT MEANS

Grammatical-historical exegesis is the hermeneutical attempt at scientific control of meaning. It attempts to recover the literal or historical base of meaning, the author's original intent. Berkeley Mickelsen claimed that "principles of hermeneutics are valid or invalid depending on whether or not they really unfold the meaning a statement had for the author and the first hearers or readers."[1] But should we stop here? Does our bias against any extension of meaning that might be castigated as "allegorism"[2] stem from biblical norm or from our scientific worldview? Does not any attempt to move from "what it meant" to "what it means" involve the whole Bible, as well as a changed situation, and will this not take us beyond what grammatical-historical exegesis can accomplish?

The NT certainly finds meanings in the OT texts that go beyond meanings recoverable by strict grammatical-historical method which focuses on the human author and his immediate audience. As we have argued in chapter 3, we need to take our own methodological cue from the Bible itself. Paul seems to suggest in 2 Corinthians 3 that a veil lies over the minds of those who do not believe in Christ, so they cannot understand the real meaning, and in 1 Corinthians 2 he claims that only those who are "spiritual" can understand the spiritual things of God's Word. There are also indications in the OT itself that it had a greater divine purpose than just addressing the immediate situation. Jeremiah and Ezekiel were both told to prophesy even though they would not be listened to. Presumably a later audience was the intended beneficiary. The fact that the Bible is not just individual units but is a whole, behind which lies a divine authorial intent, suggests that grammatical-historical exegesis by itself is not enough.

The NT writers' approach certainly confirms this.[3] If God is the author of the entire Bible, and if that Bible is a coherent communication from God, then His earlier statements will have some relationship to His later statements and thus mean more than would have been perceived by the human authors of those earlier statements. As Paul says regarding the commandment (in Deut. 25:4) not to muzzle a working ox, "Is it for oxen that God is concerned? Does he not speak entirely for our sake?" (1 Cor. 9:9-10)[4] Further, as we have seen in chapter 2, the NT presupposes that the OT *events* (such as the Exodus) and *institutions* (such as the sacrifices), as well as the explicit *prophecies,* were leading up to and pointing toward fulfillment in Jesus Christ. This is central to the NT faith, and if we hold to that faith, we too must see the OT as leading up to and pointing toward Christ.

According to Paul, only the Spirit of the Lord can remove the veil which blinds people to the Word of God. If the Spirit is the one who removes the veil, can we not rely on Him to guide us to the true meaning of Scripture for us today?

But we can also identify certain aspects of seeing the full import of the Word of God once the veil is removed. This is exciting, because it means experiencing not just ancient documents but a living Word speaking to us today. But it is also dangerous, because all kinds of our own ideas can be read into the Word. Safely going beyond grammatical-historical exegesis involves four tasks: First, we must sort out how the biblical texts transcend their original historical setting (sec. 6.1). We must also identify the ways in which earlier events and institutions point to the later and fuller fulfillment (i.e., the "typological" correspondences) (sec. 6.2). Third, we must observe the context of the canon as a whole, or application of the so-called "analogy of faith" (sec. 6.3), and finally, we need to identify how changes in the redemptive-historical situation have affected the texts' applicability to the present situation (sec. 6.4).

6.1 History and Beyond

All texts that have become "classic" (i.e., texts which help shape society and culture) speak to the human condition in such a way that changes in culture and history can adapt the text to the new situation. An author of a text originates a text's meaning, but with time and changing circumstances the functional meaning of a text can grow beyond the conscious intent of the author. Even among students of the Constitution of the United States who wish to preserve the "framers' intent" as the basis for the Constitution's interpretation, there is an admission that many of the problems we face today could not have been envisaged by the original framers. Somehow the interpreter of a text must recast the text to address the contemporary age in such a way that it preserves the integrity of the text in relation to its original context and author. A trans-historical meaning must be extrapolated from the historical meaning.

If such a thing is true of classic human works, how much more the text given by God for His people. The human author's inten-tional meaning must be preserved, but if the Scripture is going to address our problems today its meaning cannot be limited to what may have been in the original human author's mind. Paul ad-dressed his exhortations to specific people with specific problems; to the degree that our situation regarding those issues parallels that of Paul's original recipients, we can transfer the reference of those exhortations to ourselves, even though our situation is out-side the bounds of what Paul could have envisaged. God speaking through Moses addressed the Ten Commandments to His people at Sinai; to the degree that our situation regarding the issues addressed in the Ten Commandments parallels that of the Israel-ites at Sinai, the commandments also command us. Most Chris-tians make the transfer unconsciously. The Ten Commandments address such universal human conditions that very little transla-tion is necessary (except perhaps with regard to the Sabbath; most Christians observe the first rather than the seventh day, and the observation itself takes a different form).

But when Exodus goes on in chapter 22 to prohibit lending money at interest, much more effort is required. Somehow the underlying principles at work in the specific case laws of Exodus 22 have to be extrapolated, then such principles may find some application in our contemporary situation. With regard to interest, in a modern free-market society where money is itself a commod-ity and not just a medium of exchange, the prohibition of interest would create an unfair advantage for the wealthy; it would elimi-nate the middle class and ensure that the poor were permanently poor.[5] It is also true of course that in our society exorbitant inter-est and the encouragement of unnecessary borrowing continue to be means of exploitation of the poor. But for ancient Israel, which was an agrarian rather than an industrial society and had the cor-rective of the Sabbath year, the Jubilee, and the land inheritance, money lending at interest was primarily an exploitation of the poor.[6] The historically transcendent meaning would be derived by observing the principle of fairness in business relationships and the prohibition against exploitative practices. All of God's Word applies to us, but the way in which it applies is not always easy to see.

It is not simply the ordinary need for legal texts to transcend their original historical context which prevails in the Bible. Divine authorship implies that the earliest parts of revelation have something to do with the later parts. The divine plan implies that earlier events give indication of later events, even as the floor plan of a building gives indication of what the finished building will look like. As we earlier pointed out, the meaning which God intended in the earlier events and words only comes out with later events and words. As Paul says, the OT read by itself was a "mystery," but this mystery has now been made known (Col. 1:26; Eph. 3:9).[7]

6.2 Typology and "Fuller Meaning"

This "increase" of meaning can be looked at in two ways. From the standpoint of history, later and more important events, persons, and institutions are foreshadowed by earlier ones. We call this *typology*. From the standpoint of language, if we look at the meaning of a text "growing" or unfolding as God's plan develops, we refer to the "fuller sense," or *sensus plenior* which a text takes on.

6.2.1 Typology

Typology is "the interpretation of earlier events, persons, and institutions in biblical history which become proleptic entities, or 'types', anticipating later events, persons, and institutions, which are their antitypes."[8] It is thus actually a way of looking at history.[9] Typology cannot exist without history; in particular, it requires a history that is under God's sovereign control and is proceeding according to a divine plan.

The history upon which typology may be founded is not something purposeless, aimless, or going nowhere in particular. It cannot be an infinite circle, as the Greeks imagined. Biblical history is linear,[10] and the events which happen are indicative of where all history is moving. Thus typology is only possible on the biblical notion of history having a purpose, that purpose being ordained by an intending Person who controls it and who intimates within it where it is going (see Eph. 1:9-10).

This "intimation" is not just a construct "after the fact" when similarities can be noticed between recent past and ancient past. As Gerhard von Rad eloquently observed, Israel's prophets projected their hope for the future in the form of analogies from the past, which built Israel's tradition of expectation.[11] What God had done in the past was an indication of the greater deeds of God in the future. When Israel faced exile, the hope of deliverance from exile was cast in the language of the Exodus. And the hope for a final redemptive work of God was also cast in these forms. Thus, Christ is the ultimate fulfillment of Israel's tradition-building process. Israel's past was constantly redirected toward the coming deliverance by God's anointed, the Christ. He fulfills Israel's ultimate "exodus" (Luke 9:31; cf. also pp. 52–54). Not only is christological typology possible, it is necessary to truly understand the ultimate point of the OT history as well as prophecy.

Thus, typology implies that, just as earlier revelation is only ultimately understood in the light of later, so the later revelation can only be understood in relation to the earlier. As Leonhard Goppelt pointed out, "Typology demonstrates not only the nature of the new in comparison with the old, but it also shows that the new is founded directly and solely on redemptive history."[12]

It is, therefore, not surprising that the NT understands events and institutions of the OT to be "types." This is explicitly stated in a few texts (1 Cor. 10:6, 11; Rom. 5:14; Heb. 9:24; 1 Peter 3:21), but is implied in many places, because the NT writers understood Christianity as the fulfillment of OT expectation and understood the OT as pointing to Jesus.[13] When Jesus declared that He must be killed and rise on the third day because of the Scriptures, it established an essential relation between His redemption of His people and the expectations of the OT. If the NT fulfills the OT tradition, then we cannot understand the NT apart from the typological expectations of the Old.

Typology is evident in the OT both in prophetic texts and in historical and descriptive material. Hebrews specifically informs us that the OT sacrificial system was a type or "shadow of the good things that are coming" (Heb. 10:1), and proceeds to show how the sacrificial system clearly pointed beyond itself to a more perfect sacrifice (Heb. 8–10). Old Testament predictive prophecy often has a built-in indication that there is both a typological fulfillment in the near future, and a more complete fulfillment in the distant future. For example, the Prophet Nathan speaks God's word in 2 Samuel 7:12-16 to David, promising that one of his offspring would "build a house for my Name, and I will establish the throne of his kingdom forever. I will be his father and he will be my son." This has a preliminary reference to Solomon, but the language of the passage indicates the coming of a person who would far exceed Solomon in his accomplishment of the dominion of God, and so Hebrews 1:5 can quote this passage as referring to Jesus the Christ. Sometimes people speak of this as "double fulfillment" or a two-part fulfillment, a typological and an antitypological (see below, p. 220).

6.2.2 "Fuller meaning"[14]

If the divine plan gives early indication of later events through history by typology, when we look at the recorded words of the older stages from the standpoint of the completed revelation in Christ we may expect to find there a "fuller sense" than would have been evident to the first hearers. *Sensus plenior* is thus simply another way of looking at the way later revelation relates to earlier. By showing how the later revelation reflects and completes the earlier (typology), the earlier revelation itself can be seen to take on an expanded meaning *(sensus plenior),* evident to us but not to its first readers. The events, people, and words of the new revelation fill up or "fulfill" the OT as Jesus fills up the promises. The typology of promise fulfillment "permeates the thinking of Jesus and the early church and is the ultimate validation for their extensive use of the Old Testament to depict and characterize their own situation."[15] This idea of "filling up" the meaning of the OT is not restricted to prophecy; Jesus says that He came to fulfill the Law (Matt. 5:17). Even the commandments strain toward fulfillment in Jesus Christ, and this is why Paul can refer to the Law as "our custodian until Christ came" (Gal. 3:24).

To some this sounds suspiciously like reading things into the text that are not there. And indeed this can happen. Justin Martyr, along with many other early church leaders, believed that the scarlet thread that Rahab hung out her window typified the blood of Christ.[16] True *sensus plenior* is organically related to the historical meaning. That is, it should be a "fuller" sense, not an entirely "other" sense. It is like the oak tree within the acorn. Just looking at an acorn, one could not see the full end result, although one could tell that the acorn is intended to grow into something bigger, and from a later standpoint one can look back and see how the oak tree grew gradually out of the acorn. But the "meaning" of the acorn is only "fulfilled" in the tree, not in the acorn itself. Thus the meaning of Genesis 3:15, which prophesies that the seed of the woman shall crush the head of the serpent, is only fulfilled in Christ's victory over Satan.

One way in which an "organic" relationship between original meaning and the fuller meaning may be recognized is by referring to the distinction between sense and reference made in the previous chapter. The reference is the specific thing, person, or event which is in the author's immediate purview. The sense is the meaning of the sentence which transcends the immediate situation. The linguistic context defines the sense; the historical context defines the reference.

For example, in Psalm 2:7 the Lord says, "You are my son, today I have begotten you" (RSV). The *sense* of this is that the person being addressed bears a filial relationship to the person speaking, and that on the day of speaking the speaker has either established, recognized, or reaffirmed that relationship. The *reference* would be determined by context. When the psalm was written, it probably referred to the king of Israel, whose special representative relationship to God was being affirmed. But as the prophetic word of the Lord, it ultimately refers to the special relationship of God the Father to Jesus, the ultimate king of Israel (Heb. 1:5). The organic relationship is clear because the linguistic sense remains the same, but the little referent (like the acorn) has grown into the much greater referent (like the oak).

Contrast this with a comparison of a young oak tree and a lamppost. These things superficially have more resemblance than an oak tree and an acorn, but they are not organically related, and the lamppost will never grow into the oak.

Thus, another test of an alleged "fuller sense" of a text is not just to see some resemblance, but whether that text itself, or its larger context, points forward to and expects a future development of the material in that text. Genesis 3:15 clearly looks to a future development; Rahab's thread offers no organic connection to the blood of Christ.[17]

We must admit that there is one NT case which appears to exceed an organic relation between the historical meaning and the NT meaning. This is the allegorical interpretation Paul gives of the Genesis story of Sarah and Hagar in Galatians 4. Not only does Paul actually use the term "allegorically interpret,"[18] but the several items of the story are all taken as representing something entirely different. The history of the OT is taken as a symbol for a theological distinction pertinent to Paul's audience. However, a close examination of this passage shows that, although this is indeed an allegorical interpretation, it does not violate the overall contextual intent of the original Genesis story. Rather, Paul's opponents very well may have used the literal meaning of the Sarah and Hagar story to undercut the larger Genesis message.

The *referent* of the original story is the literal individuals of the patriarchal family and the fact that God's elective purpose was for Isaac, not Ishmael. A Judaizer[19] could very well have pointed to this passage and argued that, since only Isaac's descendants and not Ishmael's inherited the blessing, Gentile converts need to become descendants of Isaac by being circumcised and taking on the obligations of Moses' covenant.[20] But the larger *sense* in Genesis is that God's blessing is not by works of the flesh (illustrated by Abraham's attempt at bringing about God's promise by intercourse with Hagar), but by faith in God's promise (the miraculous birth by Sarah, which was outside even the illusion of human control). Paul's citation of Isaiah 54:1 ("Be glad, O barren woman"), which was itself perhaps a commentary on the miracle of Isaac, bears this out. To us Paul appears to be finding a meaning unrelated to the historical, but in a way this can be regarded as simply a bigger view of the one original sense. Even at that, this is the only instance of full-fledged "allegorizing" in the NT[21] and is possibly a result of the abuse of the text by Paul's opponents.[22]

6.2.3 Identifying types

May we find "types" and fuller meanings in the OT which are not explicitly mentioned in the New? Jesus taught His disciples that the whole OT looked forward to His death, resurrection, exaltation, and the preaching of the Gospel to the Gentiles. Since the NT writers do not cover everything in the OT, we may expect large areas where the typology or *sensus plenior* has not been stated explicitly in the NT.

But identifying types is somewhat risky, since we are going beyond the ordinary use of language. We have warrant from the NT, however, and also an indication as to what qualifies as a genuine type or genuine *sensus plenior*. If we look at NT examples of typology, we identify at least three controls:

(1) To be identified as a type, an event's redemptive-historical function must be known and must show an organic relationship to the later redemptive history it allegedly foreshadows.

(2) The nature of the type must lie in the main message of the material, not in some incidental detail.

(3) An antitype (the fulfillment) must be greater than the type (the foreshadow).

We offer three examples of types or fuller sense that are not explicitly spelled out in the NT.

First, it has often been noted that Joseph in Genesis behaves in a very Christlike manner, and it has been suggested that he serves as a "type" of Christ. But the NT nowhere draws that conclusion. May we? Let us apply the three tests.

The Joseph story is of great redemptive-historical significance. The purpose of the story in Genesis is to show how God preserved His people, saved them from famine, and furthered the fulfillment of the Abrahamic promises. This certainly is organically related to the deliverance Christ wrought for His people, since His was the ultimate fulfillment of the Abrahamic promises according to Paul.

Second, the main events and central details bear resemblance to the activity and character of the Christ. As Christ was betrayed by His own people and given over to Gentiles, so Joseph was betrayed by his brethren and sold to Gentiles. As Christ endured humiliation and death to rescue His people, so Joseph was enslaved and then imprisoned so that he could rescue his people. As Christ's faithfulness was rewarded with exaltation to the right hand of God, Joseph's faithfulness was rewarded with exaltation to the right hand of Pharaoh. And in both cases the wicked deeds done against them were things which God purposed for good (compare Gen. 50:20 with Acts 2:23). In these respects the story of Joseph is typologically representative of Christ. The story taught the Israelites what God was doing. On the other hand, incidental details such as the animal blood on Joseph's coat, Joseph's leaving his garment in the hand of Potiphar's wife, and his use of a cup in Benjamin's sack are probably not to be seen as having any fuller sense. But Joseph's life as a whole "pre-patterns" the ultimate Man of God. Finally, of course, Christ's deliverance is much greater than Joseph's.

Our second example is the story of Moses striking the rock in the wilderness. The first incidence of Moses' striking the rock is recorded in Exodus 17, where God commands him to strike the rock. Moses did so, and water came forth to satisfy the people. A similar situation arises later in Numbers 20, where the Lord this time commanded Moses to speak to the rock, but Moses in exasperation (or unbelief, thinking that speaking would be inadequate, see v. 12) strikes the rock twice, and as a result is forbidden to enter the Promised Land with his people.

Now we have some explicit NT warrant for understanding this rock as a type of Christ. In 1 Corinthians 10 Paul tells the Corinthians that the "rock" of the wilderness wandering was Christ and that it was by this rock that the Israelites ate of the same spiritual food and drank the same spiritual drink of which Christians now partake.[23]

If the rock "was" Christ in a typological sense, the reason for God's anger with Moses over striking the rock becomes clear. The first time, when Moses was commanded to strike the rock, the rock represents humiliation,[24] and Moses strikes the rock because unless the Christ be stricken the living water cannot flow to God's people. But the striking occurred once for all and from then on only speaking was necessary to renew the supply.[25] Moses' impatient disobedience resulted in his dislodging of some of the symbolism of the rock. Now it is likely that Moses did not realize the full typological symbolism of his actions; his punishment was for his unbelief in the effectiveness of doing exactly what the Lord commanded, not for destroying the symbol. This text by itself therefore serves only as a reminder that exact obedience is what God requires. But taken as a part of the whole OT which points to the expected Redeemer, and as a part of the whole Bible which recounts the Redeemer's appearance, the story looks to Christ. The integrity of the historical meaning is maintained, although its ultimate meaning in the context of the whole Bible is christological.

Typology is not only found in the OT. It provides the key to understanding certain NT material as well. In Matthew 10, for example, Jesus sends the 12 Apostles on a mission, which is restricted to Israel according to verse 5. But in verses 16-42 the description of the mission and its results clearly addresses the situation of the church's mission after the ascension of Jesus. The Twelve did not "stand before governors and kings as a witness to them and the Gentiles" (v. 18, authors' trans.) when they were restricted to Israel. Matthew apparently understood the mission to Israel by the Twelve as a "type" of the greater mission of the church to the world.[25]

6.3 The Bible Interprets Itself

If we allow that the meaning of a text can be more than is recovered by grammatical-historical exegesis, then once again the specter of relativism begins to arise. Is there any means of control over extensive exegesis?

We already discussed part of this control in the previous section. The original human meaning (the linguistic sense) must be organically related to any more extensive meaning, and all meaning must be related to the redemptive-historical purpose of God.

The other primary control is the concept of scriptural internal consistency and self-interpretation. This is sometimes called interpretation according to the "analogy of Scripture" *(analogia scripturae)* or the "analogy of faith" *(analogia fidei)*.[26] Augustine's maxim that "Scripture is interpreted by Scripture" is simply to say that God determines the meaning of His own words. This is not an opening up of a "Pandora's box" but a control on meaning. It confines the meaning of any text to that which fits with the rest of Scripture. This has an obvious result in two important hermeneutical principles: (1) that obscure passages of Scripture should be interpreted in the light of the clear passages, and (2) whenever a NT writer explicitly interprets an OT text, this interpretation is true.

The first of these is rather universally acknowledged (although not universally practiced) and fits with general interpretive practice with any text. In general, an interpretation begins life as a hypothesis which accepts some things which appear to be clear and then proceeds to build on that base. There is a little bit of danger, because the "obscurity" of the obscure text may be being generated by the improperly understood "clarity" of the ostensibly clear text, but if the interpreter is aware of this danger and maintains humility with respect to the interpretation, he or she can make progress up the hermeneutical spiral by using the clear to look at the obscure.

The second obvious principle is that, while the NT interpreters do not always interpret exhaustively, they do interpret rightly. This bears mentioning, because some Christians think that, while it is proper to understand the NT in light of the OT backgrounds and presuppositions, it is quite improper to understand the older revelation in the light of later.[27] Except for direct and explicit predictive prophecy, the OT is said not to speak about the NT events. But this is both ridiculous from a general hermeneutical point of view and perverse from a theological one. If God is the author of the whole (both the history and the text) then surely the later is latent in all the former, and meaning in the former is expanded by the appearance of the later. Do we not as authors expect that our readers will understand our first chapter in the light of the later ones? Was Peter in error in the way he used Joel in Acts 2 or Psalm 16 in Acts 3?[28]

Further, one cannot become an eighth-century B.C. Jew and read Isaiah as an eighth-century B.C. Jew. One may be a Christian pretending to be an eighth-century Jew or a modern Jew pretending to be an eighth-century Jew, but in both cases the actual modernity makes this impossible, even with study and a sane imagination. And this is not only because of the big cultural and social gap, but especially here because of the redemptive-historical gap. After the coming of Christ, part of the meaning of Isaiah 9, for example, must include either an acceptance or rejection of the proposition that the redeemer of Isaiah 9 is Jesus Christ. Sc a modern interpretation is necessarily different from any ancient one.

So the "analogy of faith" for Christians dictates both that obscure texts are understandable in the light of the clear and that the NT gives the correct understanding of the OT.

But it also serves to indicate that *the meaning of any part of the Bible must be understood in the context of the Bible as a whole*. This principle is sometimes called "canonical" interpretation. Texts which might have been understood in one way if they occurred in isolation from Scripture are shown by their inclusion in Scripture to have a somewhat different meaning.

The Song of Songs is an excellent case in point. Until recently, almost all Christian and Jewish interpretation regarded this book as an allegory of the love of God for His people (Christ for His church). Since the nineteenth century increasingly it has been regarded rather as an example of ancient Near Eastern love poetry, delighting in the sexual aspect of love. Considered strictly by itself, this latter does appear to be the genre of Song of Songs. But if the Song is strictly and nothing other than a sexually enticing love poem, then why is it in the Bible? What has the Song to do with the rest of the Bible? What is God communicating in the Song?

Here the totality of Scripture provides the context. The relationship of man and woman is patterned after the relationship of God to His people (Eph. 5:32; this is also implied in 1 Cor. 11:7). Song of Songs is indeed a song about human love, but its ultimate function in the Scripture is to elucidate and emphasize the depths of complete, committed, and exclusive love which God has for His people and which His people are expected to have for Him (and which, when His people do not have it, results in loss).[29]

Further, there is another love song in Scripture, Psalm 45. Since this psalm is explicitly cited in Hebrews 1:8-9 as referring to Christ, we have inspired evidence that the "king" in Psalm 45 has an ultimate reference to Christ, and of course His bride is the church.[30]

This kind of exegesis does not exhibit the absolute methodological control that science demands and thinks it can achieve; it operates by a "faith" control which depends on hermeneutical sensitivity and submission to God for its results. Total human control is impossible; life is still God-determined, not man-determined, as Job learned and the author of Ecclesiastes deduced. Such interpretation does not negate our earlier assertion that it is the human author's meaning which is the basis for discovering any further meaning, but it does recognize that God's intent, especially in the OT, often went beyond anything that the OT writer himself could have envisioned.

6.4 Redemptive History and Present Application

Ethical changes from OT to NT are sometimes due to changes in cultural context. This is mainly true where we are dealing with understanding case imperatives (for distinction between case law and principial or apodictic law, see sec. 8.2). But culture does not change the ethical principles behind case laws.

Thus, a basic principle of ethics of marriage is its permanence, according to both Testaments (Mal. 2:14-16; Mark 10:2-12; and parallels; and as Jesus points out there, by implication Gen. 2:24). But in the OT provision was made for regulating divorce and remarriage (Deut. 24:1-4); there is a so-called "exception" clause in Matthew 5:32 and 19:9; and Paul appears to allow divorce and remarriage in the case of a deserting, unbelieving spouse. There were cultural reasons for the variations in the case applications, but these variations still have invariable principles behind them. The controversies over the matter of divorce in our own time is due not only to disagreement about what the invariable principles are, but over how the principles should be applied in our own cultural context.

But sometimes a change in ethical applicability is due rather to the change in the redemptive-historical situation. Principally here we may note the change regarding circumcision and the "ceremonial" aspect of the law.

6.5 Conclusion

The meaning of any text is based on the way that text functioned in its own original linguistic and cultural context. Since any text is understood according to its human context, the Bible must also be so understood. Grammatical-historical exegesis is the means to finding this original core meaning. This task involves the study of the language elements of the discourse (words and syntax), the necessity of distancing ourselves from the text, the study of contexts both textual and socio-cultural, and the identification of a text's genre.

However, grammatical-historical exegesis only establishes the initial base, not the total meaning of a scriptural text, not only because of the historical transcendence of all classic texts, but also and more importantly because history was going somewhere, and Scripture speaks of God's gradual unfolding of His plan. The older revelation anticipates and points to the later revelation. This is predicated on divine authorship. Thus Paul can understand "seed" in Galatians 3:16 as pointing toward Christ, because ultimately there is only one true seed of Abraham, only one individual who truly qualifies as the inheritor of the promises, and that is Abraham's descendant Jesus Christ.

But if we allow for the meaning of the text to go beyond what may be established by grammatical-historical exegesis, the question arises as to what controls can be set in place to ensure that a non-grammatical-historical meaning is indeed the true divinely intended meaning. The principles we have noted are:

(1) The divinely intended meaning of any text must be clearly *organically* related to the human author's meaning. The human author's meaning is knowable by reference to his context, and this is our initial access to the larger divine meaning.

(2) The divinely intended meaning must be *consistent* with the total revelation in the Bible. It is precisely the total revelation in the Bible which enables the expansion from the human author's starting point.

(3) The divinely intended meaning must in some way or another point to (not necessarily speak directly about) God's redemption of His people in Christ; that is, it must find its place in redemptive history, be christologically focused, and apply to the church.

(4) An individual interpreter must, in humility, always hold as tentative his or her perceptions of the divine meaning, subject to the Holy Spirit's directing of the church.

PART THREE

INTERPRETATION IN PRACTICE

I n the first part of this book, we looked at the way our presuppositions and general knowledge provide a context within which we understand the Bible. And in the second, we discussed in a theoretical way what is involved in interpretation. Now we are ready to raise questions of how we interpret, questions of method and technique. But it should be clear that technique is not the solution to every problem. Technique only facilitates reaching certain goals, and unless the goals are the right ones, the technique will only make it easier to get to the wrong interpretation.

Nevertheless, technique or method can offer some controls and can help give interpretive guidance on specific texts. Method provides clarity and consistency, and often yields new insights on Scripture, so chapter 7 will give a general outline of what steps to take in exegeting passages.

But *general* guidelines often will not meet the specific requirements of specific texts. The Bible is made up of several different *kinds* of literature, and each kind or *genre* of literature requires its own special treatment. Chapter 8, therefore, will discuss the most important broad categories of writings in the Bible.

SEVEN

STUDYING GOD'S WORD

In an age of television, most people have been programmed to expect predigested and entertaining content from any book, with no labor and little thought required. But the Bible does not yield many of its treasures to those unwilling to expend effort. Up to this point we have focused on the nature and character of biblical interpretation; now we will discuss the "how to."

7.1 Spiritual Preparation

It is an interesting experience to meet the author of a book while in the middle of reading it. The book suddenly becomes much more "alive" and personal, because the reader can "hear" the author speaking in it. In order for the Bible to communicate with us in this alive and personal way, we must know God and hear Him speaking in it. Thus, one of the very first things any Christian should do to understand Scripture is to prepare the heart to hear and submit to God.

To fail to come in this way is to have a veil over one's mind, as Paul puts it in 2 Corinthians 3:15. Although the true sense of Scripture may be ascertained by analysis, "hearing" and submitting to that sense will only happen by the Spirit at work in us. Furthermore, without this "hearing," it is quite possible that, for all our analysis, we may miss the true sense of a text. A book may contain wonderful insights on the meaning and background of biblical texts, and yet altogether miss the spiritual import of the passages it professes to interpret. Study is useless if the reader does not first submit to Scripture's author, expecting to hear God's voice and obey it. Luther put it rather strongly.

> You must, therefore, straightway renounce your own sense and understanding, for with these you will not attain the truth, but only with your own presumption precipitate yourself, and others along with you, from heaven into the abyss of hell, as happened to Lucifer. On the contrary, kneel down in your chamber and pray with real humility and earnestness to God to give you, through His dear Son, the Holy Ghost to enlighten, guide and instruct you.[1]

Luther tended to overstate things. Understanding Scripture does not mean totally "renouncing your own sense and understanding"; certainly Luther did not do so (see sec. 4.4). But practically speaking, Christians need to ask God to reveal the meaning of a text to them, not in order to escape the labor of exegesis or to get some guarantee of correctness, but in recognition that all genuine insight comes by God's providence.

Remember the Parable of the Sower? To the disciples it was given to know the secrets of the kingdom; but to others it was not given. Why? Because they "asked" Jesus the meaning of the parable (Luke 8:9). And as the psalmist said, "Who may ascend the hill of the Lord? . . . He who has clean hands and a pure heart" (Ps. 24:3-4). Any endeavor to understand God's Word should begin with sincere petition to God to "open my eyes, that I may see wonderful things in your law" (Ps. 119:18).

7.2 Analyzing Passages

Dependence on God for exegesis does not mean that no labor is involved in understanding. The Holy Spirit sanctifies us but not without our struggling (and sometimes failing) to be holy; similarly the Holy Spirit leads us into truth, but not without our struggling (and sometimes failing) to interpret correctly.

Analysis, the first stage in the struggle to interpret, is the practice of grammatical-historical exegesis. It is the foundational work needed to distance ourselves from the human author, bridge that distance, and then appropriate his meaning into our own interpretive framework. Unfortunately, even this beginning analysis is not a scientifically precise operation. Everyone who has had to learn "rules" of language has also had to learn that there are always exceptions to the rules, and since exegesis is dealing with language, its rules also are not precise. This is a chapter not of rules but of guidelines to the *art* of exegesis.

7.2.1 Using translations

The first item on the exegetical agenda must be to select what version of the Bible to use. Naturally, for readers who know Greek or Hebrew, the original language text should be foremost on the desk. But those who do not know the original languages need not despair, because the best English translations generally encapsulate the best that modern scholarship has to offer. Even those who know Greek and Hebrew well often benefit from referring to English translations.

What are the best English translations? There are actually differing philosophies about what constitutes a good translation, revolving around two poles, the "literal" and the "dynamic." The literal school strives to preserve as much as possible of the grammatical structure of the original and attempts to match up Greek or Hebrew words to a few English equivalents, sticking with these equivalents as much as possible. This has an advantage of conveying to the reader a sense of the flow and style of the original and keeps interpretive decisions about what a passage means to a minimum, allowing the reader to make such decisions. It also enables the reader to see some of the verbal connections and "plays on words" which are apparent in the original. The disadvantage is that sometimes a literal rendering makes no sense at all in English, which leads to confusion or risqué exegesis, and even when a literal rendering "makes sense," that sense may be different in English than in the original.[2] An example of a literal version is the *New American Standard Bible* (NASB), or to a much lesser extent, the so-called *Authorized (King James) Version* (KJV).[3]

The other pole, the dynamic approach, relinquishes any hope of conforming to the original grammatical structure and makes no attempt to provide a word to word correspondence; it tries to reproduce the sense of whole sentences by "dynamically equivalent" sentences in the target language. This has the advantage of conveying the meaning of sentences much more clearly than the literal type. On the other hand, since the dynamic equivalent translator must make more decisions about what the sentences in fact do mean, the reader is somewhat less able to see what alternative meanings may be possible. Possibly the best examples of dynamic translation are the (occasionally hazardous) *New English Bible* (NEB), and its more even-handed revision, the *Revised English Bible* (REB). Also, the dynamic translation of the New Testament by J.B. Phillips, while idiosyncratic, is frequently unsurpassed in clarity and forcefulness.

Most modern translations fall somewhere in between. Three well-known and excellent examples are the *Revised Standard Version* (RSV), its recent update, the *New Revised Standard Version* (NRSV), and the *New International Version* (NIV). All three of these evidence occasional bias in their translating decisions (how could

they do otherwise?), but they are almost always reliable in conveying into English the sense, and to some extent the form, of the
originals. The reader may use these translations with a *great* deal
of confidence. Both the NIV, RSV, and the NRSV were prepared
by teams of scholars who generally kept each other in check, and
limited the degree to which questionable or idiosyncratic translations occur. When we read these versions, we may be confident
that they indeed convey the Word of God, not perfectly, but certainly faithfully.

With this in mind, we recommend that the Greekless or
Hebrewless student use at least two English translations. Those
with original languages, even those who are highly competent, are
advised to use a translation along with their original texts. At the
very least, a dynamic or mixed translation will indicate what some
excellent and knowledgeable scholars thought the original meant.

7.2.2 The "grammatical" side of exegesis: Discourse, sentence, and word

It is arguable that, before analyzing the passage itself, one should
examine the historical and cultural background in which to understand it. On the other hand, if the interpreter does not have some
idea what the passage is talking about, he or she would not know
what kind of background to look for. A careful interpreter will
probably alternate between examining the passage itself and inves-
tigating its background.

Some textbooks on exegesis start with the analysis of the
words. This is not unreasonable, because sentences are composed
of words, and the meaning of these words is obviously important
to the meaning of the sentences. But although it is reasonable,
there is a certain danger in that it is easy to become so enamored
of the words that we forget the sentences in which they appear.
Words only designate a few possible fields of potential meaning
and function in relation to other words; they do not "mean" on
their own. The meaning of a word is the result of an interaction of
its "fields of potential meaning" with the context within which it is
used. The context specifies the particular meaning of the word
which is intended. So word studies must be carried out with their
sentences in mind. Likewise sentences should be understood
within their paragraphs, and paragraphs within the basic complete
unit of meaning, the "nuclear discourse," or all the material coher-

ing around a particular subject or topic.

Therefore, we recommend starting with a look at the discourse, working down to words, and then back up to discourse. Before doing any formal analysis, an interpreter should read through a large part of the biblical book within which the passage occurs, preferably the entire book. While doing this, it is a good idea to ask oneself constantly, "Who, what, when, where, and how?" This will place in the reader's mind the discourse context and open up answers to the question "why?"

7.2.2.1 Discourses

What makes a paragraph is the relations between a group of sentences. *Discourse* sense involves the connection of paragraphs to form an entire argument, development, explanation, story, and so on. A discourse is characterized by *coherence*, a coherence that involves both sequence (order) and relation to a topic, and is bounded by sentences which indicate the opening and the closing of the argument. Although there may be divergences from order and digressions from the topic at hand, the whole is tied together by sequence and topic. Thus a discourse is usually understood to be the unit of complete meaning, with a beginning (introduction), middle (development, exposition, argument), and end (conclusion, summary).[4]

However, this definition is still somewhat open-ended. In a sense, the Book of Isaiah comprises several discourses. The messianically focused prophecies of Isaiah 7–12 are of a somewhat different character than the woe oracles and apocalyptic visions of 13–35. And the narrative about Hezekiah in 36–39 appears to be a different topic and sequence than the servant songs of 40–55. But on the other hand, there is a unity of purpose and character to all of these sub-discourses that also unites the whole. All have to do with God's judgment and the restoration of His people.

Similarly, the epistles of the NT sometimes jump from topic to topic in an unrelated fashion and in no clear sequence, yet are also units of discourse held together by the fact that they are letters addressed to particular people and circumstances. Jesus' "Parable Discourse" in Matthew 13 appears to be a single sermon, comprising several parables which are themselves discourse units, but these are tied together by comments about the meaning and purpose of parables. And, of course, Matthew 13 is part of the larger discourse of the Book of Matthew. Finally, the Bible as a whole, God's Word (singular) to humanity, has a huge variety of material and topics, but has a coherency in its primary subject matter (God's relationship to man) and an identifiable sequence; it has an introduction (Creation and Fall), development (redemptive history), and conclusion (the consummation in Revelation) that mark it as being in its entirety a single though multiplex discourse.

Just as a complex sentence has many "nuclear sentences" or thought-units within it, a complex discourse such as the Book of Isaiah or Matthew, or the Bible as a whole, has many identifiable "nuclear discourses" in it. This nuclear discourse or *basic* discourse concerns a single topic or story and has a beginning, development, and conclusion. It is the smallest unit that is classifiable according to genre. When studying the Bible to see what it has to say to us, the nuclear discourse is the unit from which we should work. Naturally we relate it to the larger discourses, and of course we study the smaller pieces, the paragraphs and sentences, that make up that discourse. But our questions of meaning should be directed at nothing smaller than the nuclear discourse. Although a Bible study or sermon may concern itself with a smaller unit, the discourse should control what we understand and glean from whatever smaller unit we study.

Both to identify the boundaries of the nuclear discourse, and to perceive its genre and the development within it, the first thing to do is to identify its "plot" or structure. Stories have plots, with beginning, development, climax, and conclusion. Other discourses also have initiatory or introductory material which marks them off from any previous material, a development, usually involving argument and/or explanation, and a conclusion which wraps up the purpose of the discourse and marks a disjunction from any succeeding material.

Most readers will have some help here. Frequently within the Bible, some of the chapter divisions will mark the breaks between discourse units. In the Book of Daniel, for example, it is fairly easy to recognize the introductory "historical setting" sentences—"In the _____ year of the reign of _____" (1:1; 2:1; 7:1; 8:1; 9:1; 10:1), or where there is a different ruler (5:1; 6:1), and these changes occur at chapter breaks in Daniel. But chapter divisions are not always such a good guide. For example, the conclusion of the opening discourse of Genesis 1 runs into chapter 2; the new nuclear discourse begins at 2:4. And in Colossians, Paul shifts from his opening doctrinal doxology to the subject of his sufferings and concern for his readers at 1:24, not the beginning of chapter 2, and this subject in turn goes on past the chapter division to 2:6.

Similarly, many modern translations have space breaks between discourse units, but these too should be examined carefully. They are usually better indication than chapter divisions, but are not, of course, infallible.

Within a discourse, as within paragraphs and sentences, it is helpful to pay attention to the connecting words which spell out how paragraphs are related: "for" and "because" (indicate cause), "however" and "but" (indicate contrast), "therefore" and "thus" (indicate conclusion), "furthermore" and "in addition" (indicate continuation).[5] These identify the purpose of particular paragraphs or sentences, and serve as indicators of the progress, sequence, and structure of the development.

One way of perceiving the flow of a discourse is to "paragraph" it. A paragraph is a group of related sentences. Just as a real sentence may comprise subsentences which add, argue, specify, or elucidate, a paragraph consists of real sentences which add, argue, specify, and elucidate. Even more than sentences, paragraphs "say" something.

Of course, the original text of the Bible was not marked into paragraphs; paragraphs and verses were added by later translators. It is therefore an excellent exercise to copy out the sentences of a text line by line without paragraphs, and then attempt to regroup the sentences into paragraphs. Doing this forces the reader to catch the meaning and flow of the text in question. It is useful to do paragraphing simultaneously with other students. Then, if most attempts at re-paragraphing correspond to a high degree, especially when done by people who have never before seen the text in question, then one can be more confident that there is understanding. The meaning of sentences in relation to one another is "connecting" in the minds of the readers. One cannot paragraph without some measure of understanding. And the paragraph divisions show something of the discourse's structure.[6]

An extension of paragraphing is to place the paragraphs in hierarchical relationship and then also to subdivide paragraphs into subunits. Outlining the structure of a passage is especially helpful if one pays attention to these connecting words and discourse markers. Once an outline is in hand, the interpreter can see how any part of the discourse relates to the whole, or how a "nuclear" discourse relates to the entire discourse. This too helps in constructing the "framework of understanding" by which the meaning of a text is integrally perceived.

For example, Ephesians 3 (like most of Ephesians) seems to go on without break, but the connecting phrase "for this reason" (v. 14) seems to provide a marker of a shift from one topic to the next, although it also draws the connection between topics. And verses 20-21 make up a doxology which shifts subjects, although there is no clear marker as such. So Ephesians 3 could be broken up into two main parts, with a doxology at the end. By then examining what thematic content coheres within these units, yet marks them off from each other, we can identify their main subject and assign a title to the parts of this chapter:

A. 3:1-13 — Paul as minister to the Gentiles
B. 3:14-19 — Paul's thanksgiving and prayer
C. 3:20-21 — Concluding doxology

By examining the content within these sections, we could further outline as follows:

A. 3:1-13 — Paul as minister to the Gentiles
  1. 3:1-6   Paul is recipient of God's "mystery," that Gentiles are fellow heirs
  2. 3:7-9   Paul's task is to make known the mystery
  3. 3:10-12   So that the church might display God's wisdom and plan
  4. 3:13   Therefore Paul's suffering is good
B. 3:14-19 — Paul's thanksgiving and prayer
  1. 3:14-17a   That Father, Son, and Spirit would strengthen and dwell in the Ephesians
  2. 3:17b-19   That they may know the love of Christ
C. 3:20-21 — Doxology

A discourse's genre is apprehended more intuitively. Sometimes the genre is specified, either explicitly (e.g., "So he told them this parable." [Luke 21:29] or "The beginning of the gospel about Jesus Christ." [Mark 1:1]) or implicitly by formal indicators which are used only with specific genres (e.g., "Paul, Silas, and Timothy, to the church of the Thessalonians." [1 Thes. 1:1]). In Luke 10, it is not stated that the story of the good Samaritan is a parable, but we recognize it because Jesus is replying to a scribe's question "who is my neighbor" with a story, ending with an application question. The story presumably answers the scribe's question, and bears similarity to other parables. We thus understand it as a parable, an illustrative teaching story, not as a historical recounting of an actual event.

But sometimes genre is identified only by setting, which means understanding and genre identification happen simultaneously. It is possible to misidentify a genre unless we hear the entire content and setting, which is why one should not try to interpret a text smaller than a complete "nuclear discourse unit" in its context. When Nathan told David a parable about a rich man who stole a poor man's sheep, David at first thought it was an actual literal event. Only when Nathan completed his discourse with the words "you are the man" (2 Sam. 12:7) did David correctly identify its genre and "understand" Nathan's story.

As we noted in chapter 6, genre *can* be a difficult matter because we, unlike the original readers, may not be able to recognize the literary clues to genre in a text. But in our view this is not a common problem, and the difficulties ought not to be exaggerated. In chapter 8 we will examine some specific biblical genres.

In addition to identifying a discourse's structure and genre, it is helpful to fill in the details. Basically, this means simply asking: "Who, what, when, where, why, and how?" In other words, one determines the reference of the discourse, in order to get at the sense of it. Some of this involves the historical side of exegesis, but to a large degree, this is simply a matter of paying attention to what the sentences say.

7.2.2.2 Sentences

The basic unit of verbal communication, of meaning, is the sentence. A sentence, unlike an isolated word, does something; it states, commands, requests, and so on. But just as a word should be understood within the context of its sentence, a sentence should be interpreted within the context of its paragraph and discourse. These identify the larger topic under discussion and the ultimate reason for the sentence. The most basic question an interpreter should ask about a sentence is: what does this sentence contribute to the overall discourse?

Thus, when 1 John tells us that "God is love," this sentence says something about God. Outside of its context it might be understood as an equation of God and love, and how many young Christians who are "in love" have rationalized disobedience to God's commands by appealing to the "fact" that God is love? But within its context this statement is simply an indication of a certain *attribute* of God which Christians need to imitate, not a statement about God's *essence*. It tells us that, if God is in us we will manifest God's character by our love for one another; it does not say that if we feel love it means God is in us.

Sentences (even more in Greek than in English) can be quite long and complex, and thus sentences repay closer looks. In grammar school many of us learned to diagram sentences, and this may be helpful sometimes, but the grammatical structure may not always precisely correspond to the semantic or "meaning" structure, or express the relations between parts of a sentence very clearly. A better method of analyzing sentences is to break them down into what Cotterell and Turner call "nuclear sentences" or basic thought units.[7] In other words, identify each "thought deed" which a sentence does and then see how each of these "deeds" are linked or connected.[8] Earlier we gave a content outline of Ephesians 3. Within this chapter, 3:14-19 (part B of the outline) is one sentence in the RSV.

> For this reason I bow my knees before the Father, from whom every family in heaven and on earth is named, that according to the riches of his glory he may grant you to be strengthened with might through his Spirit in the inner man, and that Christ may dwell in your hearts through faith; that you, being rooted and grounded in love, may have power to comprehend with all the saints what is the breadth and length and height and depth, and to know the love of Christ which surpasses knowledge, that you may be filled with all the fullness of God.

A rough breakdown of this might be as follows[9]:

1 For this reason [because of what I said earlier], I bow my knees before the Father [i.e., I pray]
2 [interjection] Every family in heaven and on earth is named from this Father.

3 [I pray] that he may grant you to be strengthened.
4 God grants according to the riches of his glory.
5 God strengthens
6 with might
7 through his Spirit
8 in the inner man.
9 And [I pray] that Christ may dwell in your hearts.
10 Christ dwells in hearts through faith.
11 The result of being strengthened is that you may be able to comprehend.
12 What is to be comprehended is the breadth and length and height and depth [of God's love].
13 Such comprehension is a result of the fact that you are rooted and grounded in love.
14 You should comprehend this together with all the saints.
15 Another effect of God's strengthening is to know the love of Christ.
16 [even though] The love of Christ surpasses knowledge.
17 [This is desirable, because] To know Christ is to be filled with all the fullness of God.

Breaking this down into its constituent "nuclear sentences" forced us to notice and resolve the relations between them. The relations are of four basic types: *addition* (which links elements of equal prominence, see line 9); *argumentation* (which provides the grounds for another nuclear sentence; no example in this passage, but the "therefore" in line 1 shows that what went before this passage is grounds for what follows); *content specification* (which gives further precision; see line 12); and *elucidation* (which explains; see line 10).

Sometimes the links between the pieces are not perfectly clear. For example, "to know the love of Christ" (line 15) might go back further, to Paul's prayer, rather than to the strengthening, in which case line 15 would read, "I also pray that you might know the love of Christ." Also, "in the inner man" (line 8), which we took to be a content specification regarding God's strengthening (line 5), might rather be an elucidation of "through the Spirit," explaining how the Spirit's mediation works. Although these variations do not *radically* alter the sense, establishing the relations between the nuclear sentences clarifies the sense and flow of the passage. Here is something to think about: Romans 1:17, Galatians 3:11, and Hebrews 10:37-38 all quote Habakkuk 2:4 which in the original reads ambiguously: "The just by faith shall live" (authors' trans.). Does "by faith" go with "just" or "live"? That is, does this sentence say that the one whose righteousness is by faith shall live, or does it say that the one who is righteous shall live according to faith?

7.2.2.3 Words (and phrases)

As with any discipline, control of a subject entails paying close attention to detail. The details of a sentence are its words. There are three types of references useful for doing word study. The most basic is the dictionary. Greek and Hebrew students, of course, are familiar with Greek and Hebrew lexicons, which give a range of suggested English equivalents for various uses of the Greek and Hebrew words. But users of an English translation should also be ready to acknowledge their deficiency if they are unsure of the meaning of an English word. An English dictionary will clarify the possible meanings of a word, although again readers must decide which of the *possible* meanings is appropriate to the context in which the word is found. Generally only one of a word's possible meanings is appropriate.

The second reference for word study is the concordance. A complete concordance lists the words which appear in the Bible in alphabetical order and then lists each instance where that word appears. Some "complete" concordances may minimally list words such as personal pronouns and conjunctions, but as these are usually not the significant words, this is not a drawback.

Scholars have certain standard Greek and Hebrew concordances, but several of the major English versions also have concordances prepared for them. The KJV has *Cruden's*[10], *Strong's*[11], and *Young's*[12]; the rsv has *Nelson's*[13] and *Eerdmans*[14] (and, for the NT only, *Clinton Morrison's*[15]); the *New American Standard Bible* has the *New American Standard Exhaustive Concordance*[16]; the NIV has *Goodrick and Kohlenberger*[17]; the new concordance to the *New Revised Standard Version* was also prepared by Kohlenberger.[18] Naturally the reader will benefit from having a concordance which corresponds to the version he or she most frequently uses. Many people use concordances to help them locate passages uncertainly remembered. But the primary purpose of a concordance is to assist in word study.

For serious work, it is difficult for the English student to surpass *Young's* (for KJV) and the new *Eerdmans* (for RSV), which not only list all occurrences of every English word in the Bible, but do so according to what Greek or Hebrew (or Aramaic) words correspond to the English, and have indices to enable the user to track down other locations of the Greek or Hebrew word, however translated. The "exhaustive" concordances for the KJV *(Strong's)*, NASB, and NIV cover the ground perhaps even more thoroughly, in that they list every single word, including pronouns and conjunctions, and include a key which identifies which Greek and Hebrew words are used, but in our opinion these are more difficult to use than the "analytical" type. Users of other versions can still use these concordances to track down how a Greek or Hebrew word is variously used in certain contexts. As long as one bears in mind that the translators had good reasons for translating the same word differently in different contexts, such concordances are a tremendous help.

For example, suppose one reads the commandment of Exodus 20:13, which the RSV translates "You shall not kill." A look at *Young's* will indicate that the word "kill" here is not the general or common term for "kill," and a look at other passages where this particular word is used shows that, (1) it is always used of killing a human being, not an animal, (2) it is not used for killing in warfare, but only of one individual slaying another, and (3) it usually occurs in contexts that imply hatred or murder, although it can also be used for accidental manslaughter. This helps the reader perceive the meaning of the commandment. It does not prohibit the killing of animals, nor even killing of humans in warfare; it prohibits murder.[19] Of course one *could* deduce this without reference to the original language or an analytical concordance, but the concordance does make it easier.

Contrary to the advice of many textbooks on interpretation, in our opinion not too much time should be spent on word study. In fact, a great deal of dubious interpretation gets its start here. For this reason, before we leave the subject of words it is appropriate to issue some warnings against certain improper word studies.[20]

Error #1: Etymologizing

One of the most common forms of dubious exegesis is the treating of the etymology of a word as somehow key to the "real" meaning of a passage. Although the history of a word is very often related to its present meaning, it is not necessarily related. An undertaker is not "someone who undertakes," nor does he "take someone or something under." Butterflies fly but have little to do with butter. And "understanding" is not "standing under." As we pointed out in section 5.1.1, the history of "how a word got to be" is not the real question; it is rather "how the word is being used now." Even where the etymology is related to the meaning of a word, the user is hardly ever conscious of it. Do we really mean a "speaking place" when we talk about the Parliament, or think of "coming together" when Congress is mentioned?

A very famous example of bad etymologizing is the treatment sometimes accorded the word *hyperetes*, which is translated "servants" in 1 Corinthians 4:1 (and elsewhere). This word is supposed by some to have derived from *hypo* (meaning "under") and *eresso* (meaning "row") so that the "real" meaning of the word here is said to be "under-rower," like the lower-level rowers of a trireme. The conclusion is drawn that Paul is likening the apostles to the very lowest level of slaves, and some sermons have even developed the theme of squalor and death in the triremes as somehow related to this passage. But the use of the word, at least in Paul's time, had nothing to do with boats or rowing; it always referred to a servant acting as an assistant, often with an implication of delegated authority. The sentence of 1 Corinthians 4:1 is asking that the apostles be regarded as Christ's *assistants*, because they are "stewards of God's mysteries," that is, conveyors of the truth which God had formerly kept hidden but now has revealed. The context of the paragraph demonstrates that Paul is certainly not trying to convey a lowly image of the apostles to the Corinthians.

Another popular etymological conclusion is that the Greek word for "sin" means "missing the mark." That this is what it meant for Homer's archers six centuries before the NT is undoubted. It is unlikely, however, that the biblical authors saw sin as simply being a bit off target. Its usage is always in contexts demanding a meaning of "offending God."

Such etymologizing of the Greek may not occur to the English Bible user, but we mention it here because readers may encounter such things in commentaries or sermons and be unduly impressed.[21] Further, some etymologizing has even been done with English words. How many times has the meaning of the word "atonement" been specified by reference to its English etymology, "at-one-ment." This may *illustrate* a certain aspect of the meaning, but hardly helps us *identify* what the biblical writers meant.

Another kind of English etymologizing tries to define Greek words by reference to English words that are etymologically derived from them. This is unfortunately extremely common even among the best preachers. The Greek word for "power" or "ability" is the source for the English "dynamite," so preachers love to talk about "God's dynamite power." This may add color to the concept, but the apostles did not conceive God's power as something which blows things up. Another example is the word for wrath, which is popularly (though incorrectly) thought to be etymologically related to the English word "orgy." This is supposed to shed light on the intensity of God's wrath. But, of course, the English word "orgy" does not mean wrath, but an uncontrolled sensual frenzy, with connotations of sexual abandon. God's wrath is neither uncontrolled nor sensual; the English word must not be allowed to determine the meaning or connotations of the Greek word from which it came.[22] Finally, the Greek word for "cheerful" is the root for the English word "hilarious," but 2 Corinthians 9:7 is not telling us that the "hilarious" giver is the one the Lord loves, as though one had to be a comedian to give in a way that pleases God.

Error #2: Finding a "basic core"

Words that have more than one potential meaning often tempt a creative exegete to try to find the common ground that unites the multiple meanings. This sometimes ends up drawing emphasis away from the specific meaning a word has in its context, and stressing its more general or common meaning, as though, for example, the "Spirit of the Lord" (*pneuma kyriou*) really meant "master's breath." Certainly, in Jeremiah 18:11 ("I [the Lord] am shaping *evil* against you. . . . Return, every one from his evil way" [RSV].) the word "evil" has two distinct meanings. To try to come up with a single meaning for both occurrences could have dangerous results.

Error #3: Totality transfer

Earlier we warned against confusing the *meaning* of a word with its reference or usage. A complementary error in word study is to assume that in a specific occurrence of a word, everything which that word *can* mean is brought into the sentence. James Barr called this "illegitimate totality transfer."[23]

This is a particular temptation with theologically significant words. For example, the word "flesh" can mean either physical body (Ps. 38:3; Acts 2:31), human beings (Isa. 40:5; Matt. 24:22), humanness (John 1:14), meat (1 Kings 17:6; Prov. 23:20), genetic relatedness (Rom. 9:3), and sinful nature (Gal. 5:13). "Totality transfer" would allow us to read Romans 8:3 ("For what the law was powerless to do in that it was weakened by the flesh" [authors' trans].) and bring all the possible meanings of "flesh" to bear in that particular occurrence. Thus we could say the law is powerless because of our physical incapacity, it is powerless to help humans, it is powerless because meat is high in fats and cholesterol and weakens us, it is powerless because we are genetically related to Adam, and it is powerless because of our sinful nature. This may appear to be deriving a "rich" exegesis, but in fact it simply confuses things. Only one meaning, "sinful nature," is actually in view.

Error #4: Overanalysis

Once the reader knows the ways in which a word was generally used, there is usually little problem in identifying the specific usage in the passage in question. Sometimes it is beneficial to wonder, "Why did the author use this word rather than that one," but there may be no particular reason, other than stylistic preference or the fact that the author heard someone else use it more recently. While close "synonym" studies like that of R.C. Trench can be helpful in specifying the potential fields of meaning of words, they can also be misleading.[24] Authors rarely consider a range of possible synonyms to use for each word when they write. And when they do consider alternative words, it is more often for purposes of style or clarity rather than for precision. This is not to say that the exact words are unimportant, but words are only important because they make sentences. All the words which together make up the sentence must be considered together, not in isolation.

Another example of overanalysis which commonly appeals to Greek students is the treatment of the verb *agapao* as "special, divine, elective, altruistic love" or the like, and a distinction is made between this and *phileo* which is said to be ordinary friendship. Even great scholars have been carried away, finding enormous quantities of theological meaning in this single word.[25] But why then does 1 John 2:15 tell us not to love (*agapao*) the world? Is it wrong to love the world with a divine, elective, altruistic love?

Is not John rather warning us against a sinful, selfish, manipulative love of the world? Just as our English word "love" can be used in a variety of ways with both good and bad objects, so can both the Greek words *phileo* and *agapao*.[26] Our point is that it is not the individual *word* which is by itself imbued with meaning which it brings to the sentence; it is the sentence, the particular combination of words, which focuses the words into specific meaning. The meaning of Scripture is found in its *statements*, not its vocabulary.

Finally, overanalysis can attempt to achieve more precision than the language itself directly indicates. We earlier made reference to the "of " in the phrase "Gospel of Jesus Christ." The "of " simply specifies which Gospel is in view; it is the Gospel which has some relationship to Jesus Christ and is defined by that relationship. The "of " leaves open whether that relationship is possession (the Gospel which belongs to Jesus), source (the Gospel which comes from Jesus), subject (the Gospel which Jesus Christ preached), object (the Gospel which is about Jesus), or all these. The Gospel writer did not need to specify which, because such specificity was unnecessary. We often refer to "our dog" rather than "our golden retriever," so long as specificity is not required for what we wish to say.

This kind of overanalysis is particularly acute for the Greek student who feels the need to put his or her knowledge to some use and overloads the tenses of Greek verbs with meaning. Granted, the tenses (or better, *aspects*) of the Greek verb do have a semantic function, and this function is somewhat different from English tenses, which are primarily concerned with time.[27] But just as we are not usually *consciously* making fine tense decisions when we say "he's done it" rather than "he did it," the NT writers would not have been trying with their tenses to inject subtleties into their arguments or accounts.[28] Even in English, under certain circumstances we use the present tense for the future ("the Lord is coming"), the future for the imperative ("you shall not kill"), present for past ("Calvin says in his *Institutes* "), and the past for present ("what has the Lord required of you"). Tense study is valuable, but one must remember again that it is not the tense of the verb, but the sentence in which it occurs, that says things.

Our main point here is not that words or other details are unimportant. Careful attention to details can always be of benefit. Most people who read in 1 Corinthians 3:10-15 of the man who will himself be saved even though his works be burned up as wood, hay, and straw assume this is speaking of a Christian who has done unworthy works in his life. Some have even used this passage to defend the idea that good works are optional in the Christian life. But by paying attention to the words, we note that it is the one who *builds* with different materials whose *building* is being judged. And in the context, the *building* in question is the church, God's people (vv. 9, 16). Paul is concerned that church *leaders* be careful in edifying and enlarging the church according to God's intent and directives (note v. 10b).

But paying attention to detail is not the same as constructing hypotheses on the basis of a lone detail, such as the etymology or tense of a word. Interpretation should aim for simplicity, and avoid excessive subtlety. As Moisés Silva put it, "No reasonable Greek author, when wishing to make a substantive point, is likely to have depended on his reader's ability to interpret subtle syntactical distinctions."[29] Word study is valuable because each word in a sentence is a relevant detail regarding the meaning of the sentence as a whole, but isolated words by themselves do not say things, and theological conclusions cannot be drawn from single words.

In summary, the "grammatical" side of exegesis focuses on discourses and understands discourses by noting their structure and genre as well as studying their sentences and words. Something discovered in a word study may provide a more exact appreciation for the meaning of a sentence, even though it is always the sentence as a whole which determines the exact use of the word. And that sentence's meaning will give new perspective on the meaning of the paragraph and discourse. Analysis is thus both "top-down" and "bottom-up."

7.2.3 The "historical" side of exegesis: Historical and cultural background

Discourses have meaning within the context of human situations. Fortunately for interpreters of the Bible, the *topical* interest of the biblical discourse as a whole addresses humans in their universal situation of sin, their relationship to God, and their relationships with each other. It can thus easily speak to anyone. Further, many of the historical events and situations within which the Bible was written are explicitly described in the Bible itself. Thus, much of the Bible's message can be understood to some degree without a great deal of knowledge of the historical and cultural background beyond what is found in Scripture itself.

Nevertheless, the interpreter who desires a firm grasp of the meaning of a nuclear discourse within the Bible will need some knowledge of that background. Fortunately there are reams of material readily available which can fill in this background.[30]

Bible encyclopedias (sometimes also called *Bible dictionaries)* are useful for identifying items and themes in the Bible which are unfamiliar to the modern world. There are many plants, animals, and things which simply draw a blank in our minds. For example, in 1 Kings 10:11, the fleet of Hiram brings some "almugwood" to Solomon. What is almugwood? A good Bible dictionary will relay whatever scholars presently know about it. Even more important, though, are theme words which may seem more familiar to us by virtue of their frequent usage, but about which we may actually know little. Persons, places, and things in the Bible, biblical concepts and terms, chronology, and loads of other information are all available. Further, these works have summary introductions to the authorship, date, circumstances, and character of the books of the Bible. Just browsing a Bible encyclopedia can make one a better exegete. And, if one needs to find quickly "what the Bible says about" some biblical theme (e.g., "suffering"), often a Bible dictionary or encyclopedia will help. Finally, these Bible encyclopedias or dictionaries also often have articles on subjects which modern scholars frequently bandy around as having something to do with interpreting the Bible (e.g., "Dead Sea Scrolls"or "Gnosticism").

Two excellent conservative works are the *New International Standard Bible Encyclopedia*[31] and *The New Bible Dictionary* and its successor *The Illustrated Bible Dictionary.*[32] *The Interpreter's Dictionary of the Bible*[33] is also good, but is older and has less respect for the historical integrity of the Bible. But all are excellent; any of them should handle the needs of most nonprofessional exegetes. We recommend that anyone involved in serious interpretation of Scripture purchase one of these reference works.

For more specialized or detailed information than is found in the encyclopedias, Bible atlases, Bible histories, and Bible introductions are available.

Bible atlases contain maps which give information about the geography and demography of biblical times and events. One of the best is *The Macmillan Bible Atlas.*[34] Virtually every historical event involving geographic movement in the Bible has a corresponding map showing the developments. The story in Genesis 14 about the battle between the five kings and the four kings can be very confusing, but a look at the map in the Bible atlas gives the reader the overall picture very quickly.

Bible histories are not as easy to use for quick reference. Usually a Bible encyclopedia will answer a "quick question" more quickly. But a good Bible history will provide an overview of the history of biblical events in a comprehensive fashion and can make the biblical world "real" to the interpreter.

For the NT, the best and also most readable work is F.F. Bruce's *New Testament History*.[35] Bruce respects the historical integrity of the NT, and so his historical reconstruction and fitting of the NT events in with the events of the Roman world is trustworthy.

There is not to our knowledge any Bible history of recent vintage that fully respects the historical trustworthiness of the OT, but one which is relatively conservative is John Bright's, *A History of Israel*.[36]

Introductions to the NT and OT also provide background information, as well as information about the biblical books themselves. "General introduction" covers the general background of the NT or OT periods, and gives overviews of the Bible in its historical and cultural contexts. Of value here are such works as Eduard Lohse, *The New Testament Environment*[37] and W.F. Albright, *From the Stone Age to Christianity*.[38] Both of these books are fairly easy reading. "Special introduction" focuses on the circumstances of particular books, that is authorship, date, place, occasion, unity, style, and sources. Very thorough "special introductions," both of which defend the integrity of the Bible's own claims regarding authorship, are Donald Guthrie's *New Testament Introduction*[39] and R.K. Harrison's *Introduction to the Old Testament*.[40] Much of these works consists of presentation of and rejoinders to alternative scholarly opinions.

Also of note here are two new works, *Old Testament Introduction* by Tremper Longman and Ray Dillard (Grand Rapids: Zondervan, 1994) and *An Introduction to the New Testament* by D.A. Carson, Douglas J. Moo, and Leon Morris (Grand Rapids: Zondervan, 1992). These works provide not just the historical background for each book, but also an introductory literary analysis and discussion of each book's theological purposes.

Commentaries, which would include *study Bibles,* usually provide introductory material as well, and are often useful for conveying other background information with regard to specific passages. Study Bibles (recommended are the *NIV Study Bible*[41] and the forthcoming *New Geneva Study Bible*[42]) and single volume commentaries (such as the *New Bible Commentary: Revised*[43] and the *International Bible Commentary*[44]) can provide basic help, and until the student can acquire more adequate coverage these help to "fill in the blanks." But study Bibles and one-volume commentaries are of necessity so brief that they cannot give an adequate representation of even their own position, let alone alternatives.

More adequate are commentaries on single books or groups of books.[45] However, even they do not always reliably present all the background that may be needed. Since commentaries are presenting interpretations, they sometimes tend to convey whatever background is compatible with their particular interpretation. And commentaries are notorious for answering every question except the one which the researcher was interested in.

Nevertheless, competent commentators have done the background and analytical work on their portion of Scripture already, and usually have a deep knowledge of its context, historical setting, and purpose. Thus a commentary will frequently point out things which otherwise would have been missed and provide ways of looking at the text previously unconsidered.

Consulting a commentary sometimes seems like a "quick fix," a way to shortcut directly to the solution, without having to struggle with the problems of exegesis. But there is something curiously unsatisfying about simply eating someone else's pie. Further, commentaries suffer from a disease called "novelitis." Commentators frequently feel they must come up with something novel to justify the publication of the commentary, and the result is that they sometimes obfuscate what earlier seemed quite clear. Charles Spurgeon used to complain about commentators who tried constantly "to fish up some hitherto undiscovered tadpole of interpretation, and cry it 'round the town as a rare dainty." Finally, if we go to the commentaries too quickly in the course of our investigation, we will probably allow the commentaries to determine the questions or problems we address, and these questions may not be the questions which really come from the text itself. Therefore, we urge readers to save commentaries for the last step in their exegesis. Then they will be equipped to evaluate and incorporate the valid insights of commentators, and their interpretation will still be their own.

The intent in listing these resources is not to overwhelm the reader. The point is not to indicate that one must look at all these references in order to glean the background to a particular passage, but to indicate that there are many, many ways to find out that background, in whatever detail the interpreter may need.

7.3 Understanding the Bible on Its Own Terms

So far in this chapter we have focused on grammatical-historical exegesis, the task of discovering the meaning which a specific text would have had at the time it was written. But since God is ultimate author of the Bible as a whole, it is also necessary to discover what God is communicating in a particular text by relating that text to the whole Bible.

7.3.1 When Scripture uses Scripture

The most obvious application of this principle is when one passage actually refers to another. If the NT quotes an OT text, to understand what the NT writer was saying one must go back and see what the passage was saying in its original context. This will usually clarify and elucidate what the NT writer was saying. Very often a NT writer will quote only a short excerpt from a passage in Scripture, expecting his readers to know the content of the entire passage. For example, Matthew 3:3 and Mark 1:3 quote Isaiah 40:3 to describe the significance of John the Baptist (Luke 3:4-6 quotes a bit more of Isaiah). Looking at the whole passage of Isaiah 40:1-11 shows what was so exciting to the Gospel writers. And, of course, Isaiah 40 is the beginning of the prelude to the great "servant of the Lord" prophecy of Isaiah 42–55 which is climactically fulfilled in Christ. But even if the NT writer quotes a text rather fully, looking at its larger context can still lead to valuable insights. First Peter 3:10-12 gives a rather extensive quotation from Psalm 34:12-16, and at first blush this seems to do little more than give the advice that we should live peaceably with everyone. But the quotation occurs in a context in 1 Peter that deals with Christian suffering. A look at the entirety of Psalm 34 shows that it too is concerned with suffering, putting that suffering in the context of God's hearing His people and delivering them from suffering. Peter would have expected his readers to know this and see the relevance of the psalm to his exhortation.

This principle also works the other way; if one is looking at an OT text which is referred to in the NT, it is obviously of some importance to see how the NT writer used the passage; this will often indicate how the OT passage may be christologically focused and ecclesiologically applied. When we read Genesis 2:2-3, we learn that God's finishing of His initial creation was the divine pattern that led to the hallowing of the seventh day. But we might not see the connection to the Israelites' typological entry into the Promised Land and the final entry into the eternal rest of the true people of God, if it were not for Hebrews 4. Hebrews gives us a better understanding of the meaning of God's rest on the seventh day in Genesis.

7.3.2 Unifying themes of Scripture

Even if no quotations or allusions are involved, one should relate a passage to its whole Bible context. To a large extent, this is not something that can be taught. It comes with increasing familiarity with the Bible. One passage will often bring to mind another which teaches on the same subject, or addresses a similar problem. But perhaps we can point out a few "themes" which seem to arch over the Bible, and give a general frame of reference for seeing how passages relate to one another. By no means is this an exhaustive list, but these are some of the important themes.

7.3.2.1 Covenant

In the OT, one of the principal ways of describing God's dealing with His people is that of *covenant*. The word occurs over 250 times, spread through all the parts of the OT. As we noted in section 2.3.2.1, a covenant is simply the formal expression or establishment of a relationship. In the OT, almost all references to covenant are to God's formal relationship to His people.[46]

The covenantal form in the OT was patterned after other ancient Near Eastern covenants, so that Abraham, Moses, and the rest could grasp what God was doing. Covenants typically had (1) a historical prologue which named the parties and gave the background to the relationship, (2) a statement of the nature of the relationship, (3) stipulations about the obligations of the parties in the covenant, and (4) sanctions, or blessings and curses to be brought to bear upon fulfillment or violation of the covenant's terms. Covenants were usually ratified by some oath-taking ceremony which represented the curses, such as a killing of animals or circumcision.[47]

Sometimes an awareness of covenants can help in understanding what is going on in certain OT passages. One well-known text in the OT is Genesis 15:6, "Abram believed the Lord, and he credited it to him as righteousness." But not many realize that this occurs in the course of a covenant-making. The Lord had promised Abraham descendants as numerous as the stars. And following on the heels of Abraham's "justification by faith," is a covenant-making ceremony. The Lord tells Abraham to divide some animals, and when Abraham goes to sleep, he hears the promises of descendants and land reiterated, and then "a smoking firepot with a blazing torch passed between the pieces. On that day the Lord made a covenant with Abram and said 'To your descendants I give this land' " (Gen. 15:17-18). The smoke and fire were representative of God's presence (like the pillar of cloud and of fire); this ceremony was one in which God took the covenant oath.

Now this may seem strange to us, but it would have seemed *very* strange to an ancient Near Eastern person. Ordinarily it was the *inferior* who took the oath of loyalty to the superior in a covenant. But in this case God took the oath, invoking the curse on Himself as guarantee of the fulfillment of His promises. So justification by faith was possible because of God's sworn promise, not because of Abraham's greatness of faith. And when Abraham's descendants rebelled against the covenant, the curse of death devolved upon God Himself incarnate.

The NT does not much use the word "covenant" per se. The Greek word for "covenant" (sometimes translated "testament") only occurs thirty-three times in the NT, and seventeen of these occurrences are in the Book of Hebrews. Most of the recipients of the NT had either forgotten or never knew about ancient covenants, and such language would not have meant much to them. But the concept is still there, and the fulfillment of God's promises in Christ is occasionally called the "new covenant." This is, of course, a reference to the prophecy of Jeremiah 31:31-34, where God predicts a new covenant which He will write upon the hearts of His people. When Jesus instituted the Lord's Supper, He indicated that His blood (i.e., His sacrificed life) secured this covenant for His people (Luke 22:20; see Matt. 26:28; Mark 14:24). And Paul in 2 Corinthians 3 indicates that now God's Law is written on the hearts of believers.

Finally, Hebrews, addressing Jewish Christians who were more familiar with the nature of covenants, reminds its hearers of the better covenant, which has been ratified by a better sacrifice, is mediated by a better priest, and secures better results than the old covenant of Moses (Heb. 9:15-22).

Much more common in the NT is the concept of being "in Christ." All people are "in Adam" by virtue of their descent from him (Rom. 5). Just as all Abraham's descendants are incorporated under Abraham so that they share in his covenant, so are Adam's descendants incorporated into Adam, so that the curse upon his disobedience is shared by us (Rom. 5:12). But believers are also "in Christ." "For as in Adam all die, so in Christ all will be made alive" (1 Cor. 15:22). We partake of the "new covenant" in His blood, which Paul calls our "fellowship" or "communion" of the blood of Christ (1 Cor. 10:16). The blessing of Christ's obedience, therefore, also is shared by us (see Rom. 8:16-17). The blessing covenant to Abraham has come to the Gentiles "in Christ Jesus" (Gal. 3:14).

As in the OT, the concept of covenant explains certain things in the NT. The covenant to Abraham was ratified by God's oath in Genesis 15, but in Genesis 17 Abraham underwent a covenant oath ceremony as well, namely circumcision (Gen. 17:10). In the NT, the death symbol which is equivalent to this acknowledgment of God's promise covenant is not circumcision but baptism. This is why Jesus calls His death a baptism (Luke 12:50), and why Paul says in Romans 6:3 that we are baptized into Christ's death. By being covenantally linked to Christ's death we share as well in His resurrection (Rom. 6:5).

7.3.2.2 Kingdom of God

God is King over Israel (His people) and also the whole world. Adam (humankind), God's son, is set as crown prince to rule over this kingdom as God's vicegerent. After the Fall and disqualification of man, God chose a particular family (the descendants of Abraham) and location (Canaan) to exercise this vicegerency. But the regency of Israel in Canaan is only partial and representative.

Furthermore, it is subject to constant failure. But this little "kingdom of God" points toward the reestablishment of the full reign of God on earth through humankind and stands in opposition to the "kingdoms of men" who attempt to rule not as God's vicegerents but in their own power (e.g., Dan. 4) or by the power of other gods.

This is clear from the expectations of Daniel. The kingdoms of men, or "kingdoms of beasts" (see e.g., Dan. 7:12) overthrow one another until the kingdom of God crushes all the rest (Dan. 2 and 7), and God's human vicegerent, the "Son of Man," receives the everlasting dominion that shall not pass away (7:14). God is clearly sovereign over the whole historical process (Dan. 2:21), but it is only in the future that "the God of heaven will set up a kingdom that will never be destroyed" (Dan. 2:44).

When Jesus begins preaching, He proclaims that "the kingdom of God is at hand" (Mark 1:15, RSV). Jesus was not saying, of course, that up until that point God was not sovereign. He was saying that up until that point the proper vicegerency of man as crown prince under God was not being exercised; man's kingdoms were bestial or demonic. And now that *the* particular "Son of Man," God's Son, had come, this proper reign of God through His Son was about to begin. In fact, with the casting out of demons, man's proper vicegerency has already begun (Matt. 12:28; Luke 11:20). Jesus did what Adam should have done; He threw Satan out of the Garden.

Thus we "enter" the kingdom of God not by going to a certain location, but by becoming part of this reign of Jesus on earth, participating in His reign, and ruling earth under His overlordship (Eph. 2:6). This requires us to be linked to Jesus, undergoing rebirth (John 3:5-7) and tribulation (Acts 14:22; see Rom. 8:17).[48]

7.3.2.3 Already but not yet
Closely associated with the "kingdom of God" expectation is the fact that in the NT time, after Jesus had been killed and raised, this reign of God through His Son had indeed begun (Jesus has been seated at the right hand of the Majesty on high), and yet its full effects are not yet manifest.

In the first half of the twentieth century a debate raged about whether Jesus taught that the kingdom of God was purely future (Albert Schweitzer) or that the kingdom was purely already present (C.H. Dodd). Now, most scholars recognize that they were both right in their assertions and both wrong in their denials.[49]

Even when Jesus was on earth, the fact that He cast out demons by the power of God was evidence that the sovereignty had been given to the Son of Man, and the kingdom "had come" (Matt. 12:28; Luke 11:20). But on the other hand, the kingdom is yet to come in its fullness, as is clear from, for example, the Olivet discourse (Matt. 24–25; Mark 13; Luke 21).

The tension between "already" and "not yet" is even greater now that Jesus has ascended and sent the Holy Spirit. The reign of God is already here in that Christ the Son of Man now rules in heaven (see Eph. 1:20-23), and Christians now also are already raised and rule with Him (Eph. 2:6). Yet creation, and we along with it, still groans, as we anxiously await the full manifestation of God's reign which, interestingly enough in Romans 8:19-25, is a manifestation of the "sons of God," our "adoption as sons." We are already sons (8:14) but yet still await our adoption (8:23). The reign of God through His son mankind is already here, but not yet here. Geerhardus Vos[50] illustrated it this way.

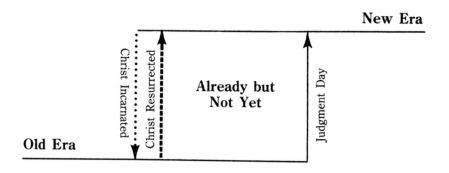

The new age is already here, even though the old has not yet passed away. This tension is evident throughout the entire NT, which was written after Jesus' ascension but before His coming again in judgment. Virtually every passage is illuminated by a recognition of this tension between already and not yet.[51]

7.3.3 Canonical analysis
In relating a passage to the whole of Scripture we should always ask the three questions based on the purpose, focus, and applica-

tion which we have noted several times: (1) How does the passage fit with the overall redemptive history of the Bible? (2) How does the passage relate to the whole Bible's focus on Jesus Christ? and (3) How does the passage apply to or instruct the church?

The redemptive-historical situation of NT texts is clear, because all the NT texts were written during the same stage of redemptive history, the stage of fulfillment, which is yet prior to the final judgment. This is the period we now live in. Further, all of the NT has to do with that stage, since it is the last stage prior to the consummation of history. A few texts in the NT relate to the very end or just before the very end of history, and the beginning of the eternal day, but even these were *originally* addressed to Christians now in this present age.

But for OT texts, the redemptive-historical question must be asked vigorously. All the material in Exodus and Leviticus on OT worship in the tabernacle cannot be understood except by way of reference to its place in redemptive history, as the Book of Hebrews so eloquently shows. Historical events such as the Exodus and the Exile cannot properly be understood except as stages in the redemptive-historical development of the purposes of God. When we read in Exodus 22:18, "do not allow a sorceress to live," does this mean we should kill the woman on our street who reads palms and holds séances, or expect the state to execute her? No, because the literal application of that prohibition pertained to a particular redemptive-historical circumstance, when the typological people of God were also a political entity which was to reflect in an external way the purity of the ultimate reign of God.[52]

Similarly, we should ask of every passage, "How does it point to Jesus Christ?" As we noted in chapters 2 and 6, this is not an expectation that every passage will speak directly about Him, but it does mean that every passage in some way relates to His person or work. And this question is just as relevant to NT passages as to OT. If we find ourselves discussing the millennium of Revelation 20 without referring it in some way to the accomplished work of Christ, we are missing its purpose. Or if we exegete the Song of Songs as "purely" a human love poem, without relating it to the overall purpose of the OT in moving toward the Christ, we are missing something of its ultimate point.

Finally we must ask, "How does the passage teach the church?" Without an application to us, why have we bothered to try to understand it? A passage may relate by informing the people of God as to who they are, or it may teach the church something about God, or it may teach what our responsibilities are, but in some way the Bible is for the church, God's people. It is not there for idle curiosity, or purely historical interest, or philosophical speculation.

7.4 Priorities of Interpretation

A chapter on "technique" needs to include some means of prioritizing results in interpretation. The message of Scripture is one and, when properly understood, no passage of Scripture contradicts another. But, given our fallibility, it is helpful to have some guidelines about where we are more likely to go wrong, and where we are less likely to go wrong, so we may give priority to the latter. There are five general priorities, many of which we have already discussed in some form.

(1) The near context is more determinative of meaning than the far context. A statement of Paul should be related to other statements of Paul before being compared to statements of Matthew or Isaiah.

(2) A didactic or systematic discussion of a subject is more significant for that subject than a historical or descriptive narrative. It should be obvious that when a historical narrative reports something as happening under some specific circumstance, one cannot draw theological conclusions from it. It has often been noted that the Jerusalem church's "having all things in common" because of its severe exigency is not necessarily a positive indication that all churches should do likewise. The fact that the first coming of the Holy Spirit was accompanied by "speaking in tongues" does not mean that all receptions of the Holy Spirit must be so accompanied; to argue so would also entail that tongues of fire be visible over the heads of receptors.

This is one reason why the idea of emulating the life of Christ can be misleading. Of course we want to be Christlike. But should we emulate His celibacy? Should we drive out money changers with a whip? Should we all engage in exorcism? Should we be circumcised as He was on the eighth day? Ought we all to restrict our preaching to Palestinian Israel? Is it appropriate for us to preach to the general public only in parables? Should we enter Jerusalem on a donkey or claim to be the Christ? Some of these are ridiculous, of course, but they illustrate that emulation of a narrative without the didactic application needs to be done very carefully.

This does not mean we cannot apply narrative material to our lives. The historical books have a purpose other than describing what happened. We can see the godliness of Joseph, David, Hannah, and we can see the godlessness of Omri, Herod, Athaliah, and the mistakes of Solomon, Uzziah, and Miriam. Watching the godly and the godless in action can help to set our own character. Further, in the whole story we see the grace of God at work, bringing His redemptive purposes to bear, and leading inexorably toward the final redemption in Christ. But these applications are indirect. The fact that godly David had several wives and committed adultery is no indication that godly men should have many wives and commit adultery. The narrative must be understood in the light of didactic material elsewhere in Scripture.

(3) Related to number 2 is *the principle that explicit teaching is more significant than supposed implications of a text.* Frequently the Bible uses concrete language in such a way that a false inference might be drawn. When Abraham demonstrated his trust in God by his obedience in offering Isaac, God says, "Now I know that you fear God" (Gen. 22:12). Should we infer from this that God did not know the true state of Abraham's heart prior to this event?

When we look at Galatians 3:28, which tells us that in Christ there is neither male nor female, we might infer from this that for Christians the distinctions between male and female have disappeared or are irrelevant for the church. After all, the distinctions between Jew and Gentile, and slave and free, have disappeared in the Gospel. But whereas Paul argued vigorously for breaking down the barrier between Jew and Gentile, he did not argue for a dissolution of slavery, though he certainly could have. The non-distinction between Jew and Gentile was of a different kind than the non-distinction between slave and freeman. Thus the non-distinction between male and female might be of a different kind than either Jew and Gentile or slave and free. We cannot conclude, therefore, that Galatians 3:28 automatically obviates all sexual differentiation on earth. If it did, Paul would have no grounds for regarding homosexuality as a mark of degradation of humanity in rebellion against God (Rom. 1:27). And the explicit indications in Ephesians 5:22-33, 1 Peter 3:1-7, 1 Corinthians 11, and 1 Timothy 2:11-15 are that Galatians 3:28 does not annihilate order in family or church in this life.

(4) Literal passages are more determinative than symbolic ones. Thus, passages which are highly symbolic in nature (such as the end of Dan. 9, the "Olivet Discourse" of Mark 13 and Matt. 24, or the Book of Revelation) should be interpreted in line with what is clearly and unambiguously stated in other passages.[53]

(5) Later passages reflect a fuller revelation than earlier. The most obvious application of this principle is that the NT takes precedence over the OT. Again, there is no real conflict between the Testaments when properly understood in their whole biblical and redemptive historical contexts, but the later revelation is fuller and clearer and occurs in our own redemptive historical context.

One more principle might be mentioned, that teachings in contexts which are central to the Bible should take precedence over teachings in more peripheral ones. The difficulty here is, who is to say what is central and what is peripheral? Further, just because a teaching is peripheral in the Bible does not mean it is not true. The central doctrines of the Bible never contradict the peripheral ones, when they are properly understood.

But it is true that central doctrines should control the interpretation of more peripheral material. Central doctrines can usually be recognized by the fact that they are frequently reiterated and assumed in Scripture, and therefore are less subject to misunderstanding. Central teachings also serve as grounds for other teachings, and the more central a doctrine is, the more likely it will be shared by Christians of many communions.

However, a central teaching should not be taken as actually in contradiction to a less central one. Many people argue that 1 Timothy 2:1-15 is less central than Galatians 3:28. Galatians 3 is dealing with some of the most important issues of Christianity, while 1 Timothy 2 is giving instructions about church order and public prayers, which would appear to most to be of less central importance. Furthermore, Paul was passionate about the matter in Galatians 3; 1 Timothy appears relatively cool. Therefore, it is argued, the *inference* from the central passage of the equality of men and women before God should overrule the *explicit* statement in the less central which forbids authoritative teaching by women in the church. But we must take great care, however, that we do not end up with one Scripture contradicting another. We cannot say that Paul was correct in Galatians but mistaken or inconsistent in 1 Timothy. We can only say that our understanding of a less central context should be less significant in building our overall interpretive framework by which we understand all Scripture. So the process of focusing on that which is central is another way of referring to progress around the hermeneutical spiral. It is not a means of setting aside the less central teachings.

7.5 Two Examples

As we stated at the beginning of this chapter, techniques are only tools to help the exegete interpret. An interpreter's presuppositional framework and goals are going to determine the way the tools are used. Techniques allow for an increase in coherence and consistency in interpretation, but they do not themselves guarantee the correct result.

Thus, analyzing a passage can improve our understanding of it in two ways. The analysis can *clarify* something which was obscure or confusing, or it can *open new perspectives* on the parts which we thought we already understood. Both these results further our progress on the hermeneutical spiral and help us understand better what God intends to teach us.

We have selected two passages to demonstrate this. The first, which is the story of Jephthah and his vow, sometimes plagues Christian readers with some confusion, but close analysis here helps to clarify things. On the other hand, many folk have always thought they understood what Revelation 20 is all about, but analysis shows that there is more than one way of looking at it; and we hope that readers of all sorts of millennial positions will see both how their own positions can be strengthened and how other interpretations might very well be worth considering.

7.5.1 Judges 11:29-40: Jephthah's vow

In accord with the pattern suggested in this chapter, we shall look at the discourse, sentences, and words, then the historical and social situation, and finally how the context of the whole Bible and the revelation in Jesus Christ affects the meaning of this passage.

Discourse: Large scale

The Book of Judges relates the history of Israel between the time of original conquest and the time of Samuel, prior to kingship. The pattern which is repeated over and over again is that Israel neglects God and goes about "doing what is right in their own eyes," which results in God punishing Israel, and then when Israel cries out to the Lord, He provides a "judge," a warrior who delivers Israel from the oppression of her enemies. They are called "judges" because they bring God's justice for His people. These judges are presented as great heroes of faith — with the exception of Samson — and even he is eventually restored and regarded as a man mighty in faith.

Discourse: Small scale

The general tenor of this story in Judges is that Jephthah was God's chosen agent for the redemption of Israel. In spite of his difficult background (an illegitimate child with no inheritance) he became God's man for the very people who had spurned him. Second, Jephthah vowed a meaningful vow, and he kept that vow even though it hurt him more deeply than he anticipated. The overall tone appears to be one of commendation, not condemnation. But human sacrifice is an abomination in Israel (Lev. 18:21; 20:2-5; Deut. 12:31; 18:10) and is unknown in Israel until the importation of Moloch worship several hundred years later under Ahaz and Manasseh. How could the author of Judges present a murder in the Lord's name as an exemplary act, or pass it by without comment?

Sentences, phrases, and words

Paying careful attention to what the sentences actually say is helpful. Several items are pertinent. First, the NIV "*what*ever comes out of the door of my house to meet me ... I will sacrifice *it*" implies that Jephthah was thinking of an animal, but the phrase "go out to meet" in verse 31 is elsewhere only used of human beings. Also, the animals which were domesticated in biblical times (sheep, goats, cattle) do not come out of the door of the house to greet their owners.[54] So the assumption is that Jephthah's vow in verse 31 had in mind a human being all along. The translation should read, "*who*ever comes out ... I will sacrifice *him*" (see RSV).

Second, the daughter of Jephthah asked for two months to bewail her *virginity*, not her youth or her untimely death. And she wails "because I will never marry" rather than "because I am going to die" (v. 37). She must remain without husband and hence without child.

Third, the conclusion of the story is the words, "And she was a virgin." This is literally "and she knew no man" (v. 39, KJV, see NASB). This is superfluous if it is simply a reiterated comment about her virginity. It makes better sense if it is explanation of the preceding sentence: "who did with her according to the vow which he had made; and she had no relations with a man" (NASB). This suggests that his vow was fulfilled not by her death but by her remaining a virgin. This explanation also has the advantage of focusing on what is explicit rather than supposedly implicit. The text speaks explicitly and repeatedly about her virginity, her never marrying, her having no relations with a man, but never states that she was killed.

It thus appears that Jephthah's vow to offer as a sacrifice the first person who comes out to meet him was a commitment to dedicate that person to the Lord, not to kill him or her.

The most difficult stumbling block for the preceding suggestion is that the word which Jephthah uses in his vow is translated "burnt offering." The common use of this word is that of the sacrifice in the tabernacle worship which was burned on the altar, and a concordance will show that almost all of its many occurrences refer to the animal sacrifice which was slaughtered and then entirely burned. Those who know Hebrew might be tempted to "etymologize" here, and point out that *olah* would not by itself necessarily carry the concept of "burnt" in it. But even without the etymologizing, close study of the texts with an analytical concordance shows that the word refers to offerings which were *wholly* given to the Lord, rather than given in token, or partly burned and partly consumed by the priests. The word thus stresses the *exclusivity* and totality of the offering, not the act of burning.

Discourse again

A further look at the discourse as a whole turns up a few more things. Sometimes this story is taken to be a warning against taking rash vows, but it does not appear that Jephthah acted rashly. When offered leadership of Gilead, he does not take up the sword at once but proceeds very cautiously. And when he does accept, he makes a treaty before the Lord. Even then he does not take up the sword, but attempts to negotiate with the Ammonites. And even when he goes to war, it is not in the heat of battle that he makes his vow, but in moments of reflection prior to the engagement. The vow has the character not of a sudden or rash act, but a promise by which, whatever the outcome, Jephthah knew he would lose something of value to him.

But a vow to offer an *animal* would have been no special vow. Military leaders always offered not one but many animals in sacrifice following a victory, even apart from vows. For this vow to be serious, it must have been costly.

Now it is sometimes objected that, if all the vow meant was to dedicate to the Lord the person who came out, why did it eventuate in such wailing and grief? Again the discourse provides the answer, for this daughter was Jephthah's only child. Since he had been cut off from his father's family, his daughter was the only family he had. And since she was the only child, he therefore had no hope of any descendants. This was devastating for a person in the ancient Near East.

Historical context

So far as redemptive historical context goes, we already noted that human sacrifice was forbidden. Further, genuine whole (burnt) offerings could only be offered to the Lord at the altar of the tabernacle, mediated by priests. Would the killing of a human sacrifice in the tabernacle have been possible?

On the other hand, there were women who were dedicated to service at the tabernacle. We know about them because of a passing reference in 1 Samuel 2:22 to the fact that the sons of Eli had violated such women. So it is probable that Jephthah's daughter was given as a "whole offering" to the Lord by being dedicated for life to service at the tabernacle.

How does this story fit in with the overall message of the Bible? Redemptive historically, it points to the fact that God's deliverance comes about through the sacrifice of a representative person. Christologically, it reminds us that God sacrificed His *only* son, just as Jephthah gave up his only daughter. And the message to the church is that Jephthah, like Abraham, was willing to give up what was dearest to him in obedience to God and so reflected the character of God. We too must be willing to offer up to the Lord whatever is most precious to us and to keep our promises to the Lord, even when it hurts far more than we anticipated.

7.5.2 Revelation 20:1-10: The Millennium

For our second illustration, let us look at a passage which has resulted in the spilling of more vitriolic ink than perhaps any other passage of Scripture, Revelation 20. We have no desire to contribute to the vitriol and should begin by pointing out that any interpretation of this highly symbolic passage will necessarily be held very tentatively. But there may be no better passage to illustrate how a passage is differently conceived within different frameworks. Let us attempt to follow our path of grammatical, historical, and canonical analysis with respect to this passage, not in any exhaustive fashion (we are ignoring numerous exegetical as well as theological questions), but to get a glimpse of how the tools work.

Revelation 20 is usually interpreted as either a 1,000-year golden age following the return of Christ, but prior to the final judgment (premillennialism[55]), or as a future golden age prior to Christ's return as the ultimate expression of Christ's victory (postmillennialism), or as a symbolic way of referring to the fact that Christ already rules with His saints in the present age (amileniaalism or realized millennialism).[56]

Discourse analysis: Large scale
The chapter occurs within the larger context of the Book of Revelation, and so the overall view of Revelation is highly determinative for our understanding of this passage. There are three main ways of approaching the book as a whole: the "preterist" view regards most of the Book of Revelation, except for the ending, as focused on the situation of Christians in the Roman Empire of the first century. The "futurist" view regards everything after chapter 4 as prophecy of the (final) future. The "historicist" view regards the various visions of the book as reflecting different stages of church history, from the first century to the final judgment.

There is no exact correspondence between these approaches and one's view of chapter 20, but there are certainly perceivable tendencies. The preterist view will usually regard chapter 20 as one more picture of the situation of the early church, and is more likely to reach an amillennial conclusion. Of course, if the beginning of chapter 20, or somewhere in 19, is regarded as the shift of venue to the last judgment, the interpreter may be a premillennialist.

The historicist view is more likely to see chapter 20 as the last age in church history prior to the final judgment of 20:11ff, so most of those who take a historicist approach are postmillennial. And of course futurists are more likely to come to premillennial conclusions.

In our view, these three approaches are too simplistic. Certainly, if the Book of Revelation, written in the first century and addressed to the church of the first century, was intended to aid and comfort the church in this world, it must have said at least some things directly to them. So at least in some sense the material must be preterite. On the other hand, the book was written not only for the first-century church, but for the church of this whole age, and one might expect at least some elements of the historicist approach. But a large amount of the comfort of the Gospel comes from its hope for the future, so there also must be a great deal in the way of future expectation. The nature of this large discourse, the Book of Revelation, cannot therefore be easily decided before looking at the text in detail.

Views regarding the structure of the book also come into play. Here, there are two main approaches, a *linear* view and a *cyclic* view. Those who take a cyclic approach argue that the other example of apocalyptic in the Bible, the Book of Daniel, is cyclic. It gives various visions presenting different images of the same periods of redemptive history. Certainly the dream of Nebuchadnezzar in Daniel 2, and the visions of beasts in chapter 7, follow the same future but with different symbols. In Revelation, the "cyclists" point to features like the sixth and seventh seals in 6:12–8:1, which certainly sounds like the final judgment of 19–20, with the ultimate destruction of God's enemies, the great victory song of the Lamb, and eternal bliss, and argue that these cover the same events of final judgment. And, of course, the portent of chapter 12 seems to refer to the birth of Christ and Satan's attempt to destroy Him. This, of course, has already happened.

Those holding the linear approach, however, point to the fact that, unlike the Book of Daniel, Revelation does not have any clear changes of venue or time, marking off visions as separate. It reads as a single prophecy, rather than several prophecies brought together. They accept that the portent in Revelation 12 is a backward glance, but argue that it is a *reminder* of Satan's activities and power that happens in the future. And they note certain differences between the judgment material of chapters 6–7 and that of chapter 20.

Again the matter is not easy to solve. Let us then look in greater detail at Revelation 20:1-10.

Discourse analysis: Small scale

The only evident sub-discourse marker is the recurring phrase "And I saw." This is not completely reliable, but 20:1 does start off with these words, as does 20:4 and 20:11 ("Then I saw"), which might be considered as beginning new nuclear discourses. So we might start by considering 20:1-10 as consisting of two nuclear discourses, verses 1-3 and 4-10.

On the other hand, verses 7-10 are thematically very closely linked to verses 1-3, picking up the theme of the activity of Satan at the end of the thousand years. So the thematic progress seems to be the binding of Satan for the thousand years, the reign with Christ of "those who had been beheaded . . . and had not received the mark" (v. 4) during that thousand-year period, and then the temporary release and final judgment of Satan after the thousand years. The two sections on Satan, and the middle section on the reign of the martyrs with Christ, are joined by the theme of the "thousand years."

Sentence and word analysis

Questions now need to be asked about the meaning of several items in the passage.

(1) What is the "thousand years"? Is it literal or figurative? If it is figurative, what does it symbolize? If it is literal, when does it occur?

(2) What is the nature of the "binding" and the "casting into the Abyss" (vv. 2-3), and what is meant by Satan's "deceiving the nations"? (vv. 3, 8)

(3) Who sat upon the thrones and lived and reigned with Christ during the thousand years? (v. 4)

(4) What is meant by "living" and "reigning"? (v. 4)

(5) What and when is "the first resurrection"? (vv. 5-6)

Each of the three viewpoints can make a coherent whole out of this discourse, by answering these questions differently.

The amillennialist argues that, since numbers in Revelation clearly have a symbolic function, even if they are literal, the "thousand" is a symbolic number and simply means an age of history. He or she will point to the fact that Satan is bound specifically "to keep him from deceiving the nations anymore." Jesus indicated that His ministry of setting Satan's captives free was also a binding of the "strong man," Satan (Mark 3:27). It is therefore argued that the binding in Revelation 20 is not a general cessation of all Satan's activities, but his inability to keep the nations in the darkness of idolatry, without knowledge of the true God. The ones who sit on thrones are those who have died in Christ, especially those killed for the sake of the Gospel. Amillennialists use a concordance, and point to the use of the word "souls" and argue that this is not an instance of "souls" being used to mean "people" (as in Acts 2:41), since it is qualified by the genitive phrase "of those who had been beheaded." It makes no sense to refer to the "people of those who had been beheaded," so souls must refer to a part or aspect of people. The concordance indeed shows that in all instances where "souls" means people, it has no qualifying genitive phrase (an "of" clause). Earlier, in Revelation 6:9, the "souls of those who had been slain" is closely parallel to 20:4, and therefore both must mean *disembodied* souls. Thus their "living and reigning" means living and reigning in heaven now with Jesus while waiting for the final resurrection. The "first" resurrection is thus a "resurrection in Christ." It is a non-literal resurrection, just as the "second" death is a non-literal death. Literal (second) resurrection and literal (first) death are not qualified by any ordinal numbers in the text. Therefore, says the amillennialist, the millennium of Revelation 20 is not a literal, future, 1,000-year, semi-golden age which is spoiled at the end by the release of Satan, but rather it symbolizes the *spiritual* victory of Christ during the present age. At the end of the age, the nations will again become united under an idolatrous power, and then the Lord will return in glory and the final judgment will take place.

The postmillennialist agrees with the amillennialist on the symbolic nature of the passage, but argues that the binding and limiting of Satan must be much more evident than has been in the period from Christ's resurrection to the present. Satan is still prowling around like a roaring lion, seeking whom he may devour (1 Peter 5:8). And it is argued that the "thousand years," while not necessarily numerically precise, must have some connection with a literal period of time. For example, the twenty-four elders and the twelve tribes are symbolic numbers, but they could quite well be literal numbers too. So in this view the thousand years cannot be the present age, but must be a future semi-golden age, a foretaste of eternity, in which God's victory is accomplished in fullness *on earth*. "Those who lived and reigned with Christ" are the believers of that time, and the "first resurrection" is understood as the "new birth" rather than the state of the disembodied saints in heaven. They can point to passages like Ephesians 2:1-6 to show that conversion to Christianity is like dying and coming to life again, and that when we have come to life in Christ, we reign with Him. As the Gospel by God's power makes progress in the world, eventually most of the world will be subject to the spiritual reign of Christ on earth, until the very end when a brief but wide-spread and intense resurgence of satanic activity will be finally overthrown by the physical return of Christ.

The premillennialist agrees with the postmillennialist that the thousand years is more literal and hence future, and that the binding of Satan does not appear to describe the present state of affairs. But the premillennialist would, along with the millennialist, argue that "those who had been beheaded" does not well describe believers in this life, especially in a golden age of obedience when most of the world is Christian. Why would Christians living in such an age be beheaded and persecuted for not receiving the beast's mark? And surely the passage gives some encouragement to Christians who *now*, prior to the millennium, are being martyred. Further, both pre- and amillennialists would argue against the postmillennialist that the binding and casting of Satan appears to be a *decisive* event; the symbol does not seem to work well as a *gradual* overcoming of Satan. So premillennialists understand the thousand years as a period after the return of Christ, when believers, but not unbelievers, are literally resurrected (the "first" resurrection). They literally live and reign with Christ during the thousand years. This fits better with verse 5, where the "rest of the dead did not live *until* the thousand years was ended" (authors' trans.). The "until" would ordinarily imply that after the thousand years the rest of the dead did come to life. This is difficult for amillennialists and postmillennialists, for the "rest of the dead" would not begin life in heaven as disembodied spirits or become Christians *after* the end of the millennium.

Discourse analysis again
Each of these viewpoints can also argue from a particular perspective on the nature of the book as a whole. If Revelation 20 *chrono-*

logically follows the events of chapter 19, the premillennial view-point appears more likely, and those who hold this view can point to 20:10 as a backward reference to 19:20 and argue that therefore they are a linear, not a cyclic sequence of visions. The amillennialist can point to the way the pattern of rebellion and judgment, persecution and deliverance, occurs over and over in Revelation and argue that Revelation 19 presents a scene of final judgment, and thus is parallel to 20:10ff, but not 20:1-9. Both post- and amillennialists would argue that chapter 20 represents a deeper picture, a different view, than 19, and thus the backward reference to 19:20 in 20:10 is to draw the similarity: just as in the picture of chapter 19 the beast and the false prophet were thrown into the lake of fire at the end of history, so in 20:10 with the focus on Satan, he is likewise destroyed at the end of history.

Historical analysis

Historical analysis will, of course, be less significant for the premillennialist who holds most of the book to refer to what is still future, but even so, historical background study could also turn up some interesting material. It was, for example, not uncommon for writers in the "apocalyptic" genre to speak of "thousand year" periods as ages of the world. There were a thousand years (approximately) between Abraham and David, and another thousand years between David and the first century. From this, theologically significant millennia were extrapolated backward and forward, with the last being a golden age of God's victory on earth. For example, the Epistle of Barnabas (an early second-century Christian tract) spoke of seven different millennia, each representing an age of the world.

Therefore, the premillennialist and postmillennialist will argue that, since John the seer was using a known figure of apocalyptic genre, its meaning must be according to the popular use of it, which means a literal 1,000-year period is in view. But the amillennialist could argue that the apocalyptic genre was already using the "thousand year" periods symbolically, and in any case, John in using the symbol was under no obligation to use it in exactly the same way other apocalyptic writers were.

For the amillennialist, especially for one with a preterist approach to the whole book, the historical background is more crucial. The promise regarding the "souls of those who had been beheaded" (20:4) and those "slain because of the word of God" in 6:9 would give special comfort to those who had been bereaved by persecution, and special encouragement to those being faced with it. Life was vicious in the ancient world, and the ability to recognize Satan as its motivator and God as having already won the decisive battle through Christ was a valued fortification for Christians in their day-to-day struggles.

Canonical analysis

When it comes to understanding this passage in relation to the rest of Scripture, the issue becomes even more complicated. Some questions, such as the identity of Gog and Magog, may be answered with reference to Ezekiel 38:2 from where the language is borrowed. (There are actually several allusions to Ezekiel 38 in verses 7-10.) But the answer even so may not be clear, since Ezekiel 38 is itself quite difficult, and the use of the terms by John the seer may not correspond literally to the same Gog and Magog which Ezekiel had in mind, any more than the "Babylon" of Revelation 19 is the literal Mesopotamian city.

Along more general lines, the premillennialist will connect the passage with Isaiah 65:18-25 which describes a future golden age on earth, but which appears still to be marked by sin and death. The amillennialist will point out that the passage in Isaiah 65 begins with verse 17: "For behold, I will create new heavens and a new earth" and argue that, since this corresponds with Revelation 21:1, Isaiah 65 is not about the millennium but about eternity. But then the amillennialist has difficulty explaining how death and sin can be mentioned.

Conclusion

Our point in all this is to show that each of the viewpoints can be worked through exegetically. Each viewpoint can also give explanations for the difficulties it encounters. Only one view can be right, of course, but Revelation is not clear enough to allow certainty on this issue (and therefore millennial positions should not divide Christians). It might turn out that all parties will be surprised (although hopefully not "taken by surprise").

Solving this question is fortunately not central to the message of the Book of Revelation. This book is one of hope, which means that the victory which God will ultimately and absolutely bring to completion in the future through Christ is certain and will be unmistakable. The attempt to answer every detail about the meaning of each symbol in the book may be an interesting exercise and even be spiritually uplifting, but prophecy generally does not have the character of a newspaper written in advance. No OT prophecy that we know by NT testimony to have been fulfilled in the first coming of Christ reads like a newspaper account of what actually did happen. The focus is always on God's ordaining history and bringing His plans to fulfillment. Revelation is a revealing. It reveals to us the enormity of spiritual forces of wickedness that both now and in the future make war against God's people, but it also enables us to see the greatness and finality of the coming victory, which with the coming of Christ has already begun. This much we can see clearly in Revelation 20, as well as in the whole of the book.

EIGHT

BIBLICAL GENRES

The books of the Bible represent several genres, or types of literary composition. In the OT there are worship literature, historical narratives, love poems, prophecies, legal codes, and wisdom literature. In the NT there are Gospels, historical narratives, epistles, and an apocalypse.

Within these book genres, the authors made use of several literary forms which are also genres. A "proverb," for example, is a certain genre; a short, pithy form, dealing with ethical wisdom, which often uses metaphor or hyperbole to give it an emotive effectiveness.

An appreciation for the diversity of genres within Scripture is crucial to its interpretation, because different genres require different ways of reading them. In this survey, we cannot hope to cover all the genres that occur in the Bible, but we will here look at a few of the more common genres that sometimes give special trouble in interpretation, namely theological history, law, poetry, prophecy, parable, epistle, and apocalyptic.

8.1 Theological History

The largest part of the Bible tells a story, the story of God's dealing with humans. Most of Genesis to Esther in the OT, and the Gospels and Acts in the NT, are biblical history. But when we claim that these books are *history*, are we saying these books are the same genre as modern history books?

Most history writing has the legitimate goal of rendering a coherent account of human events which accurately reflects the participants' experience of the events and fairly interprets both their synchronic and diachronic connections. What sets "modern" history apart is that it attempts to do so by reference exclusively to the causes and effects of this world. In other words, modern history interprets the data according to a presuppositional framework which assumes that God does not directly intervene in the course of human events. The history writing of the Bible, however, does not exactly conform to either the goal or the limitation of modern history writing. Biblical writers constantly make reference to supernatural causes, particularly God's plans and activities, and they not only reflect the sensate experiences of events, but they undergird the story with theological meaning and instruction, both explicit and implicit. Biblical history is never value-free and never limited to this-worldly causes.

However, modern history and biblical history do have two things in common. First, it is still a recounting of real space-time events which are important to the existential understanding of a people. It does make connections to other contemporaneous events, as well as to the past and future. Second, both biblical and modern Western history are putting forth *viewpoints* of the *meaning* of events. The major difference is, of course, that the biblical history writers relate things from a transcendent position. They adopt a standpoint outside the world, looking down on it and elucidating the supernatural purposes lying behind the natural events. They write from the standpoint of God. This is why much of the Bible reads like a novel, with reports of conversational exchanges, glimpses of people's inner thoughts, and judgments regarding their motives. It is not because the biblical writers "made up" the events, but that reporting style was much more closely related to the story genre than is modern history.[1]

The Books of Samuel and Kings, for example, were written to answer a question vital to Israel in exile: "Why is this happening to us?" Deuteronomy 27–28 had warned the people against covenant breaking; Samuel–Kings shows how it happened and explains the exile. Later, Chronicles covers the same ground historically, but it was written for different purposes, one of which was to reassure the people of God's continuity of purpose with them. It thus provides more of an eschatological, typological cast to past events.

Although a variety of subordinate genres are used in theological history (e.g., biographical sections, royal chronologies, genealogies, parables, prophecy, riddles, apocalyptic), all theological history writing, both OT and NT, has three purposes:

(1) to show how God's activity and purposes with His people were worked out in the past — that is, *to tell a story*,

(2) to show how that past activity has constituted that people — that is, *to establish an identity*, and

(3) to teach how God's people now should obey and trust this same God — that is, *to demand a response*.

From our NT perspective, these three purposes correspond to the redemptive historical context, the christological focus, and the ecclesiological application. Biblical history relates both events and their meaning; it is both theology and history.

Many modern scholars who want to emphasize the theological nature of this history like to speak of it as "myth," particularly with reference to the so-called prehistory of Genesis 1–11. Although efforts are often made to make the term myth palatable by defining it simply as "a story (either real or imaginary) that has religious meaning," or "archetypal history,"[2] to our minds the term has certain connotations which make it unsuitable for describing biblical-theological history. First, the common meaning of the term myth in popular parlance is "a fabulous and untrue story," not a "religiously significant story." The Holocaust of World War II has enormous religious significance for modern Jews, but we suspect that if someone called the story of the Holocaust a myth many Jews would take offense. The Holocaust is of religious significance to Jews precisely because it actually happened in real space and time. And the Fall of Adam in Genesis 3 is of religious significance precisely because it actually happened in real space and time. Second, myth connotes pagan cosmologies and fables of false supernaturals (superstition). Third, the application of the term myth to an "archetypal history" stems from a comparative religions framework. It assumes that biblical religion is one religion among many, and like them has its "myths" about the origin of humanity and the human situation which are the product of a primitive socio-cultural entity, namely, ancient Israel in the matrix of a mixed Canaanite religious environment.

But the biblical writers themselves think that biblical history is *unlike* the pagan mythology (see 2 Peter 1:16: "we did not follow cleverly devised myths," RSV), in that the biblical events actually happened in *this world*. Even Genesis 1–11 is understood by other biblical writers as being about actual space-time events and people (see Matt. 19:4-5; Rom. 5:12-21; 1 Tim. 2:13-14; Heb. 11:3-7; 1 Peter 3:20). The Bible does use the linguistic forms and anthropomorphisms which also occur in pagan mythology to express religious content. Psalm 68, for example, uses imagery similar to the Canaanites' representation of Baal. But it applied those forms to God's working in history. God manifested Himself in real space and time.

Thus the Bible "demythologized" the ancient world. It is remarkable how free the Bible is of speculation about preexistence or the afterlife. The majority of the OT's dry and noncommittal statements about Sheol appear far short of the clear expectation of resurrection found in the later books of the OT and in the NT, but with Egyptian, Persian, and other speculation about the afterlife rampant, the first task at hand was to defuse such speculation. And the creation account in Genesis, unlike that of other ancient Near Eastern cultures, is very sparing with information about *how* God created the earth and its inhabitants. Biblical history is not myth, but a true story, told with theological purpose and vantage point. It may use the images and linguistic forms of its environment, but slipping in the term myth by redefinition really results in a reduction of the uniqueness of the biblical history.

When it comes to the practical matters of interpreting biblical history, the fact that it is both history and theology means that first, we must respect the historical integrity of the texts, and second, we must recognize a purpose deeper than telling "what actually happened" from a human standpoint. Both OT and NT historical books *interpret* history, and they give us the divine viewpoint. In some cases more than one historical vantage point is necessary for us to get the full meaning of events, which is why we have four Gospels and two accounts of the monarchic period in the OT. Biblical history not only records the events of redemptive history, but explains the redemptive meaning of those events. This means that, when dealing with a historical text, we must ask, "What is the theological *purpose* of this text, and in *what way* is it relating the history?"

8.2 Law

Nestled in the redemptive history, particularly in the OT but also in the NT, are several indications of the ethical standards which God has for His people. This should indicate the appropriate hierarchy of genre. Biblical law is subordinate to biblical redemptive history.

This is hardly to say that law is unimportant. Perhaps no more significant indication of the importance of the Law for redemptive history can be found than the words of Jesus on this very issue. In Matthew 5 Jesus sharply refutes any notion that the Gospel does away with the Law. "Do not think that I have come to abolish the

Law or the Prophets . . . but to fulfill them" (v. 17). And, "not the smallest letter, not the least stroke of a pen, will by any means disappear from the Law until everything is accomplished" (v. 18). But the idea of the Law being *fulfilled* means that it looks beyond itself. It exists not for itself but in relation to that which fulfills it. Actually, the Hebrew for Law is *torah*, which means "instruction." The Law is not just a recounting of ethical standards but is part of the story of God's redemption and His covenant with His people.

The Law is thus not abrogated or reduced to unimportance, but it is bound up with redemption. Our obedience to God is a result of His relationship with us, not a means of gaining that relationship (Gal. 3–4). The Law then is given by God as a part of His redemptive activity. Divorced from the redemptive activity of God, the legal material becomes something other than redemptive. This was the mistake which had to be combated first by Jesus (Matt. 23:13-36), and later by Paul (especially in Romans and Galatians). Thus the first principle in interpreting a legal or ethical passage in the Bible is to place it in its redemptive historical context. This identifies in what way the passage now relates to the church.

Particularly with regard to OT law, the legal material of Exodus and Deuteronomy were addressed to a specific situation, where the people of God spiritually were also a political entity. In order to determine how a specific "law" may apply to God's people today, we must first ask how that law functioned in its redemptive historical context. Two types of distinctions emerge from this inquiry. First, a law may be a *case* law or *apodictic* law. Second, law in the theocratic typological kingdom of God in Israel involved laws having to do with governance and administration (civil law), and laws having to do with the cult (ceremonial law), as well as moral laws.

8.2.1 Case versus apodictic law

Apodictic law expresses general principles. The Ten Commandments of Exodus 20 are an example of apodictic law: "You shall have no other gods before me" (Ex. 20:3) is a *general principle*. On the other hand, the Ten Commandments are followed (Ex. 21–22) with laws which address specific cases, often beginning with an "if" or "when" or "whoever" clause. These are case laws: "When a man causes a field or vineyard to be grazed over, or lets his beast loose and it feeds in another man's field, he shall make restitution from the best in his own field and in his own vineyard" (Ex. 22:5,

RSV). Case laws are applications of apodictic law, and often express means of identifying and rectifying specific violations of apodictic law.

It is usually recognized that case laws in the OT are often not pertinent to the present cultural situation, and even if they appear to be pertinent, case laws first require an extrapolation of the principle(s) lying behind them. In the case of Exodus 22:5 above, the principle is, of course, that of Exodus 20:15: "You shall not steal." (Note, however, that the Ten Commandments are marked out as special—God spoke them directly to the people and wrote them on the tablets. The case laws were given only to Moses as mediator.)

8.2.2 Civil, ceremonial, and moral law
The second type of distinction, amongst civil, ceremonial, and moral law, is more difficult. There is no easy way to tell whether a law is in one category or another. There are no typical linguistic forms that mark off one type from another, and the different types are all mixed together. For example, Leviticus 19:18 ("love your neighbor as yourself") which Jesus declared to be the second most important principial law of the OT, is followed immediately by the injunction not to interbreed cattle, sow a field with two different kinds of grain, or make garments of mixed material (Lev. 19:19). The only guide to classification is content.

Also, the ethical/civil/ceremonial distinction is not indigenous to the OT itself. Nevertheless, it is useful because it spells out specifically the ways in which the relation of the OT laws to the people of God has changed with the changing of the redemptive historical situation.

Each of these types of law has its meaning in Christ, and each points to Christ, but in different ways. With the fulfillment of the *whole* Law by Christ, that aspect of the OT Law which functioned primarily as a formal symbol of His redemptive work is "ceremonial," and it is no longer appropriate to perform or observe it. In fact, to require its performance now would negate the meaning of the symbol, in that it would deny that Christ had fulfilled it. That aspect of the OT Law which functioned as a civil law for the OT theocracy served as a symbol of the coming reign of God, the reestablishment of human vicegerency on earth. It too is fulfilled in Christ, who has in fact already reestablished the true kingdom of God, His sovereign reign, although it is not yet fully implemented. The "civil" aspect of the Law does not relate directly to contemporary civil governments which are not the kingdom of God. Even the moral Law relates differently now to believers since it is no longer a "custodian" (Gal. 3:24, RSV) or "pedagogue," but is written on our hearts by the Spirit (Jer. 31:31-34; 2 Cor. 3:6). Christ's fulfillment of the moral aspect of the Law results in "the righteous requirements of the law [being] fully met in us, who do not live according to the sinful nature but according to the Spirit" (Rom. 8:4).

8.3 Poetry

Samuel Taylor Coleridge defined a poem as "that species of composition which is opposed to works of science, by proposing for its immediate object, pleasure, not truth."[3] Modern poetry seems to delight in ambiguity and uses the evocative power of words to generate a mystical "aesthetic" experience. But such an idea of poetry is modern. Ancient — and especially biblical — poetry is not a purely aesthetic object, but is indeed concerned with the communication of truth. So although we call it biblical "poetry" because it is artistic and beautiful language, it is not deliberately ambiguous or mystical.

8.3.1 Old Testament

The distinguishing mark of poetry in the OT is not primarily rhyme, alliteration, or meter (although these occur from time to time), but what is commonly called "parallelism."[4] Parallelism occurs where two (or more) lines of approximately equal length in numbers of syllables and similar grammatical structure deal with the same subject. The second line advances a bit more information or a different depiction than the first line, either by addition, contrast, or specification.

Fortunately, almost all modern translations and even original language editions of the OT now set out poetic sections in strophic format, so readers can easily see the poetic lines. When interpreting an OT poetic text, it is often useful to ask, "In what way does the second (or third) line add to or advance the material of the first?" The fact that lines are at least partly reiterative also helps to clarify the meaning of cryptic lines. The meaning of "I am like a flourishing olive tree in the house of God" (Ps. 52:8) can be understood because the next line is parallel: "I trust in God's unfailing love."

Poetry occurs in historical material (e.g., Ex. 15; Jud. 5), prophecy (most of the work of the writing prophets is poetry), and wisdom literature (which is also in mostly poetic form). But the poetic form is most consistently used in worship literature. Poetry was sung (note how the heading of a psalm frequently specifies the tune to be used), and singing was intrinsic to worship. The Psalms are, of course, entirely poetry. And the great praises of the historical books, which were sung (e.g., Ex. 15:1), are psalm-like.

Within the Psalms there are several different types. The pioneer of classification of Psalms, Hermann Gunkel,[5] distinguished five major types: hymns (e.g., Ps. 103), communal laments (e.g., Ps. 44), royal psalms (e.g., Ps. 2), individual laments (e.g., Ps. 22), and thanksgiving psalms (e.g., Ps. 138). He also identified other minor types, of which the most clearly identifiable is the wisdom psalm (e.g., Ps. 1) and recognized a large class of "mixed" types which contain elements from more than one type. Subsequent to Gunkel, other scholars have argued for other particular types, such as psalms of Yahweh's kingship (Pss. 47; 93; 96–99), psalms of confidence (e.g., Ps. 23), and historical psalms (e.g., Ps. 106).

Whether or not we adopt Gunkel's classification system,[6] it is often helpful to look at a psalm in comparison with others, to see in what ways it is similar to and different from them. But since classification is largely on the basis of content, it cannot help too much in identifying what that content is. And the historical reconstructions which some scholars attempt seem to us so speculative and tentative that little weight can be placed upon them.[7] So, when anyone is interpreting a psalm, it is better to attempt to recognize its character before looking at any commentaries to see what its classification is "supposed" to be. Some psalms defy grouping with any others, and forcing them into a classification can obscure rather than elucidate their meaning.

8.3.2 New Testament

Although there are no books of a poetic genre in the NT, there are several places where poetry occurs.[8] The songs of Mary, Zechariah, and Simeon in Luke 1 and 2, and the victory songs throughout Revelation, are clear examples, because they follow the form of OT parallelism. And Paul introduces the hymnic extract in Ephesians 5:14:

Wake up, O sleeper, rise from the dead,
and Christ will shine on you.

with the words, "this is why it is said," which suggests it was derived or adapted from an early Christian hymn already known to his addressees. But simply because there is evidence of poetic form does not mean the author is necessarily borrowing at that point. First Timothy 3:16 has a repeated parallel grammatical structure that marks it as some kind of poetry:

He appeared in a body
was vindicated by the Spirit,
    was seen by angels,
was preached among the nations,
was believed on in the world,
    was taken up in glory.[9]

And perhaps this reflects a creedal formula already known in the church, although it equally well might be Paul's own formulation. Certainly, 1 John 2:12-14 is an instance where it is apparent that the author himself used a poetic structure in the course of his writing:

I write to you, children . . .
I write to you, fathers . . .
I write to you, young men . . .
I write to you, children . . .
I write to you, fathers . . .
I write to you, young men . . .

So it is not at all clear that instances of poetry are borrowed. Surely other authors of the NT were also capable of writing a poetic line or two in the course of their literary work.

Other possible instances of NT poetry are not as clear.[10] The most famous example of a *possible* poem is Philippians 2:5-11.[11] If this passage is Paul's recitation or adaptation of a previously existing hymn, it might explain the cryptic vocabulary, the short anarthrous phrases, and the non-Pauline style; and awareness of its hymnic origins may warn us against making too much of the use of a particular word. It also would demonstrate that the NT ideas of Christ's preexistence and deity did not originate with Paul.

However, since scholars are far from agreement on what the marks of Christian hymns in the NT are, and since the interpretive benefits from the recognition of such hymns are not obvious, in our opinion it is better not to worry overmuch about discovering or identifying NT poetry. Philippians 2:5-11 is valuable and has meaning *in its present context* in Paul's letter, not as some independent hymn outside of the letter. The question then is not "what did the hymn mean before Paul used it?" but "what does Paul mean by this hymn?"

8.4 Prophecy

Prophecy has a notorious reputation for being difficult to interpret. This is not surprising, in that prophecy, even that which is not directed toward the future, tends toward highly metaphoric language.[12] And the visions of the future that God sent His prophets on occasion seem filled with difficult pictures and symbols.

But in our opinion a great deal of this notoriety comes not from the difficulties of the symbolic language (although that is hard enough), but from misconceived notions about what kind of information prophecy is conveying.

Like all Scripture, prophecy is "useful for teaching, rebuking, correcting, and training in righteousness" (2 Tim. 3:16). In the OT, most prophecy's immediate concern was the condemnation of wicked behavior, threats of punishment, and the exhortation to repentance. These condemnations, threats, and exhortations were sometimes accompanied by a reiteration of the promises of God, lest the punishment overwhelm the people (as with Isaiah and Jeremiah). And sometimes prophecy came in the midst of the punishment, when the people needed encouragement (as with Daniel and Ezekiel). Such prophecy is profitable because it reminds us also of our obligations to obedience, our liability to punishment, and our need to repent. And it encourages us with regard to the future as we look forward to God's ultimate deliverance and the destruction of all his and our enemies.

But the way in which this "encouragement regarding the future" helps us is not by giving us the news headlines in advance, but by pointing to the victorious God who has already won the decisive heavenly battle. As noted earlier, the OT prophecies which the NT says have been fulfilled in Christ are not in the form of a precise historical account ahead of time. Even where prophetic details turned out to be historically fulfilled, they occurred in symbolic settings where it would have been impossible to tell which details would be literally fulfilled. For example, Micah 5:2 prophesies the detail of the Messiah's birth in Bethlehem, but its context speaks only symbolically of what the Messiah will be like or accomplish. Psalm 22:16-17 mentions two details that were literally fulfilled in history: the piercing of Jesus' hands and feet, and the casting of lots for His garment (John 19:24). But the piercing was not done by literal dogs (v. 16) and there is no record of any bulls (v. 12), lions (v. 21), or swords (v. 20) at the crucifixion. And Psalm 22 is perhaps not even a prophecy in its original intent, but a lament of a righteous sufferer, which *became* prophetic because of Christ being the ultimate and only truly righteous sufferer.

Thus, when we interpret prophecy, just as with other material, we must try to understand the metaphors and symbols in *historical* and *canonical* context. Symbols are highly adaptable and easily subject to myriads of different interpretations. The only controls available are first, to ask what the symbols would have meant to the author and his audience, and second, to ask how a symbol functions in the Bible as a whole. For example, what would the symbol of the sun darkening and the moon turning to blood mean? If we look at, for example, the contexts of Isaiah 13:10; Joel 2:10, 31 (see Acts 2:20); Amos 8:9; Matt. 24:29 (= Mark 13:24 = Luke 21:25); Luke 23:45; and Revelation 6:12, we see that heavenly portents were a sign of events of great significance and change. Sometimes they were literally manifested, as in the case of Jesus' crucifixion, but sometimes they are only figurative, as in Acts 2:19-20, where Peter by inspiration says that the prophecy of Joel 2 was fulfilled at the coming of the Spirit (Acts 2:16). This may mean that Matthew 24:29/Mark 13:24 is referring not to the literal destruction of *physical* entities in outer space, but to the upheaval and overthrow of *political* entities and/or *spiritual* forces on earth.

With regard to prophecy we should again ask one further question: Can prophecy have multiple fulfillments? Earlier we argued that, instead of referring to double fulfillment we ought to speak of preliminary and complete, or typical (shadow) and antitypical (real) fulfillment. In other words, the earlier fulfillment is itself prophetic of the later fulfillment. Second Samuel 7:14 had a preliminary but incomplete fulfillment in Solomon, and an extensive and complete fulfillment in Christ (Heb. 1:5). The preliminary fulfillment acts as a "down payment" on the final and ultimate.

When we come specifically to NT prophecy, this same mode may be operating, and perhaps this is the key to the Olivet Discourse of Matthew 24/Mark 13/Luke 21. There are clear references in the discourse to events that happened in A.D. 70: the temple left with not one stone on another and Jerusalem besieged. But there are also elements that seem to go beyond what happened in the Jewish war: Matthew 24:14 — the Gospel preached throughout the world before the end; 24:30-31 — the sign of the Son of Man appearing in the heavens and the angels gathering the elect. This has led some interpreters to see the entire discourse as somehow symbolically fulfilled in A.D. 70 and others to see the entire discourse as literally fulfilled (or re-fulfilled) at the end of history. And various attempts have been made to apportion up one paragraph to A.D. 70 and another to the end. But it might be simpler to take the whole as immediately but partially or typically fulfilled in the destruction of Jerusalem in A.D. 70, but also to recognize that the events of A.D. 68–70 themselves point forward to the ultimate denouement of God's power and the Son of Man's sovereignty at the end of history.

8.5 Parables[13]

Parables are a particularly interesting genre because Jesus taught by using them, and sometimes those parables are difficult to understand. Although sometimes a proverb or saying can be called a "parable" (e.g., Luke 4:23 literally reads: "Doubtless you will quote to me this *parable*, 'Physician, heal yourself' "), most parables are *stories or depictions of earthly life which both illustrate spiritual truth and provoke a response to it*. They occur in the OT (see e.g., Jud. 9:7-15; 2 Sam. 12:1-6; Ezek. 17), and were often used by Jewish teachers in Jesus' time.

Up until the nineteenth century parables were generally regarded as allegories, and interpreting a parable was a matter of identifying how each item in a parable matched up with some truth. Augustine of Hippo, for example, explained the Parable of the Good Samaritan as follows (in *Quaestiones Evangeliorum* 2): The man going down to Jerusalem from Jericho is Adam (humankind), who is descending from the heavenly city to the world. The robbers (the devil and his angels) attack him and leave him half dead in sin. The priest and the Levite are the OT Law, which cannot help Adam in his sinful state. And the good Samaritan is Christ Himself, who takes Adam into the church (represented by the inn), and gives Paul (the innkeeper) the two greatest commandments of love to God and neighbor (the two denarii), promising to return again.

However, the context of the Parable of the Good Samaritan is the Pharisee's question, "Who is my neighbor?" (Luke 10:29) In other words, somehow the parable is an answer to the Pharisaic attempt to minimize the obligations of Leviticus 19:18 and to narrow the scope of responsibility for the welfare of others. It is not a sermon on how Christ redeemed the world. It seems likely that all these allegorical correspondences have little to do with the original meaning of the parable.

In the latter part of the nineteenth century Adolf Jülicher argued that parables are not allegories.[14] According to him, a parable has only one significant point, and other details are simply for the sake of the story telling. The details of the robbers, the innkeeper, and the payment of money are all incidental to the singular point, which is that, unlike standard Jewish thinking, responsibilities toward one's "neighbor" extend across racial, ideological, and geographical boundaries. Jülicher's criticism was undoubtedly proper with respect to the kind of allegorical approach dominant in his own time. Unfortunately, the "one point" which Jülicher himself tended to find was some obvious and simple moral didacticism, reflective of his own liberal theology, but the "one-point" approach has dominated parable interpretation during the twentieth century.[15]

However, the principle of "one point" seems a bit overstressed. Some parables, such as the Vineyard Tenants in Matthew 21:33-43, clearly have several points of correspondence, and the Parable of the Sower in Matthew 13/Mark 4 is interpreted by Jesus, who gives the seed and each of the soils a point of correspondence.[16] Only by removing all evidence of allegorical meaning as "inauthentic" can it then be "proven" that "authentic" parables have only one point.

The more recent studies of Madeleine Boucher[17] and John Drury[18] have approached the parables with more recognition of allegorical elements. It is better, therefore, to think of parables as usually having one *main* point, to which other points must be subordinate.[19]

The problem with the old approach was not that it interpreted allegorically but that it interpreted anachronistically, reading contemporary concerns and doctrine into the elements of the parable, without any indication that that is what Jesus was really talking about. Again we are back to the symbol problem; a symbol is extremely adaptable, and the true meaning of a symbol can only be decided on the basis of its literary contextual use and the cultural background within which it is used. A parable is a "symbol story," and whether it has one symbolic point or several, it will only properly be understood with reference to the cultural situation in first-century Palestine and the particular concerns of Jesus in the context within which the parable was spoken.[20] The Gospel writers themselves will usually indicate something about the "life setting" of a parable, and it is crucial to interpretation to pay attention to this setting.[21]

Jesus' parables often have an unexpected or surprise element in them. Most parables project a familiar world, but then introduce some radically unfamiliar element, something unexpected. It is this surprise element which provokes a hearer into a reexamination of his worldview, and thus which is the "main point" of the parable. For example, in the Parable of the Workers in the Vineyard (Matt. 20:1-16) it is surprising that the employer pays his hirelings the same amount, regardless of the time spent working. This surprise leads us to rethink the matter of "rewards" for what we do in serving God. Unfortunately, much of what would have surprised an original hearer no longer surprises us, and we must put ourselves into the place of a Palestinian Jew of the first century in order to appreciate where the surprise lay. For example, when we hear the Parable of the Pharisee and the Tax Collector (Luke 18:9-14) we are not surprised at the outcome. To us, the Pharisee comes across as a despicable, self-righteous hypocrite. But the average first-century Jews admired Pharisees as the godly folk. Even his prayer, "I thank you that I am not ... like this tax collector" (v. 11) would not have been regarded as hypocritical arrogance, but as genuine gratitude that God had kept him from a life of sinful wretchedness.[22] On the other hand, Palestinian Jews regarded tax collectors as being several rungs lower on the ethical ladder than we would regard child molesters. They were not only dishonest, they were traitors to their people. The outcome of the parable, that the tax collector and not the Pharisee was *declared to be righteous,* was shocking. It shifts from a worldview that looks at righteousness as something we accomplish (which was a universal assumption) to one where righteousness means abandoning all thought of our own righteousness. Jesus' parables surprise, because they confront the hearer with the sovereign reign of God, which operates differently from the world.

Many parables explicitly, and perhaps all of Jesus' parables implicitly, teach something about the coming manifestation of the sovereign reign of God. "The kingdom of God is like a man who . . ." does not mean that the kingdom resembles specifically the man in question, but that the story as a whole illustrates something about the kingdom.

The most important collection of "kingdom" parables is in Matthew 13/Mark 4. Here we learn a surprising thing about parables: they not only *clarify* the nature of the reign of God, they *obscure* the understanding of those who oppose Jesus. When the disciples asked Jesus about the parables, He told them:

> To you the secret of the kingdom of God has been given, but for those outside everything is in parables; *so that* they may indeed see but not perceive, and may indeed hear but not understand, lest they should turn again, and be forgiven" (Mark 4:11-12, RSV, emphasis added).

It is difficult to accept, but the parables have an elective purpose, in moving faith to greater faith, and moving unbelief to greater unbelief. Jesus is citing Isaiah 6:9-10 here, indicating that this is a judgment of God. The hidden reign of God is revealed to those who follow Jesus, but is hidden even deeper for those who do not.

So, in interpreting a parable we should ask:

(1) What is the main purpose or point of this parable? How does it address the historical situation in which it was spoken?
(2) How would the symbol(s) of the parable have functioned in first-century Palestine?
(3) What would have been surprising or uncomfortable for the first hearers?

Having done these, we may ask:

(4) How does the parable provoke us into rethinking our understanding of God and His reign?

8.6 Epistles

Most of the NT consists of epistles. Although the letter form was as well known in the ancient world as in the modern, using letters for religious instruction was apparently a Christian invention.[23] These are not simply private correspondences of only occasional significance, but were intended by their authors for circulation (Col. 4:16) and public reading (1 Thes. 5:27). Even the letters addressed to individuals such as Timothy and Titus have indications (e.g., the fact that they conclude with a blessing to "you" in the plural) that these were meant to be read to the church.[24]

However, many characteristics of the letter are still evident in the NT epistles. The structure of address, opening, body, and closing greetings attends most of the NT epistles. And this structure is sometimes helpful in interpretation. For example, the opening thanksgiving in Paul's letters appears to be an allusive précis to the entirety of the letter.[25] Philippians 1:5 mentions Paul's thankfulness for their "partnership in the gospel," which may allude to the thanks for the monetary contribution mentioned in chapter 4; and his prayer in 1:8 for the abounding of his addressees' mutual love may prepare for the exhortation to love in chapter 2 and the urging of Euodia and Syntyche to get along in 4:2. The opening gives a clue regarding the content of the letter.

Secondly, most if not all of the NT epistles were actually written down by a scribe. Sometimes, the scribe is named (e.g., Rom. 16:22), and sometimes the apostle wrote a verifying line in his own hand (Gal. 6:11). Since it is not unlikely that at least sometimes the scribe may have had some hand in the actual wording of a letter,[26] we may expect that at least sometimes there would be stylistic differences between letters from the same apostle. Thus the fact that the Pastoral letters exhibit a slightly different vocabulary than most of Paul's writings may indicate nothing more than a different secretary, or an increased need to allow the secretary to do the wording. And the easily noticed (even in English) stylistic differences between 1 Peter and 2 Peter is not of itself conclusive evidence against common authorship.

But the most crucial aspect of NT epistolary writing is that these letters were usually written for a very specific audience and thus addressed specific situations. Even letters intended for circulation (e.g., 1 Peter) have in mind the specific circumstances of the first readers. Therefore, the interpretation of certain details within the epistles depends on a reconstruction of the circumstances of its first readers. The problem is that these circumstances are usually unknowable apart from the letter itself, which usually assumes rather than describes such circumstances, and the necessary reconstruction is often haphazard guesswork. If we were to read someone else's correspondence today, some of it would be clear, but some would be totally dark, because we would not know what the correspondents both knew. As a general rule, the more an epistle appears to address a specific situation or question, the less certain is our understanding of it. On the other hand, material which appears in more than one epistle is likely to be less circumstance-specific, and our interpretation of it more sound.

8.7 Apocalyptic

Apocalyptic is susceptible to various definitions; for our purposes we will define apocalyptic as that literary genre which interprets earthly events, especially the struggles of God's people, as manifestations of the heavenly warfare between God and the forces of evil, and depicts the coming ultimate victory of God over those forces by means of highly symbolic images. By this definition, the only examples of apocalyptic genre in the canonical Bible are certain parts of the Books of Daniel and Revelation,[27] although perhaps the beginning of Job (1:6-12), the judgment prophecies of Isaiah, and the visions of Ezekiel and Zechariah were precursors to the type.

Distinctive of apocalyptic are its peculiar forms of symbolism, dualism, and messianism.

Symbolism

Once again the use of *symbol* is crucial. Apocalyptic, like other biblical materials, was addressed in some way to the contemporary situation. That Daniel was told in 8:26 to "seal up the vision, for it concerns the distant future," and in 12:4 to "close up and seal the words . . . until the time of the end" is not to say that the book had no meaning until later, but that the exact nature of the symbolism would not become clear until later. In the meantime, the symbols of both Daniel and Revelation provided comfort and encouragement to the saints who were currently enduring the onslaughts of Satan. The great world powers, which even Daniel saw from Babylon, were playing ferocious politics, but God was orchestrating their play and would ultimately restore the sovereignty of His people.

Therefore, although we may expect that the meaning of the symbols will not be exhaustively known until the final judgment, they need to be examined in light of the connotations the symbols would have had in their original cultural context and what connections the symbols have to previously written parts of the Bible. They should *not* be construed according to what *modern* associations the symbols might generate. So, when we read in Revelation 9:7-10 about the giant locusts, we should not interpret these in terms of what they resemble to us (some recent enthusiasts suggested helicopters), but what such imagery would have meant to John and his readers, and what connections with other biblical events such imagery evokes (e.g., the plague of locusts in Egypt, or the locust swarms of Joel 1). Symbols may remain obscure and identifications tenuous, but the encouragement of the apocalyptic books—that God's victory is sure—is clear.

Dualism

Dualism in Daniel and Revelation is not a philosophical dualism of real and ideal, but a religious and moral dualism between good and evil, God and Satan. Actually, dualism is not quite the right word, because Satan in the Bible is not the opposite of God, but Satan does set himself up as a cheap imitation of God, by counterfeiting His authority and works. Therefore an important dimension to apocalyptic symbolism in the Bible is the contrast between the true and the counterfeit. In Revelation 1:4, Jesus is the one "who *is* and who was, and who is to come." On the other hand, the sea beast of 17:8 "was, now *is not*, and will come." This sea beast was mortally wounded, yet healed (13:3), and obtained its authority from the dragon (13:4). The earth beast exercised the authority of the sea beast, and does great signs, even making fire come down from heaven (Rev. 13:12-13). In chapters 12–13, Satan (the dragon), the sea beast (Satan's image), and the false prophet (the earth beast, who persuades people to worship the sea beast, 13:12), are set up as an unholy trinity in counterfoil to God (the Father), Christ (God's image), and the Holy Spirit (the persuader).

Messianism

The third characteristic of biblical apocalyptic is that the great victory of God over Satan is brought about by a messianic figure.[28]

227

Already we saw in Daniel the divine figure, one who "like the son of man" receives dominion in the future (7:13-14), and who "like a son of the gods" stands with his people in their adversity (3:25), and who as the anointed (Messiah) prince is even "cut off and will have nothing" (9:26).[29] But Revelation is completely dominated by this figure, who is now identified as Jesus. He is described in language identifying Him unmistakably as God (1:12-18), who has authority over the churches (chaps. 2–3), who is worshiped by the heavenly creatures (5:8), who is worthy to open the scrolls which bring history to its fulfillment (5:9), and who executes judgment on unholy Babylon (19:11-16). As with the Bible as a whole, apocalyptic in the Bible is focused on Jesus Christ; He is the victor of the heavenly conflict, and any interpretation of the symbols in Daniel or Revelation which loses sight of this focus on Christ is undoubtedly missing the mark.

Naturally there are many other genres and forms within the Bible which we have not even touched upon, particularly wisdom literature. But we hope this survey has provided a beginning into how the various genres of the Bible testify of the God who saved us, is saving us, and will save us, through His Son Jesus Christ.

NINE

THE BIBLE IN WORSHIP
AND WITNESS

We have already described the spiral of growth that takes place as a reader is transformed by his or her interpretation and so in turn becomes a better interpreter. The change is often subtle and subconscious, taking place at the level of presuppositions and theological frameworks. But it would be a mistake to assume that this is the only mechanism for growth.

A more conscious effort to live out the Bible's message is both expected and demanded by the Bible itself (e.g., James 1:22-25). Deliberate obedience is essential. It is not simply one of several options for enhancing Christian growth; it is fundamental to the Christian life, from its starting point of repentance and faith to the last breath a Christian draws before being finally transformed in Christ's presence. It is an element that can be easily lost in many popular presentations of "the Gospel." Indeed, Christians are those who *obey* the Gospel of our Lord Jesus Christ (see 2 Thes. 1:8; 1 Peter 4:17), not merely "vote for Jesus." Maturity is not found in an advanced knowledge of doctrine but in experienced discernment between right and wrong (Heb. 5:11–6:3); doctrine has not been "known" at all until it has been lived out (James 2:14-19).

Thus a book on interpreting the Bible should not fail to address the question of how to apply it practically. We shall focus on three areas of life: worship and witnessing will be covered in this chapter and guidance in the next chapter. These have been chosen because they are often the areas in which the Bible is most needed and yet, paradoxically, are often subordinated to human ideas.

9.1 Scripture and Worship

By worship we mean the conscious expression of praise for God privately or publicly, although we shall emphasize the public or congregational context. We are aware that worship in its fullest sense is expressed through a whole life which brings praise to God and that it is possible to go through the motions of "worship,"

229

privately or publicly, while failing to live a consistent life. But here we are restricting ourselves to those times when worship is articulated, both in private devotions and in the church's corporate life.

We shall consider two aspects of the place of Scripture in worship: firstly, the specific matter of biblical teaching and secondly, the more general application to forms of corporate worship.

9.1.1 The teaching ministry

We can only worship the God we know. In fact, we shall always worship the "god" we know, whether it be the true God or not. If our god is of our own making, then we shall worship accordingly. If we are to give God acceptable worship then we must seek to know Him better, to discern what pleases Him and, since He is transcendent above all natural human comprehension, this is possible only insofar as He reveals Himself.

In John 14:21, Jesus says, "Whoever has my commands and obeys them, he is the one who loves me. He who loves me will be loved by my Father, and I too will love him and show myself to him." This raises the question of how the Lord will show Himself. Will it be by some form of contemporary revelation? This would be necessary if God's existing self-revelation in the Bible were incomplete. However, this is not the case; certainly our understanding may be incomplete, but we must be clear that in the pages of Scripture God has delivered all we need. While this does not logically preclude any extra-biblical revelation, it strongly implies that it is unnecessary.[1] Rather, this text, John 14:21, reveals a cycle of transformation whereby the more the interpreter's presuppositions and goals are improved by exposure to Scripture, the better will be one's interpretation and the more he or she will discover about the Lord. Once again, it is the spiral of growth in interpretive skill; the Lord manifests Himself to those who obey His commandments because obedience transforms their minds so that their philosophical and theological frameworks change, their hermeneutics improve, and their eyes are opened to see more of God's self-revelation in His Word.

As we seek to worship God, then, exposure and obedience to His Word is a sine qua non if we are to do so intelligently. We have already argued that every individual has the right and obligation to study, interpret, and apply Scripture, under the guidance of the Holy Spirit. But in addition, certain people have been entrust-

230

ed with the privilege of teaching in the church (Rom. 12:7; Eph. 4:11; 1 Tim. 4:11-14; 5:17; 2 Tim. 2:24; 1 Peter 4:10-11), and for this reason the regular exposition of Scripture has been a vital component of corporate gatherings of the Christian church since the first century (see Acts 2:42).

Theologically, the importance of teaching is justified on the grounds that people are not capable of pulling themselves up morally by their own boot straps, and so God has once again stepped in with the provision of a gift for His people (Eph. 4:11[2]). The history of redemption is one of God reaching down to people, speaking by word, deed, and incarnation in order to rescue humanity from its own self-inflicted catastrophe; the Gospel is interventionist, both in its initial impact on the unbeliever and in its lifelong effect on the believer as he or she *is taught* and grows toward Christlikeness through obedience. Spiritual maturity cannot be manufactured; it is grown from within by the work of the Holy Spirit, using the understanding gained through God's Word and bringing conviction of truth (John 16:8; 2 Tim. 2:15). At both an individual and a corporate level, human beings cannot "reach God" merely by sitting in silence, as if emptying the mind would bring God closer; a time of silence will produce true worship only if it has first been fed by God's Word so that it is in fact a time of meditation. Anything else will merely allow the human heart to go astray (Matt. 15:17-19). We are not arguing at all against the practice of silence. Most people today have the opposite problem of a lifestyle that precludes valuable times of quiet reflection, but the point here is that mere navel-contemplation will lead only to great ungodliness (Matt. 12:34; Jer. 17:9).

And yet there is a constant temptation to reduce the impact of God's Word in the life of our churches. There are two discernible tendencies: either the Bible is not used enough, being displaced by the more "interesting" aspects of worship, or it is used naively so that there is an appearance of commitment to Scripture while in fact superstitions eviscerate its message. Let us now examine these two problems.

9.1.1.1 Use the Bible!

The first tendency, not using the Bible enough, happens surprisingly easily. Life becomes busy with a variety of "good" activities; youth activities retain teenagers' attention by emphasizing entertainments; home fellowship groups spend increasingly longer time sharing news and prayer requests before turning to the Bible; corporate worship meetings are livelier and in some cases better attended when music, drama, discussion, and liturgy are preferred above "tedious sermons." We hasten to add that each of these can be good and often vital activities, but they should not displace the Bible.

In some cases "tedious sermons" should indeed be blamed. There has been a misunderstanding about the meaning of the word *preach*. It has been assumed that this means a monologue delivered to a congregation, in a certain style or tone, with a minimum of visual aids, lasting between ten and sixty minutes. It would not take much to stretch the definition in some cases to include a wooden pulpit, an eleven o'clock starting time, a suit and tie, and a hymn sandwich. But there is nothing sacrosanct about such forms of preaching; there is room for variety and innovation. Preaching in the NT is simply the communication of a message; it was the common method for disseminating news or instructing pupils. Indeed the words *preach* and *teach* are interchangeable for our purposes.[3] By locking the teaching of Scripture into a particular set of forms,[4] some congregations have been dissuaded from giving it a valued place in worship services. Preachers, thinking they were feeding hungry souls with biblical truth, have in fact discouraged them from using the Bible!

However, there is an appropriateness about the human spoken word as a method of teaching; it is analogous with the idea that God's communication is through language and delivered person-to-person. The Lord has not merely laid down a book of ideas for us to pick up and use at our leisure; He has addressed us as persons, urgently calling us to hear and understand Him. This is certainly not an excuse for lazy preaching, as if every other aspect of corporate worship may be lively and relevant in form but preaching must remain in the doldrums—endowed with an untouchable mystique. On the contrary, once we understand what the Bible is all about we will want to communicate its message in as interesting and sensitive a way as we can manage; correct use of the Bible stimulates an appetite for further use.

In some situations the preaching of God's message could take many different forms, while not departing from the principle of communication person-to-person via language. For example, television and other electronic devices may be used to support and enhance the delivery. We are well aware of the limitations of television and other media,[5] but the point must be made that the homiletical need is a reflection of the hermeneutical one: God's rich and beautiful revelation deserves to be expressed appropriately and imaginatively. At the time of inscripturation, the message of the Bible was often embedded in the most powerful images of the day, such as Jeremiah's land deals, Hosea's traumatic marriage, or Ezekiel's cooking with dung.[6] Similarly, therefore, it would surely be appropriate to use all reasonable means to expound God's Word for His people, "spoiling the Egyptians"[7] in our attempt to find the most effective tools of communication, provided, of course, that depth is not abandoned for the sake of style. Like William Booth who asked, "Why should the devil have all the best music?" we might ask today, "Why should the devil have all the best computers?"

Whatever the method, the church must give the highest priority to preserving a place for the teaching of Scripture so that our worship is intelligent and acceptable to God and so that it reflects the richness and profundity of His self-revelation in the teaching method.

The importance of teaching is expounded in well-known passages such as 2 Timothy 3:14-17 and Titus 2, emphasizing especially that it is the method by which godly living is engendered. Paul exhorted Timothy to employ his teaching gift (1 Tim. 4:11-16) and Peter exhorted all who have this gift to use it with authority (1 Peter 4:10-11; see also Rom. 12:7). Above all, Jesus Himself chose a teaching role at the very beginning of His public ministry, entering the synagogues in the area where He was brought up, immediately following His forty days of temptation (Matt. 4:23; Luke 4:14-27). It is also interesting to note that the importance of the teaching ministry underlies some passages which have been the subject of interpretive problems. First Timothy 2:11-15 is usually understood to be addressing the role of women, but one of its central themes is the responsibility which devolves upon anyone who exercises the ministry of teaching, recognizing that God's message carries authority and therefore will affect lives. The passages which are often regarded as "difficult" because they deal with spiritual gifts (e.g., 1 Cor. 14 or Rom. 12) are important because they are actually intended to instill a sense of responsibility in worship meetings and particularly in anyone who instructs others. One import of many such passages is: "Use the Bible!"

9.1.1.2 Using the Bible intelligently

The Bible deserves the most careful handling of any book on earth, yet so often it is treated with derisible naïveté. It can happen in churches where preaching is indeed a regular feature of congregational life, where efforts are made to teach attractively, perhaps using all of the communications techniques at their disposal. But at the same time there may be a degree of superstition attached to the use of the Bible so that, for example, it is believed that a non-Christian is certain to be affected if only he or she will come within earshot of the sermon (whether or not it is sound, relevant, logical, or delivered in modern language),[8] or that Christians will be built up spiritually in proportion to the length of time they sit listening to sermons, whether or not their teaching content is biblical.[9] On the contrary, we would reply, exposure to empty preaching may be worse than nothing.

Much that we have said already on the subjects of presuppositions, language, and methodology applies further to the ministry of teaching. Passing on the study to others repeats the dynamics of study, albeit in more dilute form. Regular listening to preaching is the aural equivalent of repeated reading, with the added benefit of the preacher's insight. The purpose is not that the hearers should learn outlines and doctrines by rote, but rather that they should interact with God's Word.

The great eighteenth-century preacher George Whitefield was accustomed to preaching to vast numbers of Welsh miners — sometimes as many as 9,000 at a time — who would congregate on the hillside above their mines after each day's shift was over, their tears of repentance running white streaks down their coal-blackened faces. Whitefield's critics, however, once accused him of wasting his time. "We have been surveying your audience," they told him, "and they cannot even remember the text you used three days ago." "My friends," Whitefield replied, "you have missed the point; they do not come here to memorize my sermons, but to come under an influence."[10]

One of the main purposes of public teaching, then, is for the hearers to interact with God's Word, to come under the influence of its Author. They would be wise, like the Bereans, having first received it with an open mind, to test the message against known biblical truths (Acts 17:11), so that they can submit to the newly understood truth; but there is an even more important process of change which then takes place subconsciously by exposure to the Author. We are all under the influence of many authors for greater lengths of time, most of them non-Christian, simply by absorbing daily media communications. And we gradually become like the people with whom we spend time; we absorb their values and standards, their likes and dislikes, their goals and presuppositions. Those who spend time with God develop not just an understanding of His ways but also an agreement with them; their values are transformed so that they are empowered both to *want* and to *do* His will (Phil. 2:13). The teaching of Scripture must therefore serve this purpose; it must accurately present biblical truths so that the Author's voice is heard above all others.

Furthermore, the Bible itself is not the final goal of our inquiry; it is an expression of God Himself and He, not merely His Word, should be the object of our worship. There is always a danger of intellectualism, of being infatuated with the minutiae of Scripture or with precise formulations of its doctrine, rather than its Author. It has been known for certain Christians, in their enthusiasm for God's Word, to attribute to it a sort of magical power whereby exposure to its pages alone will change people, as though the sound of the words themselves were effective, rather than their Author being effective through them. A biblical phrase tucked away in a longer quotation, or sung repetitively like a mantra, is thought to be irresistible. In some cases the Bible is used like an offensive weapon, the recipient finding it to be exactly that — simply offensive — while the user believes it will work automatically because it is "the Word" which "will not return void" (citing Isa. 55:11). This is naive, depending upon a trinity consisting of Father, Son, and Holy Scriptures — attributing to the Bible work that is done by the Holy Spirit.[11] Remember that Josef Stalin memorized most of the NT as a young man, but it "did not meet with faith in the hearer" (Heb. 4:2, RSV) and did him no good. It is the Author who should occupy the center of our attention; He is the only reason why we take such trouble over His book. When receiving a letter from an important person, we certainly honor the letter (and might even frame it for display) but only because of the status of the author in our eyes. The letter itself has worth only because it is an expression of and means of access to a person who has worth and whom we respect.

In order to keep the focus in the right place, therefore, it is unwise to draw undue attention in the pulpit to the hermeneutics being employed; the pilgrim's eyes must stay on the shrine, not the path that leads to it. Describing the process of exegesis leads to tedious preaching and distraction from the message itself. In any case, there is little point trying to teach study methods in the pulpit; it has a relatively minor impact compared to the unconscious transmission of the actual principles employed as the preacher speaks. We absorb hermeneutical methods all the time that we hear teaching of any kind; the preacher's hermeneutics will be transmitted subliminally to become the hearer's hermeneutics too, just as the preacher's own hermeneutics will become a reflection of the Bible's own interpretive principles if one has been exposed to it long enough.[12] Teachers therefore have a responsibility to strive for excellence in their interpretive skills, and for most of the time they should let the teaching itself be the medium for transmitting hermeneutical principles to the hearers.

It is for this reason that expository preaching has earned wide respect. By this we mean preaching which unfolds God's Word, exposing it to view, revealing its principal themes, and making the meaning clear. It does *not* mean a pedantic plodding through the Bible, dismantling texts syllable by syllable without regard to the overall intended meaning. Rather, good expository preaching gives close attention to the genre, context, style, history, and theology of each book, and flows with the themes, unpacking them in a manner consistent with the authorial intent and applying them with a thorough understanding of the present-day world.

Without encroaching too far into the subject of homiletics, we must repeat that the style of a public teaching ministry is inextricably bound up with the hermeneutics of its message. That style will include some relevance to the context of the hearers' world.[13] The teacher's exegetical work should not stop with abstract meanings but go on to identify a range of possible applications; the biblical text ought first to affect one's own life and become part of a personal transformation. This kind of hermeneutical endeavor will energize and assist the teacher in expositing the Bible as the exciting book that it is. One does not enter the pulpit as a disinterested messenger, but as a person in living unity with one's message. None of this can be accomplished, of course, without setting aside adequate time for preparation. A teacher needs first to be a student,[14] giving conscious effort to examining presuppositions (both Scripture's and ours), researching historical and cultural background (both the text's and ours), understanding genres, unpacking linguistic nuances, and identifying applications, to say nothing of the "life-preparation" by prayer and other personal disciplines which are important for a minister of the Word.

9.1.2 Assessing other aspects of worship by the Bible

It is tempting to regard the use of Scripture simply as one aspect of worship, albeit an important one; in congregational worship it might be confined to particular times in the service reserved for reading or exposition; or in private worship it might be the first portion of the session, after which time is given to prayer. But this would be to reduce Scripture from its intended purpose and we must now attempt to demonstrate that, in considering our hermeneutics, there are important applications to all aspects of worship, just as there are applications to all of life.

9.1.2.1 Public worship meetings

Scripture provides the benchmark by which all expressions of worship should be measured. It would be inconsistent for us to strive for sound interpretive skills in Bible study without ensuring that we sing hymns, recite liturgy, or pray in a manner concordant with biblical truths. In a more subjective sense, as we grow in our interpretive skills and taste afresh some of the goodness of the Lord through reading His Word, we find that the imitations taste more than a little insipid.

As an example from hymnody, let us consider the following phrase: "Emptied Himself of all but love. . . ."[15] Does this mean that Jesus divested Himself of all His divine attributes except love? This may seem a slightly pedantic example, but the question of doctrine in hymns is important if we are to honor Jesus in all His glory. Some hymns are replete with hermeneutical flaws, particularly certain Christmas carols, yet it is amazing how easily we slip into singing them without a second thought about whether we are giving God acceptable worship. Could it really have been true to say, in that primitive Bethlehem maternity room, "The cattle are lowing, the baby awakes, but little Lord Jesus no crying he makes"? Does the carol "We Three Kings" really reflect the biblical record?[16] And why do some Christians still sing "Oh, Christmas Tree" (apart from sheer pagan tradition)? With some modern hymns, the problem has reached crisis proportions.

It would be fair to say that there are some excellent modern hymns which have made an outstanding contribution to the church's worship; but there has also been a notable trend away from critical analysis in the latter half of the twentieth century.[17] What is meant by the phrase "As we worship, build your throne"? Is God's throne incomplete? Why does another one say "Worship His majesty" (almost always spelled with a small "m," as though we are worshiping an attribute of God rather than God Himself)? Does it not require careful biblical analysis before we sing these songs with gusto?

The emphasis and tone may need scrutiny also. One well-known modern song sheet has thirty-five songs beginning with "I," but only three beginning with "Lord," "God," or "Jesus" — and even these go on to put the emphasis back on "me." Many modern songs, in fact, are rather human-centered so that, even if the individual sentiments are true, the overall emphasis is not on God at all. For example, after repeating "praise His name" a dozen times, one song makes its point by saying "praise His name and you will never be the same"; this may be true, but it implies, wrongly, that the primary purpose of praise is so we can have a wonderful life-changing experience. God must be praised simply because He is worthy of praise.

When we begin to evaluate our hymns and choose those which accord as closely as possible with Scripture, and when we apply principles of hermeneutics to our understanding of the hymns themselves, our singing takes on an intentional quality and the church's music is more easily regarded as meaningful worship. Too often, without this effort, hymns and other music are treated as a means to drown out the noise of latecomers arriving, children leaving, or collections being taken; not only is this a wasted opportunity, but it is surely an insult to God to pretend to be singing His praises while in fact taking care of the congregational housekeeping duties. Rather, hymns are intended to be an expression of biblical truth applied to our lives — truth which has come to us by way of God's revelation in Scripture; otherwise, we are merely babbling like pagans, not knowing whom we worship. This is explicit in Colossians 3:16-17:

Let the word of Christ dwell in you richly as you teach and admonish one another with all wisdom, and as you sing psalms, hymns and spiritual songs with gratitude in your hearts to God. And whatever you do, whether in word or deed, do it all in the name of the Lord Jesus, giving thanks to God the Father through him.

The context of this passage is the exhortation to live holy lives based on Christ's redemptive work and in the light of our privileged status as God's chosen people; the immediate context deals with corporate relationships and the passage itself is giving practical advice on how to achieve growth in Christlikeness in these areas. The "word of Christ" is declared as the foundation for teaching, admonishing, and singing.

This actually takes the process a step further: the word of Christ is not merely a means of *evaluating* hymns and other expressions of praise, it should positively *drive* them; Scripture is not merely a "sieve" of doctrine, but should be the creative and motivating force behind our worship.

What is true for hymns is true also for prayers; they can be served or stifled by the degree to which they are consistent with Scripture. And prayer is certainly blocked by an unwillingness to obey God's law: "If anyone turns a deaf ear to the law, even his prayers are detestable" (Prov. 28:9). With prayer, however, we have the distinct advantage that there is no hermeneutical problem for God; He understands every thought and every word, even before it is formed (Ps. 139:1-4), and the Holy Spirit intercedes on our behalf when we do not know what to pray for (Rom. 8:26-27). Yet prayer is effective only insofar as it seeks God's will (John 14:13-14; 1 John 5:14), and this is known progressively by understanding God through the correct interpretation of Scripture; it is by God's Word that we discover His character, His wishes, His heart, and so are able to seek what pleases Him. It is surely no accident that the early church "devoted themselves to the apostles' *teaching* and to the fellowship, to the breaking of bread and to *prayer*" (Acts 2:42, emphasis ours); later their prayers were answered with dramatic effects (Acts 4:31) and on that occasion (Acts 4:23-31) it is even recorded that they based their intercession deliberately on Psalm 2.

Private prayer can become exceedingly meaningful by the practice of "praying through" Bible reading. That is, talking to God about the truths which are unfolding through the reading or study of His Word, as the study itself progresses. As new dimensions of God's character are revealed, they might lead spontaneously to praise, so that private prayer is driven by Scripture.

All aspects of corporate worship services can be evaluated hermeneutically. Liturgy, testimony, and sacrament can all be improved by careful comparison to biblical understanding. Even the public reading of Scripture, which is usually considered not to require great skill, can be enhanced by reading it intelligently;[18] a person who has thoroughly studied his or her text will be able to read it sensitively so that the hearers are already deepening their insight, even before a word of the sermon has been uttered; awareness of genre, structure, style, and principal themes will be transmitted subconsciously and the sermon will begin with the advantage that the congregation has a foundational appreciation of the passage.[19]

9.1.2.2 Private worship

The ministry of the Word is not always a public matter; it should be a vital part of private worship. There has been a valuable popular movement in the twentieth century which fosters good devotional habits; once the activity of only the very committed saints, particularly monks, ministers, or missionaries, it has become recognized as the privilege of every Christian to develop a system of private worship, and the forms vary enormously. While traditionalists have treasured periods of reflection and prayer, perhaps with liturgy, the simple "quiet time" has transformed the lives of millions of evangelicals.

The role of the ministry of God's Word is just as vital in private worship as it is in public. There is, in fact, a temptation to become sloppy or cavalier with matters of interpretation when they are not subject to the scrutiny of fellow believers. Perhaps pride, bringing a rare benefit, restrains us from announcing foolish interpretations in public—that is, when the audience shares a commitment to sound hermeneutics. But the restraint is off in the privacy of personal devotions and there can be a tendency to say, "What does it matter, if my reading blesses my heart and if it all leads to worship anyway?"

Many a believer has opened the Bible in private devotions and become resigned to superficial reading. There can be a wedge driven between the "quiet time" and "Bible study," the former being a time of rather shallow reflection and the latter a more serious effort to study intelligently. No such distinction should exist; the hermeneutics of Bible study should be consistent. It may be, of course, that it is necessary to limit the scope of, say, an early morning devotional time so that it is really drawing on study at other times and concentrating on committing the new day to the Lord; but even the shortest reading of Scripture must be governed by sound hermeneutical principles. It makes no sense at all to expound the prophecy of Jeremiah thoroughly for a sermon or Bible study group, only to slip back into searching the book for superficial "blessings" in times of private devotions.[20] Personal prayer and praise, just as much as congregational worship, must be addressed to God as He has revealed Himself, not in some spuriously abbreviated form that happens to suit the limitations of our devotional time.

There has been a revival of interest in some aspects of private worship which draw on traditional approaches, some of them dating back long before the Reformation. Thousands of twentieth-century Christians have gained spiritual benefit, for example, through exemplars of prayer and meditation dating back to our spiritual forebears of past centuries. There is a particular danger here, though, in the context of private worship, because so much depends on the individual's thoughts. Some popular meditation techniques appear to depend upon Scripture as their basis, but in fact depart from it and lapse into "eisegesis."[21] Typically, the reader tries to imagine oneself in the biblical situation, perhaps walking and talking with the disciples, or discussing prophecy with a prophet, or meeting Paul in the marketplace. So far so good; we have already suggested the proper place for *sane imagination* (sec. 5.2). But it is easy to move on to alter the meaning by filling in too much, by a lack of guiding background materials, or especially by creating parts that are more interesting than Scripture itself! In such cases it is tempting to apply what we think Scripture *should* or *could* have said, rather than what it actually says.

There is a similar temptation to make portions of Scripture say what we wish them to say when we have a strong personal agenda. It may be an agenda of doctrine, reinforcing our favorite systems, or it may be related more directly to behavior. Such is the power of sin in our lives that we will manipulate meanings which accord with our preferred behavior, while still feeling bound to read the Bible and seek the security of even feigned obedience. It is a genuine self-delusion; we want to convince ourselves that we really are obeying God. Thus an individual might settle for a superficial reading because it affirms a preconceived notion, a temptation which is particularly strong in private meditation since there is little public accountability. Perhaps that is why the Pharisee could so easily pray, with a mistaken sense of security, "God, I thank you that I am not like other men" (Luke 18:11); his worship was built around an understanding that suited his complacency. Here is a strong argument for the use of commentaries and other study aids; a well-chosen commentary will ask questions which might otherwise be missed, add helpful historical or cultural perspective, and point toward the central truths of passages. This is especially important when reading familiar portions of the Bible. A further safeguard is provided when private worship is associated with public worship, with the advantage of the teaching ministry behind it.

9.2 Scripture and Witness

This is not a "how-to" book on evangelism, but it is important to understand that the Bible is fundamental in the proclamation of God's deeds for humanity, and should not, consciously or unconsciously, be relegated to a secondary status.

The question of evangelism touches the very center of Christian epistemology. How can we know anything? And, especially, how can a non-Christian know enough about God to put his faith in Him? There is an obvious gap between the individual's perception and God's perception, and a moment's reflection will reveal that it is much more than a gap: it is a yawning chasm, an infinity of distance both qualitatively and quantitatively separating the omniscient, pure, and eternal God from the ignorant, sinful, and finite human being. Only arrogance leads us to minimize the distance. Most approaches in witnessing are an attempt to bridge this epistemological gap, but they succeed only insofar as they are founded on God's own approach to the problem, that is through the *revelation* which He has already given. Only God can bridge the gap and cause someone to know Him.

When Scripture is neglected and we resort to our own attempt to bridge the gap, the form is bound to be one of two principal types, or some combination of them. The first we could call the "intellectual" approach, and the second we could call the "subjective" approach.

9.2.1 The two "worldly" approaches

The intellectual approach attempts to prove by reason the logical superiority of Christianity over other philosophies, or else its compatibility with some de rigueur secular philosophy. This, of course, involves the search for some "common ground" of reason upon which Christian and non-Christian can agree. Unfortunately, once human reason by itself has been made the arbiter of truth, then our authority is no longer God's Word and we are bound to run into problems. In severe cases, the effort to be intellectually acceptable results in compromising or changing the Word in order to be compatible with reason or current trends in secular thinking.

On the other hand, the subjective approach *apparently* repudiates the intellectual approach and focuses instead on what may seem to be irrefutable because it is based on experience rather than logic. It may be some immediate and visible effect attributed to the Holy Spirit or to God's power given in support of evangelism; it may be an intensely personal but persuasive experience so that the individual "knows" God has spoken inwardly (where lies a good deal of modern gnosticism[22]); or it may simply be the social environment of acceptance.[23] Whatever the phenomenon, it is expected to impress the unbeliever and overcome his or her intellectual and philosophical difficulties. However, it too relies on a humanly-devised ground of evaluation, lacking the transcendent objectivity which has come from God by means of revelation — that is, in His Word.

Before unpacking this in a little more detail, let us note that Paul's approach was different from either of these. In 1 Corinthians 1:22-23 he mentions both of these alternatives: the Greeks, he says, admire wisdom — intellectual persuasion — and the Jews prefer signs of power. But, instead, Paul simply offers a message, a Gospel which is intellectually foolish to the Greeks (see Acts 17:22-34) and is weak and a stumbling block to the Jews. Certain miracles did occur in his ministry, but they were secondary to the message and Paul minimized their importance. The "preaching not with wise and persuasive words, but with a demonstration of the Spirit's power" (1 Cor. 2:4) is not preaching by miracle-working but preaching which is itself imbued with the power of God (2:5);

and Paul makes it clear in the context that the power of God is found in the message of the cross (1:18), for Christ Himself is both the power and the wisdom of God (1:24).

9.2.2 The underlying issue

We began this section by noting that the use of Scripture in evangelism is a subject that touches upon the central issues of Christian epistemology. In exploring this further, we must at once recognize that everyone does in fact know some truths about God. Even though we are incapable of reaching or understanding God in a saving way, we unavoidably have a basic knowledge by general revelation of God's eternal power and godhead — and this knowledge renders us inexcusable in our rejection of God (Rom. 1:18-20).

To further this knowledge, we must turn to further revelation; and, we shall argue, this is only possible on the basis of Scripture. But the very idea is repugnant to a secular mind. Every day, people discover something new — new to human knowledge, that is. Scientists unveil staggering secrets which were hitherto locked away in nature's vault; there seems to be no limit to what we can know — all it takes is time, money, effort, and expertise for the secrets to be located and exposed as trophies to humanity's omnicompetent skills. And so we begin to view the universe as ours, just waiting to be grasped piece by piece. It is easy to say, then, that among all the facts of the universe are the facts about God, also waiting to be "discovered." To be sure, as we investigate these facts, we find that God is the greatest fact of all. Further, we might argue that all reason and logic point to Him, that anyone who is willing to take an unbiased look at the facts will invariably discover the wealth of evidence which is waiting to be observed and which will lead the inquirer to God.

Such a line of thinking must be commended for its attempt to respect God's greatness and to lead unbelievers to Him, but ultimately it is a distortion of the truth. God is not merely "one of the facts"; He is not even "the greatest fact of all." We must acknowledge Him as the only original, self-existent, and complete fact (ignoring for the sake of this argument that He is a person rather than just a fact), and any other facts in the universe are derived from Him. God, rather than man, is the starting point for any understanding or argument. In the words of Cornelius Van Til:

The essence of the non-Christian position is that man is assumed to be ultimate or autonomous. Man is thought of as the final reference point in predication. The facts of his environment are "just there"; they are assumed to have come into being by chance . . . the laws of logic are assumed as somehow operative in the universe, or at least as legislative for what man can or cannot accept as possible or probable. If a god exists, he must at least be subject to conditions that are similar to, if not the same as, those to which humanity itself is subject.[24]

It is true that, as far as we can perceive with our human limitations, our world points to Him. "Ask the animals, and they will teach you . . . the hand of the Lord has done this" (Job 12:7-9). But that is only because God has chosen to reveal Himself partly by means of the creation; at the very least, the creation displays the likeness of its Creator. However, God did not need to create the universe to give Himself more meaning or significance; He did not create humanity because He needed an object to love, as though without human beings He suffered some kind of deficiency. He could have remained Himself, perfect, complete, infinite, without ever having created anything. Indeed, this is His eternal state irrespective of His founding of the world, difficult though it may be for us to grasp. God remains self-existent in the "eternally present tense." Jesus exclaimed "before Abraham was, I am!" (John 8:58, RSV), and the Scripture says of Him, "In the beginning was the Word, and the Word was with God, and the Word was God. He was with God in the beginning" (John 1:1-2).[25] Every new understanding that we gain about God from the Bible should lead us to adjust our own thinking about every other aspect of life as well, and should stand in obvious superiority to humanly based ideas. As John Calvin said in the sixteenth century: "The scriptural teaching concerning God's infinite and spiritual essence ought to be enough, not only to banish popular delusions, but also to refute the subtleties of secular philosophy."[26]

But it is often the other way round; we attempt to use minds which have been gripped in the subconscious stranglehold of secular philosophy to make arrogant predications about the being and nature of God. We go to human reason as the final court of appeal and accept God's existence only if it makes sense,[27] or we accept the Bible as God's Word only if it appears noncontradictory to our dulled and prejudiced minds. Such is the arrogance of the human condition, while all the time God graciously gives us breath with which to make such conceited utterances.

9.2.3 The biblical approach

It should be apparent, then, that the Bible has a unique and fundamental role in witnessing. It is not merely a collection of texts with which to "club" unbelievers, or a source of witty sayings to impress and entice them. It is also much more than a field of study offered to seekers so that they may discover information in their "investigation of the facts." It is much more than a record of testimonies with which they can identify and be drawn into sympathy. And it is much more than an apologetic treatise designed to marshal the arguments and persuade readers intellectually.

The Bible is, of course, all of these; it is the supreme treatise, testimony, record of theological facts, and collection of witty proverbs and aphorisms — paramount among all literature. But its role in witnessing is infinitely more than these; it is nothing less than God's self-revelation. The Almighty God is condescending to communicate with mere human beings concerning their redemption, and therefore He *shall* be heard. Indeed, when we consider the impact of this statement, it is paltry to speak of the Bible having a "role" in anything; it is incomparably GOD SPEAKING.

Accuracy in interpretation is therefore vital if unbelievers are to hear God speaking. The Bible must be understood as it was intended to be understood, and herein lies an enormous challenge in the context of witnessing. It is our belief that the most important purpose of Scripture in witnessing is *to reveal the character of God*. This is much more significant than presenting a Gospel formula. When a person begins to recognize who God is, he or she will be bound to recognize personal sinfulness and seek His mercy. Without this recognition, the Gospel formula may be a message eviscerated of a vital element — the need for God's grace and forgiveness. There is little point dwelling on people's sin in an attempt to persuade them of their guilt; they need to become aware of the holiness of God if they are eventually to collapse in repentance. When Job finally woke up to the greatness of God, he spoke (using metaphors) of the effect on his attitude: "My ears had heard of you but now my eyes have seen you. Therefore I despise myself and repent in dust and ashes" (Job 42:5-6). When the Prophet Isaiah glimpsed the Lord and His glory in the temple, he exclaimed, "Woe to me! . . . I am ruined! For I am a man of unclean lips, and I live among a people of unclean lips, and my eyes have seen the King, the Lord Almighty!" (Isa. 6:5) When Simon Peter realized that the man who produced the miraculous draft of fish must be none other than the Son of God, he fell in repentance at Jesus' knees and said, "Go away from me, Lord; I am a sinful man!" (Luke 5:8) And when Saul met the risen Jesus on the Damascus Road, he fell to the ground and asked, "Who are you, Lord?" and in turn after Jesus identified Himself, was told to await further instruction (Acts 9:5-6).

The modern equivalent of Job's or Isaiah's vision of God, or Peter's or Saul's encounter with Jesus, is the revelation which God Himself has given in His Word. An encounter with Him through the Bible will be no less dramatic for the individual concerned.

We have already alluded to the logical problem that exists when a believer and an unbeliever are engaged in dialogue, in that they inevitably find they are arguing from two self-contained positions. The Christian theistic position is, of course, the only truly rational one. But even though the unbeliever's position is ultimately irrational, he or she is not going to accept this easily, preferring the security of the apparently self-consistent position to the demands of the Gospel. Such is the experience of anyone who has tried to persuade a non-Christian that it is logical for God to have ultimate power and justice despite the existence of evil and suffering in the world, or one who has tried to proclaim that Christ is the only way to God. The unbeliever quickly opines that the Christian position is merely a "cop-out," a self-fulfilling system designed to protect naive religious faith.

The only answer is for the unbeliever to come face to face with God. Only then will any "Gospel message" make sense. But how is this encounter brought about?[28] Broadly speaking, it occurs both directly and indirectly.

Directly, the encounter with the Lord will be through reading Scripture itself. An unbeliever who genuinely searches for God in its pages will surely find Him. Here we must be clear about the purpose of such study. It is not merely to investigate the facts; God is not merely "one of the facts" or even "the greatest fact," and in any case the unbelieving mind cannot successfully arrogate to itself such a judgmental role. It is not to identify the Gospel intellectually, as though it were possible to wrap it up in a neat package, compare it with other systems of philosophy and then make up one's mind about it. What court of appeal will prevail? It is not to hold arguments with God, looking for disagreements or debates and measuring success as a kind of score, the best argument winning the prize of the individual's faith; in the unbeliever's system of presuppositions, the Bible will almost certainly appear to "fail" at some points.

The purpose of direct study of Scripture, for a non-Christian as well as a Christian, must be to meet God—to experience Him, learn of His character, and consider the implications. To be sure, multitudes of non-Christians have read the Bible with all the "wrong" motives (e.g., investigative judgment, comparative philosophy, intellectual argument), and in the end some have been met by God; their testimonies adorn many church fellowships. But sadly there are also other multitudes of non-Christians who have read the Bible, argued with it, or in some way found it wanting and rejected it, and have continued on their way even more confirmed in their unbelief. This is a discouraging blow to those Christians who expect exposure to the Bible, for whatever motive, automatically to bring conversion (doubtless quoting Isa. 55:11 or some similar text). The use of the Bible in the context of witnessing must be to invite the non-Christian to seek God in its pages. The Christian must take care to assist the non-Christian to interpret it correctly, and hence the need for sound hermeneutics to be practiced by the Christian, invisibly guiding such study. And here we can report, from our experience, that the individual who genuinely approaches the Bible with such care, searching after God, invariably finds Him.

Indirectly, the character of God is revealed most importantly through the life of a believer. God also uses both the creation and circumstances to display His character, as we have already mentioned, but it is supremely through this reflection of Christ in the believer that the indirect revelation takes place. Countless numbers of Christians can testify that it was the life of a Christian friend that impressed them and caused them to inquire further.[29] The *extent* of that indirect witness to the character of God depends upon the extent to which God's Word has been lived out in the believer's life, and here our argument reaches full circle: a Christian who is taking care to understand and apply Scripture correctly will more accurately conform to God's will. On the other hand, a Christian who habitually tinkers with words and phrases, bending them to his or her own interests, whether applying them with naive subjectivity or clever subtlety, will be robbed of some of its life-transforming power. As Paul explained to the Ephesians, the believer who has received the benefit of preparation by the divinely appointed means will mature toward the target of "the whole measure of the fullness of Christ" (Eph. 4:13). And it is this embodiment of the character of Christ in the life of the believer which is one of the most powerful and irrefutable persuasions of the unbeliever. It brings him face to face with the character of God.

Scripture, then, is not merely one of the tools in the toolbox; it is, to extend the metaphor, the hand of the mechanic Himself. And the quality of our hermeneutics will be reflected in the quality of our witness.

TEN

SCRIPTURE AND GUIDANCE

"Finding God's will" has been virtually an obsession in the modern church, yet the subject remains enigmatic for multitudes of Christians and a seemingly endless supply of teaching materials does not appear to have abated the demand for help. For many there is a feeling that the Bible somehow has not spoken to the need; even worse, it appears that God offers guidance without actually delivering it. His promise appears to be crystal clear: "I will instruct you and teach you in the way you should go; I will counsel you and watch over you" (Ps. 32:8) or "He instructs sinners in his ways. He guides the humble in what is right and teaches them his way" (Ps. 25:8-9). Yet many Christians feel this has not been their experience; they look with envy at the exiled Israelites who were told, "The Lord will guide you always" (Isa. 58:11) or "Your ears will hear a voice behind you, saying, 'This is the way; walk in it' " (Isa. 30:21). Are these passages actually promising guidance?

This is, of course, a matter of hermeneutics. An expectation that the Bible will speak directly to a contemporary subject using a modern, preconceived idiom leads people to embrace a spurious doctrine, to ask the wrong questions, and therefore to be disappointed with the outcome. In the worst cases, the price is paid in the wreckage of lives as a result of misguided decisions.

10.1 Guidance Needs to Be in Context

The first reason for the problem is that the subject of "finding God's will" has been taught in *isolation*; it has become a category of its own, and a small one at that: a topic for a little booklet, a short talk, or a conference seminar. Attention has been focused on the subject itself, but, quite apart from the fact that it is not possible simply to extract the subject and understand it in isolation; examination of the subject of guidance does not guarantee that the guidance itself will be followed. By way of analogy, we might say that a ship's navigator could study the theory of nautical navigation, and possibly understand the process perfectly, but this does not guarantee that he will follow the right course when out at sea. In the case of spiritual guidance, we cannot even study the navigation system quite so easily; it is more of a living, dynamic process.

The Lord did not give us a "formula" for finding His will in Scripture; instead, He simply commands us to "understand what the Lord's will is" (Eph. 5:17). The method of God's guidance is not at all ambiguous, as we shall see, but neither does it conform to typically human demands. It is simply a waste of time to try to find a step-by-step system of guidance in the Bible, a formula that can be called up and applied when decisions must be made, as if the topic could be selected out and treated in isolation. And yet this is what thousands of Christians have been taught to believe. Like the galactic emperors in the spoof science fiction series *The Hitch Hiker's Guide to the Galaxy*, some people spend literally lifetimes waiting for the answers to the wrong questions, eventually finding nothing but disillusionment.[1]

Another analogy may help us to understand the way forward: the subject of guidance can be likened to a magnifying glass which we use to focus light from a single source (God) and direct it on to a page (our circumstances). But the light will not focus because there are other supposed sources of light: erroneous ideas about God. These other sources are dimmer, but they emit enough light to be confused with the main source. So there is no shortage of light, but still the beam will not focus. In our frustration we examine the magnifying glass (our method of "knowing the will of God"); we refine the glass, polish it, put it in a new frame, and adjust its position. Yet no matter how hard we try, the beam will never be in focus until one light source is used exclusively and all the others have been eliminated. It must be the light of God Himself, which is expressed only in biblical truth. The others turn out to be just mirrors, dimly reflecting parodies of truth. When we make the light source clear, the beam shines brightly and our page is illuminated by a clearly focused spot. Stretching the analogy a little further, we then become enraptured by the brilliance of the true light—not merely thankful for the clarity given to our page, but filled with wonder at the light itself; our attention is no longer on the magnifying glass, nor even on the page, but on the source of the brilliance. We are attracted to God Himself. The point is that true guidance comes through our understanding of God; false understandings, like false lights, produce only confusion.

10.2 What Is "God's Will"?

Not only has the subject been taught in isolation, but the structure of the subject is usually forced into an artificial paradigm. It is often assumed that God's will is some kind of blueprint for our lives which we must somehow try to discover, often just in time for a decision. A moment's thought should make us ask why we do not need to discern this blueprint for *every* decision in daily life. We seem to be able to decide on our breakfast cereal or the color of shirt we wear, yet we feel we must "find God's will" for more important matters such as college, marriage, career, or buying a house. Some say that the difference is in the extent of the moral implications of a decision, so that certain issues are "moral" and others are merely pragmatic or "nonmoral"[2]; but it could be argued that every decision, no matter how trivial, has a moral dimension — the simplest telephone call or the choice of butter rather than margarine bears hidden moral consequences for stewardship of time or health, for example — and infringement of one small part of the law is tantamount to guilt for the whole law (James 2:10). Yet most teaching on guidance treats major decisions as a special category, needing extra divine assistance, while minor decisions are neglected; for these, the individual is on his or her own. Where is the "guidance threshold"? The question implies the answer: it has something to do with accrued wisdom which we can apply safely in familiar areas, but not in less familiar areas.

The major decisions are usually then subjected to a routine process of "finding God's will." By this it is meant that God has already drawn up the blueprint and we must now try to discover it, and the speed of discovery will be related in some way to our spiritual maturity. It is a cat-and-mouse game of guidance in which we look for hidden clues to what God wants, trying to build up a composite picture and making a decision based on a judgment as to what He appears to be saying at a particular time. Typically the elements are the Bible, counsel, circumstances, and inner "peace," especially through prayer. The Bible is used something like a recorded weather forecast or, at worst, a horoscope.

God does indeed know the next step for each of our lives, but there is no mandate in Scripture by which we should seek to know it. On the contrary, we are explicitly commanded to avoid all kinds of divination.[3]

Confusion has probably been caused by semantic coincidences.

In our current translations, there are two NT Greek words which are commonly rendered "will" in English. One of them, *boule* (and its cognates), primarily signifies God's purpose; it is unchangeable and irresistible, and in this respect these future plans for our individual lives are unavailable to our inquiry. For example, the word occurs in "Who resists his will?" (Rom. 9:19), or "this man was handed over to you by God's set purpose and foreknowledge" (Acts 2:23).[4] There is indeed a blueprint for our lives, but it is God's prerogative alone and has no part to play in the subject of guidance — except to give us reassurance of God's sovereignty; we shall consider this aspect later in the chapter.

The other word which is usually translated "will" in English is the Greek word *thelema* and its cognates, occurring more than fifty times in the NT. It refers to something that is desired or that one wishes to happen. It is this "will" that we are commanded to know (Eph. 5:17), although in our sinfulness we often disregard it. We are commanded to "stand firm" in God's *thelema* (Col. 4:12). In every instance of its use in the Bible, it signifies God's wishes as to how we should conduct our lives. For example, "it is God's will that by doing good you should silence the ignorant talk of foolish men" (1 Peter 2:15).

It is no accident that a misuse of the word "will," wherein the idea of "seeking God's will" has come to mean finding out His blueprint for the next decision, is often accompanied by similar misuse of words in looking for clues to that guidance in the Bible. The horoscope mentality leads people to find double meanings in words and phrases, and doubtless many readers will be able to cite instances both humorous and tragic. Various missionary enterprises seem to have been led by passages such as: "Enlarge the place of your tent, stretch your tent curtains wide, do not hold back; lengthen your cords, strengthen your stakes. For you will spread out to the right and to the left" (Isa. 54:2-3). And many an earnest Christian has searched the Scriptures daily looking for God's will about marriage. One of the authors of this book observed the shock and confusion of a young woman who was approached by a man claiming that God had selected her to be his wife on the basis that guidance had been given through no less than a hundred texts. (To the relief of everyone except this man, she later married someone much more suitable.)

Often a promise in the Bible does have an obvious contemporary application because of a great fulfillment in Christ or a continuing meaning in the modern age. "Honor your father and your mother, so that you may live long in the land the Lord your God is giving you" (Ex. 20:12), for example, does have contemporary application (though not an exact one), as is apparent from its citation by Paul in Ephesians 6:4. But the practice of claiming biblical promises without reference to their redemptive-historical context generally reveals a disregard for the hermeneutical principles that should obtain.

God's will—*thelema*—has been made clear in the Scriptures; He has revealed His preference, His wishes, for the way we should conduct our lives. It requires effort to understand and absorb God's wishes, but they are not obscure; the process of studying His Word reveals all His will (2 Tim. 2:15) and no "cat-and-mouse" game is necessary. It is no surprise, therefore, that Paul commended the Ephesian elders "to God and to the word of his grace, which can build you up" (Acts 20:32), and that he commended the Scriptures to Timothy as all he needed for growth and ministry (2 Tim. 3:15-17). Finding God's will is a matter of understanding His Word.

Since this book deals to some extent with methods of study and interpretation of God's Word, we shall not expand on the point here. But it must be said that there is often a temptation to avoid the effort involved. Quite simply, good students of Scripture become sound decision-makers; in the words of a popular proverb, there is no feast without a sacrifice. Understanding God's Word is a lifelong process, never complete of course, but the effort is richly repaid in the ability it brings to choose God's will. When we consider great and godly people in the church, those who have evidently lived out God's will with all its satisfaction and fruitfulness, we find invariably that they have been assiduous students of Scripture with a passion to understand it correctly. Here then is the connection between hermeneutics and guidance in the Christian life.

Implicit in this pursuit of biblical understanding is the commitment to *obey* God's will. Study is not merely for the purpose of savoring doctrine in the abstract. The industrious searching for biblical truth, the daily meditation on the Word, and the striving for sound interpretation are useful only if driven by a desire to please the Lord, to submit to His wishes.

10.3 Submission to God

The hermeneutical problem in "finding God's will," therefore, first begins with submission to God's Word, with a willingness to listen to its message rather than merely play with the semantics. It is an attitude of yieldedness and repentance which opens up the whole vista of God's will, since it represents our desire to know his wishes and follow them. A repentant Christian has no interest in manipulating texts in search of a bit of expedient guidance, preferring to find out what God really wants. The unrepentant person withholds obedience until he or she has more knowledge; but of course such knowledge is never completed. Jesus said that He would be recognized by those who first choose to do God's will (John 7:17); in other words, by those who have begun their way up the hermeneutical spiral by first committing themselves to obeying Him.

Here, then, is one of the underlying presuppositions of the traditional approach to "finding God's will": that God is at our service, and we open the Bible with a view to its serving our purposes rather than with a view to our serving God's purposes. Sometimes this attitude begins at conversion, or rather with a form of conversion that we suspect is spurious, that is, a superficial decision to "accept Christ" without the necessary repentance and faith. In the worst cases, it is a response to a message which is nothing more than an appeal to "vote for Jesus," which, of course, is no Gospel at all. The true Gospel is a matter of obedience, as we have already noted, and true faith is bound up with yieldedness and commitment to doing God's will. This is the historic, apostolic Gospel. Herman Ridderbos, commenting on Paul's view of saving faith, points out that "faith as *obedience* is of central significance for Paul's conception and is repeatedly defined as such as his epistles."[5]

10.4 Understanding God and His Ways

Knowing God's will—His wishes—is more than just knowing a code of ethics or following a list of rules for behavior. It is true that, in the Bible, His will is often expressed in the form of laws and commandments, and the Decalogue is certainly a definitive summary of the law. But if all we had was a set of commandments, we would be obliged to develop a casuistry in our attempt to cover every eventuality. But even with the highest intentions to please God, there would be many situations for which a rule had not been written and the best we could do would be to extrapolate the law to meet the situation.

The Bible, however, is not just a codebook; it testifies to the character of God. And the Christian has even more: the living Holy Spirit indwelling and interpreting God's will. This phenomenon is much more than some kind of inbuilt Bible commentary; it is a means of access to the character of God Himself. It is the most dynamic, we might say *organic*, way to empower us to know God's will. The Prophet Ezekiel described it this way.

> I will give you a new heart and put a new spirit in you; I will remove from you your heart of stone and give you a heart of flesh. And I will put my Spirit in you and move you to follow my decrees and be careful to keep my laws (Ezek. 36:26-27).

It is therefore paramount that we develop an understanding of God's character and foster a direct, personal relationship with Him; we must take advantage of the Holy Spirit's ministry in quickening our minds, convicting us of biblical truth, and empowering us to obey.

Here, in fact, is the crux of the whole question of finding God's will: it is a matter of knowing God, of understanding His ways. There is no shortcut to this. Just as in a good marriage the couple learn to know each other's likes and dislikes, in ever increasing detail, and are then able instinctively to choose what pleases the other, similarly a Christian who is growing in the knowledge of God is able to choose what pleases Him. He or she begins to know God's wishes, His pleasure, His *thelema*, more and more instinctively. All decisions in life have an ethical dimension—none of them are "nonmoral"—and therefore all decisions need to be made on the basis of moral principles. The only ultimate, perfect, moral standards are those contained in the character of God Himself as He is revealed in Scripture, and knowing Him by way of His Scripture is, therefore, the only way to establish a moral framework for decision-making.

Here also is the relevance of counsel from fellow believers. In making decisions, it is wise to seek the advice of others (see Prov. 24:6), but this does not mean adding their human wisdom to God's in the hope that the resulting "wisdom soup" will be nourishing; clearly there would be a radical disparity when trying to mix human wisdom with divine. Rather, it means drawing on the counselors' knowledge of God and His ways, which itself will have been based on His self-revelation in Scripture. Going for counsel is not an excuse to find someone who agrees with you; it is to find further insight into the character of God. Counseling may begin simply by turning to the Bible together, not to seek a direct answer to a problem but to seek the character of God.

We must also note that the study of God's character should be undertaken for its own sake; it is not merely a device for decision-making. Certainly, a major benefit of knowing God is the ability to make sound decisions, but God Himself should be the focus; anything else would be self-centeredness. Similarly, in living out God's will, the point is to grow in godly character, not merely to make right choices. God is more interested in building our character than our career. It is significant that this theme infuses Ephesians 4 before we are given particular ethical instructions and eventually commanded to "understand what the Lord's will is" (Eph. 5:17). For example, chapter 4 says:

> Then we will no longer be infants, tossed back and forth by the waves, and blown here and there by every wind of teaching. . . . Instead, speaking the truth in love, we will in all things grow up into him who is the Head, that is, Christ (Eph. 4:14-16).

In exhorting us to make right decisions in all our behavior, this passage later says, "Be imitators of God, therefore" (Eph. 5:1); decision-making is not a matter of applying a formula, but of living out the character of God. We must know God if we are to imitate Him.

Certain aspects of God's character have a particular bearing on the question of knowing God's will, and yet some of them seem to be the subject of widespread misunderstanding in the church today. We could summarize the problem by saying that much of popular theology is reductionistic; God is not seen as transcendent, immanent,[6] or self-existent.[7] Above all, although lip service is given to God's sovereignty, He is not seen as truly sovereign in real life, and we shall therefore treat this aspect in more depth.

10.5 Understanding God's Sovereignty

Just as fear can bring crippling symptoms of panic, the assurance of God's sovereignty brings calmness and confidence. The Bible teaches us that God is actively sustaining and maintaining every atom in the universe (Col. 1:17). He is especially concerned about His people (Matt. 10:29-31); we need His merciful protection moment by moment, and without it we would be annihilated (Lam. 3:22). We depend upon Him, not merely when we think we need guidance, but for everything all the time.

Most people in the world have experienced some kind of political ruler over them; the degree of power may vary, but the concept of sovereignty as "supreme power and the right to exercise it"[8] is hard to escape. However, we must beware of extending our human analogies in order to construct our concept of God. He can never be reduced to something less than infinite. His sovereignty is not merely a greater version of the human ideal; He possesses total and original power and has all the right to use it. Unlike earthly sovereigns, any veiling of His person is not to protect Him from our scrutiny, but to protect us from annihilation when confronted with His dazzling glory (Ex. 33:20).

Paul proclaimed God as sovereign when he stood before the advanced thinkers of his day at the Athenian Areopagus, and he did so without the slightest attempt to rationalize this doctrine. He knew that they would not be able to "reason their way up to God" (as their "altar to the unknown God" implied), but that he should simply declare God to be what He is:

> The God who made the world and everything in it is the Lord of heaven and earth and does not live in temples built by hands. And he is not served by human hands, as if he needed anything, because he himself gives all men life and breath and everything else. From one man he made every nation of men, that they should inhabit the whole earth; and he determined the times set for them and the exact places where they should live (Acts 17:24-26).

It is difficult to grasp the fact that when we woke this morning it was in the exact place where the sovereign Lord has decreed that we should live at this time. We may ask why we were each born on our particular birthdays rather than on someone else's or in some other century, and the answer is that God decreed these things. No other sovereign is capable of such power and authority. The unbeliever will object "*I* chose my house, no one knows when I will die, and the date of my birthday was determined by my mother and father." The reasons for God's sovereign choices may not be accessible to us, and the unbeliever will certainly have difficulty accepting the fact of God's sovereignty, but this does not alter the fact that it is true. In short, we must be willing to let God be God, to accept His sovereignty. It is too tempting to start our thinking process with the problems that this doctrine appears to create. That is, our experience tells us that certain things happen in our world which seem irreconcilable with the idea of God being both wholly good and wholly sovereign, so that we are tempted to build a doctrine which squares with our experience.

Nor is the problem confined to our experience; the Bible itself occasionally *appears* to make contradictory assertions. Perhaps the most well-known case is the apparently paradoxical relationship between God's sovereignty and human freedom and responsibility, a problem with many manifestations. For example, all people are affected by the Fall of Adam and are subsequently doomed to sin throughout their lives (Rom. 5:12ff), but the Bible also speaks of human responsibility for sin; all people are without excuse (Rom. 1:20) and will be held accountable to God (Rom. 3:19). If we juxtapose these truths they lead to a raft of apparent contradictions: humans are held responsible for their decisions, yet they have no choice but to sin; God cannot sin, yet He allows sin in His world; God gave people the ability to commit sin, yet He maintains true sovereignty over everything that happens in the world. So to come to a resolution we are tempted to modify our concept of God's ultimate sovereignty.

When we look at how the Bible tackles questions like this, we are struck immediately by the fact that it makes no attempt to explain away the apparent contradictions. Peter and John, leading the early believers in prayer, described Jesus' crucifixion in what looks like paradoxical language.

Herod and Pontius Pilate met together with the Gentiles and the people of Israel in this city to conspire against your holy servant Jesus, whom you anointed. They did what your power and will had decided beforehand should happen (Acts 4:27-28).

In his letter to the Romans, addressing the matter of God's sovereignty and man's free will, Paul simply dismisses the question.

One of you will say to me: "Then why does God still blame us? For who resists his will?" But who are you, O man, to talk back to God? "Shall what is formed say to him who formed it, 'Why did you make me like this?' " (Rom. 9:19-20)

The kind of an answer cited here reveals our own arrogance. It maintains that, rather than pleading for justice (as we perceive it), we should be thankful for God's mercy which is freely given to the elect, even though they are totally undeserving. The priorities are reversed, so that the surprising thing is not that God should fail to elect some, but that He should elect any at all. The main point of this passage is that God's purposes cannot be brought down to the level of our human understanding and then validated only if they seem rational to our minds. That would be to make us judges of God — a supreme blasphemy! The truths about God are not offered to us in order that we should try to explain them away; they are offered to us in order that we should accept them and obey them, recognizing that, although we can indeed know "true truths" about God,[9] He, and His self-revelation in Scripture, includes elements that are incomprehensible to us.

Many Christians have tried to work out the processes that must have taken place in God's mind in coming to His decisions. Attempting to explain the apparent contradiction between God's sovereignty and human freedom, there is a popular notion in which God waits to see how we will make our choices and then declares these to be His will. The principle is extended to everyday decisions. A chronological distinction is made so that, after giving men and women "true" freedom, God observes how they use it; then, foreknowing their choices, and being the eternal God who is able to move backward and forward through history, He makes these choices into the predestined plan for their lives. But this is reading a human approach back into Scripture in an attempt to make it comprehensible. It is the way a human sovereign would behave, separating his intelligence reports (foreknowledge) from his executive power (predestination), and basing the latter upon the former. Even with the very best information and with the most extensive powers, a human must make some logical or chronological separation between these functions; it is the only way to make rational, fair decisions.[10]

We are tempted to reduce God from His infinity to something

within our frail comprehension. Instead, we should let God be God, and accept that some of the truths we read in Scripture will be beyond our comprehension. This is not to say that we should give up trying to understand them; we can believe a truth and seek to understand and apply it, while not grasping it fully.

This is supremely true in the matter of God's sovereignty. As if to tantalize us in the extreme, Scripture teaches that God sovereignly ordains even the three aspects of life which seem most undetermined: those things we often regard as "chance" happenings, those things which we choose freely, and those things which seem to us to be evil. We shall now examine these more closely.

10.5.1 God's sovereignty over "chance" happenings

The roulette wheel spins, the die is cast, and the cards are dealt so that fortunes are gained or lost in seconds. A patch of ice on a dark road delivers its deadly effect to an "unlucky" driver. A stock exchange punter happens to buy the right shares on the right day and walks away with a million dollars. A mother's cherished dreams are shattered by the death of her young child. How can God be in control of such chance occurrences? Yet in the OT "lots" were cast in order to make decisions — decisions which God then declared to be His own deliberate plan.

> The lot is cast into the lap, but its every decision is from the Lord (Prov. 16:33).

> Casting the lot settles disputes (Prov. 18:18).

> Then Saul prayed to the Lord, the God of Israel, "Give me the right answer." And Jonathan and Saul were taken by lot, and the men were cleared. Saul said, "Cast the lot between me and Jonathan my son." And Jonathan was taken (1 Sam. 14:41-42).

> Then the sailors said to each other, "Come, let us cast lots to find out who is responsible for this calamity." They cast lots and the lot fell upon Jonah. . . . Jonah prayed to the Lord his God . . . "*You* hurled me into the deep" (Jonah 1:7; 2:1, 3; emphasis ours).

On the Day of Atonement, God accepted the scapegoat which was chosen by lots (Lev. 16:10). The Promised Land was allocated to the Israelites by the casting of lots, not just distributed according to the size of each tribe (Num. 26:52-56; 33:54). The Israelites decided to fight against the people of Gibeah "as the lot directs" (Jud. 20:9).

There are many other situations in the Bible where "lots" determined the course of events. Indeed, a man's whole direction in life was seen by the writer of Ecclesiastes to be a kind of random distribution of benefits from God; man is "to accept his lot and be happy in his work — this is a gift from God," and later he says "this is your lot in life" (Ecc. 5:19; 9:9). John the Baptist's birth is heralded by the appearance of an angel of the Lord to his father, Zechariah, as he served at the altar of incense in the temple. Luke's narrative seems to make a point of the fact that Zechariah was on duty at the temple that day seemingly by chance, since he had been "chosen by lot, according to the custom of the priesthood, to go into the temple of the Lord and burn incense" (Luke 1:9). The implication is that while his presence at the temple was a matter of chance, God had the whole thing arranged so that he could deliver His message by means of an angel.

The Urim and the Thummim were decision-making devices in the OT. Few details are known, but possibly they were objects which were picked out of the priest's breastplate much as one would "draw straws" to make a random decision today. This was a means of making decisions "before the Lord" (Ex. 28:29-30); the priest did not do it furtively behind the tent wall, but openly and with God's full approval.

The believers in Acts 1 used a similar device when faced with the need to elect a replacement for Judas. They had reduced the options to two nominees and then they drew lots. They prayed, asking God to "show us which of these two you have chosen to take over this apostolic ministry" (Acts 1:23-26) and then they accepted the selection as from the Lord. For a decision of this magnitude, and considering that Jesus Himself spent all night in prayer before choosing the original Twelve (Luke 6:12-13), this appears to have been a most haphazard method; but evidently it had God's approval. This occurred, of course, before the NT had been written and therefore without the benefit of God's will fully revealed (e.g., in the instructions regarding the selection of elders in 1 Tim. 3; Titus 2; Acts 20); it also occurred before the outpouring of the Holy Spirit and, therefore, without the benefit of His conviction and testimony. However, it is noteworthy that these early disciples trusted implicitly in God's sovereignty over "random" selection by means of casting lots; they knew that God was in control even when the outcome appeared to be a matter of pure chance.

Other "chance" occurrences in the world around us are also declared to be ordered by the Lord. What could be more random than all the billions of waves out on the open sea? They are the very symbol of chance and uncertainty (James 1:6). Yet each one is ordained by God (see Ps. 42:7; 107:25; Jonah 2:3; Mark 4:41). Or the stars, seemingly scattered throughout the universe, have in fact been placed there by order: God "stretched out the heavens . . . and marshaled their starry hosts" (Isa. 45:12). And we have already noted that God chose the exact places where people should live (Acts 17:26).

The only biblical conclusion is that chance is only "chance" from our limited human point of view; nothing is truly random; everything has order and purpose. The combination of God's holiness, omniscience, omnipotence, omnipresence, and immanence requires us to recognize that every minute detail of the world has been positively determined by God. To use the words of John Calvin, "We call a chance occurrence only that of which the reason and cause are secret."[11] God has left *nothing* to happen in a purely random way; everything is His sovereign will. There is "no suggestion in the Bible that God is the celestial chess-player, awaiting the unknown move, who by 'infinitive contrivance draws some good out of every cross-accident.' On the contrary, God knows every detail . . . not a quantum of energy moves outside his plan."[12] We cannot explain or understand it; we must simply accept that it is no problem for Almighty God to allow the two principles of "apparent chance" and "God's control" to operate simultaneously. At the end of the day we have no right to know what God has ordained and why He has ordained it, but this should not stop us rejoicing in the truth of it.

What does this mean for the subject of guidance? It means we must recognize that God's constant, comprehensive control underlies all the circumstances of our lives, even those circumstances which appear to be the result of pure chance. Nothing is an accident. Having prayerfully considered all facets of a decision and studied Scripture to find out God's will (God's wishes), and in submission to His will decided upon a certain path, the believer must then rest in the knowledge that he or she has done everything possible under God's guidance. If the results of the decision later take an unexpected direction, perhaps because of some apparent accident or chance occurrence, it would be wrong to conclude that the individual was "out of God's will," or in some kind of "second-best" situation.

We know a woman, a believer, who has suffered a series of tragedies. She was the victim of an abusive relationship and was eventually abandoned. After considering biblical principles, she concluded that she had made a poor choice of partner and determined to seek God's will for similar decisions in future; she recommitted her life to Christ. Shortly afterward she was the victim of a serious car accident, one of those freak occurrences where she happened to be in the wrong place at the wrong time. Recovery took more than a year, and in fact she remains slightly disabled. Adding to her suffering, her employer faced financial difficulties and she lost her job. Then she met a wonderful Christian man; they fell in love and became engaged to be married, and this time she carefully handled the decisions biblically. But tragedy struck again; her fiancé died suddenly of a rare disease, and she was again crushed with grief. She plunged, understandably, into questions about God's sovereignty. How could God allow this to happen, when she had submitted everything to His guidance? Was He not in control over car accidents and diseases? Why had she been the victim of apparently random evil? Why was life beginning to feel like Russian roulette? It was an important step in her pilgrimage of faith to learn that God is indeed fully in control of all circumstances. Though she had failed to make right decisions earlier in life, she was not left to cope with "God's second best"; she was being entrusted with difficulties which God in His wisdom sovereignly ordained.

10.5.2 God's sovereignty over human choices

Not only are apparently chance happenings under God's sovereign control, but free human choices are also subject to His total control, as paradoxical as this may seem.[13] The issue goes right back to Adam and Eve in the Garden of Eden. They had been granted the responsibility of managing the earth.

Fill the earth and subdue it. Rule over the fish of the sea and the birds of the air and over every living creature that moves on the ground (Gen. 1:28).

The Lord God took the man and put him in the Garden of Eden to work it and take care of it (Gen. 2:15).

This commission was given to man and woman as a matter of solemn stewardship, and we have been working at it ever since. The curse, given as a result of the Fall, merely added difficulties to the task, in the form of "painful toil," "thorns and thistles," and so on (Gen. 3:17-19). Yet elsewhere in Scripture the fruit of the earth is regarded as a direct result of God's work: "He has shown kindness by giving you rain from heaven and crops in their seasons; he provides you with plenty of food and fills your hearts with joy" (Acts 14:17).

We can imagine that the people of Lystra and Derbe, listening to this sermon by Paul, might feel a little offended at that statement. Had they not produced abundant crops by their own hard work and efficient farm management? Granted, God makes things grow, but without their own efforts it is doubtful that a crop would be produced spontaneously, and it certainly would not be harvested unless it developed some kind of miraculous self-harvesting ability. How can God take *all* the credit for it? Was it not a *human* decision to choose the fields, crop, planting technique, and the time for sowing and reaping?

We also know that Jesus Himself recognized people's skill in agricultural decision-making.

Do you not say, "Four months more and then the harvest?" (John 4:34)

When evening comes, you say, "It will be fair weather, for the sky is red," and in the morning, "Today it will be stormy, for the sky is red and overcast." You know how to interpret the appearance of the sky (Matt. 16:2-3).

How, then, can God take the credit for the crops? Here again is this great paradox[14] of God's sovereignty—that He can be totally in control of every aspect, while not diminishing human free responsibility at all. It is, in fact, much to our discredit that we fail to recognize God's sovereign hand in the provisions of life. One of the great exponents of this theme was the Puritan writer John Flavel.

> O it is your duty to observe His hand and disposal. When God gives you comforts, it is your great evil not to observe His hand in them. Hence was that charge against Israel: "For she did not know that I gave her corn and wine and oil, and multiplied her silver and gold" (Hosea 2:8); that is, she did not actually and affectionately consider my care over her and goodness to her in these mercies. And so for afflictions, it is a great wickedness when God's hand is lifted up not to see it (Isa. 16:11). "The ox knows his owner, and the ass his master's crib" (Isa. 1:3); the most dull and stupid creatures know their benefactors. O look to the hand of God in all; and know that neither your comforts nor afflictions do arise out of the dust, or sprint up out of the ground.[15]

Other examples abound. The disciples had chosen freely to follow Jesus, yet it was also plain that Jesus had chosen them (John 15:16). Think of Peter's feelings when he made an intelligent, rational declaration that Jesus was "the Christ, the Son of the living God," only to be told immediately by Jesus that it was "not revealed to you by man, but by my Father in heaven" (Matt. 16:16-17). Think too of the Thessalonians who welcomed the message brought by Paul, Silas, and Timothy and accepted it as the word of God, choosing of their own volition to obey the Gospel of Christ. Some time later, when they received Paul's first letter to them, they read the puzzling sentence on the first page, "we know . . . that *he* has chosen *you*" (1 Thes. 1:4, 6; emphasis ours; cf. 2:13).

Of course, this truth applies to all believers everywhere! Our faith is a rational choice to believe in Christ and to repent of sin; indeed we are told in Scripture that those who do not *obey* the Gospel (a matter of choice) will be held accountable and punished accordingly (2 Thes. 1:8-10). Yet we are also described as "the elect" (e.g., Col. 3:12, KJV), and we are told that God chose us before the beginning of the world (Eph. 1:4). Somehow, God's choice and our own choice both operate concurrently; they are not a synergism, in which we and God combine our efforts to produce the necessary result; nor are they a phantasm, in which one acts and the other merely appears to act. Both are truly active and both are efficacious.[16]

When our minds finally yield to the coexistence of these (apparently) mutually contradictory powers of choice, all we are doing is bowing to the infinitude of God. The rationalism of our age—the desire to submit everything to human reason, and to deny anything which cannot be comprehended by human reason—often prevents the acceptance of such paradox. Secular rationalism cannot accept God as He is; it can only accept a reduced version of God, one that will bow down and submit to human reason.

If we accept that God does sovereignly predestine our free human choices, what does this mean for our approach to guidance? There are two main implications:

Implication # 1

Firstly, we are responsible to use our minds. God's sovereignty has not made our brains obsolete; on the contrary, Christians should develop and use their mental capacities to the fullest potential. We have already mentioned God's promise of guidance: "I will instruct you and teach you in the way you should go; I will counsel you and watch over you" (Ps. 32:8); sometimes this promise is treated as permission to sit back and let God do it all. But the passage goes on to challenge such passivity by adding a command: "Do not be like the horse or the mule, which have no understanding, but must be controlled by bit and bridle or they will not come to you" (Ps. 32:9).

In other words, while God promises to guide us, He also warns us against idleness of mind. In the OT, there was an emphasis on "the way of wisdom." In preparing the priestly garments, God called for "skilled men to whom I have given wisdom" (Ex. 28:3). Israel was taught God's decrees and laws and was commanded to obey them carefully "for this will show your wisdom and understanding to the nations" (Deut. 4:5-6). The young king Solomon, faced with the weighty responsibilities of his throne, asked God to give him "wisdom and knowledge" so that he might govern God's great people (2 Chron. 1:10); his wisdom later became legendary and "the whole world sought audience with Solomon to hear the wisdom God [had] put in his heart" (1 Kings 10:24). The Psalms are full of references to the way of wisdom, and sometimes this is connected with the influence of God's Word; "The mouth of the righteous man utters wisdom, and his tongue speaks what is just. The law of his God is in his heart; his feet do not slip" (Ps. 37:30-31).

Perhaps most striking of all is the number of references to wisdom in Proverbs and Ecclesiastes. The early chapters of Proverbs, in fact, are a prolonged exhortation to walk in the way of wisdom. We are told that it must be sought after diligently, and yet also that it is the gift of God.

> Turning your ear to wisdom and applying your heart to understanding . . . you will understand the fear of the Lord and find the knowledge of God. For the Lord gives wisdom, and from his mouth come knowledge and understanding (Prov. 2:2, 5-6).

In Ecclesiastes, the "Teacher" (Ecc. 1:1) experiments with wisdom, its sources and its results. Many times he reflects on the apparent futility of life, so that at first reading wisdom appears to be wasted. But in fact his argument serves to strengthen the need for godly wisdom. It is self-interested learning that leads to futility, and it is a heart to obey God that is rewarded with the right kind of wisdom — "To the man who pleases him, God gives wisdom, knowledge and happiness" (Ecc. 2:26).

The idea is developed further in the NT; in fact, it is strengthened in light of the Holy Spirit's ministry in our lives. Wisdom should not become a source of presumption in our relationship with the Lord, for only He can transform our minds so that true spiritual discernment becomes possible.

> Do not conform any longer to the pattern of this world, but be transformed by the renewing of your mind. Then you will be able to test and approve what God's will is — his good, pleasing and perfect will" (Rom. 12:2).

Consider this example of what can happen when Christians believe they must obtain God's directive for every decision. Some years ago, one of us was organizing a party of volunteers to help in the renovation of a Christian conference center. Part of the work involved transporting debris from one side of the estate to the other, and for the first few days this was done by means of a tractor and trailer driving round the perimeter road, taking about half an hour each run. Then a shortcut was noticed, an old courtyard with a path through the middle; it would reduce the journey time to about five minutes. There was only one obstacle: large locked gates on each side of the courtyard. When permission was sought to unlock the gates, the proprietor deferred until a prayer meeting at 11 o'clock the following morning. Shortly after 11 the answer came: the Holy Spirit had *not* given permission for the gate to be opened. It transpired that the trustees of the property regularly put the day's decisions before God, and guidance was expected in the form of prophecies, visions, voices, or some other supernatural directives. No decision, no matter how small, could be made by means of human judgment; everything required divine intervention, and on this occasion, in the absence of a supernatural reply, it was evident that the gates were to remain shut. Thereafter, dozens of young people hauled tons of material round the perimeter road, not a little puzzled at the heavenly policy of estate management.

God's sovereignty over our free human choices, then, does not mean that we should stop using our minds to assess the way ahead; we should use all our rational powers to weigh up the implications of every decision.

Implication # 2

Secondly, our desires matter. A popular myth holds that if we desire something then it is bound to be contradictory to God's wishes. This would appear to be concordant with a doctrine of man which takes full account of the Fall and consequent depravity. But it is really a capitulation to a reductionistic view of God's sovereignty whereby it is impossible for God to govern human affairs in such a way that His will and ours might coexist in harmony sometimes. Yet this is precisely what does happen, and Scripture offers certain evidence.

The first evidence is that God's sovereignty includes common grace to all people whereby they are prevented from the worst excesses of their own sin; God restrains us in our sinfulness, even as believers, so that the world is not destroyed prematurely (Job 34:15; Lam. 3:22-23) and so that provision is made despite our unworthiness (Acts 13:34-35). When God chooses to reduce this level of control, deterioration is rapid (Rom. 1:24, 26, 31).

The second evidence is that God transforms His people so that their desires, as well as their behavior, become more synonymous with His own desires. "It is God who works in you to will and to act according to his good purpose" (Phil. 2:13; see also Ezra 1:5; 1 Cor. 15:10; Heb. 13:21). It is by being transformed by the renewing of our minds that we will be "able to test and approve what

God's will is—his good, pleasing and perfect will" (Rom. 12:2). The striking truth here is that this is presented as a realistic possibility; our own wills *can* be in accord with God's; growth in spiritual maturity brings our wills closer to His.

In seeking God's will, then, we must avoid the assumption that our desires will always be contradictory to His desires. It is not right to assume that the most odious place on earth will be God's calling for missionary service, or that He disapproves of pleasures such as watching television or playing a game of golf. Of course, neither is it true that our desires are necessarily commensurate with God's will, although there will be increasing concordance as we grow in maturity.

Thus it is perfectly possible for a Christian to exclaim, "This is what I *really* wanted!" when following God's will. Indeed, it is part of the miracle of God's working in us "to will and to act according to his good purpose" (Phil. 2:13).

10.5.3 God's sovereignty over evil

Reconciling God's sovereignty and the existence of evil is a problem that may always seem beyond our grasp. Yet Scripture indicates that this too is not a problem to the infinite God; without sinning, He is sovereign over evil. God declared through Isaiah, "I form the light and create darkness, I bring prosperity and create disaster; I, the Lord, do all these things" (Isa. 45:7).

The striking aspect of this passage is the tone of positive action; God creates disaster. Certainly, it was a *deserved* disaster, just as we can say that hell is a deserved condition. But God actually created the disaster. In the case of Jesus' suffering, although He did nothing wrong, He was imputed the guilt of our sin; we might say that, in this sense, He "deserved" His sufferings. Nevertheless, it is still astonishing to read that He was handed over to His torturers "by God's set purpose and foreknowledge" (Acts 2:23). The authorities "did what [his] power and will had decided beforehand should happen" (Acts 4:28). And, of course, we find the unmistakable truth prophesied by Isaiah: "It was the Lord's will to crush him and cause him to suffer" (Isa. 53:10).

The Book of Job is famous for its account of Job's suffering. But the truly baffling aspect appears early in the narrative, where Satan appears before God and argues the case for making Job suffer (Job 1:6-12; 2:1-6); God actually gives Satan permission to go and torture Job, which he did with alacrity. Similarly, the story of Joseph tells us that incredible suffering, though meant for evil by the perpetrators, was intended for eventual good by God (Gen. 50:20). One might ask whether God knew of any way to accomplish this objective without inflicting suffering along the way.

Suffering is not good in itself, though, of course, there may be many good results. Some will point out that all suffering, ultimately, is deserved by humanity because of sin and in fact is restrained from its full impact because of God's grace; if we received what we deserved then we would suffer very much more than we do. This does not, however, answer the ultimate question of how a holy and omnipotent God can allow evil to have any part in His created order. The important point for us to note here is that the Bible simply states the truth without defense. Somehow, in His infinite wisdom, God is sovereign over evil; this is a declared truth, not just a word game.

Here is where the Bible must inform our understanding of our lives and settle our fears in certain matters of guidance. It is possible to suffer evil and its effects even though one is, theoretically, following God's will fully. The most obedient Christian may also be one who suffers. Health, healing, freedom, security, and wealth are not ours by right, and the greatest saint may be deprived of them *under God's sovereignty*. There is a most striking example of this in John 9, the story of the man born blind, where the disciples (despite having spent more than two years in Jesus' company) asked, "Rabbi, who sinned, this man or his parents, that he was born blind?" (John 9:2) They associated suffering directly with individual sin and sought to attach blame. To paraphrase this in a modern idiom, they were asking, "Who is out of God's will, and therefore not deserving good health?" Jesus answered, "Neither this man nor his parents sinned . . . but this happened so that the work of God might be displayed in his life" (9:3).

In the matter of guidance, then, it would be wrong to assume that we are "out of God's will" when difficulties arise. Even the most obedient Christian has no right to healing or prosperity, and the wonder of healing is not necessarily a sign of God's approval. As James says, in the words of J.B. Phillips' paraphrase, "When all kinds of trials and temptations crowd into your lives, my brothers, don't resent them as intruders, but welcome them as friends!" (James 1:2, PH)

This is the third aspect of God's sovereignty that is often surprising, but must be believed if we are serious about accepting Scripture's authority and listening to what it really says. The whole phenomenon of God's sovereignty is vitally important for us to consider precisely because it *is* so alien to our natural minds; our temptation to make God understandable — or palatable — brings the risk of serious disruption to our progress on the "hermeneutical spiral." In fact, it is in the area of guidance that our hermeneutics are in special danger of being manipulated by our ulterior motives. Since our decisions are indeed personal we can easily be defensive regarding the decision-making process, and it is essential that we submit our wills to God, willing for Him to teach us His truth, as we seek to maintain good hermeneutical habits.

10.6 Conclusion

Guidance, then, is very much a matter of hermeneutics. The two subjects belong together. It is regrettable that this is not often the case in Christian conferences or study programs; as we said in the early part of this chapter, guidance is often taken in isolation and therein lies a fatal flaw. On the other hand, when God's people take the trouble to seek sound biblical interpretation, and to submit to God's will as it is revealed by it, they begin to sample the benefit of easier decision-making and, much more important, the blessing of God upon their choices.

By a delightful shift in perspectives, indeed a change in presuppositions and worldview, such people are no longer so concerned with making good decisions or receiving blessing in their lives; they are less concerned with how life pleases *them* and more concerned with how their lives might please *Him*.

CONCLUSION

The Gospel of John has been called a pool in which a child may wade and an elephant may swim. This could be said of the whole Bible. Its basic message is simple enough for young children to grasp and yet its depth and riches cannot even be plumbed, let alone exhausted, by the greatest minds. The Bible is so clear that the simplest of people can perceive its teaching, yet it is so complex that no scholar can ever presume to have attained complete understanding.

We have argued in this book that genuine understanding occurs to the degree that our basic presuppositions and operating assumptions are in line with those of the Bible. Advances in understanding occur as the Bible itself molds our presuppositions into conformity with its own. The detailed examination of how to do exegesis and of questions like whether Scripture can at a later stage have a "fuller meaning" have been to help us open ourselves to the "framework of understanding" of Scripture. Again, we must allow the Bible to mold us, not just our external behavior but our thought behavior, as well as interpretive behavior. Only then will we advance on the spiral of understanding.

Changing presuppositions is difficult. It takes concerted effort to be always examining one's assumptions, to be constantly reading and rereading the text, allowing its ultimate Author to change us. But we must be changed. And indeed we *can* be changed, because we labor not alone. Generations of Christians have gone before, building a framework of understanding which we have inherited. The framework is far from perfect, but it is much better than starting from scratch. And most importantly, the Holy Spirit Himself has guided the development of His people's understanding through history and continues to work in us now, opening our eyes to see and our hearts to obey the wondrous things that are in His Word. Indeed, He opens our minds to see the most wondrous thing of all, the true God who became true man, the Lord Jesus Christ. Like the Greeks who came to Philip, we say to the Author of Scripture, "Sir, we wish to see Jesus" (John 12:21, RSV), and He grants our request.

In all these matters of interpretation our attitude should be one of prayer. This spirit is perhaps best reflected in the early thirteenth-century poem "Day by Day" by Sir Richard of Chichester, which models a posture we would do well to emulate.

Day by day,
Dear Lord of Thee these three things I pray:
To see Thee more clearly,
To follow Thee more nearly,
To love Thee more dearly,
Day by day.

APPENDIX A

Where Is Meaning?

Where does the meaning of a text come from, or where is it located? In chapter 1 we briefly noted the differing opinions. Some say the author is the source of meaning, and interpretation is simply a matter of recovering his or her original intent. Others say that meaning is independent of the author and resides within the text itself. Still others argue that meaning comes only from the reader, whose own framework of understanding provides a meaning structure wherein the text can take on meaning. In this appendix we will describe and evaluate these approaches more fully.

A.1 Authorial Intent

The emphasis on author's intent as the locus of a determinate meaning has been championed most effectively by E.D. Hirsch, who stated his case in *Validity in Interpretation* and further defended and nuanced it in *The Aims of Interpretation*.[1] Hirsch responds to the difficulty posed by the fact that any text constantly takes on new relevance to new readers in different circumstances by arguing for a distinction between *meaning* and *significance*.[2] Just as a word or sentence has a *sense* which is distinguishable from its *reference*, so a text may have a general meaning which is distinct from its particular application. In *Validity in Interpretation*, Hirsch argues that the determinate meaning of a text is its unitary meaning intended by the author. It also has a particular application or significance to the author. Other applications of the single meaning are possible, but not more than one meaning. Thus there remains both an objective meaning to a text which began life in the mind of the author, and a subjective meaning for the reader who applies it in his own life. This approach preserves the moral right of an author to determine the meaning.

But when anyone reads a text, even if one is attempting to recover the original intention of the author, his or her awareness of the meaning of a text begins as an unreflected consciousness of meaning produced by the text as it encounters the reader's interpretive mental patterns. As J.D. Smart asks with respect to biblical interpretation, "Has the exegete any access to the original meaning of the text except *by way of the present meaning of the text for him?*" (his emphasis)[3] Hirsch recognizes this problem in his later book (*The Aims of Interpretation*) and concedes that meaning is a function of the interpreter, but he still maintains that the reader is reconstructing a *determinate* meaning, and that the "best" reconstruction is that which corresponds to the author's *single* original meaning.

But is the distinction of meaning and significance of texts as easy as with the sense and reference of words? Can a text have any meaning apart from significance?

When someone "means" something, he or she is performing a certain kind of act. This action's purpose is to generate a certain kind of effect. The intention (intended effect) is the meaning, and this includes an intended significance if the hearer has understood. If we tell our children, "The milk is bad," our meaning is not simply a description of the state of the milk; it has the intended significance of a warning not to drink it.[4] The meaning includes the significance, and without the significance the meaning is missed.

Secondly, as we noted in chapter 2, the meaning of a text only exists in an interpreter's mind. For any reader, even the author, the meaning of a text is inseparable from its significance. We cannot easily separate what a text means to us from what it "means," and in fact if we try we may miss its true meaning. No divorce can be made between them, because, unlike words which can designate "fields of meaning" by themselves without addressing anything, a text, in order to mean anything to a reader, always is taken as addressing something in particular. A text has no meaning at all apart from addressing a situation. However, in defense of Hirsch we should point out that although meaning and significance may not be *separable*, they are still *distinguishable*.

Thirdly, as Hirsch himself acknowledges, a speaker or author may *intend* a meaning of his text but he does not control the language.[5] And it is possible for someone to say something which is not quite what he or she means to say.[6] The "moral right" of an author is limited and controlled by his or her linguistic and social environment. If a man submits an affidavit in court that he saw a man wearing a green hat coming out of the bank at 4 o'clock, he cannot usually claim later that what he *meant* was that he saw a girl ("man" in the generic sense) wearing a blue hat with green lines in it coming up the river bank at what was 4 o'clock two time zones to the east (unless he can produce clear evidence that the context of his statement so indicates). So a better way of preserving an authorially determinate meaning is to find the "locus" of meaning in the linguistic context of the people to whom the author was originally addressing his work, as in Schleiermacher's canon: "a more precise determination of any point in a given text must be decided on the basis of the use of language common to the author and his original public."[7] In practice this "original linguistic context" approach recognizes the "original author's intent" as a goal, since "understanding" involves the attempt to recover the author's intent by reconstructing the original synchronic linguistic, cultural, and existential situation.

A.2 Autonomous Texts

An entirely different approach is to locate meaning in the text as an autonomous object. This view, championed by Roman Ingarden and the now old "New Criticism" school, regards texts as intentional objects, but the intention is not flowing from the author (the author is only the vehicle); a text has a life of its own. For example, T.S. Eliot claims that

> we can only say that a poem, in some sense, has its own life; that its parts form something quite different from a body of neatly ordered biographical data; that the feeling, or emotion, or vision, resulting from the poem is something different from the feeling or emotion or vision in the mind of the poet.[8]

According to Eliot, literature cannot express emotion or thought directly, it can only evoke emotion or thought. Eliot developed an idea of the "objective correlative," that particular objects, situations, or chains of events would regularly evoke certain responses. This is not to say that texts create themselves or exist independently of humans who use language, but it does argue that texts are not indissolubly linked either to author or to reader. Once they are written they are objets d'art which stand independently of their creators or appreciators (as in the New Criticism) or they are "pieces of language" which reflect the synchronic social and cultural situation but point to one or more basic human relationships (as in structuralism; see below). Using the illustration of the vinyl record, it is no longer dependent on the orchestra which first played the piece, nor does it depend on any particular phonograph. It, in its present state, rather determines what sounds will emerge from a record player. Varieties of record players will simply vary the fidelity with which the present state of the record is transformed into intelligible music.

On this approach, the original author fades into nonexistence; only the "implied" author, the assumed narrator of the text, who is really only a fictitious speaker within the text, exists, and then only as a construct of the text.

A.2.1 Structuralism

This understanding is to some extent linked with a particular approach to analyzing a text, called "structuralism." Literary structuralism also has ties to the "socio-linguistic community" approach described below (see pp. 282–83), since meaning grows not from a text per se but from the social structure. But in the modern structuralist movement, authors do not determine texts, rather language (with all its social and cultural baggage) determines authors. This leads to structuralists often finding the "true" meaning of a text in blatant disregard of what the author might have meant by it, and even in disregard of what present readers think it means.

A structural approach to a text takes its lead from the anthropological work of Claude Lévi-Strauss and the linguistic theories of Ferdinand Saussure and, more recently, Noam Chomsky. Saussure pointed out that the elements of any particular language have meaning only in relationship to the other elements in that language system, and consequently it was not the diachronic development of language which determined meaning but the synchronic state of the language at the time of utterance.[9] Since the elements of a language are thus understood as existing only as part of the *structure*, this approach is usually called "structural linguistics." Although de Saussure himself recognized that diachrony came into the picture with the later life of a story or text, structuralism has focused almost exclusively on the synchronic state not just of the language but of the social structure which in their view gave rise to the text.

Lévi-Strauss treated structuralism as an anthropological principle.[10] Human activities and social interactions were regarded as units of a framework or structure of contrasts and similarities, oppositions and identities, and any particular human activity or

278

social relation was analyzable by reference to the structure of the particular society wherein it occurred or existed. Lévi-Strauss attempted to find the commonalities of human social relations and actions, particularly as they are reflected in that society's "myths." These commonalities are now sometimes referred to as the "deep structure" level, as opposed to the particular expressions in a given society, which are "surface structure."[11]

Structural analysis of texts has applied this approach to literature in general, and later to the Bible, attempting to find the deep structure roles in every story and literary account. It thus views a text not as an act stemming from one individual, but as a unit in a particular social structure, and the "real meaning" of a text is not its "surface meaning," but the basic human roles and pieces of the deep structure of human behavioral patterns.[12]

The obvious difficulty with this approach is that it divorces texts from their only clear source of meaning; the particular people involved in the communication process. Again, it depersonalizes the text.[13] This view "forgets that a text remains a discourse told by someone else about something. It is impossible to cancel out this main characteristic of discourse without reducing texts to natural objects, i.e. things which are not man-made, but which, like pebbles, are found in the sand."[14]

Also, until recently texts were hardly ever purely art objects. People ordinarily create texts, like utterances in general, to accomplish things, without thinking about the peculiarities of creating some artistic object that goes beyond themselves. One wonders whether structuralists arguing for their particular viewpoint see their own texts as really nothing more than a reflection of the deep structures and basic roles and relations of society, or whether they expect their readers to "understand" what they want them to understand.

Up to this point we have more or less assumed that a text has *a* meaning and that the job of an interpreter was to find out that particular best meaning. But recently challenges have been issued against the idea that texts can have such a thing as a *determinate* meaning. Meaning only exists in the mind. So a text has a meaning only when an individual's peculiar mind apprehends and reacts to that text. The only meaning possible, it is argued, is therefore influenced and determined by each individual reader. So determinate meaning must be an illusion.[15]

A.3 Reader Response

Several hermeneutical conclusions have stemmed from this questioning of determinate meaning. One of the most important of modern hermeneutical theories is that of H.G. Gadamer (*Truth and Method*), who argued that the meaning of a text is produced when the "horizon of understanding" of a reader encounters and responds to the "horizon" of the text, resulting in a "fusion" of horizons. If all this meant was that the meaning of a text for today is a matter of taking the author's meaning, ascertained by reference to the author's linguistic and historical situation (his or her "horizon"), and then seeing that interpretive result from the standpoint of the present "horizon of understanding," then there would be little to quarrel with. But Gadamer is doing more than this; he is attempting to implement in hermeneutical theory the goal of Heidegger in encountering "being" by way of the encounter with texts, particularly primitive and ancient texts. Heidegger had argued that we are at the disposal of language, not the other way around, and that our encounter with being must therefore be an encounter with language. Gadamer attempted to spell out how this encounter may happen. It is not a matter simply of *applying* the distinct meaning stemming from the author's "horizon" to the present situation, but of achieving an initial meaning by the preconscious *fusing* of the horizon generated by the text itself with the horizon of the reader.

A major problem with Gadamer's theory is that it has difficulty explaining how a reader may disagree with a text, and refuse to fuse, so to speak. Somehow a reader must be able to formulate an image of a meaning with which he or she may disagree, a meaning which is not purely the result of a fusion of horizons.[16] Hirsch points out that even for Gadamer himself, for a fusing to take place at all there must be some "horizon of meaning" out there which differs from the reader's.[17] This implies the existence of a determinate meaning other than the meaning resultant from the fusion. However, Gadamer could counter by saying that, although such a "pre-fusion" meaning undoubtedly existed, it is unknowable and therefore irrelevant to the task of hermeneutics.

Gadamer's theory is at least tangentially if not directly related to the last two approaches we will mention here, the "reader-response" theory and the "socio-linguistic community" theory.

The simplest form of the reader-response theory is that meaning is engendered when a person reads a text, and is in some way affected or changed by it.[18] One of the proponents of this view calls this "the theory of aesthetic response."[19] The behavioral or perceptual "affective result" is the meaning. There is no determinate or "correct" meaning, but only meanings which arise in the reader. But two readers may agree on what a text "means" and yet differ greatly in their affective responses to it. So in this simplest form, "reader-response" hermeneutics is not very adequate.[20]

A.3.1 Deconstruction

What has found many adherents among academics is a less simple but more devastatingly consistent form of the reader-response theory called "deconstruction." Its foremost representative is perhaps the French writer Jacques Derrida.[21] The goal of this approach is not to ascertain any particular meaning, even for a particular reader, but to destroy even the illusion of any determinate meaning. Interpretation is the process of uncovering the *ambiguity* of a text as much as possible. The reason for this is that the purpose or use of a text is to open to the reader new possibilities for thought. This increases the reader's "world." There is no world apart from the one constructed by the human mind, and texts help to expand that constructed world. Since all language is metaphor, and behind metaphor is only other metaphor, therefore there is no knowledge of any objective truth, but only the increasing awareness of relative truth. It thus "de-constructs" in order to provide material for a "re-construction" by the reader.[22]

In a certain way, there appears to be some perceptivity in this approach. Meaning seems to remain personal, and the fact that meaning only exists in the human mind is appreciated. The deconstructionists want to transcend the old subject-object dialectic. Rationalism had stressed the objective; romanticism the subjective. Deconstructionists tell us that the way out of the dilemma is to focus on language, which transcends and encompasses both subject and object.

However, this approach is not truly interpersonal; people become not individuals in relationship but rather linguistic entities, separate unto themselves yet without particularity, creating their own "world" as they encounter speech and texts. Further, the absolutizing of language severs the connection between texts and life.[23] Even the objective of transcending "subject" and "object" is not reached, because this approach becomes in practice an exaltation of subjectivity. Finally, the whole idea of the reader being the *source* of meaning is closely tied to the psychological theory of the constitutive power of perception, which of course holds hands with a bias against metaphysical truth. But the rejection of the idea of metaphysical truth cuts straight across biblical assumptions, which ground truth not in man but in an absolute God. Deconstructionism is totally antithetical to the idea of an absolute knower.[24]

A.3.2. Socio-linguistic community

The other form of a reader-based theory of meaning does not find meaning within the individual reader per se, but within his socio-linguistic context. Stanley Fish has argued[25] that the author's intent is inaccessible, that a text by itself is merely sounds or figures, and that the particular reader is only a single member of a linguistic community. Just as the "meaning" of a word or phrase is determined not by absolute rules but by reference to the particular context, situation, or institution in which it is uttered,[26] so also a text being read finds its meaning according to the constraints of what meanings are "allowed" in the prevailing linguistic community. Fish, like Derrida, is operating from a basic assumption that reality has no structure other than what we give it, and he too wishes to eliminate the subject-object distinction. But unlike the deconstructionists, Fish argues that the reader is no more autonomous than the text. He does not construct his or her "world" in isolation. Linguistic reality is not constructed by the individual but by the linguistic community. Of course, the linguistic community is variable with time and place, and so Fish agrees with the deconstructionists that there are no determinate meanings and that the stability of a text is an illusion.

Fish's approach in some ways avoids the rampant subjectivity of reader-response hermeneutics. There is something outside the reader which controls his or her understanding. Further, Fish is correct to point out that words do not determine meaning; rather the structure of understanding in a given situation generates awareness of meaning. It also has the advantage of being able to explain the variable hermeneutics of the past. Why did Origen, perhaps the most brilliant and well-educated man of his day, perform interpretive feats that appear ridiculous to us? Was it not because in his social context allegorical interpretation was not just allowed but *expected* as normative? Origen's non-Christian opponent Celsus agreed with Origen that inspired texts must be capable of allegorical interpretation. Celsus' argument was that, since the Bible could not be allegorically interpreted the way Homer could be, it was not inspired![27] It was "obvious" in their interpretive community that texts of religious value would have allegorical meaning. Today, such interpretation is "not allowed" (except in certain restricted communities like the Swedenborgians) and so appears ridiculous.

But for all Fish's perception, his observations do not disprove determinate meaning; they simply indicate that the relation of form to meaning is a function of human context. It is true that a reader cannot divorce the text's significance from its meaning, but one can always strive toward the *goal* of grasping the determinate meaning, which can be sought by reference to the *original* sociolinguistic context.

A.4 Conclusion

In summary, today hermeneutics struggles with a tension between an apparently distinct meaning to a text and the fact that every interpreter comes from a linguistic environment that influences what he or she hears from the text. There is, in fact, a clash or disjuncture between the "horizon" of the text's author and that of the reader. Some cut this knot by denying the role of the reader and claiming objective inherent and obvious meaning to texts (linked either to author or to an autonomous text). Others deny any meaning to a text apart from readers, either of themselves or within their linguistic communities. But all of these approaches fail to capture the real nature of language as interpersonal communication, and they all operate from a purely phenomenological standpoint. That is, the idea of a transcendent interpretation cannot be entertained, because there is no transcendent interpreter. But we postulate that God, the inventor of language, provides the basis for interpretation which is at once both truly objective and truly subjective, upon which our interpretation can be based. This does not tell us what the correct interpretation of a text will be, but it does make possible a true interpretation that is at once the meaning of the author, the meaning inherent in the text itself, the meaning more or less faithfully apprehended by the reader, and the meaning allowed in the linguistic community. God's horizon is totally comprehensive of all horizons, which is not to say that all possible meanings of texts are God's meanings, but that the determinate meaning of any text is exhaustively known by Him. Further, God is not mutable or time bound, and so the meaning which He understands of a text is unchanging.

So it is our position that texts do have determinate meanings, with the possible exception of modern works which the author *intended* to make ambiguous and indeterminate.[28] However, this determinate meaning does not stand only on the one leg of authorial intent, but on three legs: (1) the author's intent, which is knowable by reference to his or her historical and linguistic situation; (2) the recognition of language utterances as interpersonal actions, and the continuity of people and their relationships (thus texts can have meaning even though the author and his or her original context is unknown), and (3) God's sovereign transcendency, which provides the basis for an absolute transcendent determinate meaning to all texts, most especially His own.

APPENDIX B

The Historical-Critical Method

It is curious that often those who are most insistent that the Bible be read like any other book in fact treat it as no other book has ever been treated: expending inordinate amounts of effort tracing sources, sources within sources, oral prehistory, and various stages of editorializing; while doubting every historical assertion and basically rendering its natural discourse content inaccessible. Some of this was tried on other ancient texts many years ago, but was soon abandoned as a more or less fruitless endeavor. One sometimes has the impression it is precisely the religious demand which the Bible makes that causes discomfort and generates a desire to recast its teaching into something more palatable to the modern world and its humanistic values. In any case, a word is in order here concerning the approach to the Bible sometimes called the "historical-critical method."

B.1 General Description and Evaluation[1]
It is difficult to deal clearly with this, because historical-critical method involves more than one aspect and is understood in different ways. I.H. Marshall[2] notes that it ordinarily is perceived as having a twofold task. First, the method is used to *elucidate* the meaning of the text; secondly, the text is *evaluated* in terms of its historical accuracy. Marshall says that the goal of this twofold endeavor is to recover "what actually happened."

Thus criticism is in some ways simply a more technical form of what we have been calling grammatical-historical methods. So long as a method takes the text as it stands in its integrity, and does not "evaluate" its truthfulness or accuracy, or attempt to reconstruct what "really" happened in distinction from the biblical accounts themselves, or recover levels of meaning *prior to* inscripturation, then it is a valuable set of tools. In other words, so long as criticism is confined to "judging what is the meaning of the extant text" as opposed to "judging whether the text is true," criticism is not only viable but necessary—it means the same as disciplined interpretation. Unfortunately, criticism in most circles also implies evaluation of the integrity and historical truthfulness of the text.

According to Troeltsch,[3] modern historical criticism operates on two assumptions: first, that all texts are similar, and second, that all events are similar. This is presumably an application of the "scientific" method. Actually there is a third assumption which Troeltsch does not mention, that the universe is "closed," that is, there are no causes outside the universe which have any effects inside the universe. These assumptions result in three principles of modern historical method. First is the principle of criticism based on *probability*: every historical text must be subject to a judgment based on the probability or improbability of its events and an evaluation of its historical sources. Second is the principle of *analogy*: historical events must be analogous to events that occur today. Third is the principle of *correlation*: all effects have an identifiable cause within this universe.

Now it might be argued that such an approach is appropriate for secular historiography, but it cannot be applied a priori to a text which claims to be unique and to record unique, one-of-a-kind events. To do so is to assume the falsity of its claim before testing it.[4] It is therefore odd that not just non-Christian historians but scholars who claimed to be of Christian persuasion began to apply this method to the Bible (treating it "like any other historical source"). It ultimately led to the conclusion among certain Christian scholars that Scripture was not itself the Word of God, but simply contained it, or bore witness to it, and it was the job of scholars to sort out what was good and what was true.[5]

Gerhard Maier's forthright critique, *The End of the Historical Critical Method*[6] notes six objections to this approach.

(1) It is impossible to discover any "canon within the canon." There exist no criteria to map out certain texts as having authority and other texts as not.

(2) One cannot separate divine Scripture from human Scripture. There exist no criteria to distinguish them.

(3) Revelation consists in more than simply subject matter. It is personal in nature. The historical-critical method, on the other hand, depersonalizes the text in order to study it as an object. It cannot "hear and obey."

(4) The conclusions of historical-critical method are established prior to the actual interpretation of texts. Since the method knows in advance what texts are *permitted* to say and do, the text very often is not permitted to say what it really says.

(5) The method is deficient in practicability. It yields exceedingly meager results, and there is hardly any consensus regarding most critical questions. As E. Earle Ellis points out, "although it can show certain interpretations to be wrong, it can achieve an agreed interpretation for virtually no biblical passage."[7] Further, the results are almost always useless for the life of the church. We would add that it also removes the Bible from the hands of the ordinary Christian.

(6) Historical criticism is inappropriate for a text of the nature of revelation. If the Bible really is revelation, then not critique but obedience is called for.

The last, as we indicated already, is the most damning critique of this kind of criticism. Historical-critical method which operates on antisupernaturalistic assumptions can never lead to a true understanding of the Bible, because it disallows the principal assumptions of the Bible, that God who created the world and is other than the world is nevertheless at work in the world, doing unique, one-of-a-kind redemptive deeds. Historical criticism is not "neutral ground." In fact, as Eta Linnemann has pointed out, the historical-critical approach as practiced most widely today is basically a theological system, not just methodology.[8] The assumption of many that historical criticism can be "neutral" is foolish.[9] Not only is every historian inseparable from his or her own presuppositions, but any effort to evaluate the truthfulness of the Bible implies a tacit claim that human reason is the ultimate arbiter of truth, and that the reasoner is capable of perfect comprehension.

But, one may ask, if there is no "neutral" criticism, then how does one distinguish between genuine revelation and that which falsely claims to be revelation? The proper method is advocated by Jesus in John 7:17: "If anyone chooses to do God's will, [then] he will find out whether my teaching comes from God." The truth of God is not critically discerned but spiritually discerned (1 Cor. 2:14-16), by the humble and contrite heart. There is a *subordinate* criterion of internal consistency (that which purports to be revelation must square with what is already known to be revelation), but even this is a matter of spiritual discernment.

This is not to say that there is no connectedness to the biblical history; the Bible does speak of reasons, and it assumes a normality to human existence. In fact, its miracles are to be wondered at precisely because they are outside the usual order of things. But if miracles did happen, modern criticism would still "prove" that they did not.

So long as the historical-critical method simply challenges our anachronistic interpretations, it has some value. Its "scholarly methods" (which are described below) have been beneficial in compelling us to reexamine the nature of the biblical materials and to become aware of the historical context and the cultural distances between ourselves and the original readers.[10] But the methods of interpretation are chosen according to the goal, and the goal from which historical-critical methods have been generated most typically assumes that God is *not* at work in the world. Unfortunately the incompatibility of the assumptions of certain critical methods and biblical faith frequently goes unrecognized, and many Christian scholars either end up bifurcating their lives into academic and spiritual compartments, or are arbitrarily inconsistent in their use.[11]

B.2 "Scholarly" Methods

The aspect of historical-critical methodology which has to do with discovering what the text means, or showing what it cannot mean, is nevertheless often of benefit.[12] Although these methods are more generally appropriate to professional scholars, commentaries and other books on the Bible do occasionally refer to them, so we will here give a brief description of those methods to which reference is most frequently made.

B.2.1 Source criticism

The first method to be developed was source criticism. This was sometimes called literary criticism, although that term is now applied to something quite different (see below). Source criticism attempted to recover the written sources from which the extant biblical texts grew. In the OT, this was particularly applied to the Pentateuch (or Hexateuch), where four sources were identified as having been woven together or supplemented to produce the present documents. These four were a "Yahwist" (so called because of a supposed preference for the name "Yahweh" for God), an "Elohist" (who used "Elohim" for God), the "Deuteronomist" (responsible for Deuteronomy and perhaps the "deuteronomistic history" [Joshua through Kings]), and a "Priestly" source, which was much later added into the material to make it favorable to the concerns of the priesthood in Israel. These were abbreviated J, E, D, and P, and the theory is most often identified with the name of Julius Wellhausen.[13] For Wellhausen, the spontaneous and genuine religion of patriarch and prophet was reflected in the J and E sources; D represented a late monarchical decline into monolithic absolutism, and P added the postexilic layer of cultic legalism and ceremonialism. Thus the Law was not the foundation of Israel but the product of its senility. Subsequent scholars have produced many variations on these themes, but there seems to be a consensus that there are several literary sources, of which there are at least two early strands, one or more late monarchical strands (D) and one or more postexilic strands (P).

Source-critical techniques are also applied to other material. For example, Isaiah is typically thought to have been a joining of at least two, usually three, sometimes more, sources.[14]

Now we must acknowledge that there were sources used in the production of the Pentateuch, and no doubt other OT books. Reference is made within the Pentateuch, for example, to the "Book of the Wars of the Lord" (Num. 21:14); Samuel-Kings refers repeatedly to the "Chronicles of the Kings of Judah" and the "Chronicles of the Kings of Israel" (which were different than the books we call "Chronicles"); Chronicles appears to have used Samuel-Kings; and undoubtedly there were other oral as well as written sources which informed the authors of our present Bible. But the overall effect of theories like that of Wellhausen and his predecessor Karl Heinrich Graf is to focus attention on hypothetical sources and the resultant sociological reconstructions rather than on the text as it stands.

Further, the divisions into sources which scholars make appear to be made more on the basis of theology or content than on purely linguistic grounds. And, of course, this begs questions. For example, is a source known to be late because the theology is late, or is a theological concept known to be late because the source is late? The result is that the method is haphazardly applied; everyone agrees there are sources, but no one agrees on what they are. There just is not adequate information in the texts themselves to allow a clear derivation or dating of the sources.

Most important of all for Christians who understand the Bible as God's Word, the Graf-Wellhausen approach undermines the historical integrity of the text. On this approach, no longer does the

Pentateuchal material come from God through His intermediary Moses; it only represents the spiritual experiences of people over a millennium, who were constantly rewriting their history and injecting legendary matter.

In the NT, source criticism is most often applied to the Gospels. There has been much more consensus here as to what the actual sources are than amongst OT scholars. Most Gospels critics see Matthew and Luke as having used Mark, and another source called "Q" (for the German "Quelle" which means "source"). This is called the "Markan priority hypothesis," the "Two source theory," or sometimes its variant, the "Four source theory" (which sees special sources for Matthew and Luke in addition to Mark and Q). But even this consensus is breaking down (see chap. 3, n. 15). And, even if the theory is correct, such source criticism by itself does not help us see what the present texts as they stand say. (Source criticism sometimes informs "redaction criticism" which does aim at understanding the texts as they stand; see below.)

B.2.2 Form and tradition criticism

The next type of critical method to appear was form and tradition criticism. In OT studies these are distinct. Form or genre criticism attempts to classify bits of the prewritten oral material which was later incorporated into the OT. Classifying these bits according to genre or literary type is expected to aid in understanding the purpose or function of that bit of text in its original setting. For example, certain psalms are said to be "enthronement" psalms which were sung at the inauguration or anniversary of the king's accession. Knowing the setting and literary type supposedly helps understand the original meaning of that psalm.

Tradition criticism, on the other hand, attempts to trace the history of the development and use of that bit of text in the tradition of Israel. Once a psalm was classified as an enthronement psalm, the interest would be on tracing how it was used in the life of Israel, how it developed, and so on.

In the NT, form and tradition criticism are combined. Again it is most frequently applied to the Gospels. Individual stories, parables, bits of teaching, and sayings are classified by genre, and an attempt is made to trace how they originated and developed in the oral tradition of the early church prior to their inclusion in the Gospel.

Unfortunately, form criticism depends to a large degree on a historical presupposition that the biblical documents as they stand are unreliable witnesses regarding the original verbal forms and historical settings. This is most baldly evident in the so-called "criterion of dissimilarity" which governs form critical analysis in Gospels study. The criterion of dissimilarity assumes that any saying of Jesus in the Gospels tradition which might be derived either from Judaism or from the early church is not a genuine saying of Jesus.[15] This is simply to say that Jesus must have been totally discontinuous with His own heritage and that the church was totally unfaithful to her Lord.

B.2.3 Redaction criticism

With the recognition that whoever finally put the present text into its final form must have had some theological reasons for editing it the way he did, scholars began attempting to discover those theological reasons or aims. This was called redaction criticism, because the theological viewpoint of the final "redactor" or editor is what is in view. This study bears in mind whole books or even collections of books if they are perceived to have been edited as a unit. When it looks at an individual passage, the question is: "How was the author using this bit of the tradition to develop or express his theological aims?" This approach has some value, because it attempts to understand the purpose of the writer who produced our present biblical texts. Unfortunately, too often its conclusions are based on certain dubious results of source and form criticism, and theological reconstructions which are arrived at ahead of time. However, there is no denying that, for example, the Gospel writers applied the sayings of Jesus somewhat differently (compare the context of Mark 4:25 with that in Matt. 13:12). Asking what were the inspired writers' purposes can explain these differences.

B.2.4 Literary criticism[16]

A literary-critical approach has become somewhat au courant in recent years, but there is considerable confusion as to just what "literary criticism" means. For some esoteric practitioners, it appears that literary criticism is the art of reading behind the text into what it does not say, rather than what it says. Here, however, we are understanding the literary approach as one which looks at the biblical material as texts which artistically address the human condition, using an array of literary devices and techniques. These include the means of making connections between parts of a text, the flow and structure of a narrative, character description and developments, symmetry, metaphors, settings, length of lines, and any other elements which a writer uses to communicate or cast his or her text into a form which someone will understand and/or appreciate. Observing the devices and purposes of the text as a literary document can be extremely valuable, because such analysis can show up the dynamics of the communicative message of narrative material in the Bible. In fact, since much of the Bible is classifiable under the general rubric of "story," observations regarding literary matters such as plot, the interaction between characters, the human decisions, the shift from one state of affairs to another, and the orientation around a central protagonist should highlight the central concerns of most of the Bible.[17] Further, literary analysis is a method which a "nonprofessional" exegete can easily learn and profit by, especially if he or she has some background in literary theory. On the other hand, the "literary" nature of the Bible should not be taken as warrant for treating the Bible as primarily "art" as opposed to "reality."[18]

As with other methods, the interpreter's goals will have a determinitive effect on the outcome of their application. To the degree that the methods themselves partake of the negative presuppositions of historical criticism, their results will be dubious, and frequently literary critics focus on tangential matters that obscure rather than enlighten.[19] But when used in respect of the integrity of Scripture they often will turn up insights that would otherwise have been difficult to notice.

NOTES

INTRODUCTION

1. By maximizing confusion, many of the modern trendy books on a "hermeneutic" of the Bible try to turn the Bible into a manifesto for some favored ideology. Thus we have various localized hermeneutics (African, Latin American, Asian, Western, etc.) along with specifically ideologically based hermeneutics (feminist, gay, communist, etc.). This book is not concerned directly with these. A sound biblical hermeneutic should dispel such approaches, since they seek not to conform to the Bible, but to make the Bible conform to themselves. But we should also bear in mind that *every* reader has a certain agenda, and in order to hear what the Bible actually says we must strive to transcend our agendas.
2. Many very brainy people put a great deal of effort into thinking about how we can deny a self-revealing God and still have meaning. Although we interact a little with the more important movements in general hermeneutics, this book will not systematically delve into its many complex issues and philosophical questions. Nor will we examine the many special-interest hermeneutical approaches, such as black, feminist, or Marxist hermeneutics. For a comprehensive Christian interaction with the varieties of philosophical and special-interest hermeneutics we refer the reader to the work of A.C. Thiselton, *New Horizons in Hermeneutics* (Grand Rapids: Zondervan, 1992).

PART ONE

1. J. Calvin, *Institutes of the Christian Religion*, 1.1.
2. By "presuppositions" we mean the basic commitments which give a framework to thinking, not groundless or arbitrary assumptions. While presuppositions cannot be directly *proven* by strict logic, they can be evaluated with regard to their adequacy.
3. Even the so-called nonreligious person, who regards the Bible as just another book, is caught by his or her presuppositions, because since the Bible *claims* to be the Word of God, the refusal to accord it that status is itself determinative of worldview.
4. It is instructive that the "self-evident" assumptions in Euclidean geometry turn out not to work on cosmic and atomic levels. What seems "obvious" is in fact nonworkable on these levels. The Euclidean assumptions are thus indirectly shown to be incorrect on these levels. Assump-

tions are by definition not provable, but they can be *tested*.

5. In the context, Jesus is pointing out that if one's life is oriented toward "Mammon" (money-god) then it cannot be oriented toward God.

6. Actually the individual "ego" as the starting point for thinking has now been abandoned to a large degree among philosophers. The "postmodernist" linguistically oriented philosophers such as Foucault generally see all reality as "text" which must be interpreted and understanding as a hermeneutical interaction with this "text"; the "ego" if it exists at all is simply a hermeneutical nexus or eddy in the ocean of "text." But it is still human "readings" which generate "truth." In fact, now more than ever the self, which is supposedly sunk into "text," virtually *becomes* the text; the interpretive self is not just the center of the world; it *is* the world.

Even philosophers who resist this "textualizing" of everything think of "the person in community" rather than "the individual ego" as the starting point. This latter approach is worked out in J. Habermas, *The Theory of Communicative Action* (Boston: Beacon, 1984–88).

7. C. Van Til, *A Christian Theory of Knowledge* (Phillipsburg, N.J.: Presbyterian & Reformed, 1969), 14–15.

8. Faith and reason are not at odds, nor does one precede the other; they are interdependent. We have neither space here nor expertise to develop fully the reasons behind this commitment. Its roots, we believe, go back at least to Paul (see e.g., 1 Cor. 1:18−2:16), but the nature of this faith commitment in relation to reason was particularly expounded in C. Van Til's *Survey of Christian Epistemology* (Philadelphia: den Dulk Christian Foundation, 1969) and *A Christian Theory of Knowledge* (Phillipsburg, N.J.: Presbyterian and Reformed, 1969). Unfortunately these works are not easily accessible; the approach is presented clearly in J. Frame, *The Doctrine of the Knowledge of God* (Phillipsburg, N.J.: Presbyterian & Reformed; Grand Rapids: Baker, 1987).

9. This will be discussed further in chapter 5.

10. See 2 Cor. 3:14-18, 1 Thes. 1:6, and Heb. 10:15. See also Calvin, *Institutes*, I.7.

11. This, in fact, is how the church was able to come to consensus on what books were to be included in the Bible. It was a process not of *deciding on* so much as *recognizing* the inspired books.

12. F.F. Bruce, *Canon of Scripture* (Downers Grove, Ill.: InterVarsity; Glasgow: Chapter House, 1988), 332.

13. The term "cognitive dissonance" is now a commonplace in psychology to explain why people change beliefs. The theory was developed in the 1950s by L. Festinger, *A Theory of Cognitive Dissonance* (Evanston, Ill.: Row, Peterson & Co., 1957).

CHAPTER ONE

1. Since in the eyes of some the word *man* is thought to imply male, we have ordinarily attempted to use gender-neutral language in this book, so long as it is consistent with biblical teaching and good English. But the phraseology of "man the measure of all things" is so standardized that in this section on presuppositions we will adhere to this idiom; "man" should here be understood as equivalent to "humanity," like the Greek word *anthropos* (as it was in Protagoras' original saying), or the German, *mensch*.

2. On ideological, attitudinal, and methodological presuppositions, see D. Ferguson, *Biblical Hermeneutics: An Introduction*, (Atlanta: John Knox, 1986), 13. Ferguson notes another aspect to preunderstanding, the informational, but this is not as relevant here.

3. The most important work of Kant is his *Critique of Pure Reason*. Several translations and editions exist. One is the translation by J.M.D. Meiklejohn (Everyman's Library; London, 1940). For a clear and simple introduction to Kant, see John Kemp, *The Philosophy of Kant* (Oxford: Oxford Univ. Press, 1968).

4. Thus Kant stands at the fount of both the modern "critical" approach to the Bible and the modern bias against metaphysical knowledge. Although Kant still thought that the noumenal world existed, and even called his approach a "new metaphysic," if it is unknowable it might as well not exist, and the "new metaphysic" is not really metaphysics at all.

5. Cited in M. Palsey, ed., *Nietzsche: Imagery and Thought* (Berkeley, Calif.: Univ. of California Press, 1978), 70.

6. There was, of course, a Christian involvement in the Enlightenment, since there was a shared interest in truth and understanding and the value of the individual, but the atheistic *practice* of the Enlightenment methods eventually brought the whole movement into a nontheistic mind. See P. Gay, *The Enlightenment: An Interpretation* (New York: Norton, 1977).

7. Actually modern science represents something of a fusion between the Cartesian principle of human reason as ultimate and the Baconian principle that all truth must be established by observation. See R. Lundin, A. Thiselton, and C. Walhout, *The Responsibility of Hermeneutics* (Grand Rapids: Eerdmans, 1985), 4–5.

8. "Sesquipedalian obfuscation" means "obscuring something by using big rare words."

9. A.N. Whitehead and B. Russell reduced this all the way to mathematics. See *Principia Mathematica* (Cambridge: Cambridge Univ. Press, 1910–1912). More often such claims have been made for physics (e.g., Carl Sagan), but see below, n. 11.

10. See V.S. Poythress, *Philosophy, Science, and the Sovereignty of God* (Philadelphia: Presbyterian & Reformed, 1976). Poythress has pointed out elsewhere ("Science as Allegory," *Journal of the American Scientific Affiliation* 35:2 [June 1983]: 65–71) that science itself operates with models or theories which are complex and carefully controlled metaphors to describe and conceptualize observable and repeatable physical phenomena. Scientific models do not penetrate to the "rock bottom" of reality any more than any other metaphor.

11. The well-known incompatibility of quantum mechanics, which works on the smallest scale, and general theory of relativity, which works on the largest scale, is a case in point. See S. Hawking, *A Brief History of Time: From the Big Bang to Black Holes* (London: Bantam, 1988).

12. It is precisely the rigorous denial of this which led to the most severe forms of subjectivism in the nineteenth century, as evidenced in the "Divinity School Address" of Emerson given in 1838 (see *Ralph Waldo Emerson: Essays and Lectures* [New York: Library of America, 1983], 88–89).

13. This is not the place to give full answer to the question as to how we know which view is correct, the biblical or non-biblical, but since assumptions precede the operation of reason, the answer cannot lie in human reason itself. Romans 1 and Psalm 19 assume that humans are so constituted that they cannot escape the force of general revelation, and thus everyone is always and inescapably aware of the true God, although non-Christians violently suppress this awareness.

14. A parallel English and German edition is: *Tractatus Logico-Philosophicus: the German text of Logisch-philosophische Abhandlung, with a New Translation by D.F. Pears and B.F. McGuinness* (New York: Humanities; London: Routledge, 1961).

15. M. Heidegger, *Being and Time*, trans. J. Macquarrie and E. Robinson (Oxford: Blackwell, 1967).

16. In his book *What Is Metaphysics* (1929), it appears that to him the only absolute is the Nothing, which produces Being, and to which Being goes. It is by confronting this Nothing that man has meaning. Later, Heidegger becomes even more cryptic, deciding at last that only poetry can qualify as authentic speech. But Heidegger was, alas, no poet.

17. For Wittgenstein, we already noted his direct statement in *Tractatus* 6.432. Although Heidegger to our knowledge makes no such direct a claim, for him existence is always a *path*. For God simply to *tell* man Truth which was not "under investigation" would be to deny man his freedom and meaning; indeed his very being. Man is man precisely because he knows that he does not know.

In this way Heidegger, although he denied being an "existentialist" and wished to distance himself from Sartre and Jaspers, really ends up in the same place. A God who reveals truth destroys human freedom.

18. We have focused on Wittgenstein and Heidegger because they appear to be the two most influential philosophers amongst modern hermeneutical theorists. For an exposition of these, along with the Heideggerian hermeneutics of H.G. Gadamer, see A. Thiselton, *The Two Horizons* (Grand Rapids: Eerdmans, 1981).

19. It must be admitted that ideological claims to absolute truth have often been used to support oppression and violence; for example, during the Crusades and the Inquisition. But oppression and violence can happen apart from absolute truth claims, and truth claims are not always accompanied by violence. The abuse of truth is not an argument for its nonexistence.

20. *Proslogion*, at the end of Chapter 1. For an English translation, see M.J. Charlesworth, *St. Anselm's Proslogion* (Oxford: Clarendon, 1965). The quote is found on p. 115.

21. Ferguson, *Biblical Hermeneutics*, 18.

22. "Terrifying and fascinating mystery"—the phrase is used in the influential work by Rudolph Otto, *The Idea of the Holy* (London: Oxford Univ. Press), 1936 to describe the nameless irrational fear and awe felt by people of all religions.

23. See P. Ricoeur, *Essays on Biblical Interpretation* (Philadelphia: Fortress, 1980), 58.

24. G. Ebeling, *Word and Faith* (London: SCM, 1963), 320.

25. See Augustine, *Confessions* 10.17–24.

26. From a non-Christian point of view, Noam Chomsky recognizes that language is too inherently complex for a child merely to learn it, and suggests that linguisticality must be part of the human genetic makeup; it must be "innate." See Chomsky's *Language and Responsibility* (Sussex, Great Britain: Harvester, 1979), chap. 3. Chomsky even claims that "when we study human language, we are approaching what some might call the 'human essence' " (*Language and Mind* [New York: Harcourt, Brace, & Jovanovich, 1972], 1). Our theism is able to answer the question of where such innate linguisticality came from—we are created in the image of a speaking God.

27. See P.E. Hughes, *The True Image: The Origin and Destiny of Man in Christ* (Grand Rapids: Eerdmans; Leicester, Great Britain: Inter-Varsity, 1989), 57–58.

28. For a discussion of the argument that the Greeks viewed reasoning ability and speaking ability as two sides of one coin, see D.G. McCartney, "*Logikos* in 1 Peter 2:2," *Zeitschrift für Neutestamentliche Wissenschaft* 82.1 (1991): 128–32.

29. The law of noncontradiction is the assumption that if a statement is true, its negation cannot also be true.

30. Wittgenstein wryly observed that "the confusions which occupy us arise when language is like an engine idling, not when it is doing work" (L. Wittgenstein *Philosophical Investigations*, 3rd ed., trans. G.E.M. Anscombe [Oxford: Blackwells, 1967], sec. 132). In other words, problems come not in the actual use of language but in idle discussions about "language in general." There is no "thing" which is "language in general"; there are only specific uses of language.

31. Texts are not themselves language, any more than a painting is canvas and paint. Texts are expressed in, or use, language as their medium. See F. Saussure's distinction between *parôle* and *langue* (*Course in General Linguistics* [New York: McGraw-Hill, 1966], 14–20).

32. Although P. Ricoeur does not go so far as J. Derrida in making a complete break between speech and writing, he does argue for some significant differences between them. Whereas spoken utterances are determinate, a written text is said to be thrown into indeterminacy because it has no longer a unique and specific context (see P. Ricoeur, *Interpretation Theory: Discourse and the Surplus of Meaning* [Fort Worth: Texas Christian Univ. Press, 1976], 25). However, we think even this difference is somewhat exaggerated. Some texts have less context than others (contrast Job with 1 Corinthians), but even the less precisely contextualized texts are still determinate. The main difference is perhaps simply that, whereas speech is transitory and occasional, writing is by design permanent, and is often deliberately more universal. See G. Brown and G. Yule, *Discourse Analysis* (Cambridge: Cambridge Univ. Press, 1983), 14.

33. See the definition of Brown & Yule, *Discourse Analysis*, p. 6: a text is "the verbal record of a communicative event."

34. See Gadamer, *Truth and Method*, 158. We must remark here that not all texts in our day bear this communicative character. Modern poems especially, but also some modern prose writings, are no longer attempts at communication so much as uses of language as an art medium, like an artist's paints in abstract painting. Such texts are now viewed as self-contained objets d'art to be enjoyed or reacted to rather than "understood." But ancient literature, most especially that of the Bible, was never such "pure" art; it always had some communicative purpose as well.

35. "Thoughts" and "ideas" are usually understood to be the result of *linguistic* activity. They are more than just propositions, since they would include expressions of emotions, commands, and so on. But, of course, not all mental activity is linguistic. A concert musician is intensely "thinking" her music as she performs, though not in words. But our concern here is with a text (the Bible) and its concepts or thoughts, which are, of course, verbal.

36. This is not to say that the reader is the *source* of meaning, but that he is the *recognizer* of meaning. See Appendix A.

37. We are not opting here for the so-called "intuitionist" approach which views the text's meaning as an intention which is quasi-mystically apprehended and determined purely subjectively (see H.P. Grice, "Meaning," *Philosophical Review* [July 1957]: 377–88). We would not be writing this book if we did not think it possible to give at least general "rules" or guidelines which govern the apprehension of a *correct* understanding of a text.

38. See M. Black, *Labyrinth of Language* (London: Pall Mall; New York: Praeger, 1968).

39. We stand here in direct opposition to the modern school of thought which argues that the ambiguity of a text means that limitless new possibilities of thought are inherent in texts, and that the task of interpretation is not to uncover the meaning, but to uncover its ambiguities and stress its possible inconsistencies, to call into question the text's unity and open up its multiple possibilities (See J. Derrida, *Dissemination* [Chicago: Univ. of Chicago Press; London: Athlone, 1981]). This idea comes from the modern rejection of metaphysical absolute truth, which results in the idea that the world only exists "for us," as we reconstruct it for ourselves in acts of interpretation and language.

On the other hand we must acknowledge that if language were totally unambiguous, precise, and exhaustive, then words about God would be sufficiently *in*adequate as to make them idolatrous. The flexibility of the elements of language is what enables sentences to be perfectly though not exhaustively true.

40. Ricoeur, *Interpretation Theory*, 40–42.

41. According to Ricoeur, photography "grasps everything and holds nothing," while art such as painting or engraving focuses on *essentials* (which are interpreted) and eliminates uninterpreted material. Ricoeur, of course, was not thinking of *artistic* photography, which does interpret and "re-present" by manipulating focus, lighting, and field of vision.

42. On the adequacy of language to communicate divine transcendent truth, see J.M. Frame, "God and Biblical Language: Transcendence and Immanence" in *God's Inerrant Word*, ed. J.W. Montgomery (Minneapolis: Bethany Fellowship, 1974), 159–77. Frame demonstrates that (1) language is *adequate* for speaking truly about a transcendent God, and is fully adequate for God's purpose in speaking to His people, but (2) language cannot be *comprehensively* adequate. This is analogous to the incomprehensibility yet knowability of God. A truth does not have to be stated comprehensively in order to be true. If it did there could be no true statements, since all language utterances are necessarily finite, and there would be no knowledge of anything.

43. See the seminal work of J.L. Austin, *How to Do Things with Words* (Oxford: Oxford Univ. Press, 1962). Also see J.R. Searle, *Speech Acts* (Cambridge: Cambridge Univ. Press, 1969), and *Expression and Meaning: Studies in the Theory of Speech Acts* (Cambridge: Cambridge Univ. Press, 1979).

44. For more on these different meanings of "meaning" see G.B. Caird, *Language and Imagery of the Bible* (London: Duckworth; Philadelphia: Westminster, 1980), 37–39; and P. Cotterell and M. Turner, *Linguistics and Biblical Interpretation* (London: SPCK, 1989), 38.

45. See F. Schleiermacher, *Hermeneutics: The Handwritten Manuscripts* (Missoula, Mont.: Scholars, 1977), 117.

46. See W.K. Wimsatt, Jr. and M.C. Beardsley, "The Intentional Fallacy," in *The Verbal Icon: Studies in the Meaning of Poetry* (Lexington: Univ. of Kentucky Press, 1954). Note that this is not to say that one cannot or should not gain information about the author's intention in texts. Further, Wimsatt and Beardsley were primarily concerned with the judgment of the *aesthetic* value of art literature (poetry), not with the question of meaning of texts in general.

47. This last problem is sometimes solved by making a sharp distinction between "meaning" and "significance" (see Appendix A). The "meaning" is said to be the unitary intent of the author, and "significance" is the various applications of the meaning in various situations. But as Cotterell and Turner point out (*Linguistics and Biblical Interpretation*, 59), the only access to the meaning is by way of the significance of the text for the reader; hence this distinction cannot be perfectly maintained. This does not deny that there is an authorial determinate meaning toward which understanding should strive, but it does reckon with the limitations of the reader; the meaning for a reader is inseparable from its significance.

48. Gadamer, *Truth and Method*, 158.

49. Saussure's distinction between *langue* (the language in which an utterance is made) and *parôle* (the utterance which uses language) is somewhat helpful (see n. 31). The text as *parôle* is determined by the author; but the text as an instance of *langue* is controlled by the state of the language, which in turn is a function of the socio-linguistic community. The writer determines what he says, but the language and his cultural-linguistic context is the interpretive framework which enables his text to have meaning. In that sense the cultural-linguistic context determines the meaning of what an author says.

50. B.L. Whorf, *Language, Thought and Reality* (Cambridge, Mass.: MIT Press), 1956, is credited with propagating though not inventing the old idea, common in biblical studies during the first half of the twentieth century, that somehow a language *prescribes* what a user of that language

thinks. This "Whorfian" hypothesis was mercilessly debunked by J. Barr, *The Semantics of Biblical Language* (Oxford: Oxford Univ. Press, 1961).

51. We are oversimplifying here of course; many scholars and theologians of the church tried to nuance this understanding and take into account the individual personalities and historical situations of the human authors as well.

52. See chapter 4.

53. Amos 2:4; see also Rom. 1:21-32 which shows a descending spiral of wrong thinking and debasement. One almost sees sin as a descending of the spiral of understanding here, as humanity runs further and further from true understanding.

54. Whether or not a person's conscience tells one *what* is right or wrong cannot here be discussed; if it does, it does so inconsistently — different people's consciences tell them different things. Conscience, therefore, must be at least partly dependent on outside information. Paul's point in Rom. 2:15 is that everyone is conscious of sin; not that everyone is naturally conscious of all the details of right and wrong. For Christians, of course, our understanding of the Bible ought to determine our ethics.

55. Thus two of the Ten Commandments deal explicitly with language (the third and ninth).

56. We admit that the statements in this paragraph have presupposed a great deal of hermeneutical endeavor, making claims about the "chief subject matter" and the "chief obstacle" but it seems to us difficult to find any categories which more thoroughly permeate every page of the Bible. See Isa. 59:2, where the Israelites are excoriated for thinking that the problem is God's remoteness or incapacity — the problem is their sin.

A more difficult matter is the question of what sin is. This is not the place to address this question, but we hold to the view of Augustine of Hippo and Luther that the Fall has resulted in a moral inability of man to do good, and this inability is more in view when Paul speaks of "sin" than individual acts of rebellion. Contrariwise, in the view of Thomas Aquinas, humankind has had and still has an undetermined will, and righteousness was a gift added to Adam on top of his moral neutrality. What Adam lost in the Fall was his *added* "righteousness," not his ability to choose either for good or evil. The Fall was thus a metaphysical change rather than a change in human will itself. In this latter view one could perhaps present a stronger argument for the possibility of neutrality in interpretation. But if Paul is any guide, sin has destroyed the *ability* to do right (Rom. 7:13-25), and thus to interpret aright, without divine intervention.

CHAPTER TWO

1. For a fuller exposition of different approaches to the question, see D. McKim, *What Christians Believe about the Bible* (Nashville: Nelson, 1985). Unfortunately McKim treats the view that the Bible is inerrant and direct revelation as something new and almost heretical.

2. See B.B. Warfield, *Revelation and Inspiration* (New York; London: Oxford Univ. Press, 1927), 52, and *Inspiration and Authority of the Bible* (Philadelphia: Presbyterian & Reformed, 1970). Although Calvin did not address the issue of how God inspired Scripture, he had probably already begun to move away from a mechanical dictation theory (see *Institutes of the Christian Religion* 1.6.2, and the comments by J.T. McNeill, "The Significance of the Word of God for Calvin," *Church History* 28 [1959]: 131–46).

3. This too is overly simplistic, but fairly well condenses the viewpoint of, for example, K. Barth. See *Church Dogmatics* 1/1:98–140; 1/2:457–537. Barth also understands the Word of God to be principally the person of Jesus, to whom Scripture testifies (see the next viewpoint).

The much more radical existential approach of P. Tillich understands Scripture as the matrix for encounter with the "ground or source of being," the mystery which cannot be reached by ordinary human knowledge. The Bible provides the symbols for the encounter with transcendent being.

4. See e.g., G.E. Wright, *The God Who Acts: Biblical Theology as Recital* (London: SCM, 1958).

5. See D. Ferguson, *Biblical Hermeneutics,* 32–33.

6. E.g., J. Barr, *Fundamentalism* (London: SCM, 1977; 2nd ed., 1981). See also P. Tillich, *Systematic Theology* 1:157–159, who claims that "nothing has contributed more to the misinterpretation of the biblical doctrine of the Word than the identification of the Word with the Bible." This disparagement is nothing new; it echoes the words uttered by J.S. Semler in 1771: "the root of evil [in theology] is the use of the term 'Scripture' interchangeably with 'Word of God' " (*D. Joh. Salomo Semlers Abhandlung von freier Untersuchung des Canon* [Halle, 1771–1775], 1:52).

7. The word usually translated "inspired" has become too weak in English to translate the Greek equivalent, which means "God-breathed." God's "breathing" of Scripture is His dynamic creation of Scripture (just as God created man by "breathing" into him the breath of life). The Romantic era's ideas of inspiration as sensitivity toward the non-phenomenal aspects of human existence, or the even less precise idea of a heightening of artistic creativity (as in J.G. Herder, *The Spirit of Hebrew Poetry* [Burlington, Vt.: Smith, 1833]), have nothing to do with the scriptural idea.

8. Of course, the problems of the Bible's alleged conflicts with science also need to be addressed, and here is not the place to address them in detail, but we aver that, when the Bible is *properly understood*, it will not conflict with truths which science has *properly interpreted*. See below in sec. 2.4.1.

9. We do not wish to get into the old debate about whether or to what degree language determines thought (the old "Whorfian" hypothesis, see n. 1.49), but even if thought is independent of language (about which we have some doubts) there is no escaping that the conventions and forms of the language used will at least shade and nuance the way in which the thought is expressed.

10. Notice how this encompasses two basic functions of naming: opposition or contrast, and division or classification.

11. See n. 1.25.

12. See J. Barr, *Semantics of Biblical Language*, 21–45, 264–66.

13. Deconstructionists are literary theorists that find meaning purely in the minds of readers. Interpretation is not a matter of minimizing ambiguity but maximizing the different possibilities of meaning. See Appendix A, sec. 3.1.

14. We recognize we have not given here a completely adequate defense of the equivalence of the Bible and God's Word, and have assumed that most of our readers have already settled this presuppositional matter. For further defense, see W.A. Grudem, "Scripture's Self-Attestation and the Problem of Formulating a Doctrine of Scripture," in *Scripture and Truth*, ed. D.A. Carson and J.D. Woodbridge (Grand Rapids: Zondervan, 1983), 19–59.

15. Until recently the Evangelical Theological Society had a single confessional requirement, belief in the inerrancy of the Bible.

16. The venerable *Westminster Confession of Faith* used the term "infallible" and specified that the Bible was infallible with regard to faith and practice, but the writers of the confession (authorial intent again) certainly did not separate faith from history or other aspects of life the way it is frequently done today.

17. See the "Chicago Statement on Biblical Inerrancy," in *Inerrancy*, ed. N. Geisler (Grand Rapids: Zondervan, 1979).

18. This false either-or is set up by J. Rogers and D. McKim in *The Authority and Interpretation of the Bible* (New York: Harper & Row, 1979). It has been thoroughly critiqued in J.D. Woodbridge, *Biblical Authority: A Critique of the Rogers/McKim Proposal* (Grand Rapids: Zondervan, 1982). See also D.A. Carson and J.D. Woodbridge, eds., *Scripture and Truth* (Grand Rapids: Zondervan, 1983).

19. See the "Affirmations and Denials" of the "Chicago Statement" mentioned in n. 17. It is noteworthy that these theses explicitly define

"truth" as propositional, but within that framework they attempt to define "inerrancy" in a way sensitive to the actual meaning and nature of the Bible. See also J.I. Packer, "Biblical Authority, Hermeneutics, and Inerrancy," in *Jerusalem and Athens: Critical Discussions on the Philosophy and Apologetics of Cornelius Van Til*, ed. E.R. Geehan (Philadelphia: Presbyterian & Reformed, 1971), 146ff.

An attempt to deal with some of the problems of sensitive interpretation within the framework of inerrancy is found in the essays contained in H. Conn, ed., *Hermeneutics and Inerrancy: A Tradition, A Challenge, A Debate* (Grand Rapids: Baker, 1989).

20. Both the Greek and Hebrew words for "true," like the English, can refer to faithfulness and quality of relationship as well as propositional truth. "I am true to my wife" does not mean my wife finds me to be a true proposition.

21. M. Luther, *Bondage of the Will* (Edinburgh: T & T Clark, 1957), 67. On perspicuity as a hermeneutical principle in Luther, cf. F. Beisser, *Claritas Scripturae bei Martin Luther* (Göttingen: Vandenhoek & Ruprecht, 1966).

22. See *Westminster Confession of Faith*, 1.7: "All things in Scripture are not alike plain in themselves, nor alike clear unto all: yet those things which are necessary to be known, believed, and observed for salvation, are so clearly propounded and opened in some place of Scripture or other, that not only the learned, but the unlearned, in a due use of the ordinary means, may attain unto a sufficient understanding of them."

23. As human writings, the Scripture comprises a large number of discrete discourses with discrete contexts, and these separate discourses must be interpreted within their contexts. But the Scripture as a whole also occupies a larger context of divine self-revelation and the unfolding "plot" of God's plan in human history. For this reason we speak of a coherency of the whole as well as of the various discourse units.

24. See Cotterell and Turner, *Linguistics and Biblical Interpretation*, 232–33.

25. The form of 1 John 5:7-8 found in the KJV was a late addition to the text. No Greek manuscripts written before A.D. 1500 have the reference to "Father, Word, and Holy Spirit," and none of the Greek fathers cite it.

26. Note that the repentance and faith of the Gentile church is, according to Jesus, one of the main messages of the OT. The NT church is not some kind of afterthought unforeseen in the OT.

27. See M. Hengel, *Judaism and Hellenism: Studies on Their Encounter in Palestine during the Early Hellenistic Period* (London: SCM, 1974), 1:173–75. When speaking of the beliefs and activities of the Pharisees we must be rather cautious. They themselves did not write down their oral tradition. Their spiritual descendants did, but by then the wars of A.D. 70

and A.D. 135 had changed Judaism radically, and it is not easy to cull the earlier traditions from the later.

28. See J. Weingreen, *From Bible to Mishnah: The Continuity of Tradition* (Manchester: Manchester Univ. Press, 1976). This is not to say that the Rabbis paid *no* attention to the "history-ness" of biblical history; they did recognize a historical continuity with the people of the OT stories.

29. H. Raisänen, *Paul and the Law* (Tübingen: Mohr [Siebeck], 1983), 201.

30. The most accessible introduction to Philo's technique and orientation is S. Sandmel, *Philo of Alexandria: An Introduction* (New York and Oxford: Oxford Univ. Press, 1979). See esp. pp. 17–28.

31. Some modern writers contend that since the biblical writers had different ideals of historiography, they therefore were not concerned with historicity. This is clearly a foolish non sequitur. First John 4:3 tells us that every spirit which does not confess Jesus having come in the flesh is not from God, but is antichrist. And Paul says, "If Christ has not been raised, your faith is futile, you are still in your sins" (1 Cor. 15:17).

32. A covenant is a solemn promise made binding by an oath, and as such has the purpose of establishing or formalizing a relationship, and bears a historical character, but it also establishes the terms of the relationship (laws) and specifies the nature of the parties in the covenant. See G. Mendenhall, "Covenant," in *Interpreter's Dictionary of the Bible* (New York: Abingdon, 1962), 1:714–23. W. Eichrodt, *Theology of the Old Testament*, trans. J.A. Baker (London: SCM, 1961–67) defined and worked out a system of theology around the idea of covenant, which according to him underlaid the entire OT. The Ten Commandments are called a "covenant" in Deut. 5:2. Note that the commandments start off with a historical referent (v. 6, also v. 15) and include promises (vv. 10, 16). The first four commandments are oriented exclusively around the maintenance of a *relationship* with God, and even the last six are tied up with that relationship, for a relationship with God determines the character of one's relationship with other people as well.

33. See F.F. Bruce, *Biblical Exegesis in the Qumran Texts* (Grand Rapids: Eerdmans, 1959) who notes that whereas both the NT and the Qumran literature understand the OT eschatologically, "the NT interpretation of the OT is not only eschatological but christological" (p. 68). Although the Qumran community did expect a messiah, or rather actually two messiahs, a kingly and a priestly one (1QS [Rule of the Congregation] 9.11), their exegesis in general was not focused as it is in the NT. It is this christological dimension that chiefly differentiates NT exegesis from that of Qumran. This subject is highly informative, because the Qumran literature uses many of the same texts as are used in the NT, but in quite different ways.

34. For more on Jesus' citation and use of the OT, see R.T. France, *Jesus and the Old Testament: His Application of Old Testament Passages to Himself and His Mission* (London: Tyndale, 1971).

35. See S. Amsler, *L'ancien testament dans l'eglise: Essai d'hermeneutique chrétienne* (Neuchâtel, Switzerland: Delachaux et Niestlé, 1960), 91–99. The first half of the book deals with the NT writers' use of the OT.

36. Some have noted that the fulfillment of Hosea 11:1 is placed by Matthew not at the return from Egypt in 2:19-21 but at the escape from Herod. Perhaps "Egypt" in Matthew refers not to literal Egypt (where ironically Jesus escaped *to*) but to Herod, the latter-day counterpart to Pharaoh who also killed babies in an attempt to prevent God's deliverance of His people.

37. Richardson and Schweitzer observe, "It is agreed that the unity of the Old and New Testaments is not to be found in any naturalistic development, or in any static identity, but in the ongoing redemptive activity of God in the history of one people, reaching its fulfillment in Christ. Accordingly it is of decisive importance for hermeneutical method to interpret the Old Testament in the light of the total revelation in the person of Jesus Christ, the incarnate Word of God, from which arises the full Trinitarian faith of the church" (A. Richardson and W. Schweitzer, eds. *Biblical Authority for Today* [Philadelphia: Westminster, 1951], 241).

38. K. Barth (*Church Dogmatics* 3/1:23ff) appears to overstate the case when he claims that "the whole circumference of the content of Scripture, including the truth and reality of the creation of the world by God, can be understood only from this centre" [i.e., that "the whole Bible speaks figuratively and prophetically of Him, of Jesus Christ"]. This has led some scholars to charge him with "christomonism," seeing nothing except Christ in Scripture. Perhaps this is a valid charge. Barth seems to suggest that the concept of God as creator cannot be understood apart from reference to Christ. But surely an ancient Israelite who heard Genesis 1 would correctly perceive God as creator, even though he knew only a little of God's plan for a messianic deliverer, and even though he made no clear connection between creation and what he did know about the expected redeemer. Knowledge does not have to be comprehensive in order to be true. But certainly Barth is right to say that Jesus is "the primary and ultimate object of [the Bible's] witness."

39. The *Epistle of Barnabas* written in the second century saw the number 318 as a direct reference to Jesus, because in Greek the number is represented by the letters TIH, and the T is the shape of the cross, and IH are the first two letters of the Greek for "Jesus." But this sort of sophistry has nothing to do with the meaning of the OT text.

40. For a discussion of this christological focus to the NT's use of the OT, see D. McCartney, "The NT Use of the OT" in *Inerrancy and*

Hermeneutic, ed. H. Conn (Grand Rapids: Baker, 1988), 101–16.

41. R.B. Hays, *Echoes of Scripture in the Letters of Paul* (New Haven and London: Yale Univ. Press, 1989), 162. As Hays points out, this is not because Paul is uninterested in Jesus or that christology for Paul was subordinate to soteriology, but because "for Paul's communities, Jesus' identity was not the contested issue. . . ." But Hays has probably overstated his point. A text's intended application is not the same thing as its chief subject matter. For this reason we prefer to restrict the suffix "-centric" to Christ.

42. See F. Delitzsch, *Commentary on the Song of Songs and Ecclesiastes* (Grand Rapids: Eerdmans, 1984), 1–3. For more extensive discussion of Jewish exegesis of the Song, see M.H. Pope, *Song of Songs: A New Translation with Introduction and Commentary*, The Anchor Bible Commentaries (Garden City, N.Y.: Doubleday, 1977), 89–112.

43. Literally, "light and heavy" or "a little and a lot." It is one of the seven methods of interpretation ascribed to the first-century rabbi Hillel.

44. Contrast Philo's interpretation of this same passage: Isaac is said to be wisdom; Ishmael is sophistry; Sarah represents perfect virtue; and Hagar means "intermediate training" (found in *De Cherubim* 8–9 and *De Post. Caini* 130). This allegory has no connection to the historical lesson of Genesis at all.

45. C.K. Barrett, "The Allegory of Abraham, Sarah, and Hagar in the Argument of Galatians," in *Rechtfertigung* [Festschrift E. Käsemann] ed. J. Friedrich, W. Pohlmann, and P. Stuhlmacher (Tübingen: Mohr [Siebeck], 1976), 1–16 has suggested that Paul's opponents were the first to use the Sarah-Hagar story, and Paul was responding in kind.

46. Paul's use of the OT is the subject of countless books. For starters, see: E.E. Ellis, *Paul's Use of the Old Testament* (Edinburgh: Oliver & Boyd; Grand Rapids: Eerdmans, 1957); R. Longenecker, *Exegesis in the Apostolic Period* (Grand Rapids: Eerdmans, 1975); and R.B. Hays, *Echoes of Scripture in the Letters of Paul* (New Haven and London: Yale Univ. Press, 1989).

47. Although most translations mistranslate this verse as "To you who believe he is precious," virtually all commentators recognize that v. 7 actually reads, "to you who believe there is honor, but to those who do not believe . . . [there is dishonor]." See e.g., W. Grudem, *1 Peter*, Tyndale New Testament Commentary (Leicester, Great Britain: Inter-Varsity; Grand Rapids: Eerdmans, 1988).

48. The original here is not the "sufferings *of* Christ" (*ta tou Christou pathemata*) but the "sufferings *unto* or *for* [the] Christ (*ta eis Christon pathemata*).

49. Almost all modern commentators agree that the first recipients of 1 Peter were largely Gentiles (see e.g., R. Michaels, *1 Peter* [Waco: Word,

1989]). First Peter 1:18, 2:10, and especially 4:3 imply that the readers were of pagan background.

50. Note that this sets NT and OT apart from later books that claim to carry the biblical revelation further, such as the Qur'an and the Book of Mormon.

51. Some Christians argue about whether there are "brute facts" out there which exist by themselves in an "un-interpreted" state. If "brute fact" simply means "a reality which is not contingent on *human* perception or awareness," then yes, there are such facts, but if one means "a reality which is independent of *all* awareness or perception" then we have to say that no "fact" exists apart from its perception by its Creator, and the meaning He has given it (see Van Til, *Survey of Christian Epistemology*, 6).

Furthermore, facts can only be presented as predications of language and so cannot be known as uninterpreted entities. Factual predications are propositions formulated in human language, formulations which are analogues of our perceptions within a defined context. A fact can either be true by definition ("a ball is spherical or spheroid"), by observation within a certain context ("these ripe tomatoes are red," where "ripe," "tomatoes," and "red" are all previously defined), or by extrapolation or inference ("all red tomatoes are ripe; these tomatoes are red; therefore these tomatoes are ripe"). All of these except the first (which is not a statement about reality but a statement of convention of speech or description) involve perception and interpretation. And even the first type requires a preexistent framework for understanding. "A tomato is a vegetable" is a definitional fact within the culinary framework; "a tomato is a fruit" is a fact within a botanical one. Thus no "fact" or predication about reality can be known, let alone stated, without a framework of understanding.

52. The practical starting point of our selves appears at first to condemn the spiral into inescapable subjectivity. But if the Bible is true, and we are indeed created "in God's image," then our very beginning consciousness is in some way analogous to God's knowledge, and some initial continuity between God's thought and ours is guaranteed. This would be the source of our innate ability to learn language. In this case, although our practical starting point is our selves, the philosophical starting point, the starting point for true knowledge, is in God who created us (see sec. 1.1). There is no way to prove this, of course, other than by pointing out that without it all human knowledge is sunk in hopeless subjectivity.

53. See A. Alexander, *Evidences of the Authenticity, Inspiration, and Canonical Authority of the Holy Scriptures* (Philadelphia: Presbyterian Board of Publication, 1836), 10.

54. One could also view this spiral as a function of, or at least analogous

to, the old "generals and particulars" problem. One must know the general to interpret the particulars (deductive reasoning), but one must construct the general out of the particulars (inductive reasoning). Neither is ultimate.

55. T.S. Kuhn, *The Structure of Scientific Revolutions* (Chicago: Univ. of Chicago Press, 1970).

56. See Warfield's comment, "Without special revelation, general revelation would be for sinful man incomplete and ineffective. . . . Without general revelation, special revelation would lack that basis in the fundamental knowledge of God as the mighty and wise, righteous and good, maker and ruler of all things, apart from which the further revelation of this great God's interventions in the world for the salvation of sinners could not be either intelligible, credible or operative" (Warfield, *Inspiration and Authority of the Bible*, 75).

57. Note that this tension is always the result of some misunderstanding somewhere. It is not a dialectic of paradox where it is precisely the contradiction that is "true."

58. J.R.W. Stott, *Between Two Worlds: The Art of Preaching in the Twentieth Century* (Grand Rapids: Eerdmans, 1982), 127–28.

59. Of course, many interpretations do stem from willful rejection of a text's teaching.

60. Note that accounts can be different without being contradictory. P. Ricoeur, *Interpretation Theory*, 40–42 points out that all writing, not least history writing, "re-presents" reality, it does not reproduce it. Transcription necessarily involves some interpretive metamorphosis. Thus writing (including history) is more analogous to a painting than a photograph.

61. The pessimism of that most prolific writer of world history Will Durant is illustrative: "Most history is guessing; the rest is prejudice" (Will Durant, *The Story of Civilization: Our Oriental Heritage*, vol. 1 [New York: Simon & Schuster, 1935], 12). However, this is undoubtedly deliberate hyperbole. History can be "relatively" true when it presents material in an intelligible way whereby a person who directly experienced the events could recognize the account and acknowledge that its explanation is a fair and reasonable one. An account could even be absolutely true if it corresponds to the perception of the Person who knows all the events and material relevant to the events, although we would have no way of knowing that it was absolutely true unless the account is recorded in the Bible.

62. In India, and perhaps many other places in the world, they still build enormous and beautiful buildings by constructing around and within it a thick network of scaffolding as it is erected. The scaffolding is actually so thick that one cannot see the building underneath until it is finished and the scaffolding removed. World history is like the scaffolding used to

build God's people, the object of specifically redemptive history. Someday the scaffolding will be removed to reveal God's church in all its glory.

63. For some other Scriptures where God sovereignly uses all human activity, even human wickedness, to accomplish His purposes, see Gen. 50:20, Esther 4:14, Acts 17:24-27, Rom. 8:28, and Phil. 1:12.

64. See I.H. Marshall, "Historical Criticism," in *New Testament Interpretation: Essays in Principles and Methods,* ed. I.H. Marshall (Exeter: Paternoster, 1977), 126. The phrase "what actually happened" is, as Marshall recognizes, problematic, because it assumes facts can be known without being interpreted.

65. We say "resonance" rather than "correspondence" because the perceptions of people that were there are as much the result of interpretation as are those of people looking back at the event from a later perspective, and are thus subject to incompleteness and error. Only God's interpretation can be confidently expected to "correspond."

66. In a historical text, "the historian claims — asserts — that the projected world (the story) of the text *together with the authorial point of view* counts as a story and an interpretation of events as they *actually* occurred" (Lundin, Thiselton, and Walhout, *Responsibility and Hermeneutics,* 69 [emphasis added]).

CHAPTER THREE

1. " 'Method' is inherently a limited instrumentality and, indeed, a secondary stage in the art of interpretation. More basic are the perspective and presuppositions with which the interpreter approaches the text" (E.E. Ellis, *Prophecy and Hermeneutic in Early Christianity: New Testament Essays* [Tübingen: Mohr, 1978], 163).

2. B. Chilton, "Commenting on the Old Testament" in *It Is Written: Scripture Citing Scripture,* FS B. Lindars; ed. D. Carson and H. Williamson (Cambridge: Cambridge Univ. Press, 1988), 122–40.

3. J. Fitzmyer, "The Use of Explicit Old Testament Quotations in Qumran Literature and in the New Testament," *NTS* 7 (1960–61): 297–333 (also in revised form in J. Fitzmyer, *Essays in the Semitic Background of the New Testament* [London: Chapman, 1971; Missoula, Mont.: Scholars, 1974], 3–58). See also R. Longenecker, *Biblical Exegesis in the Apostolic Period* (Grand Rapids: Eerdmans, 1975); and F.F. Bruce, *Biblical Exegesis in the Qumran Texts* (Grand Rapids: Eerdmans, 1959; London: Tyndale, 1960).

4. R. Longenecker, *Biblical Exegesis in the Apostolic Period* (Grand Rapids: Eerdmans, 1975).

5. Longenecker, *Biblical Exegesis*, 219.

6. For the Talmudic rabbis as the successors to the Pharisees, see M. McNamara, *Palestinian Judaism and the New Testament* (Wilmington: Glazier, 1983), 162–64.

7. See J. Bowker, *Targums and Rabbinic Literature* (Cambridge: Cambridge Univ. Press, 1969).

8. For more on Philo, see S. Sandmel, *Philo of Alexandria: An Introduction* (New York: Oxford Univ. Press, 1979). On the allegorical approach and its relation to philosophy, see R.P.C. Hanson, *Allegory and Event* (London: SCM, 1959).

9. See W.H. Brownlee, "Biblical Interpretation Among the Sectaries of the Dead Sea Scrolls," *Biblical Archaeologist* 14 (1951): 54–76.

10. See chapter 2 n. 33 and n. 3 above.

11. The most extended Qumran interpretation is found in the "pesharim," which are like running commentaries, usually on prophetic material, which find in every verse some reference to the community or its immediate history. See M. Horgan, *Pesharim: Qumran Interpretations of Biblical Books* (Washington: Catholic Univ. of America Press, 1979).

12. Method as a function of "what works" is not different in kind from language function as a whole. The "meaning" of a word, phrase, or sentence is a function of how that word, phrase, or sentence is being used (Wittgenstein); its value by itself out of context is only approximately definable, and the possibilities of its use are highly flexible. So also with method; its functions are approximately definable, but the result is determined by the use to which the interpreter wishes to put the method. Further, different methods can be used to obtain the same result, just as different words can be used to say the same thing.

13. This presuppositional argument may not persuade a non-Christian Jew, but neither will some kind of rationalistic exegesis.

14. See the conclusion of Longenecker, *Biblical Exegesis*, 88.

15. Although occasionally some writers may refer to certain "assured results of biblical criticism," such assured results are almost always doubted by scores of other professional exegetes. An excellent case in point is the hypothesis in Gospels criticism that Mark was the first Gospel, which was used, along with another document called "Q," in the composition of Matthew and Luke. For decades this was regarded as an "assured result," and demurral was disparaged, but recently, increasing numbers of scholars are doubting this construction. See W. Farmer, *The Synoptic Problem: A Critical Analysis* (New York: Macmillan, 1964); B. Gerhardssohn, *Memory and Manuscript: Oral Tradition and Written Transmission in Rabbinic Judaism and Early Christianity*, trans. E.J. Sharpe (Lund, Sweden: Gleerup, 1961); B. Reicke, *The Roots of the Synoptic Gospels* (Philadelphia: Fortress, 1986); R. Riesner, *Jesus als Lehrer*

(Tübingen, Germany: Mohr [Siebeck], 1981); J. Wenham, *Redating Matthew, Mark, and Luke: A Fresh Assault on the Synoptic Problem* (London: Hodder & Stoughton, 1991), *inter alios*.

16. M. Barth, "The O.T. in Hebrews: an Essay in Biblical Hermeneutics," in *Current Issues in New Testament Interpretation: Essays in Honor of Otto A. Piper*, ed. W. Klassen and G.F. Snyder (New York: Harper, 1962), 78. A "Schandpfahl" is a pillory.

17. See E.E. Ellis, "How the NT Uses the OT," in Marshall, *New Testament Interpretation*, 209.

18. Babylonian Talmud, Tractate *Pesach* (Passover), 66a.

19. First Vatican Council, Session 2.

20. See Gadamer, *Truth and Method*, 239ff, who complains that such prejudice deprived tradition of its hermeneutical power.

21. "Every interpreter comes to the text bearing those complex histories of effects we call traditions. There is no more a possibility of escape from tradition than there is the possibility of an escape from history or language" (D. Tracy, *Plurality and Ambiguity: Religion as a Test Case for Hermeneutics* [New York: Harper & Row, 1985], 16).

22. The quote above of Pope Pius I in the First Vatican Council has an inherent absurdity, because there is extremely little in the way of "unanimous consent of the fathers."

23. For an interesting discussion of some of these issues see Rex A. Koivisto, *One Lord, One Faith: A Theology for Cross-Denominational Renewal* (BridgePoint/Victor Books, 1993), 151–179.

24. See John 16:8-11. Also, see Calvin, *Institutes of the Christian Religion*, 1.7.

25. This section makes no claim to be a general study of the work of the Holy Spirit. His activity involves much more than simply that of guiding God's people into truth. See A. Kuyper, *The Work of the Holy Spirit*, trans. H. DeVries (New York: Funk & Wagnalls, 1900; reprint, Grand Rapids: Eerdmans, 1966, 1975). Further, even the subject of the Holy Spirit's hermeneutical activity cannot be exhaustively treated here. Unfortunately, neither is it exhaustively treated in any other book that we could locate, but see B. Ramm, *The Witness of the Spirit* (Grand Rapids: Eerdmans, 1960).

26. The text is uncertain; it might read "you know all things."

27. As the reader can see by comparing the NIV, this text is sometimes understood to say that Paul is expressing spiritual truths in spiritual words, i.e., words given by the Spirit. But in our judgment this would simply be redundant with the first part of the verse, and Paul's point here, as is evident in v. 14, is that it is only the Spirit-led person who can receive the content of the Spirit's teaching.

28. This passage in 1 Corinthians is rich, and the reader who studies it will reap many rewards.

PART TWO

1. See R.P. Martin, "Approaches to New Testament Exegesis" in Marshall, *New Testament Interpretation*, 222.

CHAPTER FOUR

1. Justin Martyr, *Dialogue with Trypho*, 77–78, trans. T.B. Falls, in *Fathers of the Church: A New Translation. The Writings of Saint Justin Martyr* (Washington: Catholic Univ. of America Press, 1948), 270–73.

2. Irenaeus, *Against Heresies* 4.26.1; see also 1.8.1.

3. Ibid., 2.27.2.

4. For an overall examination of Origen's method, see R.P.C. Hanson, *Allegory and Event: A Study of the Sources and Significance of Origen's Interpretation of Scripture* (London: SCM, 1959); or J.W. Trigg, *Origen: The Bible and Philosophy in the Third Century Church* (Atlanta: Knox, 1983).

5. See *Stromateis* 6.15.126; 7.16.96.

6. *Against Celsus* 7.22. Interestingly enough, a very similar explanation to these verses was given by C.S. Lewis, *Reflections on the Psalms* (New York: Harcourt, Brace, 1958).

7. Note that this sets Origen sharply apart from the philosophical idealism of secular Hellenism, for whom the body was a prison, and the bodily resurrection both ridiculous and undesirable. Note the reaction of the philosophers to Paul in Acts 17:32.

8. See D.G. McCartney, "Literal and Allegorical Interpretation in Origen's *Against Celsus*," *Westminster Theological Journal* 48 (1986): 281–301. Only when the literal meaning was embarrassing to Origen did he offer allegories in *Against Celsus*.

9. On the Antiochene school of interpretation, see chapter 2 in D.S. Wallace-Hadrill, *Christian Antioch: A Study of Early Christian Thought in the East* (Cambridge: Cambridge Univ. Press, 1982).

10. Text may be found in J.P. Migne, *Patrologiae Cursus Completus*, series *Graeca* (Paris: Migne, 1857–1891) [hereafter MPG], vol. 66.

11. MPG 66:229, 232.

12. MPG 55:327f.

13. *Sermons in the Epistle to the Philippians* no. 10; MPG 62:257.

14. The now classic work on medieval exegesis is that of B. Smalley, *The Study of the Bible in the Middle Ages*, 3rd ed. (Oxford: Oxford Univ. Press, 1983).

15. T. Aquinas, *Summa Theologica* 1.1.10, trans. the Fathers of the En-

glish Dominican Province (London: Burns & Oates, 1947), 7.

16. Ibid.

17. Ibid.

18. For a brief but suggestive study of Luther's hermeneutics, see A.S. Wood, *Luther's Principles of Biblical Interpretation* (London: Tyndale, 1960).

19. M. Luther, *D. Martin Luther's Werke* (Weimar, Germany: Böhlaus Nachfolgen, 1883–) [hereafter *WA*] 42.173. Translation ours.

20. *WA* 18.1588.

21. Luther allowed allegories as "adornments" but insisted that allegories be based on the historical account. *WA* 42.173.

22. See Wood, *Luther's Principles*, 26.

23. *WA* 7.97.

24. Wood, *Luther's Principles*, 12.

25. *Luther's Works*, American Edition, ed. J. Pelikan (St. Louis: Concordia, 1958–1986, hereafter Am. Ed.) 13.17.

26. M. Luther, *Bondage of the Will* (Edinburgh: T & T Clark, 1957), 67. Luther was responding to Erasmus' claim that nothing can be clearly known, even in Scripture.

27. Am. Ed., 25.405; see *WA* 8.236, 10.576.

28. See Wood, *Luther's Principles*, 8; and Luther's own account in *WA* 54.185–87.

29. *Martin Luther's sämmtliche Schriften*, 2nd ed., ed. J.G. Walch (St. Louis: Concordia, 1880–1910 [hereafter *Walch(2)*]) 9.1800.

30. *Walch(2)* 3.1895.

31. *WA* 2.279, trans. in J. Mackinnon, *Luther and the Reformation* (London and New York: Longmans, 1930) 4.296.

32. *WA* 40.593, cited in Mackinnon, *Luther* 4.299.

33. *WA* 5.184.

34. *WA* 50.660.

35. Erlangen edition 4.144, cited in Wood, *Luther's Principles*, 14.

36. See Wood, *Luther's Principles*, 14–15.

37. *TischReden* #5443, trans. in *Luther's Works* 54, American Edition (Philadelphia: Fortress, 1967), 424.

38. See *WA* 16.363–93.

39. For an excellent survey of Calvin's hermeneutic, see R.C. Gamble, "*Brevitas et Facilitas*: Toward an understanding of Calvin's Hermeneutic," *Westminster Theological Journal* 47 (1985): 1–17. Also see H.J. Kraus, "Calvin's Exegetical Principles," *Interpretation* 31 (1977): 8–18.

40. Calvin, *Institutes of the Christian Religion*, 1.7.1. All citations from the *Institutes* in this chapter are from the translation of F.L. Battles (Library of Christian Classics 20, ed. J.T. McNeill; Philadelphia: Westminster; London: SCM, 1960).

41. *Institutes* 1.7.4.

42. *Institutes* 1.7.2.

43. *Institutes* 1.7.5.

44. Jules Bonnet, comp. "Farewell to the Ministers" in *Letters of John Calvin* (Philadelphia: Presbyterian Board of Publication, 1858), 4:375.

45. Calvin, *A Harmony of the Gospels Matthew, Mark, and Luke*, vol. 3, trans. A.W. Morrison (Edinburgh: St. Andrew, 1972), 177.

46. Calvin, *Harmony*, 66.

47. *Institutes* 1.7.4.

48. *Institutes* 1.7.5. Calvin also discusses this internal conviction by the Holy Spirit under the topic of redemption in 3.1.1, 3.1.3–4, 3.2.15, and 3.2.33–36.

49. *Institutes* 1.7.5.

50. For NT, see Stephen Neill and Tom Wright, *The Interpretation of the New Testament, 1861–1986* (Oxford: Oxford Univ. Press, 1988); or W.G. Kümmel, *The New Testament: The History of the Investigation of Its Problems* (Nashville: Abingdon, 1972; London: SCM, 1973). For the history of modern OT study, an English translation of H.J. Kraus, *Geschichte der historisch-kritischen Erforschung des Alten Testaments* [A History of the Historical-Critical Investigation of the Old Testament] 3 Aufl. (Neukirchen, Germany: Neukirchener Verlag, 1982) is due to be published soon.

51. *Hermeneutics: The Handwritten Manuscripts*, ed. H. Kimmerle, trans. J. Duke and J. Forstman (Missoula, Mont.: Scholars, 1977), 58.

52. Ibid., 59.

53. Ibid., 42.

54. Ibid.

55. Ibid., 70. Restated on p. 117.

56. Ibid., 127.

57. Ibid., 69.

58. Ibid., 113.

59. Ibid., 148.

60. Ibid., 150.

61. Ibid.

62. Ibid., 64.

63. Ibid., 42.

64. Ibid., 68.

65. Ibid., 42.

66. It is perhaps for this reason that Schleiermacher preferred the Gospel of John as the most reliable. In Schleiermacher's eyes it gave the "best" insight into the inner consciousness of Jesus, and it did not get entangled in very many "miracle" accounts or history narratives which only distracted one from awareness of Jesus' inner self-consciousness.

67. R. Morgan with J. Barton, *Biblical Hermeneutics* (New York: Oxford Univ. Press, 1988). The entire book is deliberately constructed around the tension between "secular, rational frameworks of modern scholarship" and "its [the Bible's] own and subsequent believers' religious framework" (p. 22).

68. R.A. Makkreel, *Dilthey: Philosopher of the Human Studies* (Princeton: Princeton Univ. Press, 1975), 361.

69. On Bultmann, see R.C. Roberts, *Rudolf Bultmann's Theology: A Critical Appraisal* (Grand Rapids: Eerdmans, 1976; London: SPCK, 1977). Particularly on demythologization, see P.E. Hughes, *Scripture and Myth: An Examination of Rudolf Bultmann's Plea for Demythologization* (London: Tyndale, 1956).

70. English translation by Carl Braaten (Philadelphia: Fortress, 1964).

71. R. Bultmann, *Faith and Understanding*, ed. R. Funk and L.P. Smith (New York: Harper & Row, 1969), 31.

72. Ibid., 187.

73. Heidegger regarded himself not as an existentialist but as a phenomenologist. But his concern with human *Existenz* and "being in the world" has led many to regard him as a *de facto* existentialist, and Bultmann did not repudiate the term.

74. Roberts, *Rudolf Bultmann's Theology*, 23. Roberts refers to *Faith and Understanding*, p. 52.

75. R. Bultmann, *Theology of the New Testament*, 1, trans. K. Grobel (New York: Scribners, 1951), 165.

76. *Glauben und Verstehen* 4 (Tübingen: Mohr, 1965), 128ff, cited by Roberts, *Rudolf Bultmann's Theology*, 25.

77. R. Bultmann, *Essays Philosophical and Theological*, trans. J.C.G. Greig (London: SCM, 1955), 81.

78. Ibid., 153.

79. *Glauben und Verstehen* 3 (Tübingen: Mohr, 1960), 170, cited by Roberts, *Rudolf Bultmann's Theology*, 40.

80. Bultmann, *Essays*, 8.

81. R. Bultmann, *Kerygma and Myth: A Theological Debate*, trans. R.H. Fuller (New York: Harper & Row, 1961), 11.

82. Ibid., 1f.

83. Ibid., 9.

84. Bultmann, *Essays*, 241.

85. R. Bultmann, *Jesus Christ and Mythology* (New York: Scribners, 1958), 84.

86. Bultmann, *Kerygma and Myth*, 210.

87. R. Bultmann with K. Jaspers, *Myth and Christianity: An Inquiry into the Possibility of Religion without Myth*, trans. Norbert Guterman (New York: Noonday, 1958), 69.

88. R. Bultmann, *Jesus and the Word*, trans. L.P. Smith and E.H. Lantero (New York: Scribners, 1958), 85.
89. Bultmann, *Faith and Understanding*, 53.
90. E.g., the works noted in n. 69 above.
91. Bultmann, *Faith and Understanding*, 283.

CHAPTER FIVE

1. The so-called "historical-critical" methods available to scholars are, when properly used, tools to help in answering the questions of semantics, cultural distance, context, and genre, but they can also be used to undermine scriptural authority. These specialist's methods will be discussed in Appendix B.
2. Saussure, *Course in General Linguistics*, 79–100. Saussure's *Cours de linguistique générale* was first published posthumously in 1915. For a clear explanation of these terms and the nature of the discussion, see M. Silva, *Biblical Words and Their Meaning: An Introduction to Lexical Semantics* (Grand Rapids: Zondervan, 1983), chap. 1.
3. De Saussure, *General Linguistics*, 88–89.
4. As should be clear from what follows, this is not warrant for establishing the meaning of NT words in general from their Hebrew equivalents. See Silva, *Biblical Words and Their Meaning*, 53–68.
5. M. Silva, *God, Language, and Scripture* (Grand Rapids: Zondervan, 1991), 59, gives the well-known example of the Greek word usually translated "daily" in the Lord's Prayer. It occurs only once in the NT and never outside the NT until the Church Fathers used the word because it was in the Lord's Prayer. Proposed meanings based on etymology are the only ones available, and they abound. An easier example is the word *promartyromai* in 1 Peter 1:12. It too occurs only once in extant Greek literature until much later; but the term *martyromai* means "to bear witness, testify," and *pro* means "before" or "for," so it is a fairly simple thing to ascertain that the word means either "bearing witness ahead of time" or "bearing witness toward" someone. The former fits the context in 1 Peter.
6. See below, sec. 7.2.2; also Silva, *Biblical Words*, 35–51; D.A. Carson, *Exegetical Fallacies* (Grand Rapids: Baker, 1984), 26–36. Even when etymology is valuable, it is only a help toward understanding the synchronic meaning, not a means of expanding a meaning diachronically. Again to take the chess game example, an examination of the earlier moves can often help in understanding the dynamics of the present situation, but the situation is there quite apart from the history, and any skilled chess

player can, without knowing the earlier moves, properly understand the current dynamics.

7. Barr, *Semantics of Biblical Language*, 129–40.

8. The extra-linguistic reality need not be something in the actual universe; they can be "realities" created by the text itself, particularly in fiction.

9. Ricoeur, *Interpretation Theory*, 19. Meaning as "sense" and "reference" was first introduced into philosophy by Gottlob Frege. See "On Sense and Reference" in *Translations from the Philosophical Writings of Gottlob Frege*, trans. M. Black (Oxford: Blackwell, 1970), 56–78.

10. C.K. Ogden and I.A. Richards, *The Meaning of Meaning* (New York: Harcourt & Brace, 1945), 11. K. Baldinger, *Semantic Theory* (Oxford: Blackwell, 1980), pt. 2 objects to the triangle because it makes no distinction between the linguistic sense of a word and the extra-linguistic concept. Baldinger proposes a trapezium of word, sense, *concept*, and referent. But this assumes that a concept can exist without language, which is debatable. And so far as we can see, the trapezium adds nothing of help.

11. Cotterell and Turner, *Linguistics and Biblical Interpretation*, 85 argue that frequently words may not have true referents. "I'm off to shoot a pheasant" would not (ordinarily) refer to any particular pheasant. But this over-specializes the term "referent." The referent in this case can be one of the class of pheasant without being more specific.

12. "Under certain circumstances" because even technical terms might have a narrower reference than sense: e.g., in the sentence "Have my lab assistant fetch me that sodium," the reference of sodium is to the sodium found in a particular jar, but in the sentence "Salt is composed of sodium and chloride," sodium's reference and sense are very close if not identical.

13. See J. Lyons, *Language, Meaning, and Context* (London: Fontana [Collins], 1981), 75.

14. Cotterell and Turner, *Linguistics and Biblical Interpretation*, 153.

15. See n. 3 above.

16. J. Trier, *Der deutsche Wortschatz im Sinnbezirk des Verstandes. Die Geschichte eines sprachlichen Feldes* (Heidelberg: Carl Winters, 1931), 6; cited in Silva, *Biblical Words*, 161.

17. M.A.K. Halliday, *Halliday: System and Function in Language: Selected Papers*, ed. G.R. Kress (Oxford: Oxford Univ. Press, 1976), 73.

18. G.B. Caird, *Paul's Letters from Prison* (Oxford: Oxford Univ. Press, 1976), 14. Thus the argument suggesting that the difference in "meaning" to the word *mysterion* in Colossians and Ephesians implies different authors is groundless.

19. Many fine exegetes have lined up on opposite sides of this fence. See especially W. Grudem, "Does *Kephale* ('Head') Mean 'Source' or 'Author-

ity over' in Greek Literature? A Survey of 2,336 Examples," *Trinity Journal* 6 (1985): 38–59, who argues that "head" does not mean source; and G. Fee, *The First Epistle to the Corinthians*, NICNT (Grand Rapids: Eerdmans, 1987), 502–4, who argues that it does. Cotterell and Turner, *Linguistics and Biblical Interpretation*, 141–45, contend that Fee confuses the meaning and the usage here.

20. Related in G.B. Caird, *Language and Imagery of the Bible* (London: Duckworth, 1980), 131.

21. Sometimes a merismatic triad is formed: heaven, earth, and under the earth (meaning the sea); see e.g., Ex. 20:4.

22. In Egypt the merism "good and evil" referred to all knowledge, not just ethical knowledge. Perhaps the temptation was to achieve omniscience and thus be no longer dependent on God for knowing things.

23. I.A. Richards, *The Philosophy of Rhetoric* (New York; London: Oxford Univ. Press, 1936), 93. See p. 94: [Metaphor involves] "fundamentally a borrowing between and intercourse of thoughts, a transaction between contexts." See also M. Black, *Models and Metaphors* (Ithaca, N.Y.: Cornell Univ. Press, 1962), 38–47.

24. "Metaphorical thought is a distinctive mode of achieving insight, not to be construed as an ornamental substitute for plain thought" (Black, *Models and Metaphors*, 237).

25. As important as metaphor is, we must be careful with statements like "all language is metaphorical," such as is argued by S. McFague (TeSelle), *Speaking in Parables: A Study in Metaphor and Theology* (Philadelphia: Fortress, 1975), 26–30 and her *Metaphorical Theology* (Philadelphia: Fortress, 1982); also see E. Sewell, *The Human Metaphor* (Notre Dame: Univ. of Notre Dame Press, 1964), 11. While it is true that all language consists of signifiers, and thus is "metaphorical" in using a human-generated sound to represent an extra-linguistic reality, it is equally true that the relationship of signifiers to the things signified can be direct, or "literal" as well as indirect, or what is usually considered metaphorical. Redefining metaphor to include all language is, we suspect, a ruse to avoid taking the direct or "literal" statements of the Bible at face value. It is more helpful to limit the concept of metaphor to the juxtaposition of thought fields (see below) which involves the indirect application of a signifier (be it word, phrase, sentence, or discourse) to something it does not ordinarily signify in order to elucidate the principal subject.

26. Black, *Models and Metaphors*, 44–45.

27. Caird, *Language and Imagery*, 145–48. Caird adopts the "comparison" view of metaphor, which limits him, but his types of "comparison" are still a valid observation about many metaphors.

28. Occasionally an exegesis is given which suggests that the birds in the

mustard bush are the harbingers of hypocrisy in the church. This is possible from the context in Matt. 13, nested as it is between the parable of the weeds and wheat and its explanation, if it is also argued that the tares in the parable are hypocrites in the church rather than simply non-Christians in general. But in Mark the mustard bush parable is not so nested and hence the idea of birds as hypocrites can only be based on the assumption that the symbolic value of "birds" must remain the same. But symbols are adaptable. The "harvest" of Matt. 13:39 can hardly have the same value as the "harvest" of 9:38.

If the birds in the parable of the mustard bush have any metaphorical symbolism other than illustrating how large the bush is, it probably harkens back to Ezek. 17:23 where the birds in the branches represent the Gentiles who take refuge in the tree of Israel which God has prospered.

29. Some translations of 1 Peter 2:2 use the term "spiritual milk" in the sense of "metaphorical milk," but the term here is a rare word in the NT and different from the usual word for "spiritual." The best translation of 1 Peter 2:2 is "As new-born babies, yearn for the milk *of the Word.*" See D. McCartney, *"Logikos* in 1 Peter 2:2," *Zeitschrift für Neutestamentliche Wissenschaft* 82:1 (Spring 1991): 128–32.

30. See Barr, *Semantics of Biblical Language*, 129–40.

31. E.g., McFague (TeSelle), *Speaking in Parables*, 38–41, 43–47. See also n. 25 above.

32. First John 2:19 answers this problem in unambiguous language: "They went out from us, but they did not really belong to us. For if they had belonged to us, they would have remained with us; but their going showed that none of them belonged to us."

33. The never-ending discussion as to whether literal or idiomatic translations are better is due to the advantages and disadvantages of each. See sec. 7.2.1.

34. This is usually, but not always, true: see Eph. 2:10 – we are created for good works.

35. See P. Davids, *James*, NIGNTC (Grand Rapids: Eerdmans, 1982), 130–32; R.P. Martin, *James*, WBC (Waco, Texas: Word, 1989), 82–101.

36. Thus a phrase being used in more than one way does not indicate that different authors are involved. Some scholars have argued that Ephesians is not by Paul because some of its phrases also occur in Colossians but with a different meaning.

37. Although the Greek word for "flesh" is used in all these cases, English translations usually have a variety of words and phrases, as they attempt to catch the idiomatic meaning. But see the NASB which consistently uses "flesh." See Silva, *God, Language and Scripture*, 133–39.

38. The idea that words can be used in a variety of ways sometimes gets overlooked with certain words that have become technical. In our mod-

ern theological tradition, for example, the word "sanctification" has taken on the technical meaning of the progressive work of the Holy Spirit in conforming a believer throughout his or her life to the character of Jesus Christ. But Paul uses the word sometimes in the sense of the "making holy" which Christ definitively accomplished on the cross (cf. 1 Cor. 1:2; 6:11).

39. A word's "range" is not only a matter of what range of things it can refer to, but also involves the range of relationships the word has to other words. We can have deep thinkers and deep water. We can also have profound thinkers, but somehow "profound water" sounds odd and except for some poetic purpose would probably be considered a misuse of the word "profound."

40. This is why translation is possible. It is true that no word in one language has exactly the same range of semantic scope as a word in some other language if considered in isolation. But in actual use the word becomes translatable because its meaning is then narrowed down, and an equivalent in the target language is then possible. Translations translate meanings, which are contained in sentences and paragraphs, not in individual words in isolation.

41. The ambiguities which are not ambiguities for people are a nightmare for those attempting to use computers to translate. A computer even has trouble with "drinking" and "ordered" leading to somewhere around twenty different possible meanings from which to decide. The difference is that competent speakers of a language understand a context, and thereby unconsciously eliminate all the irrelevant meanings. See Silva, *God, Language and Scripture*, 93–97.

42. Compare the RSV and NIV translations with NEB (REB). See G. Fee, *The First Epistle to the Corinthians*, NICNT (Grand Rapids: Eerdmans, 1987), 273–75.

43. It is also important not to try to "dig up" ambiguities, which might be possible but are not clearly attested. This is an especially pertinent warning for those who know the biblical languages. The stimulating commentary on Psalms by M. Dahood, a specialist in Ugaritic (a Canaanite language very similar to Hebrew), is very valuable in providing insight from Ugaritic into the meaning of poetic words and phrases which were previously baffling. But Dahood often suggests a new meaning based on Ugaritic where the "old" or common meaning of a word already makes perfectly good sense. E.g., the word for "shield" in Ps. 3:3 ("You are a shield around me."), Ps. 84:11 ("The Lord God is a sun and a shield."), and Gen. 15:1 ("Do not be afraid, Abraham; I am your shield.") is taken by Dahood to mean "suzerain" or "overlord," based on some rather thin comparative linguistic evidence. Even worse is Dahood's argument on even slimmer evidence that the very common Hebrew word for "way" or

"path" in Psalm 1 and many other places really means "assembly." Not only does such esoteric sophistry vitiate the poetic power of the Psalms and reduce their vibrant metaphors to platitudinous pedantry, it is completely unnecessary; "shield" and "path" fit their contexts just fine.

44. This sort of problem is much more common for those who work with the original languages. E.g., Silva, *Biblical Words and Their Meaning*, 153–56 makes reference to the ambiguity of *pascho* in Gal. 3:4, which could either mean "Did you *suffer* so many [bad] things in vain" or "did you *experience* so many [good] things in vain." Only by knowing the social history of the Christians in Galatia could this ambiguity be resolved. But again, the sentence's ambiguity does not disrupt its function in the larger context; whichever meaning is correct, the sentence stands as a rebuke to the Galatians for their irrational abandonment of grace as the ground and faith as the medium of their relationship to God.

45. The phenomenon is treated in Barr, *Semantics of Biblical Language*, 218, 222, who terms it "illegitimate totality transfer." See sec. 7.2.2.

46. See e.g., P. Ricoeur, "The Hermeneutical Function of Distanciation" in *Hermeneutics and the Human Sciences* (Cambridge: Cambridge Univ. Press, 1981), 131–45. Ricoeur argues that distanciation must be practiced when interpreting *any* text, not just ancient ones, because no author is identical to ourselves. Distanciation does not mean alienation, however. It is in dialectic with the opposite process, making a text one's own, which Ricoeur calls "appropriation." See Ricoeur, *Interpretation Theory*, 43–44, 89, cited earlier.

47. This use of a "sane imagination" resembles the effort at "empathy" advocated by Schleiermacher, who thought that the interpreter should attempt to identify with the author's desires and aims by way of an artistic imagination. See Schleiermacher, *Hermeneutics*, 113, 150. Schleiermacher has often been accused of "psychologizing," and it is true that he did thereby spearhead the efforts of nineteenth-century theologians to "get into the mind and heart" of Jesus, but Schleiermacher's "empathy" is also an expression of his view of understanding as art, as an intuitive linking of persons in communication. If we wish to regard texts as interpersonal communication, it seems to us that the only final bridge of the distance between authors and readers is their common humanity and "imageness," which enables genuine understanding once the distance has been recognized.

48. Often reference is made to Luke 17:21 which in the KJV reads "the kingdom of God is within you," but Jesus was speaking there to the unbelieving Pharisees, declaring that *His presence* meant the presence of the kingdom, and so most modern translations correctly read "the kingdom of God is in your midst" or the like (see NIV, RSV).

49. See R.T. France, "The Church and the Kingdom of God" in *Biblical*

Interpretation and the Church: Text and Context, ed. D.A. Carson (Exeter: Paternoster, 1984), 30–44.

50. See E.D. Hirsch, *Aims of Interpretation* (Chicago: Univ. of Chicago Press, 1976), 39.

51. See P.E. Hughes, "The Truth of Scripture and the Problem of Historical Relativity," in *Scripture and Truth*, ed. Carson and Woodbridge, 173ff. Since the heart of the human predicament remains the same in all ages, so the heart of the biblical message does not change with culture.

52. See Stott, *Between Two Worlds: The Art of Preaching in the Twentieth Century*. The book was published in England under the title *I Believe in Preaching*.

53. See below, n. 57.

54. The personal pronoun variation is due to the ambiguity of the vowelless Hebrew text. The Massoretic textual tradition understood it as "she"; the Dead Sea Sectarians understood "you"; the Septuagint translators understood "they." The pronoun difference, of course, matters but little to the meaning of the whole.

55. This could not have been Hezekiah. The indications of 2 Kings 18:1 and 16:1-2 are that Hezekiah was born some time before Ahaz became king. This evidence is usually discounted by critics who argue that the ages and dates of Kings are worthless; but E. Thiele has shown that, with the practice of co-regency and the different counting of accession years in the Northern and Southern kingdoms, a consistent chronology is possible (E. Thiele, *The Mysterious Numbers of the Hebrew Kings: A Reconstruction of the Chronology of the Kingdoms of Israel and Judah*, 2nd ed. [Grand Rapids: Eerdmans, 1965; Exeter: Paternoster, 1966]).

56. E.g., E. Kraeling, "The Immanuel Prophecy," *Journal of Biblical Literature* 50 (1931): 277–97.

57. Endless needless discussion has been generated over whether the Hebrew word in Isa. 7:14 means "virgin" (kjv) or "young woman" (most modern translations). Ordinarily the Hebrew word simply refers to a young unmarried woman, and her virginity in most cases would be *assumed* though not explicit. At least the LXX translator of the passage into Greek thought it meant virgin. In any case, it would not appropriately apply to Isaiah's wife, who was not unmarried. Also note that in the Massoretic text of 7:14 it is the woman and not the father who names the child (contrast 8:3, Hosea 1:4, and Luke 1:63); this might suggest that a father was presumed not to be present.

58. Many modern translations (e.g., rsv) have "when" He knows, but the Hebrew is an unambiguous "in order to" (*lamed* plus infinitive). Acknowledgment must be given to Bruce Waltke for pointing out to me the significance of eating curds and honey, as well as the syntactical construction here.

59. Of course, the Jews in Jesus' day were not literally living off the fatness of the land anymore, but Jesus Himself did, in a manner of speaking. He and His disciples gleaned from the fields and had nowhere to lay their heads.

60. There are, of course, parallels between Maher-shalal-hash-baz and Christ. But it is not infrequent in prophecy to look at an immediate future event as a forecasting of God's more ultimate plan for redemption. Isaiah's son is himself a "sign" pointing to the greater "sign" of the one who would *personally* be called "God with us" (as opposed to the corporate "Immanuel" of Isa. 8:8, which cannot be Maher-shalal-hash-baz).

61. See secs. 6.3 and 7.3.

62. This head covering is probably not quite the veil seen on Islamic women today, since no such veils are evident in any paintings or other art works of the ancient world. Here again, a cultural shift can confuse a modern reader unless he or she knows something of the ancient culture.

63. This seems to be implied from 1 Cor. 11:10, but unfortunately this verse, and indeed this entire passage in Paul, is extremely cryptic. (The English translations usually make weakly warranted exegetical decisions for the sake of clarity.) Further, we really do not know what the social meaning of wearing or not wearing a head covering was. See Fee, *First Epistle to the Corinthians*, 508–12.

64. Hirsch, *Aims of Interpretation*, 68 points out that there are two ways of looking at genre. One can either think of a finite number of speech act types and then classify a particular utterance according to one of those types or a mixture of more than one (J.L. Austin), or one can think of an infinite continuum, where each text is *sui generis*, a unique genre bearing only resemblances to other texts (L. Wittgenstein). Actually this is a silly argument. We have no difficulty calling red, blue, and green distinct colors, even though they exist on an infinitely finely graded continuum. And we are able to define and classify words and categories of thought, even though they all overlap and intermingle on a continuum.

65. E.g., L.C. Allen, *The Books of Joel, Obadiah, Jonah, and Micah* (Grand Rapids: Eerdmans, 1976), 175–81. Allen (p. 178) claims that Luther viewed Jonah as nonhistorical.

66. Jesus' reference to Jonah's being in the belly of the fish three days and nights as a sign looks like an indication on the side of historical genre. This may not be strictly necessary, since the sign value of the story of Jonah might not depend on its being historical. Modern preachers can exhort their audiences to "be like the good Samaritan," even though they do not regard the good Samaritan as a historical person.

On the other hand, the signs in the Gospels are usually miracles, and if Jonah is only a parable it would not be a miraculous sign. See further T.D. Alexander, "Jonah & Genre," *Tyndale Bulletin* 36 (1985): 35–59 who argues that in fact Jonah does not bear the linguistic markers of a parable. Also see B.S. Childs, *Introduction to the Old Testament as Scripture* (London: SCM, 1979), 421ff, who points out that Jonah bears certain features which are not at all characteristic of the parable form.

67. In the ancient Near East there was a recognized genre known as fictional royal autobiography, which readers would recognize and not attribute to their ostensive authors. See T. Longman, *Fictional Akkadian Autobiography: A Generic and Comparative Study* (Winona Lake, Ind.: Eisenbrauns, 1991). No deceit was intended. Note that the opening to Ecclesiastes, although it makes several allusions to Solomon, never explicitly states that it is the work of Solomon. There are also other indications in the text that indicate that Solomon is not the author (e.g., the use of the past tense in 1:12: "I, the Teacher, *was* king over Jerusalem."). In the words of E.J. Young, "Wisdom, therefore, is here presented as embodied in a person, and that person is Solomon. Hence, it is in an ideal sense that Solomon is introduced, and so the author is not guilty of a literary deception" (E.J. Young, *Introduction to the Old Testament* [Grand Rapids: Eerdmans, 1964], 348). Thus, this is quite different than the assertion that *pseudepigrapha* are a recognized genre and therefore could occur in the Bible. Pseudepigrapha actually *claim* to be written by a particular author and hence are deliberate misinformation.

68. See n. 70 following.

69. For this reason the relevancy of authorship for interpretation is not of equal importance for different biblical works. Understanding Corinthians demands that we know that Paul wrote it to a particular church; Hebrews is more general and it is not necessary to know who wrote it to understand it. This also warns against too specific a set of generalized hermeneutical theories. One set of paradigms may work well with one text and be disastrous with another.

70. For this reason it is wise to be cautious about finding a text to be of a particular genre when it has never been previously recognized as such, unless one has at hand some new evidence never before considered. A rather spectacular example of what is in our opinion a misapprehension of genre is the suggestion made by M.D. Goulder, *Midrash and Lection in Matthew* (London: SPCK, 1974) that Matthew was not history at all but a liturgical midrash which simply took the historical elements as a point of departure. This approach was furthered by the commentary on Matthew by R. Gundry, *Matthew: A Commentary on His Theological and Literary Art* (Grand Rapids: Eerdmans, 1982). He too understands Matthew to be a "midrash" on the historical Gospel known from Mark and Luke, a "reinterpretation and application," but sees it as a mixture of true history and theologically embellished "history." But it is questionable whether there is such a genre as midrash (midrash is simply a Hebrew word

meaning "interpretation" and has a variety of uses in Talmudic Judaism), and the Gospel of Matthew itself does not itself give indications within itself that it is an instance of such a mixed historical and nonhistorical genre. Such an unusual or unexpected genre must somehow identify itself as such or it will not be understood. See the review by D.A. Carson in *Trinity Journal* 3 (1982): 71–91.

71. Allegory is technically not a genre per se but a rhetorical device, where a particularly apt metaphor is expanded with several points of symbolic correspondence to the main subject. But genre identification includes recognition of these devices, of course, so we can refer to a deliberately allegorical piece as being generically allegorical.

72. In addition, there are certain so-called "critical" methods which can help scholars in the task of identifying the contexts, in identifying the genre, and elucidating the cultural difference. We have briefly discussed these critical methods in Appendix B, but knowledge of these is not essential to good interpretation and further they presuppose original language ability and require professional training, so we will not discuss them here.

CHAPTER SIX

1. B. Mickelson, *Interpreting the Bible* (Grand Rapids: Eerdmans, 1963), 6. Mickelson's purpose was undoubtedly pragmatic and pedagogical rather than philosophical, but he appears not to have raised the question of how much can be subsumed under "authorial intent," nor whether this category is adequate when dealing with a text with divine as well as human authorship.

2. Perhaps one of the strongest diatribes against any meaning beyond the purely historical is found in F.W. Farrar, *History of Interpretation* (1886; reprint, Grand Rapids: Baker, 1961). His obloquy and unrelenting sarcasm suggests that the whole history of Christian and Jewish interpretation is nothing more than material for ridicule. Admittedly, excesses were rampant prior to the Reformation, but Farrar seems to have had no appreciation for transcendent meaning.

3. J. Barr, *Old and New in Interpretation: A Study of the Two Testaments* (London: SCM, 1966), 131 argues that "where the question is one of methods, such as typology and allegory. . . these methods themselves partake to some extent in the once-ness of the incarnation." I.e., the NT writers' strange exegesis is bound up with their particular interpretive worlds of meaning. Certainly the NT texts partake of the "once-ness" of the final revelation in the incarnation of Jesus Christ, but their interpre-

tive methods are not unique, even within the Bible. And once again, if we do not take our interpretive principles from the Bible itself, they must come from the "enlightened" autonomous reason, which cannot fully apprehend the Word of God.

4. The word "entirely" could also mean "undoubtedly." This is not a denial that the words ever had any meaning for anyone other than his readers, but an identification of their primary significance.

5. This is not the place to justify or condemn modern economic practices, but the reader can no doubt imagine how impracticable private enterprise would be for all except those who were already wealthy.

6. The Sabbath year and Jubilee effectively created a substitute mortgage loan system, because a man could "sell" his land for a period of time (up to the next Jubilee); he got the use of the money and the "buyer" got the proceeds from the land for that period. Our society obviously has no such system; our land title deeds include the ridiculous word "forever."

7. Paul's idea of "mystery" was derived from the Book of Daniel. The LXX used the word *mysterion* in its translation of Daniel (2:18-19, 27-30, 47), and of course the concept of God's secret plan being unfolded is contained in Daniel.

8. S.G. Sowers, *The Hermeneutics of Philo and Hebrews* (Richmond, Va.: Knox, 1965), 89.

9. See D. Patte, *Early Jewish Hermeneutic in Palestine* (Missoula, Mont.: Scholars, 1975), 161.

10. For the contrast between the Hellenistic notion of history as circular and the biblical view of history as linear, see O. Cullmann, *Christ and Time*, rev. ed., trans. F.V. Filson (London: SCM; Philadelphia: Westminster, 1964).

11. G. von Rad, *Old Testament Theology II: The Theology of Israel's Prophetic Traditions* (Edinburgh and London: Oliver & Boyd, 1965), 367-70. The entire section entitled "The Old Testament in the New" (pp. 319–429) develops von Rad's view of the way the OT points to and is fulfilled in the New. We should note that von Rad's view of history and the Bible is not the same as ours, and he stresses that typology does not lie in the OT thing or person, but in the progress or development from one thing to another. There is always a tension between promise and fulfillment that points to greater fulfillment. Thus David, Joshua, the tabernacle, and the Passover are not "types" of Christ in themselves as historical entities, but only as they are marks on the line of progress toward fulfillment in Christ.

12. L. Goppelt, *Typos: The Typological Interpretation of the Old Testament in the New*, trans. D.H. Madvig (Grand Rapids: Eerdmans, 1982), 151–52.

13. See S. Amsler, *L'ancien testament dans l'eglise*, and D.A. Koch, *Die Schrift als Zeuge des Evangelium: Untersuchungen zur Verwendung u. zum*

Verständnis der Schrift bei Paulus (Tübingen: Mohr [Siebeck], 1986).

14. Our use of the term "fuller meaning" or *sensus plenior* is somewhat different from that of some Roman Catholic theologians who regard the extra-biblical doctrines of the church as definitive for the fuller sense of Scripture. We are speaking of an *intra*-biblical fuller sense.

15. D. Moo, "The Problem of *Sensus Plenior*," in *Hermeneutics, Authority, and Canon*, ed. D. Carson and J. Woodbridge (Grand Rapids: Zondervan, 1986), 196.

16. *Dialogue with Trypho*, chap. 111.

17. The Rahab story does indeed occur in a typological context. The spies' preparation for the taking of Canaan does bear a typological relation to the church's preparation for taking the world away from Satan. But the nature of the typology would lie more in Rahab's sheltering of the spies (which was an act of faith) rather than in the incidental use of a scarlet cord.

18. *allegoroumenon*

19. The Judaizers were apparently Christians from Jerusalem who insisted on Gentile converts being circumcised and keeping the OT law in an OT fashion. Paul had to fight this not just because it denied the reality of the new age which had resulted from the coming of Jesus, but because it implied that relationship with God was accomplished by obedience to a code rather than by faith in God.

20. C.K. Barrett, "The Allegory of Abraham, Sarah, and Hagar in the Argument of Galatians," in *Rechtfertigung*, Festschrift E. Käsemann, ed. J. Friedrich et al. (Tübingen: Mohr [Siebeck], 1976), 1–16 argued that the Judaizers had produced their own allegorical interpretation of this text, and that Paul responds in kind with an *ad hominem* argument of his own, as if to say, "if you want an allegorical interpretation, here is a better one." This is possible, but there is no indication in Galatians itself that this was the case.

21. Other quasi-allegorical interpretations such as 1 Cor. 9:9 (= 1 Tim. 5:18), and 1 Cor. 10:1-6 (see p. 214) are not full-fledged allegories of history, but pick up on single typological elements as a means of drawing larger connections. Only here in Galatians (3:16) do we have anything else approaching allegorical interpretation, and as is explained in chapter 2 (pp. 55–56), this allegory is rooted in the actual identity of Christ as the ultimate "seed" of Abraham.

22. See n. 20.

23. Since Paul refers to the "spiritual" rock following Israel and says that "the rock was Christ," R.P.C. Hanson, *Allegory and Event: A Study of the Sources and Significance of Origen's Interpretation of Scripture* (London: SCM, 1959), 79 argues that Paul does not mean that the physical rock allegorically *symbolizes* Christ but that Christ was spiritually and really

there with His people. Their consumption of manna and the water from the rock was spiritually the equivalent of the Christian Lord's Supper. In any case the christological nature of Paul's reference is clear, and there must be some connection between the rock which Moses struck which gave the people water and Christ who gives spiritual drink.

Paul may have known certain rabbinical legends about the "rock"; these crop up in the later writings of Judaism. But even if he did, his use of the rock in the wilderness bears little resemblance to those recorded in rabbinic literature, and, unlike them, Paul's use is christologically focused.

24. The Hebrew word for "rock" in Ex. 17:6 usually refers to a low-lying rock, whereas the different word for rock in Num. 20:11 generally means a high, overhanging rock.

25. We are not sure whom to credit for the observation that the different rocks represent Christ's humiliation and exaltation. We first first heard it from Dr. Stuart Sacks, now a pastor in eastern Pennsylvania.

26. This also provides the key to understanding the difficult v. 23: "you will not complete the towns of Israel before the Son of Man comes." Just as the "finishing the towns of Israel" is a paradigm for completing the world mission, so the "coming of the Son of Man" has a first fulfillment in His ascension (or perhaps in judgment in A.D. 70), and an ultimate fulfillment in the Second Coming.

27. The phrase is based on Rom. 12:6 where the one who prophesies is encouraged to do so "in proportion [analogue] to the faith" (authors' trans.). This could mean that a prophet must prophesy as a result of his faith in God, but is more likely to mean that any prophet in the church must prophesy in accordance with the content of faith that has already been revealed. Prior to the completion of the Bible, this was a specialized application of Scripture as the interpretive rule for any other Scripture.

28. A well-known proponent of this view in the U.S. is W. Kaiser, who reiterates this thesis in many of his works. See his Toward an Exegetical Theology (Grand Rapids: Baker, 1981), 136.

29. Those who hold to this "one way" theory, if they believe Scripture to be true, can only escape from this conundrum by suggesting that the human authors of these OT passages had in mind Jesus Christ's resurrection and ascension. But getting these things from the contexts in Joel and Psalm 16 is not easy.

30. In our opinion there is a hint of this larger meaning in the references to the "daughters of Jerusalem" or "daughters of Zion" which recur throughout the Song.

31. Of course, not all interpreters agree that the christological nature of the love song of Psalm 45 gives sanction to the christological interpretation of the Song of Songs. See G.L. Carr, "The OT Love Songs and their

Use in the NT," *Journal of the Evangelical Theological Society* 24:2 (June 1981): 97–106. But to reduce this portion of Scripture to its lowest level (human love) raises the question, "Why is it in Scripture at all, and what has it to do with God's redemption of His people?"

CHAPTER SEVEN

1. Luther, *WA* 50:659; cited in J. Mackinnon, *Luther and the Reformation*, vol. 4 (New York: Russell & Russell, 1962), 304.
2. This is particularly true with idioms, but can also be true of words. A clear example of an unfortunately over-literalistic translation is the sectarian *New World* translation. To take one example, by insisting on always translating the Hebrew word *nefesh* as "soul," Jehovah's Witnesses are led by Gen. 9:4 and Lev. 17:11 into the belief that the "*soul* of the flesh is in the blood." Consequently they refuse blood transfusions and allow themselves and their children to die prematurely, all because of a literalistic translation error.

Notice that the KJV translates the word *nefesh* as "life" in over a hundred instances. When God tells Moses (Ex. 4:19) that "all the men are dead who sought thy *nefesh*," he clearly means "physical life," not "soul," and the *lex talionis* (Deut. 19:21) has to be "life for life, eye for eye, etc." not "soul for soul."
3. The KJV (which was never actually "authorized" by any duly constituted church or state) is not an overly literal translation; the scholars who translated it were competent, and if there was a conflict between the form and the meaning, usually made sure to reproduce the *meaning* in the English of their day. Although it has certain deficiencies, it is still a reliable translation.
4. See Cotterell and Turner, *Linguistics*, 230.
5. See G. Fee, *New Testament Exegesis: A Handbook for Students and Pastors* (Philadelphia: Westminster, 1983), 60–77.
6. A special kind of structure that occurs fairly frequently in the Bible is called "chiasm." A basic chiasm is an A-B-B¹-A¹ structure, where the sequence of two or more elements in the first half is echoed in reverse order in the second half. Usually the second half involves a progression or shift, not just a reverse order reiteration. A good example is 1 Peter 2:17 (RSV).

> Honor all men;
> > Love the brethren;
> > Fear God;
> Honor the emperor.

Chiasm can also tie together extended narrative sections. For example, the end of 2 Samuel closes with a chiastic narrative structure:

A   Saul's sin against the Gibeonites and its collective punishment (2 Sam. 21:1-14)

   B   David's heroes and their exploits (21:15-22)

      C   David's psalm (22:1-51)

      C¹ David's psalm (23:1-7)

   B¹ David's heroes and their exploits (23:8-39)

A¹ David's sin against the census prohibition and its collective punishment (24:1-17).

For another e.g., see Heb. 5:1-10.

7. Cotterell and Turner, *Linguistics,* 197–203. See also J. Louw, *Semantics of New Testament Greek* (Philadelphia: Fortress, 1982), 67–158.

8. See Cotterell and Turner, *Linguistics,* chap. 6, to whom we acknowledge our debt for much of this chapter. We refer readers interested in this approach to their discussion and examples in pp. 197–224.

9. This passage was only roughly done, and not all the nuclear sentences as defined by Cotterell and Turner are separated out as distinct units here. Further we have made no attempt to develop or relate a terminology for the different relations between the nuclear sentences. The reader interested in more detailed instruction regarding this type of analysis is advised to consult chap. 6 of their book.

10. A. Cruden, *A Complete Concordance to the Holy Scriptures of the Old and New Testament,* 3rd ed. (London: n.p., 1769, republished many times since).

11. J. Strong, *The Exhaustive Concordance of the Bible* (New York: Hunt & Eaton; Cincinnati: Cranston & Curtis, 1894; also republished many times).

12. R. Young, *Analytical Concordance to the Bible,* rev. W.B. Stevenson (New York: Funk & Wagnalls, 1873, etc.).

13. *Nelson's Complete Concordance of the Revised Standard Version Bible* (New York: Nelsons, 1957).

14. R. Whitaker, ed., *Eerdmans Analytical Concordance to the Revised Standard Version of the Bible* (Grand Rapids: Eerdmans, 1988).

15. C. Morrison, *An Analytical Concordance to the Revised Standard Version of the New Testament* (Philadelphia: Westminster, 1979).

16. R.L. Thomas, ed., *New American Standard Exhaustive Concordance of the Bible* (Nashville: Holman, 1981).

17. E. Goodrick and J.R. Kohlenberger, *The NIV Complete Concordance: The Complete English Concordance to the New International Version* (Grand Rapids: Zondervan, 1981; London: Hodder & Stoughton, 1988); and *The NIV Exhaustive Concordance* (Grand Rapids: Zondervan, 1990). The latter, like Strong's, has a key to the original language words.

18. J.R. Kohlenberger, *The NRSV Concordance Unabridged* (Grand Rapids: Zondervan, 1991).

19. Of course, some Christians believe that all killing of humans is morally wrong, but such teaching cannot be derived from Ex. 20.

20. For more on the fascinating subject of exegetical "false steps" with regard to words, see D.A. Carson, *Exegetical Fallacies* (Grand Rapids: Baker, 1984), 25–66.

21. Even famous scholars have fallen prey to this error. Particularly Hebrew scholars were susceptible, partly because of the ease with which the "root" of a Hebrew word is identified, and partly because the legitimate use of etymology in the defining of rare words is much more frequent in OT study.

22. Actually the English word for "orgy" does not come from the Greek word for wrath, which is *orge*, but from a similar word *orgia*.

23. J. Barr, *Semantics of Biblical Language*, 218, 222.

24. R.C. Trench, *Synonyms of the New Testament*, 9th ed. (London: Macmillan, 1880; often reprinted).

25. G. Bromiley, trans., *Theological Dictionary of the New Testament* [TDNT] 1, s.v. *agapao, agape* by E. Stauffer (Grand Rapids: Eerdmans, 1964). This sort of thing is the inevitable result of so-called "theological lexicography," which attempts to discuss theological *subjects* or *concepts* under the rubric of *words*. But then passages where the word happens not to be used but which are highly relevant to the subject matter may be overlooked, and passages where the word is used tend to get loaded up with the entire theological concept. Since TDNT groups cognates together there is the further problem of having quite divergent and unrelated subjects discussed under the same heading. It is like discussing the word "marinade" under the subject "marine" simply because of its common etymology.

C. Brown, ed., *New International Dictionary of New Testament Theology* (Exeter: Paternoster; Grand Rapids: Zondervan, 1975) is somewhat better, since it groups several Greek words having to do with subjects under a single subject heading, with indices for cross reference. But it would have been better had it not been called a "dictionary," which implies it is defining words rather than collating the New Testament teaching on certain subjects.

26. It is thus questionable whether John means anything special other than stylistic variation in the alteration between *agapao* and *phileo* in John 21:15-17.

27. Tense, or "aspect" in Greek, is related primarily to the nature of the action. Generally speaking, "present" tense (or "progressive aspect") is used for continuous or repeated actions, and the perfect tense or aspect for completed ones. In the indicative mood, the aorist tense ordinarily

indicates past time, but indicates nothing at all in the other moods. The aorist is the "default" tense. It is not, as some grammars misleadingly say, a "punctiliar" tense.

28. Tense in Hebrew, even more than in Greek, is uncertain ground for conclusions.

29. M. Silva, *Philippians* Wycliffe Exegetical Commentary (Chicago: Moody, 1988), 13; also see his *God, Language, and Scripture* (Grand Rapids: Eerdmans, 1990), 11–15.

30. In the section that follows we are not attempting to offer anything like a comprehensive bibliography. Two excellent guides to secondary materials for Bible study are F.W. Danker, *Multipurpose Tools for Bible Study* (St. Louis: Concordia, 1970), and J. Fitzmyer, *An Introductory Bibliography for the Study of Scripture*, rev. ed. (Rome: Biblical Institute, 1981). These works are to some degree oriented toward theological students and original language study, but there is much for English Bible students as well. Danker not only lists the tools, but gives examples of how to use them.

31. *New International Standard Bible Encyclopedia*, 4 vols. (Grand Rapids: Eerdmans, 1979–1988). It is based on the earlier encyclopedia ed. by J. Orr (1915).

32. *The New Bible Dictionary*, ed. J.D. Douglas (Grand Rapids, 1962); *The Illustrated Bible Dictionary*, 3 vols. (Leicester, U.K.: Inter-Varsity; Wheaton, Ill.: Tyndale, 1980).

33. *The Interpreter's Dictionary of the Bible*, 4 vols. (Nashville: Abingdon, 1962).

34. Y. Aharoni and M. Avi-Yonah, *The Macmillan Bible Atlas*, rev. ed. (New York: Macmillan, 1977).

35. F.F. Bruce, *New Testament History* (London: Nelson; Garden City, N.Y.: Doubleday, 1972).

36. J. Bright, *A History of Israel* 3rd ed. (Philadelphia: Westminster, 1981).

37. E. Lohse, *The New Testament Environment* (London: SCM; Philadelphia: Fortress, 1976).

38. W.F. Albright, *From the Stone Age to Christianity* (Garden City, N.Y.: Doubleday, 1957).

39. D. Guthrie, *New Testament Introduction* (Downers Grove, Ill.: InterVarsity, 1990).

40. R.K. Harrison, *Introduction to the Old Testament* (Grand Rapids: Eerdmans, 1969; London: Tyndale, 1970).

41. (Grand Rapids: Zondervan, 1985).

42. (Nashville: Thomas Nelson, hopefully to appear in 1994).

43. D. Guthrie and J. Motyer, eds., *New Bible Commentary: Revised* (Grand Rapids: Eerdmans; London: Inter-Varsity, 1970).

44. F.F. Bruce, ed., *International Bible Commentary* (Basingstoke, U.K.: Marshall, Morgan, Scott; Grand Rapids: Zondervan, 1986).

45. The best and most up-to-date commentary surveys, which include evaluation and critique of important commentaries, are D.A. Carson, *New Testament Commentary Survey*, 3rd ed. (Grand Rapids: Baker, 1990), and T. Longman, *Old Testament Commentary Survey* (Grand Rapids: Baker, 1991).

46. There is a debate in some Christian circles as to whether there is basically *one* redemptive covenant between God and man, with two aspects (an unconditional promise and a conditional law), or whether there were *two* distinct covenants, one being unilateral and unconditional, the other being bilateral and conditional. In our view this issue is largely a quibble over words. Certainly Gal. 3:17, 4:24, and Heb. 8:7 imply two covenants, an old and a new (the "new" being older than the old according to Paul); but they resolve into one *relationship* to God through Jesus Christ (see Gal. 3:20).

47. Cf. M.G. Kline, *By Oath Consigned* (Grand Rapids: Eerdmans, 1968).

48. For more on the idea of the kingdom of God as the restoration of human vicegerency under God on earth, see D. McCartney, "The Kingdom of God as the Restoration of Human Vicegerency," *Westminster Theological Journal* 56 (Spring 1994): forthcoming.

49. Actually, before the argument was fully underway, Charles had already noted that the kingdom in Jesus' conception was both already present yet still future. See R.H. Charles, *A Critical History of the Doctrine of a Future Life* (London: A & C Black, 1913).

50. G. Vos, *The Pauline Eschatology* (pub. by the author, 1930), 38.

51. For a marvelous example of how this illuminates the teaching of Paul, see H. Ridderbos, *Paul, an Outline of His Theology* (Grand Rapids: Eerdmans, 1975).

52. This is the reason why we must reject the so-called "theonomic" movement, which argues that the OT civil laws apply in their entirety to the civil state today. The modern civil state is not the church, and it is entirely inappropriate to apply OT casuistic civil legislation directly to the modern state. See W. Barker, ed., *Theonomy: A Reformed Critique* (Grand Rapids: Baker, 1990).

53. Of course, this begs certain questions about what constitutes a "literal" passage. See sec. 5.1.3.

54. Dogs were not kept as pets until fairly recent times.

55. There are, of course, two branches of premillennialism, which are so disparate that they are usually considered as separate views, but the differences are not so much related to the specific exegesis of Revelation 20 as the relation of the millennium to other material in Scripture.

56. Our discussion here makes no claims to present adequately any of

these views, nor to treat all of the exegetical problems of Revelation 20. It is for illustrative purposes only. We have therefore made some effort to conceal our own viewpoint(s) on this passage.

CHAPTER EIGHT

1. This is a statement about *style*; we do not concur with the postmodern blurring of the distinction between history and fiction.

2. There are actually a variety of ways of understanding the term "myth." See J.D.G. Dunn, "Demythologizing – The Problem of Myth in the New Testament" in *New Testament Interpretation: Essays on Principles and Methods*, ed. I.H. Marshall (Grand Rapids: Eerdmans, 1977), 285–88.

3. S.T. Coleridge, in *Bibliographia Literaria, The Portable Coleridge*, ed. I.A. Richards (New York: Viking, 1950), 522.

4. The degree to which meter functioned in ancient Hebrew poetry is hotly debated, but not a single extant piece of OT Hebrew poetry exhibits the kind of regularity which marks Greek poetry. Efforts have been made to identify the number of syllables as a constant (as in our modern Western hymns), but such efforts must always amend the Hebrew text very heavily and are generally unconvincing.

5. H. Gunkel, *Einleitung in die Psalmen. Die Gattungen der religiösen Lyrik Israels* (Göttingen: Vandenhoek & Ruprecht, 1928). See A.R. Johnson, "The Psalms" in *The Old Testament and Modern Study*, ed. H.H. Rowley (Oxford: Oxford Univ. Press, 1951), 162–209. Gunkel was motivated by the desire to reconstruct the original historical setting of the Psalms.

6. Scholars subsequent to Gunkel have recognized the several types of psalms and although they have modified and adapted his classification system in various ways, Gunkel's method is the starting point for most modern psalm study.

7. Gunkel's own reconstructions differ widely from, e.g., those of S. Mowinckel, *Psalms in Israel's Worship* (Oxford: Blackwell, 1962), who finds the historical setting of the Psalms in the various cultic activities of Israel, most especially in the purely hypothetical "Enthronement Festival of Yahweh."

8. For an elegant brief overview of hymns and poetry in the NT, see R.P. Martin, "Approaches to New Testament Exegesis," in Marshall, *New Testament Interpretation*, 235–41.

9. The structure is even more obvious in the Greek.

10. There are also several other instances where a parallelism *may* re-

flect borrowed or adapted poetry (e.g., Rom. 1:3-4; 1 Cor. 3:17; 1 Cor. 15:3-4; 1 Peter 2:10; 3:18-22), but with only one "couplet" and no indications of its source it is difficult to know whether these are borrowed, or simply a poetic device on the part of the author of the book.

11. Since the publication of E. Lohmeyer, *Kyrios Jesus: Eine Untersuchung zu Phil. 2, 5–11* (Heidelberg: C. Winters, 1926) it has been de rigueur to regard this as a hymn, although different investigators come to different conclusions regarding what its hymnic elements are. See R.P. Martin, *Carmen Christi: Philippians ii. 5-11 in Recent Interpretation and in the Setting of Early Christian Worship* (Cambridge: Cambridge Univ. Press, 1967).

12. An excellent introduction to the subject of biblical prophecy is P.E. Hughes, *Interpreting Prophecy: An Essay in Biblical Perspectives* (Grand Rapids: Eerdmans, 1976).

13. Parables are one of the most interesting and challenging of biblical genres. An excellent introduction to the nature of parables and problems of their interpretation is C. Blomberg, *Interpreting the Parables* (Downers Grove, Ill.: InterVarsity, 1989).

14. A. Jülicher, *Die Gleichnisreden Jesu*, 2 vols. (Tübingen: Mohr, 1899). Jülicher (1:93–98) made a distinction between similitudes, parables proper, illustrations, and allegories on the basis of Greek rhetorical categories. The clearly allegorical parables (Matt. 21:33-43; Matt. 22:1-14) and the interpretations which give an allegorical meaning (Matt. 13:18-23, 37-43) are castigated as not possibly authentic, because they are allegorical! These classifications have been maintained in the mainstream of German scholarship (with the exception of J. Jeremias). See E. Linnemann, *Parables of Jesus: Introduction and Exposition* (London: SPCK, 1966), 3–8. But there is little to suggest that Jesus or the early church thought of these as distinct categories, and frequently elements from more than one classification are found in a single parable. Like the "stylistic laws" of R. Bultmann, *History of the Synoptic Tradition*, 2nd ed. (New York: Harper, 1968), 188–92, these appear arbitrary impositions which are useful only for distinguishing the "authentic" material from the supposedly "inauthentic," thereby making the teaching of Jesus conform to modern expectations.

15. See J. Jeremias, *The Parables of Jesus* (London: SCM, 1954; 2nd ed., 1963; 3rd ed., 1972). This conviction of "one point" is held so strongly that indications to the contrary within the Gospels are regarded by some critics as necessarily inauthentic. See Jeremias, *Parables*, 66–89 (3rd. ed.).

16. Many critics do not regard Jesus' interpretation of the sower as authentically from Jesus Himself, but the interpretations which modern scholars have come up with have certainly not generated any consensus.

They rather tend to reflect the predispositions of the scholars toward what Jesus *ought* to have taught.

17. M. Boucher, *The Mysterious Parable* (Washington: Catholic Biblical Assoc., 1977).

18. J. Drury, *The Parables in the Gospels: History and Allegory* (London: SPCK, 1985).

19. Blomberg, *Interpreting the Parables*, argues that many parables have at least three points of interpretive correspondence: an authority figure (representing God), one or more protagonists, and one or more antagonists. But Blomberg also points out that no scheme can work with every parable.

20. K. Bailey, *Poet and Peasant* (Grand Rapids: Eerdmans, 1976) and *Through Peasant Eyes* (Grand Rapids: Eerdmans, 1980) give some excellent insights into the symbolic value that many of the parables would have evoked to its first hearers. (These two volumes are now published together [Grand Rapids: Eerdmans, 1983]).

21. Unfortunately, many scholars today doubt the validity of the social contexts given in the Gospels. They have therefore attempted to reconstruct an original "life setting" of the individual parables, as well as subsequent "life settings" in the church which caused the parable to develop into its present form(s). In our view, this only reopens the door to reinjecting anachronistic concerns into the interpretive process, because the scholar is able to reconstruct a church situation which gives a parable the "meaning" which the scholar wishes to find.

22. See the prayer of a scribe recorded in the Talmud (b.Berakoth 28b): "I thank thee, O Lord my God, that thou hast given me my lot with those who sit in the house of study, and not with those who sit at street corners . . . I run towards the life of the Age to Come, and they run towards the pit of destruction."

23. See E.J. Goodspeed, *The Formation of the New Testament* (Chicago: Univ. of Chicago Press, 1926), 25.

24. Only the tiny letter of 3 John has no indication of an intended readership larger than one individual, and even this letter deals with instructions to more than just Gaius himself.

25. P. Schubert, *Form and Function of the Pauline Thanksgivings* (Berlin: Töpelmann, 1939), 71–82.

26. This was argued by O. Roller, *Das Formular der paulinischen Briefe* (Stuttgart: Kohlhammer, 1933).

27. Ordinary prophecies about the end of history, such as Isa. 65 and 2 Thes. 2 are thus not apocalyptic, nor are judgment prophecies such as Isa. 24–27 and Zech. 9–14. The so-called "little apocalypse" of Mark 13/Matt. 24 has many symbolic or cryptic elements, but this is not really apocalyptic either. It bears rather the character of a farewell address,

with a series of warnings. See W. Lane, *Mark*, NICNT (Grand Rapids: Eerdmans, 1974), 445, who refers to F. Busch, *Zum Verständnis der synoptischen Eschatologie. Markus 13 neu untersucht* (Gütersloh, 1938), 44.

28. See D.E. Aune, *Prophecy in Early Christianity* (Grand Rapids: Eerdmans, 1983), 112.

29. This passage (9:24-27) has some notoriously difficult interpretative problems. Consult E.J. Young, *The Prophecy of Daniel* (Grand Rapids: Eerdmans, 1949; reprint, London: Banner of Truth, 1972).

CHAPTER NINE

1. For a helpful recent discussion on the canon of Scripture, see D. Dunbar, "The Biblical Canon," in Carson and Woodbridge, *Hermeneutics, Authority and Canon*, 295–360. Attacks on the status of Scripture among evangelicals have been gradually shifting from the question of inerrancy to the question of sufficiency.

2. In this passage the "gifts" are persons, not merely the talents, following the metaphor in vv. 7-8. "Christ gave the persons; the Church appointed to the office" (T.K. Abbott, *A Critical and Exegetical Commentary on the Epistles to the Ephesians and to the Colossians* [Edinburgh: T & T Clark, 1985], 117).

3. Although some scholars have made a distinction between *preaching* (proclamation of the Gospel and the call to repentance) and *teaching* (inculcation of doctrine), the NT makes no distinction or separation between them. Proclamation always includes doctrinal content, and teaching always has a hortatory purpose.

4. Form must not be confused with *function*. The thirty-minute sermon with three points and a poem is a *form*; the communication of the message is a *function*.

5. Individualism, passivity, or commercialism, for example.

6. Jer. 32; Hosea 1–3; Ezek. 4:12.

7. The NIV uses the phrase "plundered the Egyptians" (Ex. 3:22; 12:36), describing the God-given opportunity for His people to take what was worthwhile from their pagan environment at the time of the Exodus.

8. In some European cities, for example, street preachers occasionally harangue the passing crowds in the belief that the sermon will be effective, even if it is unsympathetic to the hearers' mind-set, language, or culture. The most extreme example we can remember is that of a small group of men dressed in dark suits and carrying large black Bibles, passionately addressing the swimmers and sunbathers on a beach. In

front of them was the only empty expanse of sand for some considerable distance.

9. There may be an assumption that the teaching is biblical, while in fact it is shallow and platitudinous.

10. We cannot find the source of this story, but for a summary of his life see J.C. Ryle, *Christian Leaders of the Eighteenth Century* (Edinburgh: Banner of Truth, 1978), 30–63.

11. The Word and its Author are of course inseparable, but we refer here to a superstitious use of the words themselves in a way not intended by the Author. For example, a leader might announce his evangelistic plan with the phrase, "See, I have placed before you an open door that no one can shut" (Rev. 3:8), intending to generate confidence and boldness. But these words were strictly the prerogative of God alone, describing His sovereignty over opportunities, including doors which are closed just as much as those which are open (v. 7).

12. We are arguing here that good hermeneutics can be communicated to a congregation by a sound teacher. Why, therefore, is it necessary to teach the subject at college or seminary? There are three basic reasons: first, there is such a dearth of good expository preaching that few candidates for the ministry will have previously absorbed sound hermeneutical principles. They must be taught the subject deliberately, often undoing the assumptions gained from a lifetime of using defective hermeneutics. The candidate who has already had the privilege of sitting under a good expositor begins his or her training with an enormous advantage. Second, without formal identification of hermeneutical principles it is much easier for shifts to occur away from the unspoken hermeneutics of one's predecessors. And third, even the greatest teachers make interpretive blunders and violate their own canons of interpretation. Formal articulation of hermeneutics enables a critique.

13. See J.R.W. Stott, "Preaching as Bridge-Building" in *Between Two Worlds,* 135–79.

14. Stott writes, "There is no doubt that the best teachers in any field of knowledge are those that remain students all their lives. It is particularly true of the ministry of the Word . . . there is a freshness and a vitality about every sermon which is born of study" (Stott, *Between Two Worlds,* 180).

15. From "And Can It Be That I Should Gain" by Charles Wesley.

16. Matt. 2:1-12. They were not kings, but "magi" or wandering wise men; and no number is given in Scripture.

17. It could also be argued that unbiblical hymns have been written for centuries but that, with the passage of time, the older hymns have been subject to extensive scrutiny and the "unsound" ones have disappeared from most of our hymnody; and that, similarly, in a day to come the

church will exercise further discernment. We can only respond "haste the day."

18. The situation in Neh. 8:8 (where the Levites "read from the Book of the Law of God, making it clear and giving the meaning so that the people could understand what was being read") was slightly different; they were probably translating it into Aramaic and may also have been adding an expository commentary.

19. It could be argued, therefore, that the best person to read the Scriptures in a service is the one who will preach from it; indeed, this is expected in some churches.

20. A friend of ours has been heard to parody this practice by reversing the well-known beatitude to say "righteous are they that hunger and thirst after blessings."

21. "Eisegesis" is reading ideas into Scripture rather than drawing them out from Scripture.

22. Gnosticism is an ancient heresy, where salvation is supposedly attained by esoteric spiritual knowledge.

23. We refer here to the wrong kind of peer pressure, not to the legitimate attraction to a community which exemplifies God's love.

24. Van Til, *A Christian Theory of Knowledge*, 12–13.

25. Here, of course, the "Word" refers to the ultimate self-revealing person of God, the Son who became man, the Lord Jesus Christ.

26. Calvin, *Institutes*, vol. 1, 120–21.

27. The problem is that we normally assume our "common sense" to be truly objective, shared by all reasonable people, and capable of identifying true truths. But only God-given sense could accomplish this!

28. In this entire discussion we have assumed the truth that any awakening to God is the result of God's previously acting grace. It is not our intention here to address this theologically; we are simply looking at it from the standpoint of human agency, as each believer attempts to witness obediently (and in God's providence becomes the human agency of the unbeliever's encounter with Him).

29. See 1 Peter 3:1, 15.

CHAPTER TEN

1. The galactic emperors, after generations of waiting, assembled on the computer-planet to hear its reply to the question, "What is the meaning of life, the universe, and everything?" The answer was: "Forty-two." "Is that all you've got to show for seven and a half million years' work?" they asked in astonishment. It replied: "I checked it very thoroughly, and that

is quite definitely the answer. I think the problem, to be quite honest with you, is that you've never actually known what the question is" (D. Adams, *The Hitch Hiker's Guide to the Galaxy* [London: Pan Books Ltd., 1979], 136).

2. One of the most helpful books on the subject published in recent years is M.B. Smith, *Knowing God's Will: Biblical Principles of Guidance* (Downers Grove, Ill.: InterVarsity, 1979). However, he does make a distinction between "moral" and "nonmoral" decisions, placing them at opposite ends of a continuum with all other decisions somewhere in between the two extremes (pp. 16–21).

3. Ex. 22:18; Lev. 19:26, 31; 20:6; 22:27; Deut. 18:10-11; Isa. 2:6; 8:19-20; 44:25; 47:12-13; Micah 5:12; Zech. 10:2; Mal. 3:5.

4. Luke 7:30 is a special case; God's purpose had already been declared through the prophets, so that the Pharisees and experts in the Law had indeed had a preview of God's "blueprint" but rejected it.

5. H. Ridderbos, *Paul: An Outline of His Theology* (Grand Rapids: Eerdmans, 1975), 237.

6. God's immanence means that He is *actively* involved in every atom of the universe which He has created (Ps. 139:7-16); He cannot be relegated to the role of a passive consultant, as though He were absent until we decide to bring Him into the picture. See H. Bavinck, *The Doctrine of God* (Hendriksen; Grand Rapids: Baker, 1979), 137–41, 161–64; Stephen Charnock, *Discourses upon the Existence and Attributes of God* (Grand Rapids: Baker, 1979), 364–67.

7. God's self-existence means that, in contrast to His creatures, He needs nothing to help Him to be what He is. He has existed from eternity past and will continue to do so into eternity future. All that we see and know derives from Him, and He is totally self-supportive. When Moses asked God for His name, God called Himself "I AM WHO I AM" (Ex. 3:14; or "I shall be who I shall be"); see W.J. Dumbrell, *Covenant and Creation* (Exeter: Paternoster, 1984), 83–84. The Dutch theologian Herman Bavinck put it this way: "God is a personal being, self-existent, having the source of life in himself, self-conscious, and self-willing, not shut in by nature but exalted above nature, Creator of heaven and earth" (H. Bavinck, *The Doctrine of God* [Grand Rapids: Baker, 1979], 17).

8. *Oxford English Dictionary.*

9. The phrase was that of Francis Schaeffer, who used it in opposition to the "relative truth" of modernism. See chap. 1.

10. In response to a rather esoteric debate about God's own logical processes, Bavinck says, "God's decree should not be exclusively described ... as a straight line to indicate a relation merely of before and after, cause and effect, means and goal; but it should also be viewed as a system, the several elements of which are co-ordinately related to one

another. . . . As in an organism all the members are dependent upon one another and in a reciprocal manner determine one another, so also the universe is God's work of art, the several parts of which are organically related" (Bavinck, *Doctrine of God*, 383ff).

11. Calvin, *Institutes*, vol. 1, 208.

12. J. Wenham, *The Enigma of Evil* (Leicester, U.K.: Inter-Varsity, 1985), 43.

13. For a classic study on this subject, see J. Edwards, "On the Freedom of the Will," in *The Works of Jonathan Edwards*, ed. Edward Hickman (1834; reprint, Edinburgh: Banner of Truth, 1984), 3–89.

14. The reader will note that we have been referring to paradoxes or *apparent* contradictions, not actual contradictions. We do not aver that the Bible maintains truths which are *in fact* contradictory. They only appear to be contradictory to us, because we do not see the whole picture.

15. J. Flavel, *The Mystery of Providence* (1678; reprint, Edinburgh: Banner of Truth, 1985), 181.

16. In saying that both are efficacious, we are not claiming that human choice actually achieves *salvation*. Strictly speaking, God's election does not achieve salvation either—it simply sets the process in motion and it is Christ's death that achieves redemption. We are speaking now about the reality of the choice, about the fact that it is a complete choice, neither half a choice nor an illusion of choice.

APPENDIX A

1. See E.D. Hirsch, *Validity in Interpretation* (New Haven: Yale Univ. Press, 1967), and *The Aims of Interpretation* (Chicago: Univ. of Chicago Press, 1976).

2. Cf. particularly his *Aims of Interpretation*, chap. 1.

3. J.D. Smart, *The Interpretation of Scripture* (London: SCM, 1961), 42.

4. The intended effect does not have to be precisely defined in the author's mind. The situation of the reader can affect the specific form of understanding, and a variety of specific responses can all be within the range of the author's intended meaning.

5. Hirsch, *Aims of Interpretation*, 52.

6. Cf. the interesting example in Cotterell and Turner, *Linguistics and Biblical Interpretation*, 58, of a confusing phrase "not without displeasure," where the author (Lessing) clearly meant "not with displeasure," i.e., the person enjoyed the activity. No one noticed the problem for a hundred years, because what was meant is perfectly clear from the context. Usually when one says something other than what he or she means

to say, what was meant is obvious to the hearer or reader, and an automatic, sometimes even an unconscious, correction is made. Fortunately language is redundant enough that such blunders do not hinder communication.

It is an interesting question whether this is possible with biblical writers. Sometimes it is suggested that James committed such a blunder in James 2:18, getting his "you" and "I" reversed. For a better solution to this problem, cf. R.P. Martin, *James* (Waco, Texas: Word, 1990), 77–79, 86–89.

7. Schleiermacher, *Hermeneutics*, 117.

8. T.S. Eliot, *The Sacred Wood* (London: Methuen, 1928), x.

9. Saussure, *Course in General Linguistics*, 79–100.

10. C. Lévi-Strauss, *Structural Anthropology* (New York: Basic Books, 1963).

11. This terminology is based on that of N. Chomsky, who developed the theory that speech in any language has a certain "deep structure" which is perhaps common to human experience, expressing the most basic and primitive human relations and social experience, and a "surface structure" which is the grammatical structure actually used to express the "deep structure" meaning.

12. One of the clearest exponents of structuralist exegesis of the Bible is D. Patte. Cf. his little book *What Is Structuralist Exegesis?* (Philadelphia: Fortress, 1976). Patte has applied this method in a commentary, *The Gospel According to Matthew: A Structural Commentary on Matthew's Faith* (Philadelphia: Fortress, 1987).

13. P. Ricouer, *The Conflict of Interpretations: Essays in Hermeneutics* (Evanston: Northwestern Univ. Press, 1974), 27–61 ("Structure and Hermeneutics") and 79–98 ("Structure, Word, and Event"), while appreciative of certain aspects of structuralism, argues that by its reduction of language to an object of analysis and its rigorous suppression of diachrony, structuralism deliberately eliminates the speaking subject and effectively changes the natural character of linguistic communication. Structuralism depersonalizes texts, language, and ultimately people.

14. Ricouer, *Interpretation Theory*, 30.

15. Cf. S. Fish, *Is There a Text in This Class? The Authority of Interpretive Communities* (Cambridge, Mass.: Harvard Univ. Press, 1980).

16. This is sometimes complicated by discussion of "fusion of horizons" amongst evangelical biblical scholars, who when interpreting Scripture are not free to ascertain a meaning and then disagree with it. Failure to recognize that one's own "horizon of meaning" is coming into play is presumptuous, but failure to *strive* for the meaning outside oneself is equally presumptuous.

17. Hirsch, *Aims of Interpretation*, 49.

18. For an overview of various forms of this approach, cf. J.P. Tompkins,

ed., *Reader Response Criticism: From Formalism to Post-Structuralism* (Baltimore: Johns Hopkins Univ. Press, 1980).

19. W. Iser, *The Act of Reading: A Theory of Aesthetic Response* (Baltimore: Johns Hopkins Univ. Press, 1980).

20. See W.K. Wimsatt and M.C. Beardsley, "The Affective Fallacy," in *Verbal Icon: Studies in the Meaning of Poetry* (Lexington: Univ. of Kentucky Press, 1954).

21. J. Derrida, *Dissemination* (London: Athlone; Chicago: Univ. of Chicago Press, 1981). For bibliography on deconstruction, see William Ray, *Literary Meaning: From Phenomenology to Deconstruction* (Oxford: Oxford Univ. Press, 1984).

22. Deconstruction hermeneutics lies behind a plethora of "specialized" hermeneutic applications. By drawing attention away from any inherent meaning to a text and focusing it on the "meaningfulness to the reader," the philosophical path is laid for such things as Marxist, feminist, or gay hermeneutics. According to this approach, the most valid hermeneutical endeavors are those which most radically challenge the current perceptions, and hence it is the radical antimetaphysical philosophies that gravitate toward this approach. It is curious that in practice the deconstructionists still talk about "good" and "bad" interpretations, or sometimes "authentic" and "inauthentic" to use the language of existentialism. Those interpretations which radically confront the reader are considered "good."

23. Cf. N. Frye, *The Anatomy of Criticism: Four Essays* (Princeton, Princeton Univ. Press, 1973), 352.

24. For further exposition and criticism of Derrida's approach, cf. Lundin, Thiselton, and Walhout, *Hermeneutics of Responsibility*, 35–36.

25. The best-known exposition of his view is the above noted (n. 15) *Is There a Text in This Class?*

26. Wittgenstein noted in his *Philosophical Investigations* that words are like tools; they are used in a variety of ways, but the range of uses is determined by certain actions and behavior patterns that are shared in a society. So a term is understood "not on the basis of private existential experience, but on the basis of a public tradition of certain patterns of behavior" (A. Thiselton, *The Two Horizons: New Testament Hermeneutics and Philosophical Description, with Special Reference to Heidegger, Bultmann, Gadamer, and Wittgenstein* [Exeter: Paternoster; Grand Rapids: Eerdmans, 1980], 382).

27. Cf. *Contra Celsum*, 1:20; cf. also 4:21, 38, 50. Celsus and Origen agreed that allegorical interpretation is a mark of reason (*Contra Celsum* 1:27); only the less intelligent read literally.

28. In which case one could say that it is the indeterminateness which is the determinate meaning.

APPENDIX B

1. For a more extensive introduction to and evaluation of the various types of critical methods, see D.A. Black and D.S. Dockery, eds., *New Testament Criticism and Interpretation* (Grand Rapids: Zondervan, 1991).

2. I.H. Marshall, "Historical Criticism," in *New Testament Interpretation,* 126–38.

3. E. Troeltsch, "Uber Historischen und Dogmatischen Methoden in Theologie" ("On Historical and Dogmatic Methods in Theology," 1898; reprint in *Gesammelte Schriften II* [Tübingen: Mohr (Siebeck), 1922], 729–53).

4. Goldingay writes, "If it is unscientific to be gullible about what purports to be a miracle, it is also unscientific arbitrarily to rule out the possibility that an event may be unique, miraculous. Historical sources must be treated on their merits as sources, rather than prejudged by means of presuppositions" (J. Goldingay, " 'That You May Know that Yahweh Is God': A Study in the Relationship Between Theology and Historical Truth in the Old Testament," *Tyndale Bulletin* 23 [1972]: 89). Unfortunately Goldingay still allows for an evaluation of the "merits" of sources. But on what grounds can one evaluate these merits?

5. As might be expected, increasing consistency of application of the method has led the Christian scholars ever closer to the non-Christian historian's position, with the result that much modern criticism adopts the stance that anything in the Bible is assumed to be unreliable until proven reliable. In Gospels study, e.g., a saying of Jesus is assumed to be a later invention of the church unless proof can be given of its authenticity.

6. G. Maier, *The End of the Historical-Critical Method* (St Louis: Concordia, 1977).

7. E.E. Ellis, *Prophecy and Hermeneutic,* 163.

8. E. Linnemann, *Historical Criticism of the Bible: Methodology or Theology?* (Grand Rapids: Baker, 1991). Before rejecting historical-critical method as incompatible with biblical Christianity, Linnemann had achieved prominence in Germany as one of its accomplished practitioners.

9. Many, perhaps most, Christian scholars of this century struggle to maintain faith and at the same time exercise historical-critical methods which are incompatible with that faith. See R. Morgan with J. Barton, *Biblical Interpretation* (New York: Oxford Univ. Press, 1988), who attempt to build a model for bridging the tension between the "secular, rational frameworks of modern scholarship" and "its [the Bible's] own and subsequent believers' religious framework" (p. 22). Although Morgan and Barton claim that the two approaches are "inseparable" and the

tension resolvable, the diametrically opposed assumptions in the two frameworks allow for resolution only by way of the modern dialectic of rationalism and irrationalism.

10. See H. Frei, *The Eclipse of Biblical Narrative* (New Haven, Conn.: Yale Univ. Press, 1974). It is arguable that, had the Enlightenment never happened, the church would be poorer in its understanding of Scripture. To paraphrase Gen. 50:20, the rationalists meant it for evil, but God meant it for good.

11. For further critique of the historical-critical method see in addition to G. Maier's aforementioned work, P. Stuhlmacher, *Historical Criticism and Theological Interpretation of Scripture* (Philadelphia: Fortress, 1977), and the almost reactionary critique by the former "insider" Eta Linnemann, *Historical Criticism of the Bible*, mentioned above.

12. For an excellent introduction to the negative and positive aspects of criticism, see P.H. Davids, "Authority, Hermeneutics, and Criticism," in Black and Dockery, *New Testament Criticism and Interpretation*, 19–37.

13. Wellhausen was building on the earlier work of E. Reuss and K.H. Graf.

14. B. Duhm was the first to apply Wellhausen's approach to Isaiah.

15. H. Conzelmann, "Formgeschichte" in *Religion in Geschichte und Gegenwart* 3 Aufl. (Tübingen: Mohr [Siebeck], 1957), 3:623.

16. For a good introduction to literary approach to the Bible, see L. Ryken, *Words of Delight: A Literary Introduction to the Bible* (Grand Rapids: Baker, 1987). For a description of scholarly literary criticism of the Bible, see T. Longman, *Literary Approaches to Biblical Interpretation* (Grand Rapids: Zondervan, 1987).

17. See L. Ryken, "And It Came to Pass," *BibSac* 147.2 (Apr/Jun 1990): 133.

18. R. Frye, *Anatomy of Criticism* (Princeton: Univ. of Princeton Press, 1957, 1971), 3–29, 74, claims that "in literature questions of fact or truth are subordinated to the primary literary aim of producing a structure of words for its own sake," and that pleasure rather than reality is primary in literature. Although this may have been true of Homer, the way in which biblical writers refer to their own words and to earlier biblical writings suggests that the writers themselves were not writing for art but for the sake of the hearers knowing truth.

19. See the remark of C.S. Lewis, himself no mean literary critic, that "those who talk of reading the Bible 'as literature' sometimes mean, I think, reading it without attending to the main thing it is about" (C.S. Lewis, *Reflections on the Psalms* [New York: Harcourt, Brace, & Jovanovich, 1958], 2–3). A special instance of a literary criticism which usually avoids what the text says is structuralism, described in Appendix A.

AUTHOR INDEX

SCRIPTURE INDEX